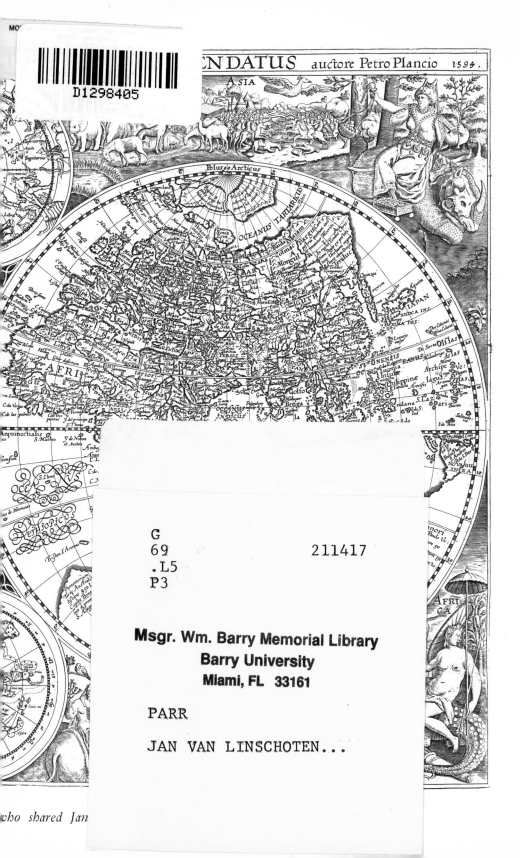

...NDATUS auctore Petro Plancio 1594.

who shared Jan

Jan van Linschoten:
The Dutch Marco Polo

with all good wishes
Charles McKew Parr
Chester, Conn.
11/20/64

THIS PORTRAIT *was made when Jan Huyghen van
Linschoten was thirty-two years old and at the apogee of
his career. He had just discovered what he and all the
Netherlands believed was the Northeast Passage to China,
and was about to sail on his second polar voyage. It is likely
that he posed for this picture in his wedding costume.*

Jan van Linschoten:
The Dutch Marco Polo

by Charles McKew Parr

Thomas Y. Crowell Company

Established 1834

New York

To the memory of
HENDRIK WILLEM VAN LOON,
distinguished son of Holland,
enthusiastic citizen of the United States,
historian, teacher,
friend of presidents and porters,
lover of freedom,
succor of countless Netherlanders in the
days of their distress,
this volume is respectfully and affectionately
dedicated

Contents

Illustrations

Illustrations

[x]

Acknowledgments

D URING the past ten years, while I have been studying the competitive relations of the Dutch and Portuguese in Asia in the sixteenth and seventeenth centuries, I have invariably met with cordial co-operation from the scholars whom I have approached for information and advice. Therefore this book would not be complete without recording my gratitude for the inspiration and guidance I have received from so many quarters.

Mr. W. J. van Balen, of The Hague, the erudite historian and gifted author of a life of Linschoten and of many other works concerning the period, and a trustee of the Linschoten Society, and Mrs. Antoinette E. van Balen, née Chavannes, Archivist, most generously read and checked the manuscript before publication. I cannot thank them enough for their detailed, constructive and creative criticisms and suggestions, which have immeasurably strengthened the book.

In the Netherlands, in addition to Mr. and Mrs. van Balen, I have been helped by: Mr. H. Th. de Booy of Amsterdam, author of nautical works concerning Dutch activities in the Orient; Dr. L. Brummel, former Librarian of the Koninklijke Bibliotheek, den Haag; Dr. G. A. Cox, Director, Nederlandsch Historisch Scheepvart Museum, Amsterdam; Professor Dr. C. F. A. van Dam, Directeur Het Spaans, Portuguees en Ibero-Amerikaans Instituut of the University of Utrecht; Dr. João de Barros Ferreira da Fonseca, Portuguese Ambassador at The Hague; Mejuffrouw L. C. J. Frerichs, Rijksprentenkabinet, Rijksmuseum, Amsterdam; Hon. L. W. H.

Acknowledgments

de Geus, Burgemeester van Linschoten en Snelrewaard, Province of Utrecht; Dr. Simon Hart, Adjunct Director, City Archives of Amsterdam; Dr. M. de Jong, Lector at the University of Amsterdam, Vice-Consul Honoraire de Portugal; The late Captain T. H. Milo, Professor of Naval History, University of Leyden; Dr. Wouter Nijhoff, Honorary Secretary of the Linschoten Society; Professor Dr. H. Howens Post, Instituto de Estudios Hispanicos, Portugueses e Iberoamericanos, University of Utrecht; Rear Admiral James Clair Shaw, Former U.S. Naval Attaché to Holland and Belgium; Mr. J. O. Spier, Distinguished illustrator; Captain C. A. A. van Werkhoven, Holland America Line, Rotterdam.

In Belgium I am particularly indebted to: Dr. Albert Schouteet Bullynck, Conservator, Stadsarchief, Brugge; Mr. H. K. Overdiep, Standard Boekhandel, Antwerp; Dr. Jan van Roey, Adj. Archivaris, Stadsarchief, Antwerp; and M. Et. Sabbé, L'Archiviste General, Brussels.

In England I owe a special tribute to the generosity of Professor Charles R. Boxer of the University of London, whose knowledge of Dutch and Portuguese history has produced many authoritative publications from which I have drawn guidance.

In South Africa I am much indebted to the writings of the late Rev. Sidney R. Welch, of Capetown, who possessed an understanding of the spirit and motives of the Portuguese pioneers in Africa.

In Spain I am first of all grateful to my friends Dr. Adele Kibre, of the Archivo General de Indias in Seville, and Rev. Dr. Pedro Meseguer, S.J., Secretario de Redaccion de "Razon y Fe," Madrid. I also wish to extend thanks to: Professor Guillermo Cespedes, of the Universidad de Sevilla; Padre Don Tomas Teresa Leon, of Madrid; Señorita Antonia Matosas, of the Museo Maritimo, Barcelona; Don Joaquin Gonzales Moreno, Conservador de la Casa de Pilatos, Seville; Rev. Dr. Manuel Marina Martin, S.J., Colegio de PP.Jesuitas, Pamplona; and Señor Dr. Jose de la Peña, Director del Archivo General de Indias, Seville.

In Portugal I owe thanks to: Professor Dr. Antonio de Almeida, Secretario Geral, Sociedade de Geografia de Lisboa; Dr. José Gaspar de Almeida, Conservador do Arquivo Nacional da Torre do Tombo, Lisbon; The Conde de Alvellos, Lisbon; Dr. Luis Benevente, Arq., Ministry of Public Works, Lisbon; Dr. Manuel Santos Estevens, Director da Biblioteca Nacional de Lisboa, Lisbon; Senhora Maria Luisa de Oliveira Esteves, Queluz; Dr. Antonio Machado de Faria, Academia Portuguesa da Historia, Lisbon; Dr. Julio Goncalves, Secretario Geral, Sociedade de Geografia de Lisboa, Lisbon; Dr. Alberto Iria, Director de Arquivo Historico Ultramarine, Lisbon; The late Dr. Americo Pacheco Jorge, Lisbon; The late Dr. Gaspar de Abreu e Lima, Ponte da Barca; and Dom Frazão de Vasconcellos, Chefe de Seccão, Biblioteca de Marinha, Lisbon.

In the United States I wish to thank: Dr. Ruth Lapham Butler, New-

Acknowledgments

berry Library, Chicago; Professor Manoel Cardozo, The Lima Library, Catholic University, Washington, D.C.; Dr. Howard F. Cline, Hispanic Foundation, Library of Congress, Washington, D.C.; Professor Bailey W. Diffie, Department of History, The City College of the City University of New York; Mr. Ray C. Dovell, History Book Club, Stamford, Conn.; Professor John Edward Fagg, Department of History, New York University; Professor Seymour Flaxman, Department of Languages, State University of New York; Dr. Melvin H. Jackson, Maritime Division, Smithsonian Institution, Washington, D.C.; Professor Lewis U. Hanke, Department of History, Columbia University, New York City; Professor Richard Herr, Department of History, University of California, Berkeley, Calif.; Professor Ronald Hilton, Department of History, Leland Stanford University, Palo Alto, Calif.; Dr. John F. Hutchins, Department of Languages, U.S. Naval Academy, Annapolis, Md.; Rev. Dr. Mathias C. Kieman (OFM), Academy of Franciscan History, Washington, D.C.; Miss Jean Rogers Longland, Librarian, Hispanic Society of America, New York City; Professor Francisco Marquez, Harvard University, Cambridge, Mass.; The late Professor Garrett Mattingly, Department of History, Columbia University, New York City; Mrs. Jeannette Mirsky, Princeton, N.J.; Dr. Boies Penrose, Devon, Pa.; Professor Francis M. Rogers, Widener Library, Harvard University, Cambridge, Mass.; Dr. Julia Sabine, Public Library of Newark, N.J.; Professor Rhea Marsh Smith, Department of History, Rollins College, Winter Park, Florida; and Dr. Lawrence C. Wroth, The John Carter Brown Library, Providence, R.I.

My thanks are also due to Mrs. Egbert Broekhuysen, Mrs. Y. Haagsma-Kramer, and Mrs. Irma Barends, my patient teachers of Dutch; because of their help I have been able to study in the ancient maritime archives of the Netherlands.

I am deeply grateful to Mrs. Frances Stillman not only for her invaluable editing of the manuscript, but also for the zeal and enthusiasm which she has lent to the undertaking, and I am most indebted to my colleague Miss Elizabeth M. Riley for her counsel and encouragement.

Librarian Mary Parr, my sister, and her assistant, Mrs. Mary Meglin, have continuously aided me, and my secretary, Miss Gertrude Conlon, has been of much help in arranging and typing the manuscript.

Charles McKew Parr

Preface

THE YOUNG Jan Huyghen van Linschoten (pronounced YAHN HOY-ggen van LIN-sko-ten) ventured into the exotic, secret Indian Empire of the Portuguese toward the end of the sixteenth century, and it was his genius for gathering, organizing and reporting all kinds of information which gave the Dutch and English the data they needed in order to oust the Portuguese and become masters of the Orient themselves. Although Jan suffered many reverses in his lifetime, his career was in the end crowned with worldly success, and since he was a self-made man this doubtless gave him much satisfaction. However, its enjoyment was cut short by his untimely death in 1611 at the age of forty-eight. In many ways—his reportorial skill, his great personal drive, his realistic attitude toward business—he was a man of the modern era, although he lived in a late Renaissance period still tinctured by medievalism.

This modest and talented clerk, adventurer and scholar enjoyed little status and was accorded no recognition until after he returned from Goa, although there he had been recognized as the trusted confidant of the Archbishop, and he had enjoyed a responsible position and the considera-tion of the governor during his stay on Terceira Island. His early friends in Goa were mostly fellow foreigners of the lower middle class, but he apparently had natural gifts of leadership and magnetism which drew such contemporaries to him. Inevitably, he was a social nonentity in the pre-tentious, self-seeking colonial circles of Goa. However, he was undaunted by obscurity and did not hesitate to put his keen perceptions to work in observing and recording the idiosyncrasies of the people around him. No historian can justly describe the polyglot world of the late sixteenth century in the Orient without having recourse to his chronicles and his inimitable drawings and charts.

Linschoten's first published book, the *Reysgeschrift*, was rushed into print ahead of the rest of the *Itinerario*, in 1595, and it had an enormous impact upon the chancelleries and countinghouses of Western Europe, particularly in the Netherlands and England, where it was translated soon after its appearance in Dutch. Its conversion into action came even before publication, as the logbook of Cornelis Houtman proves. The commander of the first Dutch voyage to the Indies recorded that the *Reysgeschrift* was given to him in manuscript form for his guidance in the accomplishment of his epochal mission.

The *Itinerario* as a whole was published in 1596, with the learned Dr. Bernard Paludanus as Linschoten's collaborator. Linschoten had been granted a license to publish it by the States General in 1594, but his work of preparing the manuscript was interrupted by his two voyages to the north in search of the Northeast Passage to the Indies, and its final preparation and publication were left in the hands of Dr. Paludanus and the publisher, Cornelis Claeszoon of Amsterdam. The first part is the "Itinerary" itself, the detailed account of Linschoten's voyage to Goa and of all he saw there, as well as his experiences on the voyage home. It is a fascinating example of travel literature, and the plates and charts by Linschoten illustrating various aspects of life in the Far East add greatly to its interest.

The second part of Linschoten's magnum opus is the *Reysgeschrift*, which, although it had been published alone in advance of the rest of the book, was included when the whole came out in 1596. It is a description of the sea routes to India, the seas of the Far East, and the coasts of America. This second part also included a summary of the possessions (domains, revenues etc.) of the King of Spain, under a separate title. The *Reysgeschrift*, called *Rutter* or *Pilot's Guide* in English and *Roteiro* in Portuguese, was the part of the *Itinerario* which had a direct effect upon the discoveries and conquests made by Dutch, English and French navigators in the Far East. Linschoten modestly described himself as the compiler of these rutters; actually, his treatment is a masterpiece of scholarly editing which could only have been accomplished by one intimately in touch with every aspect of the material, and who was competent to translate into simple Dutch the rugged sea vernacular of the Portuguese pilots who had summarized their experiences and observations over the period of the past eighty years. These reports ranged from the early logging by Vasco da Gama of the first landfall, on May 18, 1498, and continued, for instance, to a painstaking description of the approach to the Chinese island of

Preface

Sanchoan, which the British were later to call St. John, where St. Francis
Xavier had died in 1552. All subsequent English, Dutch and French navigators freely admitted their reliance upon this indispensable *Pilot Book*,
and modern seamen still give credit to its accuracy. Many of the navigational landmarks of that early period, such as groups of high trees on a
point, forested inlets, or sandbanks at a river's mouth, have of course long
since vanished, but many more lasting observations of currents and contours still hold good.

These sailing directions were among the most secret national data of the
Portuguese. They had been assembled by the government, carefully
checked and edited, zealously guarded, and given only to Portuguese
pilots. Evidently the pilots had instructions to destroy them in case of
imminent capture, for they were never found among the papers of Portuguese Indiamen taken by the Dutch and English during the latter part of
the sixteenth century. Dutch spies, such as the Houtman brothers and the
agents of Petrus Plancius, were able by bribery to get hold of important
government charts, but they could never lay their hands on these rutters.

How, then, was Linschoten able to get them? It may be presumed that
he acquired these ultra-secret documents during his two years' stay on the
island of Terceira, where the Azoreans seethed with hatred against the
Spanish usurpers in Lisbon. (It will be remembered that Philip II of Spain
seized the Portuguese throne in 1580.) The islanders had been barbarously
persecuted for their loyalty to Dom Antonio of Crato, who had attempted
to defend the Azores against Philip's conquest. The Portuguese mariners
who had been taken prisoner by the Spanish commander, the Marquis of
Santa Cruz, had been treated as rebels and had been either decapitated or
condemned to the galleys for life. Any refugee Portuguese patriots who
had survived this ruthless treatment and were in hiding in Terceira would
understandably have been eager to take vengeance upon the Spaniards by
giving Portuguese secrets to the Dutch, who were also enemies of Spain.

No one can read the old rutters which Linschoten published without
appreciating the caliber of the sixteenth-century Portuguese pilots who
composed them. There is nothing dry about their texts, which graphically
and tensely reflected the extreme hazards of sailing the routes they described. With absolutely no certainty of the east-west position of their
ships, with only an approximate knowledge of their north-south location,
and with no surety concerning the degree of accuracy of their compasses,
these seasoned steersmen relied largely upon observations such as the types
of seabirds to be seen, the abundance of sargossa or other floating seaweed,
the kind of marine life to be detected, and of course the drifts, currents
and prevailing winds, all of which varied with the seasons. It is no wonder
that the most reliable pilot might be a hundred miles or more off in his
reckoning.

Preface

The third part of the *Itinerario* is also a digest of the works of other authors; it contains descriptions of both the east and west coasts of Africa and of America. It is entitled *Beschryvinghe van de gantsche custe van Guinea.*

Successive editions of Linschoten's Dutch text were brought out, after the first edition of 1596, in 1604, 1614, 1623 and 1644, and French editions appeared in 1610, 1619 and 1638. The English translation was published in 1598, and the passages in English quoted in this biography are taken from this translation. The translator was not mentioned, but he is believed to have been named William Phillip. This English edition, published by John Wolfe of London, was in four volumes. It was endorsed by Richard Hakluyt and aroused enormous interest in England, serving, just as in the Netherlands, to encourage and to guide the commercial invasion of the markets of the Far East. Two Latin editions appeared in 1599.

The first and also subsequent editions of the *Itinerario* were illustrated by thirty-six plates drawn by Linschoten himself and engraved by the brothers Joannes and Baptista à Doetechum. These include drawings of such typical inhabitants of Goa as Brahmins and other Indian natives, and the Portuguese colonists, as well as of Chinese, Malays, Arabs, Abyssinians, and natives of Mozambique, and the customs and costumes of these people; boats of various kinds; a vivid elephant; and manufactures and natural products of the area. They also include maps and topographical plates by Linschoten: a large map of Goa island and city, a large plan of Angra, in Terceira Island, and carefully drawn profiles of St. Helena Island and Ascension Island. The book also contains six large maps which were made by Arnoldus and Henricus Florentii à Langren, as well as a reduced copy of Petrus Plancius' great map of the world. The Florentii maps were apparently made with the assistance of a group of sea-charts of the world which the publisher, Claeszoon, had obtained from Bartolomé de Lasso, the cosmographer of Philip II. The Plancius map of the world shows the northern and southern constellations, among them *Columba*, which was drawn for the first time by the great Dutch geographer.

Linschoten's drawings were those of a reporter. Had he lived in the modern era, he would undoubtedly have been an assiduous photographer. Obviously untrained as an artist, he nevertheless possessed considerable ability as a draftsman and a keen and accurate eye. There is dynamism in the depiction of movement in some of the plates, as well as a pleasing composition. The backgrounds are meticulously sketched, with notably stiff little trees; but in the sweep of a few of them one is reminded of scenes in ancient Chinese landscape paintings, with their wide stretches of water and distant hills and mountains. In general, however, the work is rather wooden. The charm of the plates resides in their naive depiction of exotic and historically interesting subject matter, and their very deficiencies as works of art render them more humanly touching. Linschoten's charts and maps are detailed and workmanlike. He was always careful to show, in his profiles of islands and coastlines, the exact position from which his view was drawn, which he indicated by picturing a ship in the correct spot.

An engraved portrait of Jan Huyghen van Linschoten serves as a frontispiece for the *Itinerario;* it is dated 1595, and his age is given as thirty-two in the border. Presumably the portrait was executed in April, 1595, at the time of his marriage and just before he embarked upon his second polar voyage. He was then at the apogee of his career, and it is probable that his handsome costume was actually composed of his wedding garments.

The portrait medallion has an oval frame of simulated metal upon which is engraved Linschoten's French motto, *Soufrir pour parvenir* (which may be translated "Endure in order to succeed"), his name in Latin, Joannes Hugonis A Linschoten Haerlemensis, aged 32, and the date, 1595. His continued loyalty to Haarlem as his birthplace is shown by its inclusion in his name, while the age and date given enable us to place his birthdate as 1563. Behind him on the medallion is a coat of arms, surmounted by a crest, upon which are shown the checkered Saint Andrew's Cross of the Province of Holland and the Lion of the United Provinces. Jan is dressed in court fashion, with a sleeveless satin jacket over a quilted silk shirt and a plain starched ruff. His curly hair is trimmed and brushed into a pompadour, and his strong nose, long moustache, and sharply trimmed beard give him a faintly military appearance, while his broad, high brow makes him look intellectual. The proportion of his head to his shoulders gives the impression that he was of small stature. Along with his courtly dress and military air, there is a certain mildness and kindness in his countenance with its widely spaced eyes, as well as a hint of fortitude and tenacity about the bearded mouth. He does not look like a vigorous, robust man, and the fact that he had only one child, who did not survive to maturity, and that he himself died at the age of forty-eight, may show that the severe sicknesses through which he passed during his overseas career had a weakening effect upon his health. The portrait medallion is supported on each quarter by oval cartouches in which appear miniatures of Linschoten's own engravings of Goa, Mozambique and St. Helena.

Where this portrait serves as a frontispiece for the *Itinerario*, it is usually supplemented on the opposite title page with a companion piece which shows, also in a medallion, two sixteenth-century Dutch men-of-war convoying a numerous fleet of herring busses. The four oval supporting cartouches have corresponding sketches depicting Enkhuizen, Middelburg, Antwerp and Amsterdam. The ensemble supplies a background of Linschoten's past and a reflection of the world in which he was living.

Preface

The other work by Jan Huyghen van Linschoten upon which this biographer has drawn is *Naar Het Noorden* (To the North), the journals of his voyages in search of the Northeast Passage, published by Gerard Ketel in 1601 in Franeker, and dedicated to Prince Maurice of Orange and to the Mighty Lords of the States-General of the United Provinces of the Netherlands. This book, containing many interesting profile-charts and plates depicting the people of the region, as well as of the flora and fauna, did not enjoy the success of the *Itinerario*, for obvious reasons, and has become extremely rare and hard to find. However, the book has been reprinted by the Linschoten Society of the Netherlands and is therefore available for study.

Linschoten also published two translations of importance. The first, published in 1598, was entitled *Historia Naturael ende morael van de Westersche Indien*, and was a Dutch version of the *Historia natural y moral de las Indias*, by Josef de Acosta, a Spanish Jesuit. This book, in line with Linschoten's interest in making public the secrets of the overseas empires of Spain and Portugal, concerned the Spanish colonies in the West Indies.

In 1609, J. Lz Meyn, of Enkhuizen, published Linschoten's last work, a translation of a letter of the King of Spain to the Duke of Lerma on the subject of the banishment of the Moriscos from Spain. It was one of two economic publications which at the time were of major importance in putting weapons in the hands of the shrewd, commercial-minded English and Dutch in their war against Philip II, a war which was more economic than military, and which was eventually settled not on the field of battle but in the bourses of Europe.

The first of these had been the searching and comprehensive analysis of the complete sources of revenue of the King of Spain included in the *Itinerario;* one cannot but wonder how, from what source and in what manner, Jan secured this vital and jealously guarded information. His feat in acquiring it parallels his achievement in learning the closely guarded details of the marine routes of Portugal. Modern commentators are apt to underestimate this non-literary and brief compilation, but at the time of publication it must have had a telling influence in the struggle.

The second such publication, now almost overlooked by critics, was this brief translation of Philip's communication to the Duke of Lerma regarding the expulsion of the Christianized Moors (called Moriscos), who had contributed so much to the economic life of Spain; their exile in a measure paralleled in its painful effects the expulsion by the Spaniards of the artisans from the South Netherlands and by the French of the Huguenots. This key confidential communication by the king to his trusted minister no doubt was welcome information to the statesmen of the northern countries.

Preface

More than two centuries went by before there were any modern editions of Linschoten's great works, and curiously enough, it was the English who first revived interest in him. In the 1880's, the Hakluyt Society, in England, decided to produce a scholarly edition of the English translation of 1598 of Linschoten's *Itinerario*. Mr. Arthur Coke Burnell, a civil servant of the East India Company at Madras, undertook the work, but unfortunately he died when but halfway through his task. Then Colonel H. Yule, the President of the Hakluyt Society, procured a Dutch scholar, Professor Pieter Anton Tiele, to complete the work. It was published in two volumes, in 1884, the first edited by Burnell, the second by Professor Tiele, with the introduction to the whole by the latter. No further edition has been published in English.

Apparently Dutch historians had given no thought to reissuing Linschoten's works until Professor Tiele began his researches for the Hakluyt Society of England. Shortly thereafter, several constructive contributions to the subject were published in Dutch scholarly quarterlies. Early in the twentieth century, a group of Dutch historians formed a society which, like the Hakluyt Society, was to devote itself to publishing previously unknown accounts of great Dutch voyages; they called it *De Linschoten Vereeniging*, or The Linschoten Society, thus recognizing the prime importance of Jan Huyghen van Linschoten in that field. The Honorary Secretary was Wouter Nijhoff, of The Hague.

The Linschoten Society then proceeded to bring out, among its other publications, scholarly editions of Linschoten's works in the original Dutch. In 1910, H. Kern edited the *Itinerario* proper in two volumes (Number II in the publications of the Linschoten Society). This was followed in 1914 by *Reizen van Jan Huyghen van Linschoten naar het Noorden*, edited by S. P. L'Honoré Naber (Number VIII). In 1934 came the third volume of the *Itinerario*, the *Beschrijving*, edited by C. P. Burger Jr. and F. W. T. Hunger (Number XXXIX). In 1939 the *Itinerario* was completed with volumes four and five, the *Reysgeschrift*, edited by J. C. M. Warnsinck (Number XLIII). Finally, in 1955, 1956, and 1957 the original publication of the *Itinerario*, as edited by H. Kern, was revised by H. Terpstra and brought out in three volumes in three successive years.

No editor or historian has been able to explain where Jan Huyghen got the surname "van Linschoten." It was not the patronym of Jan's father, Huig Joostenszn, and never appeared in connection with the names of any of his relatives. It was quite easy at that time, when surnames were only beginning to be universally adopted, for an individual to alter his patronym to some other that better suited his fancy. Almost all scholars changed their names to their Latin forms, which set an example for others to follow.

Preface

Jan's mother came from the little village of Schoonhaven, not far from the manor of Linschoten, and this no doubt influenced Jan in his choice of a surname. However, had he possessed the means, he might actually have acquired a legal patent of nobility complete with coat of arms and title, since King Philip II, chronically pressed on all sides by financial worries and desperately in need of funds, as early as 1557 was reduced to selling such titles. At that time he sold nearly a thousand patents of nobility to commoners for five thousand ducats each. The haughty hidalgos of Spain thus had to admit to their privileged ranks not only wealthy burghers, but also the descendants of Jews and Moors, and even men whose parents had marched to the stake in autos-da-fé wearing the despised habit of San Benito.

Linschoten, in the Province of Utrecht, is a picturesque old village with a church dating back perhaps as far as the tenth century. Some of the town records of the period are extant, and those of the larger, adjoining town of Oudewater have been preserved. Records of the district reveal the names of the early gentry as well as of some farmers, artisans and peasants, but nowhere has it been possible to trace any relationship of Huig Joostenszn to the aristocratic family of van Linschoten domiciled near the town of Linschoten.

Yet Jan must have been legally entitled to use van Linschoten as his patronym, because in his dedication of the *Itinerario* to the States-General in 1596 he signs his name formally in that manner.

Jan left home as a boy using the patronym of Huyghen, the son of Huig. In Spain and Portugal he may have gone by the name of his half-brothers, Tin, with whose firm he was identified. When he returned home after an absence of thirteen years, it was as the sophisticated, travelled Jan Huyghen van Linschoten. Since he was, above all, prudent, systematic and realistic, one may be confident that in adopting the name van Linschoten he had made sure of his footing.

Nowhere else in Europe were heraldic bearings and escutcheons so important, such a fetish, as in the Iberian peninsula, where even today they are held in greater esteem than in other modern countries. In both Spain and Portugal, the granting of coats of arms was a jealously guarded right of the monarch, and the patent of nobility, when granted, was cherished along with the title deeds to property. In both kingdoms there were many fraudulent pretensions, and when King Manoël of Portugal had the court heralds make a rigorous investigation of all blazons of nobility, it was discovered that many of the most prominent families were displaying inherited armorial bearings without realizing that they were not entitled to them. In Goa it was notorious that many persons claimed rank and descent to which they had no right, but their pretensions could not be exposed because of the distance from the homeland. In the Azores, where Jan spent two years, an exasperating condition prevailed whereby individuals descended from the ancient nobility were, because of an absurd but rigid technicality, debarred from using their inherited coats of arms. In all these places there were no doubt skillful artificers available who would, for a consideration, forge any desired credentials.

Since no one could advance to any important governmental post in the Portuguese service without proof of gentle lineage, the question of armorial bearings was of prime importance. It was a serious weakness, not only in the civil service but also in the armed forces of Portugal, that a subordinate of noble birth might decline to accept orders from a senior officer on the grounds of being of superior lineage.

Jan had, until the end of his stay in India, apparently planned to make a life career in *Asia Portuguesa* under Philip II, and because of this he well may have taken a convenient opportunity to have some claim, legitimate or otherwise, to the patronym of van Linschoten authenticated through the official channels then available to him. Unquestionably he could not have hoped to rise in the Portuguese colonial service unless he could qualify as to birth. In the Provinces of Holland and Utrecht, where Enkhuizen and Linschoten were located, all titles and questions of nobility still were admittedly subject to the sovereign authority of Philip II, even though the provinces had otherwise thrown off their allegiance to him. If Jan actually obtained an official *libro de sangre* in Goa, it would have been accepted without question in the Netherlands.

Jan Huyghen van Linschoten died in Enkhuizen on February 8, 1611. For some decades his contributions to the maritime and colonial development of the Republic were remembered and respected because of the outstanding worth of his great publications, as edition after edition came forth from the presses of Europe. However, in the ensuing century he was quite forgotten. A brief mention of him appeared in a rhymed history of Enkhuizen in the mid-seventeenth century, and then his name dropped out of the chronicles of his native land. About 1870, a historical survey entitled *The Land of Rembrandt* listed the names of worthies of the seventeenth and eighteenth centuries in Holland, but Jan Huyghen van Linschoten was only mentioned in an offhand way, as one of slight importance. His great achievements were apparently totally forgotten until the English, soon after that date, revived interest in his work.

Introduction

Linschoten's Influence

O N E O F the great shifts of world power in all history got under way during Jan Huyghen van Linschoten's lifetime, and it is not too much to say that he was one of its major instruments. He not only divulged to the predatory maritime nations of the North that the previously formidable Portuguese naval force had become a fleet of poorly armed, unwieldy merchant ships which would be easy prizes for swift, heavily gunned corsairs. He also, and even more importantly, presented in detail the hitherto unknown Portuguese sailing routes from Europe to the Orient, and audaciously recommended a new and untried course which completely turned the flank of *Asia Portuguesa* in both the naval and economic sense. The route which the Dutch adopted, on Linschoten's advice, led them directly to the great islands which were to become the Dutch East Indies, which for three and a half centuries were to pour their wealth into the Netherlands.

At the very date of the *Itinerario*, with its evidence of what appeared to be the decay of Portuguese might at sea, many English and Dutch adventurers had been hesitating whether to risk running the gauntlet of the supposedly potent Portuguese naval patrols in the South Atlantic and in the Indian Ocean. Linschoten's revelations were given much weight, and undoubtedly influenced the backers of the proposed intrusions.

The Dutch pioneers who planned to raid *Asia Portuguesa* followed

[xxv]

Jan's advice, and the first Dutch fleet to the Indies eschewed the established Portuguese route around the Cape of Good Hope and north by east to Goa, and instead sailed from south of the Cape due east and then north by the Sunda Strait. Thus they outflanked the Portuguese bases in the Indian Ocean and tapped the undefended source of their vital spice trade.

Most historians agree that, had the first Dutch fleet gone to the Malabar Coast or the West Coast of India instead of taking Linschoten's advice, it would inevitably have been destroyed by the formidable Portuguese fleet based on Goa. The Dutch expedition was poorly commanded, and its complement was demoralized by dissension, gravely weakened by disease, and in poor condition for heavy combat. When the fleet finally struggled back to Holland, one ship had been lost, and the total complement of the other three had dwindled to eighty-nine seamen out of the 249 picked men who had originally manned the fleet.

Linschoten's sound counsel was also important in the final Dutch economic victory because, by following the sea route which he recommended, the Dutch Indiamen escaped the hitherto unavoidable handicap of having to sail once annually, with the Monsoons. Instead, they could sail at any season of the year both to and from Java. The never failing westerlies of the far south in three weeks blew a Dutch ship a distance of six thousand miles, from the Cape of Good Hope to the longitude of the Sunda Strait. On the return voyage, the southeast trades took the ship on a course about twenty-five degrees south of the equator, as far east as the longitude of southern Madagascar. From there the Algulhas Current carried it toward the Cape of Good Hope. Then it picked up the southeast trades of the Atlantic for the homeward sail.

While such navigating details were only gradually learned by trial and error, nevertheless it was with the general guidance of Linschoten that the Dutch first undertook this course. The *Reysgeschrift*, carried in manuscript by the First Dutch Fleet under De Houtman, turned out to be indispensable to the pilots, for it gave accurate and comprehensive sailing directions establishing the practicable eastward routes from the Cape even as far north as the Japanese Islands. There was no other source of information available to the Dutch pioneers for reaching the Indonesian Archipelago.

Two testimonials to the value of Jan's book are widely separated in time. In 1613, Captain John Saris, the first Englishman to sail to Japan, wrote: "Wee found Jan Huijghen Van Linschotens booke very true, for thereby we directed our selves from our setting forth from Firando." C. R. Boxer wrote, in the *Mariner's Mirror* of 1934: "If all the printed and manuscript copies of Portuguese Roteiros which are known to exist were to disappear, leaving only Linschoten's *Itinerario*, this would still be more than sufficient to establish the fame and efficiency of those [Portuguese] pilots."

The naval benefits resulting to the Dutch from Linschoten's advice were fully as decisive as the economic ones, because while the Portuguese war fleet was bottled up in Goa harbor for half a year by the Southwest Monsoon, the Dutch war fleet, by keeping south of the equator where the Southwest Monsoon did not prevail, was free to sail where it wished. The Dutch squadrons thus had a great strategic advantage, since they operated to the windward of the Portuguese.

Portuguese and Dutch Practices

JAN HUYGHEN VAN LINSCHOTEN's experiences and opinions can best be understood against the wide background of what happened at sea and in the colonies of the Far East not only during his own century but during the entire early period when sailing ships and galleys plied the seas and oceans of the world to gain and to maintain overseas possessions. In order to provide such perspective, the author has included the following two sections on Portuguese and Dutch practices and the lot of the common seaman, in the confidence that this introductory material will add to the interest of the book.

The power shift from the Iberian Peninsula to Northern Europe was more than geographical; it was a shift in many ways from the medieval to the early modern period, from the somewhat cumbrous rationale of chivalry to a commercially motivated *Realpolitik*. Portugal, perhaps in part because only one round-trip voyage to *Asia Portuguesa* was possible each year, had developed the autonomy of its colonies there to a high degree. *Asia Portuguesa* imported practically no manufactured products from Europe, and the fleets that went out from Lisbon carried almost no trade cargo—only a little Venetian glass, a few other such items, and bars of nonferrous metal. Almost all the outgoing cargo to India was in coined silver pieces of eight. The returning pepper ships, on the other hand, were crammed to the gunwales with Oriental manufactures. India and the Orient were self-sufficient economically, and therefore the Portuguese never regarded their colonies primarily as a market. In matters of commerce and finance, the native merchants were in fact more astute than the Portuguese conquerors, for generally speaking the Portuguese were not commercial-minded, and their business even in Europe was largely monopolized by Italians and Germans. The Portuguese were still crusaders in spirit, and perhaps their primary aim in colonization was the extension of Christianity. The *casados*, or Portuguese married settlers, were given substantial benefits by the government, and frequently had high-caste native Catholic wives whose relatives were much more cultivated and able than their Portuguese husbands. In other matters as well, the Portuguese were often amazingly liberal. For example, they permitted the Venetians and Genoans, among others, to purchase native produce in Goa and various Indian markets and to ship it overland to Aleppo, and thence to Europe, in competition with the merchandise which the Portuguese themselves imported in their pepper naos sailing the long route around the Cape.

What really supported the Portuguese colonial establishment in India was the intra-coastal trade which they built up based on Goa, whose vast network of maritime freight lines fanned out in every direction. Almost all its profits remained in the colony. The owners of the freighters and manufacturing and trading depots were generally not continental Portuguese, but were either Eurasians or their full-blooded native relatives. By Linschoten's time, the Portuguese policy of intermarriage had been operative for three or four generations, and Eurasians had in consequence largely taken over the Portuguese Asian colonies. The high government posts, the captaincies and other positions of command, were held by Portuguese subjects appointed by the King. However, most of these appointees held limited terms of office, and beneath them was a strong permanent bureaucracy of Eurasians. In the Church there were many Eurasian and native priests, and at the time Linschoten was in Goa three thousand seminarians of various Oriental races were enrolled in the Jesuit college alone, all of whom presumably attained ordination.

Portuguese insistence upon continuing their proselytizing efforts proved to be a handicap later, during the hard struggle to maintain supremacy against England and the Netherlands; the ecclesiastical organization in *Asia Portuguesa* had priority over the military, and much of the local revenues went to maintain the numerous churches and convents in the colony. Vast numbers of able-bodied men of military age were seminarians and priests, and they, of course, could not be called upon to fight.

A great advantage of the Dutch in the early days was their system of promoting able seamen to high command, regardless of family rank or early advantages. The Portuguese, on the other hand, rigidly restricted naval rank to *fidalgos* with coats of arms who, even if good soldiers, rarely had the seamanship or experience to rival the veteran Dutch sea-dogs. Linschoten denounced the incompetence of Portuguese naval commanders chosen only because of their noble birth, and he also blamed the Portuguese for manning their overbuilt and overloaded naos with convicts and unemployables. However, once the Dutch had secured a monopoly of the East Indian ocean routes, they too became guilty of the latter fault.

Though the Dutch were able to overcome the lubberly crews and inexpert commanders of the Portuguese naos, as well as Spanish ships in

Introduction

the Atlantic, they faced a very different situation in the waters around the Philippines. There, the Spanish galleons were just as big and clumsy as the Portuguese naos, but their crews were composed of Basque sailors who were at least the peers of the Dutch in seamanship, and they roundly defeated the Dutch again and again.

When the Dutch, English and other colonial powers took over various territories in the seventeenth and eighteenth centuries, their attitudes were in great contrast to the old racial tolerance—and indeed, integration—of the Portuguese. The new colonists scorned all colored persons, no matter how cultivated the individual nor how high his lineage. As for inter-marriage, it was beyond the pale. Social recognition of any kind could not be given to members of the native races or to people of mixed blood.

As soon as the Dutch took over the spice trade, they destroyed spice-producing trees and vegetation in many areas, and in some cases deported entire populations from spice islands, in order to create a scarcity of spices which would drive up their market price in Europe. They also managed, by monopolistic practices, to raise the European prices of dyes, drugs and other oriental specialties.

The most bitter diatribes against the Dutch came not from Portuguese sources, but from the English, their colonial rivals who had once been such good Protestant allies and still pretended to be friendly.

Pieter Both, the first Governor of the Dutch East India Company, was sent out in 1609 with specific instructions that "the commerce of the Moluccas, Amboina and Banda shall belong to the Company and no other nation in the world shall have the least part." After having made common cause with the English against the Portuguese in the Persian Gulf and the Straits of Malacca, the Dutch did their best to drive the English out of the East. They tortured and massacred them, and they carried on a particularly relentless campaign against them in Java. An English factor in the Persian Gulf complained, "They have lately in these parts committed such inhuman acts in murdering all they meet abroad, as well friends as foes, that it is abominable before God and Man." Another Englishman wrote: "They wrong you in all parts and grow to insufferable insolences. I have tried them in East and West and know their bestiality and ingratitude." However, it is notable that in the American colonies, where the English held the upper hand because of population, they showed no consideration to the outnumbered Dutch in New Amsterdam.

The Dutch were inclined to drink heavily in the Orient, unlike the abstemious Portuguese and the relatively temperate English; this was probably due to their difficulty in enduring the climate, so unlike that at home, although the English too had to contend with the same hard contrast. The Portuguese, on the other hand, did not find high temperatures insupportable. The Dutch attempted to live in the highlands of Java and

Ceylon, where the climate was pleasant, but according to repeated official Dutch reports of the time, greed, immorality and drunkenness were rife even there.

It was no doubt the iron in the nature of Jan Pieterszoon Coen, the great Governor General, which saved the Dutch colonies and established a more moderate and civilized way of life. Coen was utterly ruthless, and although his methods paid dividends of a hundred percent to the stockholders, his spoliation of Banda, massacre at Amboina, destruction of surplus products, and exploitation of the natives represented some of the worst aspects of colonialism. His great successor, Antony van Diemen, although also stern in discipline, helped to elevate the general tone of the Dutch colonies. It was his naval strategy of continuously blockading Goa which broke the back of Portuguese resistance to the Dutch.

Once the Dutch had absolute control of the East Indies, the same short-sighted maritime policies for which Linschoten had criticized the Portuguese were adopted. One of these was the practice of allowing shipmasters and officers to carry their own private ventures on a homeward voyage, so that many a vessel sailed for home so grossly overloaded that it foundered and sank in the first storm.

It is said that the conqueror inevitably becomes like the conquered. In the early eighteenth century, the great maritime principles of the earlier Dutch were abandoned; because of the monopolistic system, high standards of naval development and construction had vanished. Dutch ships were now slow, cumbersome and awkward. Because of the shortage of long timbers, they were built short in length, but with excessive beam and great depth, with an average draft of thirty feet. Their sail plans were often undeveloped, and many of them snugged down at night even in trade winds. Consequently, passages from Holland to Java took six or seven months, even by the new route which utilized the strong west winds. The ships were crowded with men, many recruited from the slums of Europe, dirt abounded, and the mortality was grave. The hardships and loss of life on the long outward voyage from Holland were so severe that many Dutchmen decided never to return to Europe. All this happened almost two centuries after the same abuses in the *Carreira da India* had been criticized by Linschoten. Almost the same description could also be applied to the ships of the British East India Company at the same period. The cause was the same in all cases: human nature, unchecked by competition, degenerated into sloth and inefficiency. Because of the monopoly, great profits were assured. Neither the Dutch nor the British naval conditions were much better, despite the improvements of navigating instruments and nautical science, than those of their Portuguese predecessors had been in the late sixteenth and early seventeenth centuries.

Introduction

The Lot of the Common Seaman in the Age of Sail and Oar

HOWEVER LAMENTABLE the situation of the natives of the colonies, another group of men were by and large even worse off during the age of expanding discoveries and colonization. Viewed objectively and without nationalistic prejudices, it is evident that, in all the Christian countries of Western Europe and all across the oceans of the world, without exception the most abused members of society were the common seamen.

Jan, at the age of twenty, had been acquainted only with the relatively disease-free and sanitary conditions on the short coastal voyages of the fiercely self-reliant Sea Beggars and herring fishermen of the Zuider Zee. Therefore he was shocked at the caliber and condition of the maltreated, miserable crewmen on the *Sam Salvador*, upon which he shipped for Goa, and without further ado he scorned the Portuguese as a decadent maritime race. He would have been surprised to learn that the squalor, disease and distress of these poor Portuguese mariners were to be repeated until the end of the age of sail in the forecastles of the proudest Indiamen, under the flags of the most civilized nations of Europe, and particularly on those of the United Netherlands.

In the early seventeenth century, the promise of great booty in the Indies attracted the adventurous and lawless elements in the Netherlands; for although the Dutch ships were legally commissioned with letters of marque, they actually were little more than heavily armed corsairs manned by piratical crews. However, once the bonanza period had passed and the great national monopolistic East India Company, the "VOC," had begun to operate, adventure and loot no longer beckoned, and the caliber of the seamen accordingly deteriorated. Able Dutchmen no longer manned the fleets, and the crews were largely recruited from slum elements of German, French and Baltic nationality.

The life of the sailors then became as inhuman as it had been in the *Carreira da India*. After a Dutch ship was made ready to sail, it often had to lie in harbor off Texel awaiting a favorable wind. Because of the wait, unsanitary conditions frequently developed while the vessel was still at anchor; the living quarters became filthy with vomit and fecal matter. Most of this filth was not cleaned up in the next five or six months, and when the ship reached the festering heat of the tropics the ferment was accentuated. Dysentery, typhoid, and a host of other malignant diseases became rampant, in addition to the ravages of scurvy, which generally appeared after a month or two at sea because of dietary deficiency. Every morning a number of bodies were tossed overboard without religious or civil ceremony. Many a poor sufferer crawled off and hid himself to die, and the putrid, rat-eaten carcass would not be discovered for days. The sailors, although themselves in such a hard plight, were completely insensitive to the sufferings of the soldiers their ships carried. One commentator remarked that the death of a chicken in their poultry-coop caused more concern than the death of half a dozen soldiers.

The skippers of later Dutch Indiamen were no longer the bold navigators of the earlier period, and a surprising number of ships were lost on the outward voyage because of their inability to calculate their easting in the driving westerly gales of the "roaring forties." With only sandglasses to determine time, it was impossible to calculate longitude, and the pilots therefore often failed to change their course to northerly in time for the Sunda Straits and Java; hence they piled up their ships on the reefs and coasts of Australia and New Guinea, which they thought still lay hundreds of miles ahead to the east.

While the indifference of the Crown of Portugal and of the Dutch East India Company toward the sufferings of mariners on the passage to India was inhuman, their iniquities cannot be mentioned in the same breath with the fiendish barbarities with which France and Spain treated the oarsmen on royal galleys, in the days when naval control of the Mediterranean depended upon oared warships.

During the pre-eminence of Venice as a naval power, the rowers had been free citizens of the Republic with their own guild and patron saint. They were well paid by the State and possessed jealously guarded rights and privileges. After Venice lost control of the Mediterranean in the sixteenth and seventeenth centuries, the French and Spanish war galleys which took over the domination of the Inland Sea were rowed by slaves, convicts, and prisoners of war. In the beginning the slaves generally were North Africans, officially classified as "Turks" and purchased by the French and Spanish consuls at the slave markets of Malta and Leghorn. Toward the second half of the seventeenth century, the supply of Moslem captives available as slaves could not possibly meet the demand, and the galleys were largely manned by convicts; in the late sixteen-hundreds, the oarsmen in the French *Corps de Galères* numbered about 1,400 purchased slaves and about 4,900 convicts. In 1690 there were 12,000 unhappy men at the oars in the *Corps de Galères*.

These poor creatures were classed as "Huguenots, deserters from the French army, smugglers of salt, bigamists, thieves and forgers." Soon the list was expanded to include "bohemians, vagrants, beggars and vagabonds," or in other words, almost any able-bodied common man whose enemies might contrive to have him seized. A nobleman of influence could have almost anyone condemned at his whim. Sometimes if the shortage of rowers became desperate, word was passed from the Ministry of Justice in Paris to the local magistrates in the provinces to collect convicts for the navy. Under these conditions, the zealous local justice was ready to seize almost any passer-by on a pretext of begging, brawling or stealing. The culprit was kept in jail until the Collector of Convicts reached town in the spring and collected the already sick prisoners. An iron collar was fastened about the neck of each, and a very heavy chain welded to it which he had to carry. The collectors were paid so much per head for each slave transported to Toulon or Marseilles. The profit to the contractor was whatever saving he could make on his per capita price, and consequently the poor wretches were given just enough rations to keep them alive. The passage of one of these chain gangs was pitiful, but as by then the prisoners had become desperate men, like those released by Don Quixote, an onlooker dared not treat them with sympathy.

The first step in induction into the galleys was to brand the recruit's face and cut off his ears and nose. At a slightly later date, cutting off the nose was discontinued, since under intense exertion the oarsman had difficulty in breathing which rendered him less useful. Many of the wretches in the French galleys were men from the royal Spanish fighting ships who had been captured in combat. In order to maintain the crews, both Louis XIV and Louis XV at times made diplomatic arrangements whereby friendly monarchs of non-maritime countries, such as Poland, would turn over to the French all the convicts in their jails. The oarsmen were chained to their benches and rowed under the lash to the tuck of a drum. A high degree of tactical efficiency was attained, and the maneuvers and speed of a squadron of galleys were graceful and impressive.

The stench from the benches was overpowering, and when court ladies of delicate sensibilities were conveyed in the luxurious, gilded cabins at a galley's stern, the gallant commander saw to it that the ship was never rowed into the wind, regardless of the manpower expended. The French captains of galleys were proud members of the most distinguished families in that brilliant period of elegance and enlightenment, and the Captain General of the Galleys was sometimes even of the blood royal. The abandonment of this atrocious system was not due to any advancement in the Christian brotherhood of man, but was brought about in 1700 when a Bourbon of France ascended the throne of Spain, thus eliminating the costly naval rivalry between the two powers.

Contrasted with the lot of the oarsmen in the French galleys, the life of a seaman on a French sailing ship was infinitely more free. But compared to the life of a free man ashore, the sailor had a wretched existence, badly paid, miserably fed, harshly driven, brutally mistreated, uncared for and generally sick. In the case of the French, the gulf was even greater than in other nationalities between the aristocratic officers and the miserable jailbirds and conscripted fishermen who huddled in the squalid quarters of the crew. The original policy of the French, after Colbert had presented the Crown with a fleet of magnificent warships, was to acquire crews by conscripting the hardy fishermen of the channel ports. These free, masterless amphibians were essentially individualists to whom the thought of naval servitude was insupportable. They tried to elude capture, but the press gang soon developed an ingenious and effective method of recruiting good seamen. When the desired victim escaped and hid himself, the usual procedure was to quarter soldiers upon the humble hut of the absentee—something they had a legal right to do. Brutal and licentious men were especially selected for the purpose, and at once made free of the wife and daughters of the missing householder. Generally the anguished husband would be caught lurking in the area and hustled aboard ship, leaving his family destitute and without protection. This kind of recruitment meant that the King was served by seamen with implacable bitterness toward the flag. Naturally, these common seamen, full of rancor as they were, found no sympathy in their elegant, aristocratic superiors.

This ruthless French policy of naval recruitment acquired very able seamen for a brief period, but it soon resulted in the destruction of the fishing industry of the hardy Bretons. The next generation warily forsook apprenticeship in such a persecuted calling, and then there were no more skilled recruits available; the quality of the French fighting crews, except in the Dunkirk corsair frigates, deteriorated accordingly. The inhuman malpractices of the French press gangs eventually brought about their own downfall, for when the revolution finally broke out, the ill-used naval crews mutinied and seized all the high-born officers, who quickly were sent to the guillotine. Thus, when Napoleon attempted to build up an effective fleet to challenge the British navy, he was reduced to furious impotence. In carrying out his grandiose plans to conquer Egypt and reach India, he found that his newly created admirals and captains could not cope either in strategy or tactics with Nelson and his experienced commanders; and, largely for want of seasoned naval strategists and tacticians, the Empire finally collapsed in the grip of the British navy.

As long as the Hispanic powers controlled the overseas sources of wealth they were irresistible. When their maritime monopoly was broken, not so much by ships and guns as by the hardihood of the common seamen who made up the crews of the English, Dutch and French raiders, there was a scramble among the victorious northern nations for mastery. Finally it was the British jack tar, despised, maltreated, and enslaved though he was, who caused England to emerge triumphant. The sailors provided the sea power for the marine blockade that throttled their continental rivals.

It is noteworthy that, at the very inception of the modern British

Introduction

navy, even before 1590, when Jan stood upon a cliff of Terceira Island and watched England's first hesitating advances through the Spanish seas, a humane and appreciative understanding of the role of the common sailor was displayed by two farseeing Englishmen who, as much as any others, were the creators of the English navy. They were the Reverend Richard Hakluyt, Esquire, and Sir John Hawkins.

In 1583, the year in which Jan arrived in India, Richard Hakluyt was sent to Paris to serve as chaplain at the English Embassy. Born in Herefordshire and educated at Westminster School and at Oxford, he had early been interested in geography and cosmography, but his dedication in life was to social reform. In 1582 he had published a book called *Divers Voyages* in which he advocated a policy of colonization in North America to relieve the distress in England due to industrial depression. In it, he pressed for an attempt to revive English trade by finding the Northwest Passage to China. He had previously been a proponent of a search for the Northeast Passage, the chimera that was later to captivate his Dutch contemporaries Jan Huyghen van Linschoten and Petrus Plancius, but which he himself had already decided was impracticable.

In his book he also had urged that improvement in English navigation should be fostered by the founding of a school for pilots, such as Petrus Plancius advocated in Holland. Because of his consuming desire to solve the enigma of a short and safe arctic route to China, Hakluyt successfully courted the good will of those French authorities who were acquainted with the French voyages of discovery to the west, and particularly with their magnificent pioneering efforts which were to result in colonies in Nova Francia, Florida, along the Mississippi, the Great Lakes, the West Indies, Brazil, in the Indian Ocean and in farther India.

He also sought in Paris the friendship of a group of Portuguese navigators of the refugee court of Dom Antonio, Prior of Crato, who was recognized by France, England and the Dutch Republic as King of Portugal, instead of the usurping Philip II. Several of the exiled Portuguese noblemen had rounded the Cape of Good Hope and had commanded ships and squadrons in the Indian Ocean and the China Sea. To Hakluyt's chagrin, he found that both the French and the Portuguese looked with patronizing scorn and some amusement upon such navigators as then served Queen Elizabeth.

Hakluyt was stung by the opinions of these foreign veterans. He now determined to initiate a campaign to develop the potentialities of England as a maritime power. He returned home in the following year and set about arousing the interest of influential courtiers in his crusade for a school of navigation for captains and pilots, which would also start to train a contingent of English common sailors, for he recognized the importance of the man before the mast.

Introduction

He was a good publicist, possessed considerable political ability, was a man of energy, and, in that great age of Elizabethan letters, ranked as a master of English prose. In various subtle ways and through suitable channels he endeavored to enlist the Queen's support. To further his plan he wrote a manuscript entitled *Western Plantings* and had the gratification of presenting it to Her Majesty personally. His maritime crusade fitted admirably into his strongly preached economic and social program; he proposed that, with a strong navy and efficient merchant marine, England should occupy both shores of the Atlantic Ocean, grow in wealth, prestige and power, entrench the Protestant religion in the New World, and make Elizabeth pre-eminent among the crowned heads of Christendom. He gained the confidence and support of such courtiers as Secretary of State Walsingham, Lord Treasurer Burghley, Lord Admiral Howard, Lord Chancellor Hatton, and of course of Sir Walter Raleigh and Sir Humphrey Gilbert.

With prodigious energy Hakluyt translated into English and published at his own cost the *Decades of the New World* by Peter Martyr and several other Spanish works, just as he was to have Linschoten's *Itinerario* translated into English and published ten years later. In 1589, to vindicate the prestige of his native land, he wrote a manuscript of 750,000 words, corrected the 825 pages of proofs, and published one of the greatest and most influential histories of the English nation, the immortal *The Principall Navigations, Voiages and Discoueries of the English Nation*.

The book came out the year after the repulse of the Spanish Armada and became the inspiration for the transformation of the insular English into the rulers of the seas. However, although Hakluyt struck the patriotic note that aroused the English to enlist in his crusade, he was not successful in persuading them, once they had attained their goals of power and wealth, to follow the idealistic practices which were to him the real point of victory. Hakluyt's dream had been to elevate the lot of the common man and particularly the common sailor by victory at sea. His motto was: "In the numbers of skilled workmen consists the safety of the nation." He did not think it possible to succeed with untrained, conscripted crews for the fighting ships. "A class of seamen must be bred from boyhood to the sea, and they are irreplaceable if lost." He worked for an increase in the number of seamen, their education, development, and employment under tolerable and decent conditions at a fair rate of pay. They were Englishmen who deserved well of their country.

Hakluyt's enlightened program was heartily supported by Admiral Sir John Hawkins, the one man to whom, more than to any other, England owed the victory over the Invincible Armada. Hawkins, against great opposition, had built and armed, as the core of British naval defense, battleships faster and handier than Spanish galleons, able to sail much closer into

Introduction

the wind, and so heavily armed that while keeping themselves out of range they could pound the Spanish fleet at will. He held with Hakluyt that the men who manned the ships were even more important than the hulls and the cannon.

From his vast practical experience in many long corsair voyages, Sir John went further than Hakluyt. Hawkins asseverated again and again that good sanitary conditions were the secret of good crews and good fleets. He said, "In my twenty years at sea I have seen the lives of more than ten-thousand good seamen lost by diseases that might have been prevented by better sanitation."

A lack of medical knowledge cannot be used as an excuse for those losses because, as we shall see, even in those early days voices were raised and books were printed which advocated the sanitary shipboard methods recommended by Hawkins. Unfortunately, as sea power was attained for England, the nepotistic Admiralty, merchant interests, and Parliament all closed their ears to the advice of the two men to whom they owed their prosperity.

The penal regulations in the English navy, even at the end of the eighteenth century, make gruesome reading. Apart from such mild sentences as extra duty and being deprived of the grog ration, a very common penalty for a culprit was being put in irons, which meant having both ankles shackled to a long iron bar fastened to the deck. There generally would be several other seamen in irons lying or sitting alongside one another in this cramped position; some were kept there for weeks, or even for the duration of the voyage, without any sanitary provisions whatsoever.

If a man was caught spitting on the deck he was forced to carry a wooden spittoon hanging from his neck. If a sailor talked back to a petty officer, he had to submit to wearing in his mouth an iron bit like that of a horse, which was held in place by a cord about his head. The worst punishment, which was frequently meted out, was flogging with a cat o' nine tails, a stout wooden truncheon having nine pieces of knotted rope about two feet long fastened to it. It was wielded by two boatswain's mates, one left handed and one right handed, so as to crisscross the stripes. A flogging was a full dress affair, with the entire ship's company mustered in ranks to witness it and with the marines under arms to preserve order. The condemned man was lashed to an upright grating with his arms fastened over his head, and whipped on his bare back with lusty strokes. A dozen blows made his skin a bloody pulp, and eight or ten dozen were generally fatal. Condemnation to being "flogged through the fleet"—that is, successively whipped from ship to ship—was a death sentence much more cruel than being condemned to be hanged from the yard-arm.

There was no appeal, either in the Royal Navy or in the East India

Introduction

Company's fleet, from the despotic rule of the captain, who had more arbitrary power than any other officer in England. In both services, the captain was appointed through influence and lived in relative luxury on his ship. In the Indian service, he made a fortune in two or three voyages from his profits on food and supplies and even on medicines, as well as by private trading and smuggling. In neither the navy nor the Indian service was it possible for a meritorious officer without influence to rise to top command, no matter how brilliant his record of service might be; a captain appointed through nepotism might well be half his age. Being responsible to no one, and with the power of life and death over the hapless crew, a despotic or sadistic captain was in his element; his tyranny was transmitted from the quarterdeck into the forecastle, which became a living hell.

On one royal ship in the eighteenth century, the captain had a midshipman hanged from the yard-arm "because of muttering with a mutinous gleam in his eye." The poor lad's family were people of influence, and hence managed to get a naval inquiry instituted, but the guilty captain was acquitted by the Admiralty Board that heard the case.

In the *Globe*, one of the earliest English Indiamen, which left England in 1610 to trade in the East Indies, the standard punishment for fighting among the crew was to truss up the offender, haul him to the yard-arm, and drop him precipitately into the sea. Then he was hauled by a rope under the hull, almost suffocated and badly cut by barnacles. This "keel hauling" often was fatal and always was shattering to the culprit's nerves. If he survived, his right hand was then nailed to the mainmast by his own jackknife and he was left in that position until, unaided, he pulled out the knife. Finally, he was fined six months of his miserable pay which, although it rarely equalled five dollars a month, was more than was paid to a seaman in the Royal Navy.

Even several officers of the *Globe* were, for various offenses, punished by being "cast from the yard," and others were "put to the capstan," which meant being tied in a painful position to the capstan bar with a weight hanging about the neck.

The British East India Company (The John Company) prospered mightily, despite the terrible sanitary and navigating conditions of its Indiamen, the mortality rate of its crews, and the loss of many homeward bound ships due to gross overloading. The worst conditions of the *Carreira da India* were repeated, and for the same human causes. Even in the late eighteenth and early nineteenth centuries, after scurvy had been largely eliminated, the chronometer invented, the reading of longitude perfected, and many improvements introduced in naval architecture, the conditions in the English Indiamen were, incredibly, no better than those of the Portuguese three centuries earlier. The heedlessness of a monop-

Introduction

olistic trust and its single-minded pursuit of profits so retarded ship development that a crew resurrected from a British ship of 1600 would have been at home on a British Indiaman of 1790.

The John Company followed the barbarous tactics of the navy and recruited by ruthless press gangs, who flung their nets to capture any man, be he yeoman or scholar, who could be shanghaied and brought aboard. It is to the logs of some of these literate unfortunates that we owe the accounts of life in the forecastle during the Golden Age in which England's navy was developed. From their journals we draw the conclusion that in the lumbering English Indiamen the lot of the men before the mast had deteriorated in almost every respect from the level of the unhappy Portuguese seamen of whom Linschoten wrote.

In 1625, when the English were challenging the Dutch at sea, the crews of the English men-of-war were described as "human refuse, filthy, diseased and in rags." Sir William St. Leger wrote in 1625: "They stinke as they go, the poore rags they have are rotten and redy to fall off if they be touched." In addition to its hard treatment of its seamen at sea, the British navy was accustomed to put ashore in England all its sick and wounded and leave them to shift for themselves without pay and without medical attention. Before the Reformation, these destitute seamen could seek asylum in a monastery; but after these places of refuge were closed, the suffering wretches had to beg for their food, and often died from lack of medical attention and starvation. So many destitute and wounded discharged seamen filled the English ports after the defeat of the Armada, in 1588, that in 1590 the Admirals Drake, Hawkins and Howard founded a mutual fund for their medical treatment. This was called the "Chatham Chest," and many years later became the Greenwich Hospital and Soldiers' Home. The plan was quite ineffective for over half a century; while the unfortunate discharged seamen died in the streets, the large annual payroll tax was embezzled by naval administrators.

The main attraction which drew both officers and men to disregard the hardships and hazards of life at sea was prize money. In the British navy the total amount realized from the sale of a captured ship and cargo was divided into twenty parts. Three parts went to the captain, two to the lieutenants and masters, two to the marine officers, surgeon, pursers, boatswain, gunner, carpenters and chaplain, three to the midshipmen, surgeon's mates and ratings other than chief petty officers, and the remainder to the seamen, marines and boys. Since hostilities were almost always in progress and meant a sort of organized piracy on the high seas, there were great fortunes to be made in the navy, if one were a high enough officer and if his ship had luck in taking prizes at sea.

The most dreadful scourge of long sea voyages was scurvy, and the Portuguese were not alone in closing their eyes to its cause and prevention; the English, French and Dutch were equally heedless. The record of the first English expedition to the Orient under Captain Lancaster and of the first Dutch one under the Houtmans showed losses as catastrophic as any ever suffered by the Portuguese. Yet at that same early period, careful commanders were able to avoid scurvy by proper care.

In the British navy between 1600 and 1800 the deaths from scurvy amounted to the frightful minimum of four thousand a year and in the merchant marine about twelve hundred a year, and yet during this period many books or articles were published which correctly diagnosed the causes of scurvy and the means of curing it.

Captain Cook, two centuries after Linschoten, on his first voyage in the Pacific lost more than one-third of his men from scurvy; he learned from his mistakes, and on his second and third voyages he lost practically none. His contemporary, Admiral Anson, left England in 1789 with 961 officers and men, and within a year 626 had died from disease, mostly scurvy; his total loss on his voyage amounted to three-fourths of his complement. In fact, when Anson arrived at the island of Tinian, in the Marianas, he could muster only seventy-one men fit for duty.

Scurvy greatly reduced the effectiveness of Spain's Invincible Armada, and in the following two centuries it was to be an important factor in the defeat by the British of superior French fleets. It is estimated that, in the period from 1500 on, when long sea voyages began to be undertaken, to 1800, when the "seaman's fever" was checked, as many died from scurvy as the total from all other diseases plus shipwreck and naval battles. And yet, during all those three centuries, it was generally known that supplementary rations of sauerkraut, raw potatoes, raw or dried onions, currants, raisins, citrus fruits, and green leafy vegetables such as watercress, parsley or scurvy grass, as well as of fresh meats, would prevent or cure the disease. However, the only methods of preservation known were drying, salting or smoking fresh food, and generally these processes failed to preserve the anti-scorbutic elements, except in the case of sauerkraut, but sauerkraut (called in Dutch *zuurkool*, or sour kale) was served as a standard ration only on Dutch ships.

It has been known only since about 1930 that scurvy results from a deficiency of vitamin C in the human system, and that it is about a fortnight to two months before deprivation of the vitamin exhausts the natural supply in the average person. The first symptoms of scurvy are lassitude and marked weakness; swelling of the abdomen, legs and arms; very foul breath, together with softening, bleeding and swelling of the gums and loosening of the teeth; and extreme pain in moving the members. Death from heart failure, from rapid pneumonia, asthma, or complete exhaustion due to sleeplessness, then carries off the sufferer.

The sad condition of the Portuguese men before the mast was somewhat relieved by the presence as passengers on every nao of a number of priests and friars, who voluntarily and compassionately ministered to the sick and dying. The Dutch East India Company operated its ships and its "factories" on a strictly business basis, with profit as the sole motive; although Calvinistic in its principles, it avoided supporting religious establishments ashore in India, made no pretense of proselytizing, and did not count a chaplain as an essential member of a fleet's complement.

The British East India Company apparently did all it could to avoid having chaplains aboard. Parliament early passed a law requiring all passenger ships of 500 tons or more to carry a chaplain. However, the John Company for years thereafter registered all its ships as being of 499 tons, and lobbied successfully through many sessions of Parliament to defeat bills requiring an official measurement. When at last the reformers managed to bring out such legislation, it was discovered that all the Indiamen were of much greater actual size than 500 tons, and the company had fraudulently under-registered them. The John Company then had to comply with the law, and thereafter they signed on chaplains as regular officers of their ships.

On a British warship in the seventeenth century, a tapping sound heard outside the wardrooms was evidence that the officers were at a meal; it was universal custom to tap a ship's biscuit against the edge of the table to knock out the weevils before eating it. There was a grim saying that "bread without worms was so bad that even the weevils would not touch it." The standard ship's biscuit was about the size of a saucer and as hard and heavy as flint. It was made of wheat flour mixed with flour of dried peas, and every biscuit was infested with little brown grubs of two kinds. "The weevils tasted bitter but the maggots left a disagreeable cold taste in the mouth." The standard soup that was served was a puree of peas, and it was impossible to swallow a spoonful without gulping down weevils as well.

In the early days of sail, when voyages lasted for months or years, one of the desperate problems of a commander was to procure fresh drinking water. It was customary to anchor off a river mouth, or wherever a landing might be possible, and send watering parties ashore, generally under heavy guard, in order to fill the water casks at any source that was available, sometimes even from stagnant pools. As there was then no knowledge of bacteria, polluted water was often brought aboard and the entire crew would be stricken.

As early as 1612, the British East India Company appointed John Woodall as Chirurgeon General; although he never went to sea, in 1617 he published a book called *The Surgeon's Mate* which became a standard reference work. In 1598, Watson had published *Care of the Diseased in Remote Regions*, which treated of what later became known as tropical medicine.

Introduction

Captain John Smith, of American colonial fame, in 1626 brought out his *Grammar and Accidence for Young Seamen*, in which he advised that a surgeon be given a regular position in the ship's company and that his medicine chest should be stocked with medicines for physic as well as for surgery. Captain Smith's sensible suggestion received no recognition, and indeed in the year in which he published it an eighth of London's entire population died of the plague, and surgeons were too busy bleeding their thousands of patients to be much concerned that a few dozen wretched sailors might be dying because of their inability to cope with their maladies. However, medical treatment at sea could not have been given by a surgeon, who could not legally practice internal medicine; hence typhoid, dysentery, yellow fever, smallpox and food poisoning raged through the ships while the Society of Apothecaries (founded 1617), the College of Physicians and the Company of Barber Surgeons squabbled over jurisdictional questions.

It is surprising to learn that in 1572 an acute English merchant named Henry Hawkes announced his belief that yellow fever was carried by mosquitoes. However, his idea was scorned by the medical world. Although it was recorded by Hakluyt, over two centuries were to pass before the theory was proved and adopted by the medical profession.

Until the middle of the eighteenth century, British seamen received little better treatment than when the East India Company was formed in the days of Queen Elizabeth. Then the rule read that "the Chirurgion Generall's duties are to give medicine and practise surgery and also to cut the hayre of the carpenters, saylors, caulkers and laborers in a seemly manner." Another of the surgeon's duties was to give lessons to the officers and men in the application of tourniquets to men wounded in arm or leg. When the ship was cleared for action the surgeon and his mates placed piles of tourniquets about the decks for first-aid treatment. In a wooden warship, many of the casualties were from secondary missiles, or splinters which were scattered in showers when a heavy round shot crashed into the bulwarks, mast or hull. Many such wounds were very severe, and it was necessary to apply tourniquets immediately to prevent the wounded from bleeding to death.

Because of lack of antisepsis, any wound in the arm or leg was likely to fester into gangrene. Consequently preventive surgery was the rule; a shattered member was amputated with a saw, and the stump was seared with boiling tar to stop the bleeding. A stiff drink of rum was the only anesthetic, and even a rugged patient well might die of shock. Abdominal, chest or head wounds were generally fatal. The surgical cockpit or sick bay was literally a slaughter house.

Ship's crews were largely infected by venereal disease, which would today be termed an occupational hazard. Deprived of female companion-

Introduction

ship for months at a time, the men were mad with sexual hunger, and since they were almost penniless, they could only consort with the squalid, diseased dregs of the ports. Quite possibly a number of these poor creatures were the wives and daughters of impressed seamen of the Royal Navy, left penniless and with no means of support when their husbands and fathers were snatched away. As we have seen, the common seamen in the Royal Navy received no pay at all, because the Navy was in arrears as much as six years in their payments. The legal amount they should have received was about five dollars a month, but they were never paid it.

In Plymouth, the English naval base, the population of prostitutes was estimated to be in excess of five thousand, mirroring the terrible economic condition of the poor which drove women into such a profession. When the fleet was in, these women were allowed the run of the ships; this practice was not forbidden until the late nineteenth century. Naval regulations for many years authorized naval surgeons to charge for treatment of venereal disease, and this extortion was estimated to average fifteen shillings for each case, although all other medical treatment was free. This hypocrisy supplied the surgeons with their major source of income.

In the sixteenth and seventeenth centuries there were no able doctors on the ships of any nation, and if there was any surgeon at all, he was an ignorant barber who bled patients to the extent of six or seven pints in a few days. On one ship it is recorded that 400 invalids were bled in one day.

It was not until the middle of the eighteenth century that scientific studies of nautical diseases began to be made, when a group of Scottish surgeons in the British Navy commenced to diagnose the causes of crippling diseases aboard ship. The pioneer in these discoveries was Dr. James Lind (1716-1794), an observant and humane naval surgeon whose common-sense findings, although at first derided, were soon confirmed by some of his fellows. After half a century of opposition from the bureaucratic Admiralty, they were finally officially put into effect, and resulted in greatly improved combat effectiveness and navigational efficiency in the royal fleets. All of Lind's remarkable recommendations were revolutionary, but they now represent standard practice in naval hygiene. They were:

Careful physical examination of all recruits, with permanent records of the characteristics of each individual.

Bathing recruits and keeping them in quarantine for some days with physical exercises and daily baths of cold water to toughen and condition them.

Removal and destruction of old clothing and issue of new clothes—thus initiating the adoption of naval uniforms.

Introduction

In the tropics, to anchor well off shore, to send men ashore only in the daytime, and preferably to man necessary landing parties with natives if possible. (This was a very well thought-out rule, considering that the responsibility of mosquitoes for infection had not been recognized despite its discovery by Hawkes in 1572, two centuries earlier.)

To furnish lemon juice daily to every seaman.

This last rule would formerly have been impossible to carry out because of the inability to preserve fruits at sea, but Dr. Lind solved this problem by inventing a method of concentrating the juice by successive boilings, so that a heavy residue which he called "rob" could be preserved aboard ship indefinitely for dilution with water when needed. Captain Louis H. Roddis of the Medical Corps, United States Navy, wrote in *James Lind, Founder of Nautical Medicine,* published by Heinemann in 1951: "The conquest of scurvy is one of the mileposts in human progress. This scourge affected exploration, the colonization of new lands, commercial enterprises, mercantile shipping and all naval operations. If the ten greatest events in maritime history were to be selected, the conquest of scurvy would have to be included. This discovery was largely the work of James Lind, and his work affected the whole course of modern history."

Dr. Lind also developed a practical method of deriving drinking water from ordinary sea water by simple distillation.

The effect of Dr. Lind's rules of hygiene when finally adopted was striking. The average confinement of crewmen in naval hospitals dropped from a ratio of one out of three in 1779 to one out of twenty in 1807, in the crucial days of the naval struggle of Lord Nelson's navy against Napoleon's.

Dr. Lind emphasized not only that poor food and foul drinking water weakened the men, but also that overcrowding in poorly ventilated, cold, damp forecastles, loss of sleep, and fatigue all contributed to their lack of resistance to contagion and infection.

The most striking diagnosis of the Scottish medical group, which met with little credence by the Admiralty, was that one of the cruelest maladies which sapped the strength of sailors was the mental disease of homesickness felt by those kept away from their families under depressing and dispiriting conditions for periods of four to six years and more. It is now believed that homesickness was the cause of much of the mortality among the crews of the royal naval sailing ships. The term "homesickness" is too mild to describe the despairing agony of an impressed sailor who knew that his wife and family would be destitute and have to beg for food, while he not only was kept away from them by force, but was not given any wages whatsoever sometimes for as long as ten years. Being penniless, when in port he could not even buy fresh food for himself after suffering from a prolonged diet of inferior salted rations.

Even in the enlightened and relatively humanitarian nineteenth century, the best and most efficient sailors were not allowed to go back to England when their ship was ordered home after long service, but would be transferred and kept on station because of their superior skill. The better a sailor was at his job the less likely was he ever to get home at all. Many ships had been on station for three or four years when the welcome order came to return to "blighty." The captain of a ship that was to return always gave the admiral a list of his best seamen, and these unfortunates, with their hopes of returning to their families completely blasted, were then transferred to the ships that were going to remain on station.

It was for this reason that so many of the best men of the British fleets during the Napoleonic wars deserted, perhaps abandoning six years or more of accumulated pay, and shipped aboard an American merchant ship where they would enjoy more freedom. Before long the crews of American craft were substantially made up of British seamen who had deserted; and it was British insistence on searching American vessels for such deserters that brought about the War of 1812 between England and the United States.

However, the lot of the common sailor in the American merchant marine during the age of sail in the nineteenth century was also an unhappy one. The men before the mast were underpaid, poorly fed, and were called upon for the most strenuous and hazardous exertions, driven by a brutal discipline which took no heed of their exhaustion. Except for the elimination of scurvy, the forecastle hands in the American Clippers in the China or Australian trade were little better off than their Portuguese predecessors in the days of Jan Huyghen van Linschoten.

The Portuguese Speak Up

REGARDLESS of the impact which Linschoten's *Itinerario* had upon the foreign policies of the northern maritime nations, his personal contribution to the aggrandizement of his native land was little appreciated there. In 1610 he presented a humble petition to the States General for a modest annual pension in recognition of his services to the United Provinces. His plea was brusquely rejected, with the tart official comment that the renewal of copyright upon his book was compensation enough for whatever he might have done for the State.

However, even had the pension been granted he could have enjoyed it only for the one remaining year of his life. And after the patriotic author's death, although his book continued to be reprinted again and again, his name and personality were soon forgotten in the wave of Dutch prosperity which he had helped to bring about.

Ironically enough, the Portuguese could not forget him so easily. Through the centuries, his vivid pictures of sixteenth-century *Asia Portuguesa* and his descriptions of social and economic life in Golden Goa have been accepted as basic by Anglo-Saxon and other historians. This unquestioning acquiescence by nineteenth and twentieth-century northern scholars, who rarely appear to have been qualified to accomplish research in the abundant Dutch, Portuguese and Indian archives of the era, has caused bitter protests from twentieth-century Portuguese historians, who refute many of the biting and satirical passages of the *Itinerario* in regard to the Portuguese. However, what they particularly resent is the general assumption, based upon Linschoten's account, that the government of *Asia Portuguesa* at the end of the sixteenth century was corrupt and decadent and that therefore it soon fell like a ripe fruit into the hands of the vigorous Dutch invaders.

Viewed after the lapse of centuries and with an abatement of the intense religious and racial antagonisms of the late sixteenth century, when the *Itineraro* was written, the neutral reader can note two aspects of the argument. First, it is not difficult now to show from the records that, despite aggressive assaults upon the Portuguese domain by the Dutch, with their strong English and native allies, the Portuguese steadfastly held their own for several decades in the early seventeenth century, and relinquished Ormuz, Cochin, Ceylon and Malacca only after prolonged and stubborn resistance against superior forces.

History also details the repulse of the Dutch attacks upon the bastions of Portuguese power in Mozambique in Southeast Africa, Goa on the Malabar Coast of India, Macao on the China Sea, and Timor in Indonesia; over all these strong points, the Portuguese flag still waved in the mid-twentieth century, after both England and the Netherlands had lowered their own ensigns in Southeast Asia.

Second, latter-day Portuguese chroniclers point out that, far from having become decadent and ineffective at the end of the sixteenth century, the Portuguese not only succeeded in defending many of their naval bases in the Orient, but they rose up in the homeland, expelled the hated Spanish invaders, and regained their national independence. In the seventeenth century, when the United Provinces of the Netherlands were at the height of their power and were the world's strongest maritime nation, the supposedly decadent Portuguese not only invaded and recaptured Angola, forcing the Dutch to surrender that rich African province, but also actually defeated strong Dutch armies in several decisive battles in Brazil, where they captured the Dutch metropolis of Recife and made the surprised Netherlanders cede all their promising Brazilian possessions back to Portugal.

Thus modern Portuguese historians are satisfied that they have refuted the scornful and devastating criticisms of Jan Huyghen van Linschoten.

Jan van Linschoten:
The Dutch Marco Polo

CHAPTER I

Background and Boyhood

JAN HUYGHEN VAN LINSCHOTEN, the Dutch adventurer, geographer and explorer, lived during the latter half of the sixteenth and the beginning of the seventeenth centuries. Born just a year before Shakespeare, he lived during the times of Queen Elizabeth of England, King Philip II of Spain, and Prince William of Orange of the Netherlands. The great century of exploration just past had left Spain and Portugal in possession of a monopoly of trade with the Far East and the New World. The campaign of the northern nations, the Netherlands, England, France and even to some extent Germany, to supplant Spain and Portugal on the seas was beginning. In this epic struggle for power, Jan, the talented and intrepid son of the innkeeper of Enkhuizen, played an important part; for until he published his descriptive and geographical work, *The Itinerario or Seavoyage of Jan Huyghen van Linschoten to the East or Portuguese Indies,* the northern nations had no guide to the incredibly difficult passage to the profitable markets of the Orient. Published in Amsterdam in 1596, in Dutch, and soon translated into English, French and Latin, this book proved to be of crucial influence in shaping the currents of world history. Thanks in part to the alert Dutchman's directions, his country and England were able to gain the ascendancy over Portugal and to dominate the sea-lanes used in the prodigiously important European trade with the East and also within the East.

Jan was born in Haarlem in late 1562 or early 1563, and was taken to the town of Enkhuizen as a child. Enkhuizen was his permanent home; it was where he settled down after his first great period of travel and put his manuscripts in order for publication. There he married and became a leading citizen; and there his further explorations were planned.

The people of Enkhuizen used to be the most amphibious of all the Netherlanders, for the town had little but the sea upon which to depend. Because the town and its inhabitants, including Jan Huyghen van Linschoten, had such an individual character, it will be of interest to pause for a moment and consider their situation and history.

Enkhuizen

ENKHUIZEN is located in West Friesland, in the Northern Quarter of the Province of Holland, about a dozen miles to the east of its fellow city of Hoorn. It stands on a bulge on the west bank of what used to be the Zuider Zee, at the narrowest part of the great gulf which in olden times it commanded as a fortress.

Although Enkhuizen and Hoorn are now referred to as the "dead cities of the Zuider Zee," this description is fair only in relation to their former importance as seaports, for today they are both comfortable and picturesque provincial towns. The great Zuider Zee, to which they owed their prosperity up to a recent time, has now been shut off from the ocean and has become a freshwater lake called the IJsselmeer; much of it has been drained and its bed converted into farmland. Because of the withdrawal of the water, Hoorn is no longer even a port, but Enkhuizen is still an active fishing town, though it is accessible only to boats of shallow draft.

Enkhuizen, in West Friesland, is not a very old town, as Dutch history goes. Such towns as Medemblik, Stavoren or Dordrecht were already provincial centers in the early Middle Ages, whereas Enkhuizen, as well as Amsterdam, appeared in history somewhat later. However, that was even before the Zuider Zee was a sea, when it was still an inland lake that had been known from Roman times as Lake Flevo. The farmers and fisherfolk of the region were not Hollanders, but Frisians, a stalwart, blond people of Scandinavian affinity, speaking their own tongue, who had come across the lake from Friesland to the area still known as West Friesland. The earliest legend of the town, from about the year 1100 A.D., relates how the parish priest, Father Melchior, was so poor that he wore the same cassock for his whole life's service—the only one he ever possessed. There was no rectory in those days, and the priest was given lodging by various families in the town. The people of the area were freemen, and feudal vassals to no lord, although the Count of Holland, whose castle was at Haarlem, several times attempted unsuccessfully to conquer them. One hard winter when the marshes were frozen, the Count's men crossed the ice and burned Enkhuizen's few poor hovels. However, when the ice suddenly melted and the mounted invaders had a hard time getting back home through the boggy paths, Enkhuizen regained its freedom.

Then suddenly occurred one of those natural disasters which sometimes abruptly change the face of a nation. The North Sea burst through the land barriers and dunes of North Holland and overwhelmed thousands of acres of farmland. It surged into Lake Flevo, and by successive assaults widened and deepened the lake until it became a great salt sea. It was called the *Zuider Zee*, or South Sea. Enkhuizen was left on a flat, marshy peninsula, almost treeless and without hillocks, swept by the prevailing westerly wind from the North Sea—the same wind which was later to be so useful when native ingenuity developed the windmill to work the drainage pumps that freed the land from the ever-encroaching sea. Enkhuizen found itself on the shore of a navigable gulf, across which it came into contact with the prosperous Hanseatic ports of the east bank, Kempen and Deventer.

However, the swamps no longer protected Enkhuizen. In 1287, Count Floris V sailed from Haarlem in a fleet of big cog ships to add Enkhuizen to his tributaries. After a decade of war, the town in 1299 had to accept the Count of Holland as suzerain. From then on, the Enkhuizers had to fight the battles of Holland against their own kinsmen, the central Frisians; the latter quite held their own, and once even captured and sacked Enkhuizen and burned twenty-five ships in its harbor. In later years, Enkhuizen and Hoorn, although now located in the Province of Holland, held aloof and considered themselves as separate entities, comprising West Friesland, or the so-called Northern Quarter, in rivalry with Amsterdam and the rest of Holland proper.

The West Frisians, centuries later, were the core of the invincible Sea Beggars, who broke the power of Spain in the North Netherlands. Other seamen of history, the Scandinavians, Bretons, English, Genoans, Venetians, Basques and Portuguese, although born and bred to the sea, nevertheless were partly landsmen, in that behind them stood a wide stretch of terra firma. The West Frisians, however, had no such backing; except for their narrow patches of lush pastureland, fenced only by ditches amidst their fens, they sprang practically from the middle of the sea itself.

The Amphibians

TO THE ENKHUIZERS the Zuider Zee was all the world. Every child grew up with a drainage ditch or a tidal canal alongside the yard of his house, and his toys were ships made out of bits of wood with leaves as sails. He absorbed instinctively a knowledge of currents, of ebbs and flows, and of shifting winds, to which not only the sails of his own little bark but also the canvas of the ubiquitous windmill had to be trimmed. To him the primary elements of existence were water and wind. All transportation and movement were by boat, and man's life was attuned to the vagaries of the unpredictable Zuider Zee. The folk songs of West Frieslanders were entreaties to Providence to save their men from the dangers of the Zee, and their other plea was that the Benign Father might lead the schools of herring into the ready nets of His deserving children. Their folk legends are of mermaids and mermen, who in ancient times visited the fishing villages and were entrapped and Christianized.

Dutch Parochialism

THAT INTERNAL DISSENT which comes from strong local feeling is characteristic of Dutch history. Enkhuizen not only carried on warfare against the other Zuider Zee towns, but also had, in about 1400, an absurd schism between its two local Catholic parishes. This was so bitter that the members of one church would not allow their children to contract marriage with those of the rival parish. In the beginning, the farmers and merchants who lived in Enkhuizen were much better off than the poor fishermen of the town, and when they set about erecting a church (now the Zuider Kerk), they snubbed the fishermen. Therefore the latter decided to build their own church (now the Wester Kerk). Both buildings were piously put up by volunteers, and often construction was held up while the workers went off to war or when funds were lacking. Because of the rivalry between the two groups the churches were constantly being enlarged and their towers made higher. When the fishing faction suddenly became rich from the profits of the herring industry, the competition became furious indeed, and as a consequence Enkhuizen today has two very impressive churches. However, a century later, when the Calvinists took over the pulpits, the church interiors were very much changed by the removal of all the pictures, statues, and stained glass windows; the high, whitewashed naves no longer have the rich embellishments that once adorned them.

Although the little Zuider Zee towns were only a few miles apart and their fleets were in contact at sea, each community clung to its isolation. They retained their common dialect, but through the centuries a striking difference in local customs and in costume developed, especially among the women. Each town also invented its own type of sailing craft, with hulls and rigs markedly different from any other.

The Fisheries

FOR GENERATIONS, the people of Enkhuizen barely subsisted upon their hauls of mussels, smelt, anchovies, flounder, eels and shrimp, even though many of their smacks sailed out through the strait known as The Helder, past the large island of Texel and into the tumultuous North Sea, and fished dangerously with line and net along the irregular coast and as far out as the shallow Dogger Bank, about halfway to England. Some of the larger boats even went annually on the long and tortuous trip through the difficult Skagerrak, the Skaw and the Sound, until they reached the Swedish coast off the town of Kalmar to take part in the great herring catches. Even more perilous on such a voyage than storms and ocean currents were the ever threatening pirates and wreckers; the Enkhuizers learned to be fighters at sea as well as fishermen, nor did they hesitate to take an unarmed merchant ship if the opportunity arose. In those generations of precarious struggle for survival in the fierce, windswept North Sea and against the pitiless raiders of Denmark and Hamburg, the seeds developed which later came to fruition in the adventurous, piratical Sea Beggars and the great Dutch Corsairs.

In the middle of the fourteenth century, an alteration occurred in the course of the current from the Gulf Stream along the Swedish coast. The temperature of the waters changed, and the herring, deserting the Baltic region, suddenly appeared in great numbers off the coast of England. This, of course, was very convenient for the Dutch seamen, and the fishing industry began to expand rapidly.

Just at this time, Willem Beukelszoon of Biervliet invented a method of gutting and barreling herring which preserved them for many months. The process was kept secret from other nations, which permitted the Dutch to build up a large export business throughout Europe, since the preserved herring could be eaten on many days of Christian abstinence from meat. The contribution of Beukelszoon was of such importance to the economy that, two hundred years later, the Emperor Charles V formally visited his grave to do him honor and ordered that a monument be raised to his memory as a benefactor of his country.

The Herring Industry

BY THE TIME of Jan Huyghen van Linschoten (1563–1611), the Dutch herring industry had become one of the most highly organized trades of Europe. Its every operation was controlled by edicts issued by the

"Board of the Great Fishery," which had its headquarters in Delft and was financed and controlled by the municipal governments of Enkhuizen, Hoorn, Schiedam, Delft, Rotterdam and Brielle.

The ships of the herring fleet were not allowed to sail from Holland until June 15th of every year. Then, under strict supervision, they fished the Scottish waters between the Shetland Isles and the cape called Buchan Ness. On St. John's Day, June 24th, fishing started from Buchan Ness to Fair Isle; after July 25th, St. James' Day, they were allowed to fish off the Northumberland coast until September 14th, or Elevation Day; then, until September 25th, St. Catharine's Day, they fished along the English Channel as far as Yarmouth. By December they were back at the Thames estuary, and on January 31st all fishing was ordered to cease.

The herring caught before St. James' Day were always smaller, and the authorities required them to be packed separately and so marked. Every barrel of fish had to have the identifying marks of the individual fisherman who had packed it, the skipper of the smack, and the inspector at the port of unloading. The fish were packed in barrels on the smacks and then collected by light carriers and taken to port. Even the type of salt used in curing was rigidly controlled, and nothing was neglected in order to preserve not only the fish, but the Dutch fisheries' reputation for quality.

These operations along the English coast were a constant source of friction between the two countries; therefore the Dutch smacks each carried two small cannon, and the fleet was convoyed by ships of war. The English several times passed laws requiring that any boats fishing along their coasts must have an English license, and this was occasionally used as an excuse for harassing the Dutch, but was never strictly enforced.

The Herring City

ENKHUIZEN's identification with the herring-fishing industry became so complete that three herrings were represented on the town's coat of arms, and it was known as the "herring city." In Jan's day, Enkhuizen had a population of around 40,000, and operated a fleet of four hundred fishing smacks or busses (*buizen*).

The buss, a peculiar type of fore-and-aft-rigged vessel invented in Enkhuizen, was ideally suited to the shallow waters along the coast of Holland. A heavily built sloop with a broad beam and a flat bottom, it could squat in the mud without capsizing if it became stranded at low tide. It had a special feature in the vertical lee outriggers known as *zwaarden* (swords) on each side of the ship, which compensated for its lack of a keel. Busses were not only seaworthy in the turbulent North Sea, but could be handled by a very small crew; they were economical and efficient when used as cargo carriers and effective in blockade running, smuggling, and piracy. Although they ordinarily carried only two small cannon, they banded together in flotillas like a wolf pack to attack a large ship. Poor targets themselves, they could concentrate their fire on the rudder or masts of a war galleon and render it helpless to maneuver, then close upon it from all sides while their sailors swarmed aboard for the capture. Because the busses were able to use the inland lakes and rivers as well as the sea, they became the decisive factor in the war with Spain, for they could cut the communications and supply lines of the Spanish armies. These craft were, however, primarily used for peaceful fishing and cargo carrying. Roomy enough to permit families to live aboard and make them their homes, they constituted an important element in the society as well as in the economy of Enkhuizen.

Just as Enkhuizen had invented the buss, its neighboring city of Hoorn invented the dragnet. These two Zuider Zee towns prospered greatly, not only from the herring trade, but also from the general maritime activities which resulted from it.

The fishing industry was of paramount importance to the Dutch, just as agriculture was to most other nations. At the time of Linschoten, there were approximately a thousand busses employed, and the cost of each has been estimated at about $5,000. The number of people employed in the entire herring industry in Holland was estimated at half a million, twice as many as were employed in agriculture, and half as many as were engaged in all other industry.

The Carrying Trade

A T T H E E N D of the herring season, the great fleet of busses sought other employment for the interval of four and a half months before the annual cycle once more began. A few went to the Dogger Banks to fish with hook and line for cod and sole, but most were sent to the Baltic and Gulf of Finland to carry salt herring, cheese, and the products of Western Europe, and to bring back iron, grain, timber and shipbuilding supplies. This horde of small, economical ships soon managed to win most of the Baltic carrying trade, which became very important to the Netherlands.

A few of the busses were sent to load salt at the port of Setúbal, in Portugal, but the Dutch also used larger ships, yachts and flyboats, both in the salt trade and to bring back from Lisbon and Seville the products of the Mediterranean countries, of the Americas and the Orient. The herring not only served as an export commodity, but also were accepted as currency in the payment of dues and customs duties in foreign ports. This favorable two-way traffic permitted the shrewd Enkhuizers and their neighbors to operate so economically that the Portuguese soon began to charter Dutch yachts to carry their heavy traffic between Lisbon, Brazil and West Africa.

The Enkhuizen Skippers

THE ENKHUIZERS were generally recognized as the most expert of the Dutch navigators. In 1517, when the sovereign of the Netherlands, the young Archduke Charles, had to sail from Flanders through the North Sea and the English Channel, down the Atlantic and across the Bay of Biscay, to be crowned King of Spain, his advisors chose an Enkhuizen ship as the safest. Thereafter, as Emperor Charles V, he always sailed back and forth from Spain to Flanders in an Enkhuizen vessel, as did his son and successor, Philip II, in the one such voyage that he made. In 1530, when Charles invaded Tunis in North Africa, the town of Enkhuizen supplied him with four large carracks which served as transports across the Mediterranean and covered the landing of their soldiers by bombarding the Tunisian forts.

Fortifications

SINCE Enkhuizen projected into the narrowest part of the Zuider Zee and had a good harbor, Charles used it as his base when crossing the Zuider Zee to invade the Central Friesland province of his enemy, the Duke of Guelderland. He also decided to make it his bulwark against sea invasion from that quarter. He therefore made the town impregnable against land attack by having high, thick walls built, with numerous strong towers and a deep, wide moat. On the harbor side he established strong fortifications dominated by the giant brick tower now called the *Drommedaris*, which still stands as a monument of the town's past glory.

In Enkhuizen, as in all of Holland, there was no native stone for building purposes, and heavy timbers were in short supply. Both these materials could only be imported at great expense, and most of the fortifications and other structures were built of Dutch brick which, when set in depth, provided a suitable battlement against the artillery fire of the day. Because of the lack of piling to form a foundation in the marshy ground for such heavy edifices, the Enkhuizers used thousands of bales of dried cattle hides, pounding them down into the mud so that they formed relatively satisfactory foundations for military structures. Enkhuizen became the best fortified port of the Netherlands, and because of its large expenditures for defense it was granted the right to levy taxes upon the transportation in the Zuider Zee, and was also given exemption from provincial taxes.

A serene sense of security was a boon to its citizens, who jealously guarded their home rule and organized a strong, well-drilled, and adequately armed burgher guard corps.

The Reformation

THERE WAS no religious unrest in the town because, although the Reformation had been initiated by Martin Luther in Germany in 1517, it was not until about 1560 that the Enkhuizers showed any interest in the new doctrines. There were several well-liked nunneries and monasteries in the town, and the general religious atmosphere was placid. When some of the Catholic priests in both the great churches began to preach the new doctrines, they were not hindered by the tolerant Catholic town rulers. Moreover, when the diocesan authorities in Utrecht and the inquisitorial officials in The Hague began to take notice of these Protestant tendencies, the Catholic town government came stoutly to the defense of their fellow townsmen, the radical preachers, and by various measures protected them from severe penalties such as were inflicted in other towns. In one case they even winked at a jail delivery by his parishioners of a preacher who had been held in prison by the Inquisition in neighboring Hoorn.

However, the country was caught up in the religious convulsion which was profoundly shaking all of Europe, and Enkhuizen could not isolate itself from the general social disturbance. Therefore, in 1568, when ecclesiastical pressure from outside became threatening, the town government allowed about three hundred and fifty adherents to the new doctrines to leave the town en masse and peaceably to cross the frozen Zuider Zee to Friesland on their way to Emden, in East Friesland (now part of Germany), a center of the Calvinist movement.

William of Orange

IN 1568 the overt Dutch revolt against King Philip II commenced when William of Orange with three large armies of mercenaries unsuccessfully invaded the Netherlands. The movement was only partly religious, and was largely actuated by the revocation by Philip II of the traditional privileges of the Flemish and Dutch nobility and burghers. It was financed by France and England and by some of the German rulers who were enemies of Philip II, and it was led by the same Prince William of Orange who had been the favorite of King Philip's father, Charles V. William of Orange recognized the importance of Enkhuizen as the key to the Zuider Zee, and directed his efforts, both military and naval, to reaching that port with a strong force. In preparation he sent a number of secret emissaries there and also took pains to ingratiate himself privately with the leaders.

Each of these attempts by the Prince to establish himself in Enkhuizen was frustrated, but he succeeded in creating a strong hidden partisanship. This was aided by the fact that the town burgomasters, although Catholic, were also patriotic, and secretly opposed to the tyranny of Philip II.

In the meantime, a steady stream of Protestant refugees from Spanish misrule in the southern provinces (now in modern Belgium) and later from conquered Haarlem and Catholic Amsterdam had flocked into Enkhuizen. These men were for the most part Calvinists who were violently anti-Spanish, and the group included individuals of energy and ability who commenced to work secretly to influence the burghers of Enkhuizen in favor of the Prince of Orange.

The Prince arranged to have his privateer fleet, called the Sea Beggars, sail from England to Enkhuizen, from which port many of the sailors had come, but unfavorable winds prevented their passing from the North Sea through The Helder and entering the Zuider Zee. Desperately in need of food and water, the frustrated fleet put in at the harbor of Brielle and, finding the Spanish garrison away on an expedition, managed to capture that strategic port.

No sooner had the Sea Beggars hoisted the Orange flag at Brielle than a wave of excitement spread through West Friesland. In Enkhuizen the supporters of the Prince seized the city government and declared for him in May, 1572; Enkhuizen was thus the first Dutch town to take that bold and risky step. The burghers were determined, however, to keep control of the town's fortifications for themselves and to allow neither the Orangists nor the Spaniards to introduce their soldiers into the city.

The Spaniards tried by various ruses and subterfuges to gain entry, but were prevented by the alert burghers. Even King Philip himself tried his influence; he gave an audience in Madrid to a group of merchant captains from Enkhuizen whose ships had been seized in Spanish harbors, and tried to cajole them into pleading with the city rulers, when they should get home, to restore their allegiance to Spain.

The Spanish army based in Amsterdam attempted to take Enkhuizen by land, but was stopped at Alkmaar by the opening of the sea dikes—hence the Dutch saying, "With Alkmaar began victory." Then Count Bossu, the Stadtholder (or Royal Governor) of the Provinces of Holland, Zeeland and Utrecht, sailed from Amsterdam with a strong fleet to reduce Enkhuizen by sea. Under Admiral Dirkszoon, a defensive fleet of twenty-four Dutch ships, whose core was composed of the light, well-armed craft of the Sea Beggars, engaged the heavy galleons and maneuvered them into running aground on the sandbanks of the Zuider Zee. After a desperate twenty-eight hour hand-to-hand battle, two of the galleons were sunk, the flagship captured, and Count Bossu taken prisoner. This naval victory was decisive and put the Sea Beggars in control of the Zuider Zee with Enkhuizen as their base; it had an important effect on the final outcome of the war.

Jan Huyghen

J A N   H U Y G H E N (John the son of Hugh) was born in Haarlem in late 1562 or early 1563. His father, Huig Joostenszoon, had been born in the same city in 1532, and had married Marietje Tin Henrixdochter, from the village of Schoonhoven near Rotterdam, a widow with twin sons. Besides these elder half brothers, Jan also had a younger brother and sister.

The Joostenszoon family moved from Haarlem to the city of Enkhuizen, but the exact date of the move is not known. The earliest record of the family in the Enkhuizen archives is dated 1578, at which time Huig is referred to as a notary forty-six years of age. He could hardly have attained the very responsible status of a notary without having been an established citizen of the city for some years. The position of *notaris*, then as now in the Low Countries, is one of high consideration.

Well before the famous siege of Haarlem by the Spaniards in 1572, many Catholic families had been forced to flee from the city by the persecutions of the Calvinists who were in control. The Spaniards in 1572 reversed this trend; in 1573 the city surrendered to them, and there was a massacre of the foreign garrison and of some of the Protestant inhabitants. It may be assumed that Huig Joostenszoon, who was a Roman Catholic, had left Haarlem with his family and settled in Enkhuizen at some time before 1572. On February 14, 1579, we find Huig identified in the Enkhuizen archives as the innkeeper of *The Golden Falcon;* in 1581, when his son Jan already had gone adventuring, he is recorded as the innkeeper of *The Arms of Haarlem.*

The Innkeeper

H U I G evidently possessed some capital, for there are records of a number of loans made by him and secured by mortgages on ships. These transactions were of the type known in maritime law as bottomry, and in case of nonpayment the lender had recourse only upon the vessel itself and not upon any other property of the mortgagee. These were speculative loans, and accordingly bore a good rate of interest. However, as Enkhuizen's total activity was nautical and the capital of the community was almost entirely invested in ships, shipping and fisheries, no doubt Huig knew how to spread the risks.

At that time the position of innkeeper in the Netherlands was a responsible one, with recognized fiduciary functions, and it was not unusual for the innkeeper to be a notary and to act as a banker and as trustee. In Bruges, for example, the municipality was required by statute to guarantee the fiscal obligations of licensed innkeepers. This is brought out in the fifteenth and sixteenth century records of Bruges and of Antwerp, where there were many visiting foreign merchants and sea captains who found the landlord to be their best depositary and custodian. In many cases, the innkeeper also continued to act as legal agent or broker locally for overseas traders who had been guests at his inn; therefore he had to be a man not only of recognized dependability and probity, but also one of considerable acumen.

Jan's family, being newcomers, were not among the governmental leaders in the community; Enkhuizen, like all Dutch towns, was ruled by an oligarchy composed of Burgomasters, Members of the Council, Sheriffs and Magistrates, all drawn from the older wealthy families who had perpetuated their monopoly over the generations. The name of Huig Joostenszoon, his father, therefore does not appear in any of the rolls of ruling functionaries, although, as we shall see, Jan himself in later life achieved admission into that exclusive clique.

Education and Reading

THAT AN "Enkhuizen Latin School" was in existence during Jan's childhood is to be assumed from the record that one Gerard Vesterman, a member of an influential family of the town, who also served as preacher in the Church of Sint Gommarus, was installed as Headmaster in 1585. Jan was already in Goa at that date, but the school was obviously not new. Vesterman was a bibliophile and possessed numerous manuscripts and books, which tells us, perhaps, something of the tradition of the school.

It may be presumed that Jan was a pupil in the Enkhuizen Latin School and there received his grounding in reading, writing, mathematics and some Latin. He wrote that he "took no small delight in the reading of histories and strange adventures"; this leads to some speculation as to what books could have been available to a boy in his situation, apart from a few popular stories of imagined adventures. There were then no authentic books of travel in print in Dutch and very few in French, which was probably the only other language with which he was at all familiar, although perhaps he could spell out German as well. Most of the accounts of voyages at that time were written and printed in Italian, Spanish or Portuguese, languages as yet unfamiliar to him. Though he was not proficient in conversational Latin, undoubtedly he learned to read it in school, and there were many books of travel available in that language, which was still the *lingua franca* of educated men in all European countries. Books were rare and costly in those days (there was, of course, no public library!), and the atmosphere of Enkhuizen was by no means scholarly.

It is likely, too, that Jan might have borrowed books from the priests of his district, or read them at the rectory or school. There is, in the Wester Kerk (which was formerly Sint Gommarus Church), a genuine sixteenth century library still extant which is supposedly a heritage to the church from Gerard Vesterman, although some historians think it was Paludanus who founded it, because some of the books are inscribed by him. The library is of carved oak and has three bookcases of three shelves each, with a slanting shelf or table in front of them upon which an open book may be laid; there is a long bench, running the length of the room, for the readers. There is no conclusive evidence as to the date of the library's founding, and a nucleus of it may well have been in existence during Jan's boyhood.

The collection was evidently by donation, books then being very rare and costly. There is a work on anatomy by Vesalius, printed in Basle in 1543 and given by the widow of Jan's patron, Dr. François Maelson. There are also several other medical books and a few recounting the annals of the town and of its burgomasters. "The Vineyard of Saint Francis," printed in Antwerp in 1518, is a collection of legends and chronicles from which Jan may have drawn inspiration. There also is a collection of "Golden Legends" dated 1516 which may have supplied the tales of travel which Jan said aroused his wanderlust. There is an interesting volume of Erasmus dated 1522, Basle, and many other early sixteenth century publications of value.

There were three ancient cloisters clustered about the Church of Sint Gommarus, the Convents of Saint Ursula, Saint Cecilia and Saint Clara, and it is possible that these institutions, too, may have furnished books for the eager lad.

A few of the refugees from Antwerp and the South Netherlands who came to Enkhuizen to re-establish themselves were people of culture, and some of them may have taken pleasure in helping the eager boy to read any treasured volumes they had salvaged from their ruined libraries. Sea captains and merchants stopping at the inn had no doubt made long voyages and had had adventures in strange lands; besides the stories they told, they may have lent books to the wide-awake son of the host.

Whoever took pains to lend books to the studious boy must have felt repaid for his trouble in later life, when Jan won fame by making available the secrets of the fabled East, and directing his readers' attention to other exotic lands as well.

The Golden Falcon

ALTHOUGH Jan wrote of the interest in the great outer world and the wanderlust inspired in him by books, probably his unrest also was fostered by the feverish environment in which he lived. *The Golden Falcon* at Enkhuizen must have been a focal point for the political, naval and mercantile activities which took place during his boyhood years. Intensely active groups must have made the inn their rendezvous, and the intelligent, lively boy would certainly have been caught up in the atmosphere of importance and urgency.

Enkhuizen had become a boom town and, temporarily, the metropolis of the Netherlands. Impregnably fortified, with a good harbor, and located far from the storms of the North Sea, it was now safe from attack by the Spanish navy, since Count Bossu's fleet had been destroyed when he attempted to capture the town. Another land assault by the Spaniards based on Amsterdam was unlikely, since the army of Don Frederick of Toledo, who had expected to conquer Enkhuizen from the rear, had been thrown back at Alkmaar by the opening of the dikes. Therefore, the harbor of Enkhuizen was crowded with Dutch craft which had fled from Amsterdam, and *The Golden Falcon* no doubt was filled with refugees from there.

The piratical Sea Beggars made Enkhuizen the market-place at which they disposed of their loot, taken not only from Spanish ships but from hapless merchantmen of all flags. Thus many prizes of war were brought in, and their cargoes were auctioned off to the numerous merchants and speculators who came to buy distress merchandise at bargain prices.

Because the huge traffic of Antwerp, Bruges and Amsterdam had been destroyed by the war, much of their commerce was diverted to Enkhuizen. At the same time, the town's own substantial dealings in salt herring and in Baltic products were stimulated by the war-created demand.

The course of the war with Spain had now made Enkhuizen the citadel of the Calvinist cause, which suited the Sea Beggars very well, since most of them had originally come from there and from the other nearby herring ports. The little city thus served as the naval base of the Prince of Orange, and it boomed as prize after prize was brought into the harbor and its contents sold.

Jan was in his seventh year when this mercantile transformation commenced, and it continued during all his boyhood. The consuming interest in strange lands and in overseas life which he wrote moved him so strongly as a boy must have been awakened and excited by his contacts with the foreign adventurers who gathered at *The Golden Falcon.* The inn must have been a veritable trading post, and the innkeeper's lively lad may well have served as a messenger or helper, even perhaps as the notary's clerk for the flush sea raiders and the keen foreign speculators in their tense transactions. Since the boy was genuinely curious about faraway lands, he doubtless listened breathlessly to many a sea-yarn spun before the hearth of the taproom.

Wanderlust

IN THE OPENING autobiographical paragraphs of the *Itinerario* there is no mention at all of this exciting environment, now of such historical interest. To the sixteen-year-old boy, brought up in the turmoil of the times, Enkhuizen probably seemed commonplace; the faraway places beyond the horizon were where he longed to be. Therefore he made no mention of the inn, and only once referred to his family and to his town: "I took leave of my parents, who then dwelt at Enkhuizen."

Although terse concerning his early environment, he described at some length his inner conflict when he decided "to leave my native country, and my resolution overcame my affection"; he "trusted God would further my intent." It seems obvious that a prolonged struggle had taken place in the household in an attempt to keep the lad at home; it was almost inevitable that such an energetic, high-spirited youngster would be tempted to ship as cabin boy and see the world.

Jan expressed the typical restlessness of youth clearly when he said of himself: "being young, and living idly, in my native country sometimes applying myself to the reading of histories and strange adventures, wherein I took no small delight, I found my mind so much addicted to see and travel in strange countries, thereby to seek some adventure, that in the end to satisfy myself, I determined, and was fully resolved, to leave my native country."

In the Royal Archives at The Hague is a letter Jan wrote to his parents in 1584 from Goa, India, in which, reflecting upon his youth, he said: "There is no time more wasted than when a young fellow hangs about his mother's kitchen like a baby, neither knowing what poverty is, nor luxury, nor what is found in the world, an ignorance which is often the cause of his ruin."

In another letter written years later, he indicated that when he left home he yielded to his wanderlust without any definite plan except to follow a career of adventure, but at least, "When you come home, you have something to tell your children when you get old."

Presumably some hurried, perhaps secret, letters traveled from Jan Huyghen's mother, Marietje, to her twin sons, who were established in business in Seville, Spain, asking them to invite their young half-brother to come to them as an apprentice. To an anxious Catholic mother this would be infinitely more desirable and safe than to have the boy run off to sea, perhaps with one of the ruffianly Calvinist Sea Beggars. These piratical individuals were much in evidence in the taproom of *The Golden Falcon*, and she surely knew how glamorous their freebooting careers must appear to a restless youth. Apparently the boy consented to go to Seville as a compromise, without intending to devote himself to the business of the brothers Tin, for on his arrival there he wrote: "Although I had a special desire presently to travel farther, yet for want of the Spanish tongue, without which men can hardly pass the country, I was constrained to stay there to learn some part of their language."

A Hazardous Voyage

O F H I S V O Y A G E he wrote: "On the 6th of December, in the year of our lord 1579, we put out from Texel, being in all about eighty ships, and set our course for Spain." He did not say what kind of vessel it was, what shipmates he set out with, or whether he went as a paying passenger or to work his way. Like most of the amphibious population of Enkhuizen, Jan no doubt was qualified by experience to make himself useful aboard ship, and the maritime connections of his father probably served to get him a berth as ship's boy under the eye of some family friend. Marietje undoubtedly saw to it that his sea chest was well packed for the voyage and that, besides woolen clothing for the wintry climate of the blustering North Sea, he had lighter changes to suit the mild weather of Southern Andalusia. At the time of setting forth on his life's adventure, Jan was almost seventeen years old.

The young adventurer reported that the convoy stayed at Texel awaiting a favorable wind, but did not mention how long the fleet had to wait. It was customary for ships from the Zuider Zee ports to assemble in the lee of the large island of Texel to await a suitable wind before passing into the North Sea through the passage known as The Helder, and this practice continued all through the age of sail. In the winter season, as when Jan sailed, the fleets were sometimes held there for a month or more without getting out to sea.

Once through The Helder and out in the North Sea, ships might be delayed for another month or more by the wild storms which often drove the vessels ashore—or ,worse, they might be foundered by the gigantic waves. Even in the next century, when craft were much more seaworthy, some of the Dutch war fleets under the command of very competent navigators met with long delays and heavy losses on this same route. Another great risk that Jan's flotilla had to face was attack by Dunkirkers, pirate ships which were based in the impregnable harbor of the Spanish-ruled Flemish town of Dunkirk at the entrance to the "narrow seas." These corsairs had fast, well designed and heavily armed vessels under very able command, with formidable crews who dared even to exchange broadsides with Dutch and English warships. The Dunkirkers would dart out of their strongly fortified harbor, slash into and scatter a convoy of Dutch merchant ships, pick out the prizes they wanted, and herd them into their lair—and the Dutch warships that guarded the convoy could not prevent them. Their depredations became so bold that even Dutch merchant captains with a record of bravery refused to sail through the English Channel, and the regular Dover packet from England to Calais did not dare to make the passage unless escorted by warships.

Even after Dunkirk had been taken by the French in 1646, this profitable abuse continued for some time, and when the British and Dutch protested to the French Court, demanding that the Dunkirkers be curbed, they received diplomatic promises of corrective action. However, everyone knew that influential courtiers owned the corsairs and acquired their loot, just as, in England, great nobles and even royalty itself backed the sea raiders who brought their prizes to Plymouth. It had been no secret to the world that the Dutch Sea Beggars, commissioned as privateers by the Prince of Orange, captured merchant ships of all nations and brazenly brought their prizes to Enkhuizen for public auction. Indeed, in that age of official European piracy, such diplomatic protests amounted to the pot calling the kettle black.

The fleet of eighty merchantmen with which Jan sailed were all from the Zuider Zee ports that were hostile to Spain. A number of them were sailing to neutral Portugal to deliver Dutch foodstuffs and Baltic ship stores in exchange for spices and Oriental goods, and also would pick up return cargoes of salt at Setúbal for the herring packers. A second and considerable part of the fleet was destined for Spain with cargoes of Scandinavian and German products, including spars, tar, rope, resin, and even cannon and weapons for the hostile Spanish navy; these ships would bring back Spanish wool and sugar, tobacco, and silver from the Spanish Indies. It was indeed paradoxical that the Spaniards and the Dutch, although at each other's throats in the Netherlands, nevertheless permitted this commercial interchange without hostilities.

The rule of the fleet was that a ship, to participate in the convoy, must be at least of a certain minimum tonnage, have an adequate complement of men, a fair rate of speed, and an armament of about twelve to sixteen guns of medium to heavy caliber. These were necessary conditions, since experience had taught that a slow boat or a lightly armed one might handicap the entire fleet as the corsairs hung on their flanks waiting to pick up cripples or stragglers.

Once through the English Channel and away from the Dunkirkers, the merchant fleet had another danger to face as they neared the Portuguese coast, where Moorish raiders were to be feared. Since the Dunkirkers customarily threw overboard the crews and passengers of captured ships, and the Moors "put them to the oar" unless heavily ransomed, anxiety for the safety of the voyagers was reasonable.

An even greater threat than freebooters was the danger of storms in the Atlantic and the Bay of Biscay during the winter season, and the losses from tempests were very great. There was no lifesaving equipment, and the small boats which a ship carried were both inadequate for the crew and difficult to launch in a heavy sea. No way of calculating longitude was known, and the very uncertain calculation of latitude depended on the clearness of the weather; so many a ship in a storm suddenly found itself off a lee coast without warning. The losses in the Bay of Biscay were staggering, and even the best of ships might be unable to withstand the test of a Biscayan hurricane.

Many nautical risks certainly existed on the course taken by Jan Huyghen on his first ocean voyage down the hazardous, centuries-old Atlantic route from the Netherlands to Portugal, but luckily the young adventurer arrived safely and expeditiously. Several years later his half-brother, Willem Tin, was less fortunate; the ship on which he sailed for home, from Setúbal, in Portugal, following this same course in reverse, was lost with all hands without a trace, somewhere in the Atlantic Ocean. As we shall see, in due course Jan himself was later to learn, on his own homeward trip, just how difficult and troublous this passage could be.

However, this time Jan had fair weather and the best of luck, for they met no corsairs. Within three days they passed between Dover and Calais, in another three they saw Cape Finisterre, at the tip of Northwestern Spain, and in three days more they were off the bar of the Tagus River. Here many ships of the fleet left them to go on to Lisbon, while others branched off toward Setúbal to load salt.

CHAPTER II

Apprenticeship
in Spain and Portugal

San Lucar

ON DECEMBER 17, 1579, Jan's ship reached Cape Saint Vincent, the southwest point of Portugal, where the course was changed to southeast, then east. Eight days later, on Christmas Day, it crossed the bar at the Spanish port of San Lucar de Barrameda and dropped anchor at the mouth of the Guadalquivir River, in Andalusia. Some of the fleet continued on to Cadiz, the terminus of all such voyages, since the Spanish authorities did not allow Dutch ships to pass into the Mediterranean via the Strait of Gibraltar.

Given the sharp eye, keen intelligence, and ready note and sketch books of the fresh, alert young Dutchman, there can be no doubt that he kept a journal of his first impressions of Spain, but unfortunately these early records have not been preserved. That his Spanish material was not included in his *Itinerario* is not surprising. Interesting as his observations of the social and economic conditions in Spain during his stay there would be to us, to his Dutch contemporaries the subject was not particularly newsworthy, as they already had heard much about it. What the Dutch public was intensely curious to learn was the real truth about the exotic lands of the Orient, and this, by the time he began writing, Jan was supremely qualified to tell them.

[19]

Apprenticeship in Spain and Portugal

The Andalusian town of San Lucar de Barrameda was, like Enkhuizen, both a fishing port and a busy emporium. Its history as a commercial port dated from the days of Tyre and Carthage, but now it acted as the ocean harbor for the metropolis of Seville, which lay inland far up the Guadalquivir River. San Lucar no longer was the great harbor it had been in the days of Ferdinand Magellan, for nearby Cadiz had replaced Seville as the terminal for many of the deep-draft Atlantic cargo carriers. Although these ships no longer made the long journey upriver to Seville, that city still held jealously to its many legal maritime privileges and monopolies. It was a further blow to San Lucar that the thriving colony of resident English merchants who for so long had contributed to its prosperity recently had been dispersed and their trade destroyed when King Philip II broke with his sister-in-law, Queen Elizabeth of England.

Jan wrote that his ship lay at San Lucar for several days, and he no doubt eagerly acquainted himself with the features of his first foreign landfall, so different in all respects from his native city. With his eye missing no detail, the boy from the Zuider Zee must have walked the beach and inspected the tackle and equipment of the sardine and tuna fishermen. The chunky, lateen-rigged Spanish boats of cutter-like design with lofty, rakish booms and deep keels built for the furious Atlantic were very unlike the flat-bottomed, stubby, sloop-rigged herring busses of Enkhuizen, with their pivoted lee outboard *zwaarden* which, like centerboards, served for keels when lowered in the gales of the North Sea, but which could be lifted when sailing through the shallows. The swarthy fishermen of San Lucar went about with feet and legs bare, instead of wearing encumbering clothing like the wooden sabots and baggy trousers of his blond countrymen. Jan no doubt grinned at the drooling children, as happily grimy as those of home, who, instead of chewing on the ever-present smoked eels of the low countries, munched sections of succulent sugar cane.

In the city, he doubtless noticed the glazed tiles that, instead of appearing indoors, as at home, decorated the exterior surfaces of the stuccoed, pastel-colored walls. His Northern eyes must have stared in astonishment at the flat, Moorish roofs, the green latticed, harem-like upper windows and the large, iron-barred lower ones of the houses. The great iron-studded oaken doors were crowned with the family escutcheon in the stone lintel above them, and in the cobbled inner courtyards, filled with flowers and shrubs, he glimpsed the stone-curbed family well about which home life revolved.

As he went along he noted that the streets were filled with a multitude of pack mules carrying the loads which in Holland would have been transported along the network of canals in the familiar canal boats. He saw that here massive granite blocks were used, instead of warm-colored Dutch brick, in building fortifications and churches. Since he was a very young man, hardly more than a boy, he must have lingered in the public squares, among their exotic palm trees, as the whole community strolled in the evenings; he doubtless wished he could join the parade as the swaggering youths and giggling maidens perambulated in opposite directions in their separate circles. The girls wore high tortoiseshell combs and lacy mantillas, but their gay spirits were kept under strict control by the vigilant glances of grim duennas seated on the park benches.

Walking the narrow, dimly lighted streets at dusk, the lonely lad must have been moved to see a young man's figure leaning toward the outward-curving iron bars of a street window as he murmured to the strictly cloistered maiden whom he had probably been ogling in the public square earlier in the day. Jan's footsteps doubtless slowed and paused as the lover began to strum his guitar and softly sang Andalusian romances to his lady. It was indeed a different world from Enkhuizen.

Meanwhile, Jan's ship busily unloaded its casks of salt herring, its wheat, cheeses, Scandinavian copper, tarred rope, resin, pikes, halberds, and German printed books. Then they took aboard tuns of red wine, flasks of sherry, cases of dried raisins and almonds, West Indian coconuts, and cochineal dye from the Canaries. Throughout all this business, the ship from Enkhuizen, a city of rebels and heretics, flew the flag of Hamburg, and all the customs papers and harbor forms were filled in as if the ship were from that German city, so that no decrees of the Inquisition or of the royal government would be infringed on paper. Everyone winked at the pretense. The Dutch ship passed under the guns of the castle of the Duke of Medina-Sidonia, and it must have had a favorable breeze to sail in two days the sixty-odd miles to Seville, against the sluggish current, along the winding Guadalquivir. Jan probably stayed on deck through the daylight hours so as not to miss the panorama which unfolded before him.

Andalusia

NOWHERE are there more flourishing farmlands than in Andalusia, along the banks of the Guadalquivir. The young Dutch traveler observed cacti, palms, hedges of prickly pears, the unending rows of silver-leaved olive trees, orange and lemon orchards, groves of cork trees whose trunks showed scarlet where the bark had been stripped away, the terraced vineyards on the slopes, and the ever present oaks, which bore edible, finger-shaped acorns. All was new and strange to Jan. He saw numerous herds of goats on the unfenced hillsides, and shepherds leading flocks of scrawny brown sheep that were very unlike the fat white creatures at home, all snugly contained in their pastures by the canals of Holland.

The countryside was dotted by the white *casas*, or large houses, of the

Andalusian nobles and by the shooting lodges and country places of the merchants of Seville. Jan also saw castles, some of which seemed still to be inhabited, but most of the battlements and towers so picturesquely silhouetted on the low hilltops were only empty shells, burnt-out strongholds of the Moorish wars or fortresses reduced by Ferdinand and Isabella in their campaign to crush the rebellious feudal lords of Andalusia.

Seville

ON JANUARY 1, 1580, Jan got his first view of Seville, the largest city in Spain, called the "Door and Port of the Indies." As the ship slowly approached, Jan must have thrilled to the spectacle. From far away one saw the great Moorish tower, *La Giralda*, not far from the immense Gothic cathedral, one of the most impressive temples of all the world. Nearby was the splendid *Lonja*, or exchange. Next to that was the *Alcazar*, the beautiful palace built by Moorish architects for the Castilian conqueror; it was surrounded by orange groves, and in its many splendid rooms and tiled patios filled with the music of heavy-splashing fountains, Ferdinand Magellan had lived with his father-in-law during his stay in Seville. Next was the famous *Casa de Contratación*, the headquarters of the Colonial Government founded in 1503 by the famous Bishop of Burgos, Juan Rodríguez de Fonseca. Next beyond was the *Casa de la Moneda*, or royal mint, where gold and silver bars were stacked like cordwood, and which was being rebuilt to provide more space. Then came the old *Aduana*, or customhouse, through which Jan would have to pass upon disembarking; it had one door on the river and one in the city. Next his eyes were caught by the famous Moorish *Torre de Oro*, so named because the Andalusian sun, glittering on its walls of polished Arabian tiles, made it appear as if built of shining gold. Beyond were a series of docks and the *Huerta del Rey*, the King's Garden, and ahead stretched the pontoon bridge of seventeen barges that crossed the Guadalquivir to Triana, the industrial quarter across the river. It is possible that Jan Huyghen's ship tied up at the same docks of *Las Muelas*, in Triana, where Magellan had reconditioned his five ships for the circumnavigation of the globe.

Jan found one brother, Floris Tin, in Seville, but the other twin, Willem, had gone on a business trip to Madrid, where he had an influential connection at court. Jan spent eight months in Seville and devoted himself to learning Spanish. It was presumably his parents' intention that he should learn not only Spanish, while apprenticed to his half-brothers, but also the rules of European business; for this purpose, his most important textbook was doubtless that bible of both Spanish and Flemish merchants, the famous Italian text on double-entry bookkeeping by Luca Patcioli, first published in Venice in 1494, and translated into Dutch by Ympyn at Antwerp in 1543.

At that time Spain was foremost in almost every field of European activity, and Seville was its metropolis. The impressionable seventeen-year-old boy must surely have been captivated by what he saw and heard. However, the record of his observations and impressions has been lost, and one can only speculate about what must have interested him most and how he must have spent his time.

In the Andalusian dusk, after a day's work, it must have been restful to walk through some of the public plazas in the city, of which there were more than eighty, all embellished with marble and bronze statues, with fountains, pools and basins surrounded by clumps of shrubs and groves of orange trees. So many fortunes had been gained by Sevillian merchants in the American trade, and so grateful to Providence were these citizens, that the town was called "the city of charity"; at every turn, it seemed, one saw the schools, hospitals, asylums, monasteries and convents endowed by those thankful for their good fortune, and many of these foundations were ensconced in handsome gardens, as was the great Columbian Library founded by Ferdindand, the son of Admiral Christopher Columbus. The century-old University of Seville and the new Jesuit College, in their park-like surroundings, must have appealed to the intelligent boy who had himself been denied educational opportunity.

He must have gazed open-mouthed at the palaces of the Duke of Medina-Sidonia and of the Duke of Alcalá; the latter was called the House of Pilate, and had been built in commemoration of a pilgrimage to Jerusalem. Even the most sumptuous homes, however, were only two stories high, with a flat roof on which the family sat in the cool of the evening. In the daytime, the center of home life was in the delightful inner patios, with their orange trees, shrubs and flowers, and pools with fountains. Seville had inherited from the Moors their appreciation of the decorative and refreshing use of water. Among the other amenities of life left to the city by the Moslems, and one at which Jan marvelled, were the easily available and cheap public baths, reserved exclusively for women in the daytime and for men at night. As impressive to the Dutch apprentice as the homes of the nobility were the establishments of the merchant princes such as the agents of the German bankers, the Fuggers and the Welsers, and of the Florentine, Genoan and Venetian plutocrats, each of whom tried, as a matter of commercial prestige, to outdo his competitors.

After Jan became established in his brothers' house and learned his way about the great city, he must have delighted in browsing through the open-air book stalls and the bookshops of the Calle de Genoa. He must have gazed curiously at the displays of the stores in the twisting lanes of the retail quarter known as the *Alcaiceria* where, because of the richness of the stocks of the goldsmiths, silversmiths, and gem dealers, the whole section was closed off at night with locked gates guarded by armed sentries, and patrolled by watchmen. Jan, of course, had no money to buy more than the bare necessities of his life, though he was naturally better situated than an ordinary apprentice. However, he possessed gifts far more valuable than a few gold pieces, and could enjoy his close observations and draw his own sensible conclusions.

As a good son of the Netherlands of his period, he no doubt especially enjoyed the numerous pageants and parades in which the merchant guilds took part, notably the rich brotherhoods of the embroiderers, silversmiths, engravers, glaziers, and the painters of religious images. The great Easter festival saw nobles and beggars alike participating in the carnival masques; it was marked by deeply emotional religious parades, and ended with a solemn high mass at the cathedral at which the remarkable feature was the famous dance of the *seises*, six richly dressed young pages who executed a ritualistic dance before the high altar in the magnificent cathedral.

Like all the apprentices, Jan must have attended the still aristocratic bull fights, which were far superior in their challenge to dexterity and courage to the popular bull baitings or bear baitings in his homeland. Perhaps, if there was an *auto da fé* during his stay, he might have noted its ceremonious technique, in contrast to the more brutish burning at the stake or boiling in oil which in the North were such popular and grisly spectacles.

Trade and Industry

A N O T H E R and no less exciting public show was the arrival of the annual plate fleet from Spanish America, when as many as a thousand oxcarts were loaded with the precious cargo of the vessels, gold and silver and pearls, to be stored in the *Casa de Contratación*. Then the buyers from all over Europe gathered in Seville and crowded the continuous auctions held on the marble steps of the cathedral, auctions in which all the imports from the New World were sold, as well as arms and armor, tapestries, slaves, and gold and silver jewelry.

Since Jan's interest was then almost wholly commercial, he must have spent much time sauntering along the Calle Larga in Triana, the city's industrial section across the river, where there were at least three thousand silk spinning plants employing some 30,000 workers, and many linen and woolen mills as well. The numerous tanneries processed much cordovan, goatskin, and camelskin, and imported quantities of cowhides and sheepskin from America. The manufacture of hats, shoes, and particularly of gloves was extensive, and the soap factories consumed enormous quantities of Andalusian olive oil. The famous Triana White Soap was exported to all the markets of the Western World. Here also were made the glazed Sevillian tiles, or *azulejos*, which one saw everywhere, as well as the popular and cheap household crockery called Málaga Ware which no less than fifty potteries in Triana manufactured. A large and potentially very dangerous government gunpowder factory was also located here.

Since Seville had a monopoly of both the import and the export traffic with the Western hemisphere, the factories whenever possible imported their raw material from America in order to furnish return cargoes for the ships which carried out their exports. Not content with the profits from their trade monopoly, the industrial community of Seville saw to it that there should be no competitive manufacturing facilities set up in the American colonies, and managed to get strict laws passed to this effect. The silk manufacturers succeeded in having the importation of Chinese silk via Manila to Mexico legally restricted, and the vintners arranged to protect their profitable exports of sherry and other wines by having it declared illegal to plant vineyards in the New World. The young Dutch apprentice was no doubt in full sympathy with these repressive laws, for in the Netherlands, too, the theory of monopoly was the essence of good business.

The same spirit of monopoly also ruled in the colonies, for just as Seville alone was allowed to export to America, only three ports on the American Atlantic side, Vera Cruz, Cartagena, and Nombre de Dios could receive imports—plus Acapulco, on the Pacific, for imports from the Philippines.

In Seville, as in the Netherlands, speculation was the breath of trading; and someone was always "cornering" the Sevillian market on some such commodity as wheat, wine, silks, linens, ironware, wax, or velvets from Granada. Trading was feverish; the mark-up of the merchants was at least a hundred percent, and on sales to America much more. The money lenders thrived at interest rates of from sixty-five to eighty percent. Successful merchants had huge fortunes at their disposal, and their greatest ambition was to arrange marriages for their children into the nobility. They wore expensive clothes made of silk, velvet or taffeta, and dressed their wives in elaborately embroidered silk with quilting. To Jan, the contrast in apparel between flamboyant Seville and sober Enkhuizen must have been startling.

The display of fashionable styles was most notable on the public promenade called the *Arenal*, which ran along the river front outside the city walls. There not only rich citizens and nobles strolled, but also the army of beggars and *pícaros* who have infested Seville since time immemorial. Here too was the famous second-hand market, where fraud and cheating were the rule. Jan doubtless mingled with the crowd in the lively and picturesque *Arenal* whenever he was able, and must always have been glad on the occasions when some errand took him in this direction during business hours.

However, alongside all its splendors, there was much squalor and poverty in Seville. Filth, dung and garbage littered the streets, and, because there was no system of sanitation, frequent outbreaks of the plague scourged the population.

Out beyond Triana, Jan came upon the extensive ruins of the ancient Roman city of Italica, the predecessor of Gothic and Moorish Seville. Its amphitheater was still standing, and after every rainfall Roman coins, mosaics and shards were uncovered in the soil. Wide-awake modern boy as he was, he had an avid interest in all curiosities, and without doubt he sometimes lingered thoughtfully among the ruins, and picked up a rain-washed Roman coin. These ancient people, too, had carried on business, and there were probably boys like himself apprenticed to it. Perhaps for the first time, history became real for him in that spot.

An Intellectual Center

EVEN THOUGH Jan's short stay in Spain was in an humble and obscure mercantile role, the lad must have acquired an appreciation of Spanish intellectual primacy in that time of its golden age. In his later life, he translated Spanish geographical works and paid frank homage to Spanish scholarship. At the period when he was in Seville, the same dynamic force that gave Spain the best army and strongest navy in Europe also stimulated scholarly and creative work in many fields. In literature, architecture, sculpture, painting, and music, Spain led Europe; while in the field of natural and physical science, in mathematics, and in medicine, Spaniards were well in the forefront. Historians, cosmographers, and geographers produced authoritative work. Not only were the Universities of Salamanca and Alcalá respected throughout Christendom, but there also were, in almost all corners of Spain, popular smaller institutions of learning of good quality. It is impressive to read how many important chairs were filled by Spanish professors in the foreign universities of Bologna, Padua, Paris and Oxford. Jan was in Seville at the apogee of the many-sided Hispanic culture, a culture whose richness had assimilated the varied contributions of Moorish scholars, erudite Sephardic Jews, and learned Greek refugees from Constantinople. Most of Italy and all of Flanders, Brabant and Burgundy as subject provinces sent their artists and thinkers to the Spanish court; the blight of the repressive alien Hapsburgs and of the deadening Inquisition had not yet had their baneful effects upon the rich flowering of Spanish arts and sciences, although the decline was about to set in.

The Brothers Tin

J A N G A V E no inkling as to the kind of business his twin half-brothers conducted in Seville, probably under the name of Tin Hermanos, or Tin Brothers. Although he mentioned that Willem Tin had left for Madrid on business just before his own arrival in Spain, he gave no explanation of the nature of his affairs beyond saying that he had gone to the Royal Court. In writing of Willem Tin's activities in 1583, three years later, he referred to him as "my brother who followed the Court," whose "Master was one of the Secretaries of His Majesty." By that time, the partnership between the two brothers had been dissolved, and the other twin, presumed to have been named Floris, had died of the plague at Salamanca.

Although apparently the firm of Tin Hermanos had no staff of any size nor any substantial stock of merchandise, it seems that it was domiciled with some appearance of stability and permanence in Seville. Jan evidently disapproved of the short-sighted opportunism displayed by the partner at Seville when, as we shall see, he abandoned the establishment there in order to engage in a speculative venture into which he drew his young half-brother. Jan commented, "Whereupon divers men went out of Sevill and other places into Portingale, as it is commonlie seene that men are often addicted to changes and new alterations, among the which my Brother by other men's counsels was one."

King Philip the Mighty

I N A U G U S T , 1580, Philip II of Spain was preparing to enter Portugal to seize the throne. During all of Jan's stay in Seville, the commercial element had been in a ferment in anticipation of the opportunities for plunder which would arise in the wake of the intended invasion. When the king moved from Madrid with his forces to the border city of Badajoz, a horde of traders and speculators flocked there from Seville. Among them, perforce, was Jan, who accompanied his brother. All awaited the opportunity to enter Portugal, poised on the border to try to get there first.

Although Philip had long hoped to satisfy the centuries-old yearning of the Spanish Crown to establish complete hegemony over the entire Iberian peninsula, this seemed an impossibility until the death in battle in North Africa in 1578 of Philip's nephew, the half mad King Sebastian. This young monarch not only threw away his own life, but by incredi-

[27]

bly bad tactics sacrificed the army of Portugal. Among the fifteen thousand prisoners held by the Moors were the courtiers and aristocrats of the Kingdom, and the wealth of Portugal was sucked into Africa for ransoms.

The senescent uncle of Sebastian, Cardinal Henry, was crowned king, and the poor old man became the center of intrigue in which Philip of Spain, with his long purse, was the dominant plotter. On January 31, 1580, when Jan had been in Seville only a month, the feeble Cardinal died. The Portuguese nobility, demoralized and impoverished by the ransoms they had had to pay to North Africa for the return of their kinsmen, now succumbed to the lavish bribes of Philip, while the clergy already had been efficiently organized in his favor. Only the middle classes and the populace at large, all of whom bitterly hated the Spaniards, opposed Philip and supported the pretensions of the profligate Antonio of Crato, an illegitimate nephew of the late Cardinal, whose personal qualifications for the throne were weak at best.

Badajoz

JAN'S WEEK-LONG TRIP by horse or mule along the great northern highway from Seville to the border city of Badajoz must have been a fascinating experience to the observant youth, for the road was a pathway of history along which were the traces of many travelers who had gone before—Carthaginian, Roman, Goth, Moor and Castilian. Badajoz itself, with its high walls and sturdy towers, not only had participated in many stirring events in past centuries, but more recently had been a strategic point of conflict in the later wars between Portugal and Spain. Now once again it was the assembly point for a Castilian army of invasion.

As they approached its environs, they rode through orchards of lemon and orange trees and past ancient Roman fortifications; finally they emerged from a dense grove of palms to see before them a long bridge of arched masonry which led across the wide Guadiana River to the fortified city on the opposite bank. Here Jan's brother must have pointed out to him a marble tablet which bore a legend stating that a century earlier the mighty causeway had been erected by Philip I of Castile, his own countryman. Philip I, or Philip the Fair, was a royal Netherlander who had married Juana, the daughter of Ferdinand and Isabella, and become King of Spain; he was the grandfather of the present king, Philip II. At that time the plaque was still striking, but now its Latin lettering can barely be deciphered.

After crossing over the long bridge, they passed through an arched gateway between the squat towers defending the entry from the causeway into Badajoz. There they must have paused before another impressive marble tablet (today also barely readable) showing chiseled portraits of

Ferdinand and Isabella with an inscription in Latin dated 1551 stating that Philip, Prince of Flanders, Sicily and Spain, and son of Charles V, Emperor of Rome, had completed the fortification.

Now, thirty years later, this same Philip approached Badajoz to effect at last the age-old dynastic dream of adding the monarchy of Portugal to the five Spanish kingdoms, thus consolidating under the crown of Spain the entire Hispanic peninsula. In the next year, 1581, another tablet would be put up to commemorate the present event, of which Jan was now a spectator.

Riding across the great plaza, Jan must have found himself halted many times by the traffic congestion of hurrying riders, carts, and pedestrians. Perhaps he rode along in front of the heavily guarded palace of the Marquis de la Lapilla in the *Plaza de la Soledad,* where were domiciled not only the King and Queen, but also the heir apparent, Prince Diego, the Princesses, and Archduke Albert of Austria, who was later to become the Royal Governor of the Netherlands. The assumption of the Crown of Portugal, with all its world-wide possessions, was a momentous dynastic event, to be celebrated joyously by the entire royal family.

Although the prize was not yet won, Philip was confident that it was within his grasp. Later, he cynically paraphrased Caesar when he boasted, "I came, I bought, I conquered." In the flush of near victory, he little imagined that neither his Queen, Anne of Austria, his fourth wife, nor his heir, would live to see him crowned King of Portugal, or that he himself would soon lie at death's door, stricken along with them by the dread plague that was no respecter of persons, royal or otherwise.

The Invasion of Portugal

J A N , avid like all Netherlanders to witness parades and spectacles, must surely have been in the crowd that saw the King review his army on the meadows of Calatraveja before giving the order to plunge across the border. And Jan must have been stirred to see the old Duke of Alva, so hated in Enkhuizen, as he led a force of twenty-six thousand infantry with fifty-seven heavy siege guns and fifty portable river pontoons or barges on carts, as they marched off with banners waving and drums rolling, the vanguard composed of Philip's Italian regiment under the command of Pietro de Medici, brother of the Grand Duke of Tuscany.

Word came back to the Spanish speculators who were being held back at Badajoz that the vanguard under Pietro de Medici had met with no resistance in its march across Portugal; each fortress in its path surrendered until the city of Setúbal was reached. There Dom Antonio, Prior of Crato and pretender to the throne, attempted to make a stand with the aid of

British and French auxiliaries. Alva easily crushed this resistance, marched into Lisbon, and proclaimed Philip as King. Soon after, word was received that the patriot army, hastily gathered and poorly organized, had been cut to pieces and scattered by Alva, although Dom Antonio was said to have escaped. The report was that the implacable Duke of Alva was applying the same terrifying tactics to the so-called rebels, the defenders of their homeland, that he had used against the Netherlanders. At the same time, the able Spanish admiral, the Marquis de Santa Cruz, with a strong fleet was reported to be occupying one Portuguese harbor after another, apparently succeeding in terrifying some and bribing others of the defense officials.

The situation of Jan and his half-brother must have been extremely uncomfortable while awaiting release in Badajoz for their Portuguese adventure. The small city was quite unprepared to accommodate the whole court, with its attendant grandees, hidalgos and officials, with their pretentious retinues of vassals and servants, to say nothing of the self-assertive military contingent which occupied the place as a base for the invasion.

Even the richest and best connected of the merchants were unable to obtain adequate quarters in the outlying towns, and indeed did not dare to compete for them. As for the small traders like Jan and his brother, they were lucky to find a spot to sleep in the public squares. It was almost impossible for people of such minor importance to buy food from the farmers at any price, particularly since the soldiers had already raided the herds and flocks and pillaged the barns and wine cellars of the countryside. There was a complete absence of sanitation in Badajoz, filth abounded, and such water as could be reached was badly polluted. Then suddenly the plague made its appearance, and the dead and dying lay everywhere. When it was whispered that the mighty King himself had been laid low, terror became widespread.

It was difficult to get a night's sleep in a public square. Torches and bonfires flared, and the trotting of trains of pack mules, the cracking of the muleteers' whips, the creak and rumble of the ungreased wooden axles of oxcarts, the jangle and clang of cavalry patrols, and the rustle of the restless sojourners with their cries and calls, all kept one awake. More upsetting still were the moans of the sick, whom none dared, because of the danger of contagion, to succor with food or water or even to supply with necessities of any kind. After the plague became prevalent there were not even scavengers to remove the bodies, so the stench became maddening. Suddenly everyone who could do so wanted to escape from Badajoz.

In the crowded and suffering town constant rumors flew about, rumors of catastrophe of various kinds, and even of the defeat of Alva by a strong French and British force which had landed to aid Dom Antonio. This latter would not necessarily have disturbed the speculators, who would have benefited if the Portuguese had put up a strong defense. The worst news for the merchants was that the country had been pacified, that Dom Antonio was in hiding, and that all hostile ships had been sunk or captured by the Marquis de Santa Cruz.

Although the Portuguese people disliked the Spaniards and hated Philip, the popular attempt to defend the country had not possessed enough force and had now been stamped out, in spite of some aid from France and England. Members of the nobility and the Church were driven from office, and the entire administration fell into the hands of the Portuguese tools of the conqueror.

The fugitive pretender to the throne, Dom Antonio, was hidden and protected by the Portuguese people, and even though countless individuals must have been privy to his concealment, not one betrayed him. After seven months in hiding, the hunted man was able to take ship for France. Though Philip had scoured the country with spies and soldiers and had offered not only great privileges but 80,000 ducats in cash to anyone who would turn him in, he had not been able to capture him.

Because of his own illness and the deaths in his family, it was not until December, 1580, that Philip II of Spain ascended the throne as Philip I of Portugal. The Duke of Alva had crossed the border into Portugal on June 27, 1580. After the quick collapse of the resistance, there were no longer any opportunities for great profits open to the discouraged traders waiting in Badajoz, except for those few who had some influential backing.

Jan wrote that when Portugal was so quickly brought to heel his brother "presently changed his mind of travelling for Portingale and entered into the service with an Ambassador that on the King's behalfe was to goe into Italie, with whome he rode; and arriving in Salamanca he fell sicke of a disease which at that time raigned throughout the whole Countrie of Spaine whereof many thousands died and among the rest, my Brother was one." Evidently his brother, Floris Tin, had not left Badajoz early enough to escape infection, or else the cortege of the ambassador had carried it with them. At all events, the unfortunate fellow died far away from Enkhuizen and his friends and family.

Before Floris Tin had left Badajoz to enter the Ambassador's service in July, he no doubt procured a post horse or a mule for Jan's return to Seville, for return he did. Once back in Seville, Jan was not idle and soon secured employment, On August 5, 1580, he was engaged to accompany a wealthy Dutchman (or German—the text is unclear) who planned to travel through Portugal. It may be assumed that Jan's new employer was going to use both his capital and his connections and fish profitably in the troubled waters of the newly conquered kingdom, for this happened long before the days of travelling simply for pleasure—nor would the country of Portugal at that time have been indicated as a good place for tourism!

Since Jan could have known only a smattering of Spanish and no Portuguese, and had had only a brief apprenticeship in business, obviously his new position could not have been an important one. According to his own account, they left Seville on September 1st and arrived in Badajoz after eight days on the road. Upon their arrival in Badajoz, he was lucky enough to find his other half-brother, Willem Tin, the one of whom we last heard as "following the court." Apparently this was Jan's first meeting with Willem Tin in Spain, for it will be remembered that the latter had already left for Madrid before his young half-brother's first arrival in Seville. No doubt the news of Floris Tin's death in Salamanca had already reached Willem in Badajoz. Although Willem Tin was soon to assume an important role in Jan's life, the present sad reunion was brief, and Jan shortly left with his employer for the Portuguese border city of Elvas.

Portugal

A L T H O U G H as we know Jan had previously spent some time in Badajoz, this was the first time he had crossed into Portugal. The party stopped briefly at the strongpoint of Elvas, just across the boundary line from Badajoz, to which it had been opposed through a long history of border warfare. From Elvas they pushed on through several centers, and after about a week of travel they arrived at Lisbon on September 20th.

As we know, Portugal was in a very unsettled state, and it appears likely that Jan's employer was one of the carpet-baggers of that time. That is, he was probably an agent of a syndicate of foreign speculators who, with Spanish political backing, were buying distress merchandise in Portugal for perhaps as little as ten percent of its subsequent market value in Spain. They were able to buy at these ridiculous prices because of the frantic need of the Portuguese people to convert assets into cash in order to ransom suffering relatives and friends held under dreadful conditions of captivity in Morocco. For soon after the catastrophe of Sebastian's defeat and death, the Trinitarians, the monkish intermediaries who customarily negotiated with the Moslems for the release of captives, reported to Lisbon that among the prisoners were eighty noblemen of high rank whose collective ransom amounted to 400,000 cruzados, an enormous sum. There had also been about two thousand lesser nobles in the army, although of course many had not survived the battle; but the cost of deliverance even of a simple gentleman was set at not less than 4,000 cruzados, and a servant was valued at a hundred cruzados. The immensity of the Moors' demands can be appreciated when it is realized that the Portuguese government itself was then able to offer only a total of 117,000 cruzados for ransom money.

The prisoners were being treated with great inhumanity, and fatalities among them were horrifyingly numerous; consequently their families beggared themselves in offering, for any price, their jewels, heirlooms, rich clothing, furniture, and anything else that was saleable, in order to raise money.

However, soon there was no longer any market in Lisbon for these family treasures, and then the longheaded Genoan, Venetian, German and other European traders established a market in the Portuguese fortified city of Ceuta, in Morocco, on the Strait of Gibraltar. There they held daily auctions of family treasures that brought a final total receipt of the prodigious sum of 1,100,000 cruzados, but even this was inadequate to liberate more than a limited number of prisoners. The entire portable wealth of a rich empire was being auctioned away. After a period of confusion, the government established a system of taxation upon many functions and activities of the commonwealth, the proceeds to be administered for ransoms under the supervision of the clergy. This was, of course, a drain upon the lifeblood of the colonies as well as of the homeland.

Ordinarily Jan's route from Elvas would have led to the city of Evora, famous for its Roman ruins and for its university, and particularly important at that time because the banking houses which controlled much of the foreign exchange of Portugal were domiciled there. If Jan's foreign employer was traveling on business, it would have been logical for him to make Evora his first stop. On the other hand, if he was in a position competitive to the strongly entrenched financiers in Evora, he might have detoured away from the town for that reason; or he might have feared the plague then raging in the university town. If he avoided Evora for fear of contagion, the choice of Lisbon as a goal was not a happy one, for when they arrived there on September 20, 1580, the capital city was in the grip of the dread epidemic. Eighty thousand persons had died there in the past two years either of the plague or of the disease which followed it called *coccolucino*, now whooping cough but probably in that day typhus or diphtheria.

Jan came down with this disease almost as soon as he arrived in Lisbon, and with nearly fatal results. His employer was able to get a doctor for the stricken boy, but, since the medico bled him no less than seven times, perhaps he would have been better off without any attention. His vigorous young constitution saved him, but after his recovery he resigned from the service of the foreign traveler and got a position with a local merchant, desiring, as he said, to learn merchandising. He stayed in this position for two and a half years, but in the *Itinerario* he gave no details at all about contemporary Portugal nor about his activities there, although at the time the local happenings were anything but dull or commonplace.

Philip the Conqueror

ON THE OTHER HAND, Jan devoted considerable attention to the royal family and to the two military leaders of the conquest, Alva and Santa Cruz. It is evident that he was at this time, and apparently until after his return to Enkhuizen a dozen years later, a loyal and admiring subject of Philip. Jan then claimed citizenship in Haarlem, and this may be explained by the fact that he was a member of the Roman Catholic, Spanish-sympathizing group, now a minority in Enkhuizen but the dominant group in Haarlem. He may well have thought of Philip not as the King of Spain and Portugal, but as the Count of Holland, his hereditary liege lord, one of whose principal ancestral castles was at Haarlem.

After the surrender of Haarlem to Spain, many of the loyalist exiles had returned home to resume political power, but since Huig Joostenszoon had by then become well established in Enkhuizen he evidently decided to remain. However, he seems always to have retained his identification with his native city, for when he moved the location of his inn, he changed its name from *The Golden Falcon* to *The Arms of Haarlem.* Even after his return home to Enkhuizen, Jan still referred to himself as a citizen of Haarlem, and did not transfer his registration to Enkhuizen until after his marriage into the local ruling clan, just before his appointment to public office there.

Perhaps the obvious loyalty to the Spanish despot of so devoted a son of ravaged Haarlem may be regarded as a paradox typical of the confused relationship between the opposing sides in this strange revolution. At the time when Jan felt free to travel from Orangist Enkhuizen to Spain in a fleet of eighty rebel Zuider Zee merchantmen, the provinces of Holland and Zeeland were the strongest and most stubborn supporters of the rebel Prince of Orange. At the same time, their population is calculated to have still been ninety percent Catholic, and their revolutionary leaders came almost entirely from the outside, being neither Hollanders nor Zeelanders.

It is perhaps surprising that the brief part of the *Itinerario* describing the author's early stay of over three years in Spain and Portugal should have been published as it stood, revealing his respect and sympathy at that period for Philip II, who by the time the book appeared was with some justification generally depicted in the Netherlands as a despotic ogre. The publisher of the book quite obviously edited and censored it to conform to the prevailing political atmosphere in Holland and Zeeland in 1595, but for some reason allowed the evidence of Jan's early attitude to stand. It is also interesting to note that in this part, as throughout the *Itinerario*, the writer took the position of the typical Spaniard in his scorn for the Portuguese people. It is apparent that, in the dozen years during which Jan was a subject of King Philip in his Portuguese realms, he always identified himself with the Spanish overlords.

In the first part of the *Itinerario*, though nowhere else in his extensive writings, Jan displayed great interest and reverence for officialdom, and his references to the King and the royal family were almost as loyal as if he were writing a court gazette. For example, he supported the legality of Philip's seizure of the Portuguese throne by alleging that the late King-Cardinal had bequeathed it to him, a story that was not at all true, but which Jan obviously believed. He wrote with keen interest of the movements of the royal family and described with gusto the popular celebration and carnival when Philip came to Lisbon to assume the crown. He was jubilant that the theatrical presentation by the Netherlands, designed to express joyous devotion to the King, was considered the most artistic bit of the pageant.

Like any provincial lad, Jan was dazzled by the glittering splendor of King Philip, as well he might have been, since the monarch was then at the apogee of his career. He had won resounding victories against France, his affairs were not going badly, on the whole, in the rebellious Netherlands and were flourishing in Italy, and his vast overseas colonies made him ever richer. His acquisition, almost without a struggle, of the opulent, world-girdling Portuguese Empire almost doubled his resources and made him the mightiest monarch in Christendom. It was only natural that the boy who had been born in Haarlem should share with pride the glory of the regal hero to whom he could give fealty as his own liege lord, the Count of Holland.

The Marquis of Santa Cruz

J A N also wrote enthusiastically of the strong fleet organized to dislodge the patriot forces in the Flemish Islands, as the Azores were called, saying "the principal noblemen of Spain and Portugal went with their fleet at their own cost, and of their free will, in order to show the good affection they felt for their King and the honor they recognized in serving him." When the Marquis de Santa Cruz was victorious after a reputedly desperate battle with the royal fleet of France which was supporting Dom Antonio, he had all the French officers who had surrendered decapitated; many of these, as Jan said, were of the highest nobility. The Marquis also doomed all the sailors he captured to be Spanish galley slaves, yet Jan expressed no disapproval of either action. He wrote, "By this victory the Spaniards were so proud, that in Lisbon great triumph was holden for the same and the Marquis of Santa Cruz received therein with great joy."

In reality the report of the engagement released by Philip was a misleading one. The Spanish fleet of twenty-eight large ships, with 6,700 soldiers aboard, was in theory opposed by a French fleet of sixty-three ships of various tonnages, holding 5,800 soldiers, of whom 1,200 were gentlemen. However, the fact was that, because of treachery and disaffection, when the French Admiral, Philip Strozzi, led the attack, he was followed by only seven ships. All the rest of the French fleet abandoned him. Although Strozzi's small force fought with the greatest gallantry, it had no chance of winning against such vastly superior numbers. The admiral himself was wounded by an arquebus bullet and taken prisoner from a small boat after his flagship had sunk. He was then carried before the Spanish admiral and at once summarily knocked on the head and thrown overboard; just as ruthlessly, Jan said, all the noble prisoners were beheaded "as enemies of the public peace and instigators of rebellion." The rest of the French fleet returned home without having fired a cannon. Perhaps all these events were so remote that Jan did not fully comprehend their terrible reality, and hence did not criticize the conduct of the Spanish toward their captives.

The Duke of Alva

H o w e v e r , when the Duke of Alva applied the same ruthless methods of bloody repression to the Portuguese patriots who were attempting to defend their homeland as he had previously employed against the rebel Netherlands, one wonders that Jan apparently felt no sympathy for the victims. Instead, he devoted a long paragraph in the *Itinerario* to the illness, death and burial of the Duke of Alva, relating that for the last fortnight of his life the grim old martinet subsisted entirely upon woman's milk.

Modern critics may well hold that Alva, like Cardinal Wolsey, would have done better had he served his God as zealously as he served his ungrateful king, since many of the severities that history condemns were carried out in obedience to royal orders. In the judgments of history national loyalties play a great part, and perhaps a truly impartial judgment is impossible. For example, the unjust executions of the Flemish Counts of Egmont and Hoorn, for which English historians condemn Alva, were from the current moral standpoint no more reprehensible than many contemporary English political death penalties upon similarly disaffected noble politicians.

When Alva furtively abandoned his governorship of the Netherlands, he left behind him a monumental mass of unpaid personal debts; he had assumed this indebtedness because of governmental deficits, but in the eyes of his canny Dutch creditors this was perhaps his greatest atrocity.

When the fallen tyrant came home from the Netherlands he was treated with ignominy by the King. Shortly afterward he was thrown into jail because he had attempted to protect his son, Frederick of Toledo; this young blade had incurred Philip's rage by hurriedly marrying a noble heiress, and thus avoiding marriage with a highborn maiden of the court whom he had seduced and made pregnant. The King then let both the Duke and his son languish in prison until he needed to loose the bloodthirsty old warrior upon the Portuguese patriots.

The Invincible Armada

I T   W A S the superior naval skill demonstrated by the Marquis de Santa Cruz in defeating Dom Antonio's fleet in the Azores which led Philip to entrust to him the assembling of the great Invincible Armada; this incidentally stripped Portugal of its defensive naval power in India. Most experts agree that this stupendous effort, which so exhausted Santa Cruz physically that he collapsed, resulted in a poorly equipped and undisciplined fleet. Popular history to the contrary, in August, 1588, while Jan was still in India, the Armada came within an ace of defeating the gallant and superbly handled British defenders. In the opinion of many modern writers the Armada might well have been the victor if Santa Cruz, its creator and guiding genius, had survived to command it. In reality the battle of the English fleet against Philip's Invincible Armada was, as the Duke of Wellington said two centuries later of that other decisive British victory, the Battle of Waterloo, a "demned close thing."

The Subject Kingdom

T H E   S I G H T S and experiences that the young Dutchman encountered in Portugal should have been searing ones, but he was not touched by them. The countryside had been ravaged by the dreadful plague, the spirit of the nation broken by the ruthless, repressive methods of the Spanish conquerors, and the heart of the people sickened by the shameless sycophancy of those native officials who were given power by the usurper. Only the common people dared show discontent; the nobility, suddenly impoverished because of the forced liquidation of their possessions to provide ransoms for their captive relatives in Morocco, were eager to fawn upon their new rulers. Nevertheless, to a foreign traveler the nation superficially seemed the same; it preserved a façade.

Almost a century earlier, King Manuel the Fortunate had initiated an era of great interior development in Portugal, using the flood of wealth which in the beginning poured in from the Orient to build up the country. With good taste and good sense combined, he restored and renovated many of the historic but dilapidated medieval structures and declared them national monuments. He repaired highways, rebuilt bridges, improved and fortified harbors, and employed foreign architects, engineers and artists to erect handsome churches and abbeys, many in the style which came to be called, in his honor, Manoeline.

During the sixteenth century the nobility and the merchants became opulent beyond their wildest dreams, and built palaces and manor houses throughout the countryside. No doubt Jan saw many of these park-like country estates, as well as the prosperous towns where much of the wealth was centered. However, at this time many of the farmlands and vineyards lay uncultivated because of the dearth of agricultural laborers other than African slaves. Although the people were depressed and the domestic economy was beginning to crumble, still the country had experienced none of the ravages of the wars which had devastated so much of Western Europe, and its physical appearance remained magnificent.

Strangely enough, the merchants and bankers, in contrast to the gentry and landowners, temporarily were prospering as never before. At first the conquest by Spain had little effect upon the inward flow of imports which had made Lisbon the financial capital of Europe. It was not until the great Portuguese marine was impressed into the Spanish navy and destroyed in the latter's various defeats and disasters that the Portuguese bankers and merchants lost their European primacy.

Portugal the Opulent

THE MODERN READER, who almost inevitably visualizes Portugal as a small, poor country, can hardly imagine its imperial affluence when Jan first travelled through the land. The nation had an almost absolute monopoly of the rich trade with the Atlantic islands of Madeira, the Azores, and the Cape Verdes, which produced sugar, wine, fruit, timber and livestock. The imports of gold, ivory, pepper and slaves from the whole coast of West Africa, as well as the rich output of the entire East African, Arabian and Persian ports, came to Lisbon. Portugal imported the costly, delicate fabrics and rich textiles, as well as the pepper, from the enormously productive west coast of India, the jewels and cinnamon of Ceylon, the rice, other agricultural produce, and woven fabrics of the busy

Coromandel coast and of Calcutta and Madras. All these, together with all that flourishing Siam, Burma and Indonesia had to sell, the fabulous spices from the Moluccas, the silks and porcelain from China, and the silver from Japan, were exclusively marketed in Europe by Portugal, except for what was brought in overland through Asia Minor. The limited volume of Chinese goods, funneled through Manila, which crossed the Pacific in Spanish galleons to Acapulco, in Mexico, never reached Europe, but was absorbed in Mexico and Peru.

Although Portugal had busy shipyards not only at home, but at Goa and elsewhere in the Orient, the demand for bottoms to carry their trade was so great that they employed many chartered English and Dutch ships to bring in their imports from West Africa and the Atlantic Isles, to fetch huge harvests of sugar, tobacco and dyewood from Brazil, and to carry abroad the salt, corkwood and wines which were the principal native exports of Portugal to Western Europe.

The Portuguese Bankers

BECAUSE of the freedom accorded to the "new Christians," or Jewish *conversos*, by Portugal, the banking business flourished; there were very strong, largely Jewish *converso* banking houses in Lisbon, Evora and Oporto, whose foreign exchange operations were of such prime importance that for a while Lisbon outstripped Genoa, Antwerp and Rome in financial influence.

The account books of some of these banking firms have survived through the centuries. They disclose a veritable web of exchange between Portugal and the great Spanish center of Medina del Campo, as well as with Pisa, Frankfort, Antwerp, Paris, Leipzig, Venice, Rome, Leyden, Hamburg and Lyons. Many of the correspondence files of these bankers are also still intact. Since their transactions were largely on long terms of credit, a personal element comes into their correspondence to an unusual degree, and their comments concerning individual character and their cautionary expressions are numerous. Since there was no established postal service, all correspondence was by private courier; the hazards of communication are shown by the business custom of drawing drafts or bills of exchange in five copies, each viable only if the preceding copy had not been honored.

There were few payments in currency; transactions were offset against one another on the books, and the balances were finally settled in cash at the great annual or semi-annual fairs, when the transmission of funds under government protection was safeguarded. Throughout the letter files of these Portuguese merchants the speculative insecurity of the times is evident, particularly in regard to the danger of partial or total loss of fleets from overseas during the hazardous voyages. Therefore the cost of merchandise was doubled, tripled or even more in selling; but even so, bankruptcies were frequent.

In business correspondence the scribe invariably drew a cross and wrote the word "Jesus" at the top of the letterhead, and, although the style was courteous and formal, beneath the polite veneer there was a straightforward, businesslike bluntness appropriate to such transactions. One can well visualize how strictly Jan must have been held to account during his apprenticeship, according to the severe discipline of the time, as he was taught the meticulous procedure of these Renaissance merchant princes.

The Portuguese possessed great mercantile ability, but they conducted their transactions with a degree of punctilio and decorum which sometimes masked their shrewdness. In the fourteenth and fifteenth centuries there were important colonies of Portuguese merchants in Bristol, England, in Lyons, France, and in Bruges and Antwerp, Flanders, all of which were prosperous. The Portuguese also showed their mercantile genius in their trading in the Orient in competition with Chinese, Hindu, Gujarati and Arab competitors, for *Asia Portuguesa* derived most of its profit not from the Lisbon export-import business, but from buying local products in one Oriental area and transporting and selling them to another.

The Portuguese Adventurers

THE PORTUGUESE adventurers of the late fifteenth and early sixteenth centuries were men of very superior courage and endurance. The maritime achievements of Bartholomeu Dias, Vasco da Gama and Ferdinand Magellan have never been surpassed, and the military exploits of Affonso de Albuquerque at Goa, Ormuz and Malacca are almost without parallel in all the history of captures by meager forces by frontal attack on strongly held and supposedly impregnable fortresses.

Jan, like his Dutch and English contemporaries, came to the biased conclusion that Portugal's luxury and soft living, its wealth and ease, had resulted in national decadence. That there had been a certain relaxation in the fiber of the nation may have been true, but that does not explain the several pieces of sheer ill luck which afflicted the country. In the Orient, most of the early reverses of the Portuguese in their struggles against the English and Dutch attackers were not due to decadence, but to the lack of reinforcement or support from the homeland following the disaster in Morocco and the conquest of Portugal by Spain.

However, it is certain that one major effect of Portugal's good fortune in mastering such rich overseas possessions had been a mingling of races which naturally diluted the vigorous drive for power of the original conquerors. In the colonies, a hybrid upper class as well as a mixed lower-class population grew up. The mulattoes of Africa and the Eurasians in India both lacked the stamina and motivation of the original races, and because of their social handicaps their morale was not high. It also was inevitable and natural that men exiled for decades from the homeland should adopt local polygamous practices, take native consorts, and raise a hybrid progeny. At the same time, the morality of the homeland itself was affected when the ratio of females to males became disproportionate. During the late sixteenth century, when the demand for labor became imperative in Portugal, the need was met by the importation of African male slaves to perform manual labor, especially in the semitropical southern province of the Algarve.

Negro Slavery

IN THE EARLY nineteenth century, the callous slave dealers who traded with America were usually Portuguese half-breeds, the successors to the equally heartless Dutch in that field; but during the period with which we are here concerned the Portuguese were the most tolerant of the slave-trading nations, and sincerely felt that the conversion of the slaves to Christianity justified their capture. Considering the universality, both historically and geographically, of slavery and slave trading, this represented a real advance in attitude. The docile Negroes from the Congo and from Angola were easily converted to Catholicism. They were well treated, became reconciled to their captivity, and in a measure benefitted economically and socially from their servitude. The Portuguese as a people were never intolerant of darker races and were kindly masters; and since their captives adopted Christianity, they were largely assimilated into the population. Because of the acute and permanent shortage of white males, and the inability of the Portuguese women to emigrate, in rural regions there was some miscegenation among the peasantry, although this never became an accepted pattern and there do not seem to have been any legally recognized unions. The general racial effect was apparently not substantial, although there was much whispering of scandal in higher circles, where the great ladies were husbandless for periods of years.

Portuguese Diplomatic Relations

BEFORE the military debacle of 1579 in Morocco, although there had been imbalances in the Portuguese exchequer and an unsound national economy due to a neglect of agriculture, an excess of slave labor at home and the emigration of needed workers to vast colonial possessions, Renaissance Portugal was an opulent and powerful state. Its navy was the strongest in Europe and counterbalanced the superiority of the Spanish army. The foreign policy of Portugal was neutralism, diplomatic and trade relations were excellent with all Christian nations, and Lisbon was recognized as the financial capital of Europe. Although the dynasty was closely related to that of Spain, the Portuguese avoided being drawn into the international enmities and rivalries of the Hapsburgs. They maintained friendly relations with the rebellious Netherlands and chartered many Dutch and English ships as freighters.

The terms of the Treaty of Tordesillas, which divided the areas of colonial development between the two peninsular countries, had been respected for almost a century, despite the temporary strain brought about by the activities in the Orient of the Spanish fleet of Ferdinand Magellan. Under that treaty, Spain held all rights in the Western Hemisphere, apart from Newfoundland and Brazil, which fell to Portugal; the latter was given Africa and Asia, excepting the Philippines and, intermittently, the Spice Islands.

The principal source of difference in relations between the two countries lay in the relative tolerance of the Portuguese toward the Jews, despite the constant diplomatic pressure of Spain. While it is true that Jewish merchants were restricted as to immigration into *Asia Portuguesa* and the East Indies, nevertheless they were allowed to participate within Portugal in the mercantile and financial transactions pertaining to those areas; they were actually encouraged to emigrate to the Brazilian and West African colonies, where they soon became well established and influential.

This infuriated the implacably anti-Semitic Spaniards, whose general term of arrogant scorn for any Portuguese national was "Jew." One of the popular sayings in Spain was: "A Portuguese is born of a Jew's fart." Nevertheless, the Spaniards had had to respect the naval might of Portugal and recognized their own vulnerability in their Atlantic sea lanes to the Spanish American colonies.

If there had been a strong heir to the throne in 1579, Portugal could quickly have recuperated from the Moorish disaster—a disaster which had itself been brought on by bad judgment on the part of their young ruler. However, the feebleness of the subsequent administration of the Cardinal-King, coupled with the impoverishment of the nobility through stripping themselves to pay Moorish ransoms, made it possible for Philip to seize the empire with the expenditure of less gunpowder than would ordinarily have been needed to capture a small citadel. It was dynastic bad luck, more than anything else, that plagued the Portuguese nation.

Suddenly England, France and the Netherlands, who were deeply antagonistic towards Philip, changed from traditional friends to relentless enemies of Portugal as the result of its conquest by Spain. While Portugal's ships, men and resources were ruthlessly expended by Philip to support his own imperialistic European aims, the Portuguese were rendered helpless to defend their overseas possessions against predatory attacks by the Northern European maritime powers.

Another calamity whose effect upon Portuguese society at this time is difficult to imagine in its full enormity was the plague. Whole villages were depopulated, business organizations were wiped out, and many land-owning and noble families were left without an heir or successor. In some counties there were no judges, sheriffs or police left, all having been swept away into a common grave. All this made possible many fraudulent claims, and law and order, and even morality itself, were plunged into a morass of anarchy. Because of the great loss of life, it was almost impossible to find laboring men to cultivate the fields or to work in factories or shipyards, and a working man or artisan could demand and receive any price for his labor.

Under these conditions, no able seaman would enlist in the poorly paid navy or merchant marine, and in particular would not sign up for the dreary, dangerous and unrewarding voyage to India. The pepper ships so necessary for the economic health of the nation could be manned only by the press gang or by clearing out the jails; this accounts for the lub-berly seamanship in the Portuguese ships on the Indian voyage of which Jan was later so critical. Before the pepper ships could get any sailors at all, both Philip's war galleons and his oared galleys which patrolled the Mediterranean coasts against Moorish rovers had at any cost to be manned.

The Domestic Economy

J A N was in Portugal for almost three years, and it may be assumed that, with his lust for travel, he managed to be sent about the provinces on various business errands. He probably managed to see the temperate high-lands of the north, with their climbing green grapes, bitter wine, and herds of great oxen with branching horns; he must have known, too, the middle region where the purple grapes grow on bushes and flocks of brownish sheep and goats cover the land, and he no doubt visited the semitropical, Africa-like Algarve in the south. Instead of the mules of Spain there were burros, and one saw then, as now, the peasant women carrying burdens balanced on their heads with an ageless grace. Portuguese horses were good, and the roads were passable, winding through the hills amid groves of pine, oak, cork and olive trees.

The youth from the simple herring port on the Zuider Zee had gained some sophistication of taste in Seville. Now he was almost certainly charmed by Lisbon, with its many flower-bedecked public squares, its luxurious private gardens, the palatial government buildings, the picturesque ruined Moorish citadel, the wide Tagus River filled with foreign shipping, and the nearby sunny ocean beaches.

In 1583, he wrote, business was poor because of "fresh discord between the Spaniards and Portuguese." Most of the chronicles of the period did not, and doubtless dared not, dwell upon such a demoralization of spirit as would cause a stagnation of trade. On the Spanish side, the private letters of the supercilious conquerors, apart from official publications, mentioned their annexed Portuguese brethren and co-partners with patronizing scorn. It is easy to imagine the effect of such events and such an attitude on the part of the dominant Spanish upon a subjugated people who for so long had held their heads high in prestige, power and wealth. The atmosphere in the capital could hardly have been other than depressing, and Jan's old wanderlust was pricking him.

The Pepper Trade

THEN his brother "who followed the court" secured, through the influence of his "master," the royal secretary, an appointment as clerk or purser on one of the great pepper ships in that year's passage to India. This was a political plum and would, no doubt, bring in a good profit to Willem Tin, which he would, of course, have to share with his "master." A ship's clerk had to keep account of all commercial transactions, in order to see that the crown received its due share and that there was no smuggling or evasion of customs duties. This function created openings for the clerk to receive good fees for winking at irregularities. He also was the beneficiary of many time-honored perquisites, not the least of which was the privilege of engaging in private trading on his own account, with the right to a fixed amount of cargo space on the outward voyage for goods to be sold in India, and an even more valuable assignment of room in the hold for costly merchandise to be transported back to Portugal.

The system could not be condemned as graft, as it was so firmly established as to be a vested interest. The Portuguese Indian capital of Goa depended upon it. Although they received imports from Lisbon only once a year, and were perforce always twelve months behind the European styles, still that rich and pretentious vice-regal court followed the fads and fashions of the homeland eagerly, and itself set the mode for the outlying provincial centers. Consequently, if Willem Tin secured the monopoly of exporting to Goa some novelty or folly that had been the

LARGE SHIP *similar to a Portuguese nao' of the Carreira da India etched by the great Flemish artist Pieter Brueghel the Elder. Almost all sketches of ships of the period are fanciful renderings that are not technically correct, but Brueghel was a realistic draftsman, and his ship is accepted as accurate.*

DUTCH SHIPBUILDING. *Shipwrights at the end of the sixteenth century, working without blueprints or models, and using hand tools of inferior steel and wooden pegs instead of metal spikes, turned out seaworthy small vessels suitable for use not only in the shallow coastal and inland waters, but in the tempestuous North Sea as well.*

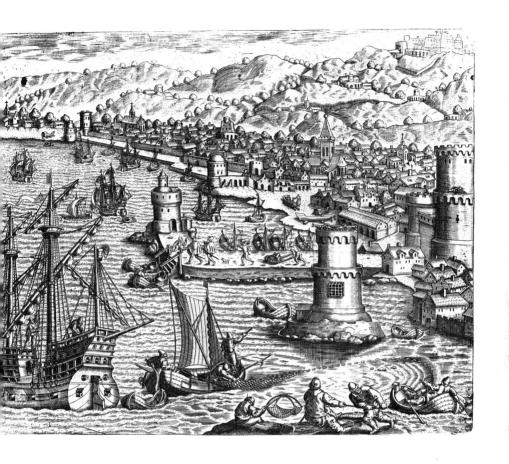

SAN LUCAR DE BARRAMEDA, *the ocean port of Seville, at the mouth of the Guadalquivir River, Linschoten's first landing outside the Netherlands. He was only seventeen, and this was his first glimpse of the great world.*

O. Leilaõ. que se Faz cada dia pola menhã na Rua direita na Cidade de Goa Feito Polo natural por Ioan de Linschoten framengo.

Xaraffo Wiselaer

Porteiro Wtroeper

Pinques Arbeiders.

Ama Voesser

Goënsi se quanta foro viden area pandat
Plana frequens tectis splendida dives opum?

Ut mercem hic properet gemmis auroque nitentem
Ille abducta procul vendere mancipia?

Congesta huc
Insulæ et

GOA'S FAMOUS MARKET, *called the Leylon, attracted traders from all over the world, as well as local potentates, ladies, and shopkeepers. Note the vista of streets in the background, the solidity of the houses, and the closed palanquin being carried in the right foreground.*

A. Misericordia

Joannes a Doetechum fecit.

et Indus
'Hoogerb.

Fori Goensis tabernarum mercium et mer catorum illud frequentantium aperta ex plicatio per N Linschoten

Claere opdoeninge vande merckt van Goa met haer winckelen waren en daegelickse Coopluyden. door I. H. V. Linschoten

44 en 45

Goa's market was drawn by Linschoten in great detail, showing the various kinds of business that were transacted. Food, garments, slaves—everything was sold there. Disputes were settled. Letters were written. Above all, the market served as a social meeting place.

Indorum casæ, villæ, et vici
circa Goam.

Indische hutte Lanthuysen en dorpen
ontrent Goa.

A SUBURBAN VILLAGE *and estate near Goa, complete with shop, domestic animals, a well, and a stream in which people bathe. Note the use of only the left hand when performing ablutions, in accord with the sanitary custom of the Orient.*

A PORTUGUESE OFFICIAL *on horseback, accompanied by his customary retinue of slaves and attendants.*

Naves celoces seu biremes, quibus Bello et transportandis
mercibus utuntur Lusitani, et eorum hostes Malabares.

Fusten welcke die Portugeesen ēn haer vianden die Malabaren
gebruycken ter oorloch, ēn om coopmanschap te voeren

46 en 47

A FUSTA, OR BERGANTYME, *rowed by Malabar prisoners of
war. The swift, shallow-draft, heavily armed coastguard boats were
very effective against native smugglers and pirates.*

rage in Lisbon or Madrid, he could make a handsome profit by selling the exclusive rights to some fashionable dealer in the style-conscious colony.

Such private traffic had grown immeasurably by Jan's time, because the great pepper fleet no longer was a crown enterprise; the ships were now owned and operated by the great German firm of Welser, under a royal patent. Because of its incurable fiscal deficit, the crown had for years hypothecated in advance to the Fuggers and Welsers its proceeds from the annual pepper fleet, then operated as a government monopoly. The royal exchequer finally got several years behind in such borrowings against future income, and the debt became unpayable. Therefore a new system was evolved in which the Welsers were allowed to administer armadas and market the imports in consideration of a guaranteed annual advance payment to the crown. Under this financial arrangement the government assumed responsibility for no losses, but had a speculative interest in profits beyond its annual heavy fee. Under such a system politics were rampant and patronage was the rule. As a secretary to Philip II, the "master" of Willem Tin no doubt had great influence with the Welsers, and there can be little doubt that Willem Tin's perquisites were substantial.

This was an age when appointment to all governmental posts of importance had to be paid for, and when many jobs were customarily sold or bequeathed; the system of privilege in the *Carreira da India*, as the Portuguese annual fleet was called, was not a corrupt one, but simply the generally recognized business procedure. In fact, both the Dutch and English East India Companies subsequently followed the same procedure; in England, by the nineteenth century, the practice of private trading by functionaries of the East India Company had assumed indefensible proportions. There is no doubt that one great drawback to the working of the system, and a major cause of most of the maritime losses of the Indiamen under all three flags, was the overloading of ships due to the heavy private cargoes of the officers which were added to the regular commercial lading of the carriers.

As soon as Jan learned of his brother's plan to visit the fascinating world of *Asia Portuguesa*, from which most Europeans, especially the Spaniards and French, were barred, his wanderlust prompted him to devise means of accompanying Willem Tin. It happened that the announcement was then made of the appointment by the king and confirmation by the Pope of a new Archbishop of Goa, who would sail to India in the pepper fleet of 1583. Jan learned that there would be openings in the prelate's retinue for lay accountants and clerks to keep the records of the extensive taxes which were to be levied upon commercial operations throughout the colonies in order to raise ransoms for the Portuguese captives in Morocco. After his three-year apprenticeship in Portuguese business methods, Jan appears to have felt qualified to act as a tax collector or bookkeeper under ecclesiastical auspices, and therefore, as he said, he began to try by every means to get an appointment.

Willem Tin's "master" was a friend of the Archbishop, and thus influence was exerted and a post secured for Jan Huyghen on the Archbishop's staff, which numbered in all forty persons. As the prelate and his retinue were booked for passage on the great galleon *Sam Salvador*, Willem Tin arranged to be clerk on the same ship. Thus, Jan wrote, they "could help one another."

CHAPTER III

The Outward Voyage

Portuguese Foreign Policy

FOR NEARLY A CENTURY, Portugal had maintained impressive, well-staffed embassies in the capitals of all the important maritime powers, embassies whose main task was to see that there was no trespassing in the West African, Oriental and Brazilian waters over which Portugal claimed supremacy by virtue of the Treaty of Tordesillas. The particular care of the Portuguese Ambassador was to make complaints against and try to prevent the outfitting of any corsair which might plan to intrude in Portuguese waters. If his protests were ignored or evaded, he tried to have the offending ship seized by its own government upon its return to home port. This diplomatic policy was backed up by a ruthless naval program which did all that was possible to capture any interloper and, once it was captured, to confiscate its cargo and to sink it with all hands battened under the hatches. Such savagery at sea then was universal—what was remarkable about the Portuguese was that they tried to forestall it by diplomatic representations.

This maritime policy in regard to the *Carreira da India* was accepted by the northern nations because the Portuguese government and many Portuguese merchants chartered English and Dutch bottoms to carry to Lisbon their imports of timber, cattle and wines from the Atlantic Islands, sugar from Brazil, and slaves, ivory and even gold from West Africa.

The Outward Voyage

Since they were given ample employment in the Portuguese trade, the northern maritime nations were, on the whole, less desirous to be competitive than they might otherwise have been.

It was also generally recognized that Portugal's general foreign policy, at least in part, was genuinely motivated by a desire to win the heathen to Christianity and to combat Islam. One of its prime goals, perhaps a survival from the chivalric ideas of the Middle Ages, was the achievement of the unity of Christendom through a revival of the Crusades. This task had been recently undertaken, unilaterally and disastrously, by King Sebastian, and its consequences were to be fatal to the power of the nation. Yet no one had forgotten that, when all maritime Christendom had been still cowering before the threat of Moslem corsairs, Portugal had been a shield against the common enemy. This had helped Portugal to gain a sympathetic acceptance of her claims to monopoly.

The Departure from Lisbon

On Good Friday, April 8, 1583, the nao *Sam Salvador*, with Jan and his brother Willem Tin aboard, dropped down the Tagus River with the tide, crossed the bar, and plunged into the Atlantic, steering for the Island of Madeira en route to Goa, the capital of *Asia Portuguesa*. All hands had attended early Mass that morning in the historic church of the Jerónimos before embarking, and the flotilla had received and answered a farewell salute from the cannons of the waterside castle at Belém. Jan wrote: "Putting our trust in God, without whose favor and helpe we can doe nothing, and all our actions are vain, we sayled forwards."

Although three quarters of a century had elapsed since the sailing of the similar fleet of Vasco da Gama in 1497, the details of the departure were not unlike those so graphically described in Camoen's *Lusiads*: the mothers and wives of the mariners wailed in grief and apprehension, and ". . . the old man of venerable air who on the seafront stood among the crowd and thrice his head, as one in grief, he bowed," as he forecast the hardships, woes and losses that would be the lot of the mariners who sailed to the blare of trumpets and waving of banners.

Now, however, there were a few differences. The sailing of the annual fleet for Goa was perhaps the greatest nautical event of the year, but it set forth upon a charted route, where its dangers were known and risks calculated. The ships were much larger than da Gama's, but unfortunately they were not any safer, if as safe. Jan Huyghen listed the ships: "The Admirall was the *S. Phillip*, the Vice-Admirall the *S. Jacob*, both new ships and bearing the name of the King and of his sonne, the other three, *S. Lawrence, S. Francisco,* and our shippe *S. Salvador."* Sixteenth-century terminology of naval rank is bound to be confusing to modern readers. It was at that time customary to call the flagship the "Admiral"; this vessel carried the commander-in-chief of the Armada, whose title was "Captain-General." The officer who was second-in-command of the Armada was known as the "Admiral"; and the ship which carried his flag was called the "Vice-Admiral."

Each of the naos was of about 1,400 to 1,600 tons burden, and each had a total of four hundred to five hundred men aboard, including a crew of about a hundred and twenty. The naos were lightly laden, since in general the people of highly civilized India had little need for European manufactured goods, which they did not consider to be in any way superior to their own. However, the lading included Venetian mirrors and glassware, pieces of coral, some cheap trinkets known as Nuremberger ware, brass basins for rice, and many bars of copper and antimony, which were always in demand in India for minting coinage. The most important cargo on each ship consisted of hundreds of casks of coins, silver "pieces of eight" or Portuguese *reales,* for which Indian demand was insatiable.

When the Portuguese had first reached India under Vasco da Gama, they had expected to be able to trade their merchandise for Indian produce. However, the Indians had no desire for the goods they offered, and this posed a frustrating economic problem for them. They were unaware, of course, that, centuries before them, Greek merchants, later Roman traders, and still later, Arabian and Venetian exporters, all had discovered that what the Indians demanded was gold or silver coins. As soon as the Florentine and German bankers who financed the importation of pepper, spices, and oriental ware into Portugal recognized these requirements, they were happy to stamp out "pieces of eight" from Peruvian and Mexican silver and to export these *reales* to India at an exchange markup of forty percent; to this was added, of course, the handsome profit reaped by the sale in Europe of the products purchased by the easily minted pieces of eight.

It must be remembered that in 1583, when Jan made his voyage to Goa, the Invincible Armada had not yet been defeated by the English, and neither English nor Dutch, except for a few reckless corsairs, had attempted to invade the maritime preserves of *Asia Portuguesa.* Portuguese naos had made the round trip unmolested for almost a century. The earliest tiny wooden sailing ships had blossomed into ocean liners that were enormous by the standards of that day, crowded with passengers and troops on the outward voyage and overladen with cargo when homeward bound.

The Outward Voyage

Deserters and Dead Men's Chests

A MUSTER of all aboard was held as soon as the ship had passed over the bar of the River Tagus and entered the ocean, as Jan Huyghen did not fail to report. Checked off on the ship's roll were the names of those who turned up missing. In accordance with regulations, every man who signed on for the voyage was required to have a surety or sponsor who guaranteed his sailing for the amount of the advance pay given him when he enrolled. Now this was recorded by the purser for later claim upon each sponsor, the sea chest of each missing man was declared forfeit, and his belongings were inventoried and given to the captain to be "disposed of at his pleasure." Jan added that the property of persons who died on the voyage was treated in the same way, and little of it ever reached the heirs of the deceased, since it was embezzled and disappeared en route. This habit of summary appropriation of a dead man's estate constituted one of the most profitable perquisites of a captain, and the heirs had to have great influence to force him to make an accounting and disgorge his plunder. When it is realized that an average of fifty percent of the complement of a nao generally died of disease on the six-month outward voyage to India, the value of the captain's pickings can be estimated.

Although the ditty box of a sailor or common soldier might contain only articles of trifling value, the chest of a merchant or of a person of rank might well yield a fortune. There was no way of transmitting valuables, specie and personal belongings to India except in one's own sea chest. Any man of importance sailing for *Asia Portuguesa* had to take with him the funds, jewelry, arms and apparel which he would need in order to assert and maintain his position in the vice-regal court of pretentious Goa, where status and Oriental "face" were of such importance.

The minimum stay required in the king's service in *India Portuguesa* was three years, and since it was almost impossible for the average person going there to have any belongings sent out to him later, and in no event except after a year's delay, most emigrants from Lisbon carried a substantial part of their portable wealth with them. Any man of intelligence who crossed the gangplank to board an India-bound nao was grimly aware that his chances of reaching Goa were, on the average, only one out of two, and that in case of his death on shipboard there was but little probability of his belongings ever being returned to his heirs.

During the voyage it was common to find a dying man surrounded by watchful shipmates, perhaps even priestly ones, waiting to pounce upon his treasure as soon as the breath should leave his body. Many a poor sufferer, once convinced that his end was approaching, would forestall the jackals by distributing the contents of his sea chest to his friends with his own hands before he died.

Rations

THE BALLAST of sand, gravel and stones in the hold was supplemented by the weight of the supplies—barrels of salt beef, cheeses, casks of wine, water, olive oil, vinegar, dried fish and sardines, and packages of almonds, acorns, chestnuts, prunes, garlic, onions and raisins. As the voyage continued and as these liquids and food supplies were consumed, the ship rode higher and higher in the water.

The drinking water became foul, and a man had to hold his nose while drinking it, even after filtering it through a cloth. Whenever the ship was becalmed, the foul element in the drinking water settled to the bottom of the scuttlebutt as sediment, and the water became clearer and lost its nauseous odor. There were drinking dippers at the scuttlebutt which were used by everybody, whether sick or well, and this was the unsuspected source of much disease. Tropical rainstorms were greeted with rejoicing, and tarpaulins were spread to catch fresh water for drinking and washing.

About a month after all the green vegetables and fresh meat and fruit had been consumed, the symptoms of scurvy began to appear among passengers and crew. From then on, the voyage became a torment. Onions would have helped hold off the scourge, or a bountiful ration of the newly discovered American tuber, the potato, but this was not understood. The crews on the Dutch ships chartered by Portugal for the Atlantic routes were more free from scurvy than those on Portuguese ships, due to their abundant servings of sauerkraut. This pickled cabbage was the only vegetable which retained much of its vitamin C content when preserved; but of course vitamins were unknown at that time. Since sauerkraut did not form part of the normal Portuguese diet, it did not occur to anybody to serve it aboard ship. Dried onions and garlic kept some of their anti-scorbutic properties, but as noted they never formed a large enough part of the rations to have much effect.

The Ship's Mess

THERE WAS little hot food served because the cooking had to be done in open hearths in a sheltered sand box behind the main mast, and whenever there was a fresh breeze the danger of fire on the wooden ship made the risk of cooking too great. On some ships, galley fires were lighted on top of the stone and sand ballast in the hold; the ballast was, of course, noninflammable, and the flames were sheltered from any wind. However, in most naos the bilge water soon infiltrated the ballast, and in any event it became noisome due to sewage; and when the vessel keeled over or pitched in a gale the bilge was likely to inundate such a galley. Moreover, it was extremely difficult to hoist cauldrons of hot food up the hatches, which was necessary when the cooking was done in the hold.

Obviously, culinary problems had to be subordinated to safety, because a fire at sea meant certain death for almost all hands; there was no life-saving equipment adequate to take care of more than a fraction of the complement, for no ship carried more than one longboat and there was generally only one skiff. The woodwork was very inflammable, and if the racing flames reached the gunpowder magazine the whole ship would explode. Consequently the galley fire was always quickly doused when the wind became brisk; and then the lack of any hot water for washing and laundry or for the sick bay was a real privation. Perhaps for weeks at a time no meat could be cooked nor any soups or stews be prepared. Neither tea nor coffee was known at that time, so their lack was not felt.

In the torrid or temperate zones, the lack of warm food meant only boredom and distaste, but in the often prolonged, storm-bound cruising in the freezing latitudes below the Cape of Good Hope this deprivation was keenly felt, particularly as there were no braziers or other sources of warmth for chilled hands and bodies.

Light at Night

THERE WAS little illumination aboard ship at any time because of the risk of fire, and at best only dim, swinging oil lamps were used. To the seamen who lived and slept on the open waist-deck, the stars and moon, when not obscured, gave adequate light; but the little cubicles which served as cabins were gloomy even in the daytime. In windy weather the lamp in the cabin was extinguished, and the occupant had to grope for his belongings. Reading or writing at night under such conditions was out of the question. When the pilot wanted to scan his chart, he had to hold it under the feeble glimmer of the shrouded binnacle lamp, often the only source of light aboard the whole ship.

In a good breeze, apart from the binnacle lamp the only light for the steersman came from the huge wax candle or torch of impregnated reeds in the stern. This was well sheltered by the horn, shell or glass panels in the wooden stern lantern, eight or ten feet high and elaborately carved and gilded, which stood firmly fixed in its bracket in the poop as a signal to the consorts in the fleet. If the ship was sailing alone, the poop lantern was generally not lighted.

The Outward Voyage

Construction

B U I L D I N G ocean-going ships was still a relatively new art in Europe. It was only a century since the frail, undecked or single-decked lateen-rigged caravel of Bartoloméo Dias first encountered the frightening gales off the Cape of Good Hope, and even less since Portuguese ships had braved the terrifying typhoons of the China Sea. In design and construction ships such as the fifteen hundred ton *Sam Salvador* were a triumph of naval architecure. In its building over two thousand oak trees and hundreds of pines were used. The trees had to be felled up in the forested hills, floated down rivers, and hauled by oxen over difficult roads to the shipyards at Cascais, near Lisbon, or other yards at Oporto. After due seasoning of the timber, the planks were sawed out by hand, shaped by adze and draw-knife, and formed and bent in kilns. The fitting, joining, bracing and drilling were all done by hand; only a few simple tools were available, and their steel cutting edges were of limited sharpness. There were no blueprints and few clear-cut diagrams or specifications; a great hull was constructed largely by rule of thumb and by eye, and sometimes took two or three years to build. But at last, when the finished hulk slid down the ways into the water, it was truly a thing of grace and beauty. Knotty problems of buoyancy, stability and oscillation had been correctly solved. Strains had been foreseen, watertight subdivisions constructed, and workable pumping, draining and ventilating facilities had been provided.

The thick wooden hull was much heavier, in proportion to the size of the ship, than is a trim modern steel one. The thrust against the decks of the towering masts when strained by the titanic pull of canvas in a gale, the tremendous weight of rows of ponderous cannon, and the vulnerability of innumerable caulked seams in the planking of the hull were all dangerous disadvantages. However, the dead weight of the iron cannon was balanced and supported by trusses and stanchions, and provision was made for the shuddering vibration and straining of the bulkheads when a broadside was fired. Protection also was devised for the powder magazine in the ship's vitals. The powerful leverage of the masts against the decks under the press of the mighty sails was offset. The planking of the hull was closely fitted to insure tight seams against the hammering of the waves at the Cape of Good Hope, especially when, being heavily overladen on the return trip, the nao had to plow straight into the pounding seas, instead of being lightly loaded and able to ride along on the surface.

Several disadvantages were inherent in the design of a nao. With its very high poop, it presented a vulnerable broad surface to the suddenly

[53]

shifting blasts, and through the tiller slot in the stern there was always danger of being pooped by a following wave. The very low freeboard at the waist was continually waveswept in a storm, and if a hatch covering was torn loose the ship took water and was doomed. The sails were made of light cotton and were easily damaged. In addition, the crude wooden pumps were weak and ineffective; their valves, subject to shrinkage or swelling, often lost suction if they became clogged or jammed by floating bits of oakum, dregs of sediment or loose masses of pepper from damaged cargo. If the pump went out of action, the hold often filled with water and the vessel inevitably sank.

Many of the features of the building of these great wooden ships were kept secret by the family of the designer or builder and were handed down from father to son. Later on, the first step of the English Admiralty, or of the Dutch, when a captured Portuguese Indiaman was brought into port, was to have shipwrights study its design and make sketches and detailed plans of it for copying.

Although the naos had been developed originally in Portugal, it was not long before the best ships were being constructed in the colonies. In Jan's day, the most seaworthy naos and galleons were built of teak in India by native labor under Portuguese supervision. Several thriving independent shipyards in the various ports along the Malabar Coast of India attained a high degree of technical proficiency. Since each was located in a different native state, the rivalry between the various rajahs became acute. Each shipyard attempted to underbid its rival, with the result that the industry, caught in the grip of cut-throat competition, suffered such losses as to wipe out its working capital and forced almost all the great Indian shipbuilders into bankruptcy. Only two yards survived the price war, and these established a monopoly. Competition ceased, but so did progress; with the stimulus of business rivalry removed, the quality of their production soon suffered.

The race between Portuguese naval architects to design larger and larger naos also became suicidal, since they refused to recognize one serious technical limitation which should have established a maximum practicable size. The available timbers were only of a certain length, and that length should have governed the size of the ships. It was structurally impossible to fashion a wooden hull of the extension and beam necessary for a fifteen-hundred-ton cargo ship of sufficient strength and durability to hold together in a hurricane when grievously overloaded. The fatal absurdity of flouting the laws of simple mechanics became so obvious that, in 1570, the Crown belatedly became disturbed by the series of losses. Too many overladen pepper ships, homeward bound, were unable to withstand the gales at the Cape. Therefore definite orders were issued concerning the size of naos in the *Carreira da India;* henceforward they should be of not less than three hundred tons nor more than four hundred and fifty tons burden. Later the decree was amended to make the upper limit six hundred tons and to reduce the number of flush decks from four to three. However, until almost a century later, the vested interests, which included shipbuilders, owners, shipper and crews, completely ignored the wise governmental rules. They all persisted in their blind folly, gambling their lives and possessions against the fury of the sea in ships that were structurally unsound because of the mania for size.

Excessive size likewise proved a fatal disadvantage when another hazard was added, that of attacks by English privateers, which became acute during Jan's time. The unwieldy bulk of a nao flaunted an invitation to capture. No matter how well gunned and well manned a fifteen-hundred-ton nao might be, it was impossible for the slow, unhandy craft to fight off the attack of a squadron of three-hundred-ton warships. This was first demonstrated a few years later, in 1592, when the well-handled and adequately armed sixteen-hundred-ton *Madre de Dios*, returning with over a million dollars worth of cargo, was attacked off the Azores by six English privateers; after a desperate defense it was rendered helpless and had to surrender. The prize was brought to Dartmouth, England, where its design and construction excited universal admiration.

Because of the jealously guarded secrets of the trade, little was printed about ship construction, and no certain knowledge now exists of the design or build of sixteenth-century ships, their rig, or the cut of their sails. Unfortunately, the many drawings, engravings, and paintings of ships used to embellish maps and charts or included in paintings or tapestries showing marine scenes are not accurate in technical details. Artists often depicted a vessel merely by copying an older picture which was at hand, and since the aim was imaginative rather than scientific, everybody was satisfied. The earliest accurate pictures of sailing ships date from the seventeenth century, when Dutch marine artists began to accompany the war fleets in order to paint their pictures from the deck of a ship at sea. The drawings and the numerous modern models of the craft of Christopher Columbus, Vasco da Gama, Ferdinand Magellan, and Sir Francis Drake are hypothetical and cannot be accepted as authoritative.

In the fifteenth century the tops of the masts had not been accessible by ratlines from the deck, for fear the enemy might scale them, but had Jacob's ladders for access which could be lowered or drawn up. The tops also were provided with heavy bags in which ammunition or supplies could be raised. During the sixteenth century, the builders of Portuguese naos gradually assimilated features from the Hanseatic cogs, the Genoan and Venetian *carracas* (or carracks), and the lateen-sailed caravels and galleys of the Mediterranean. The ships appear to have had only four sails. The platforms or tops of the masts in the early sixteenth century were only incidentally used for crow's nests or lookout stations, but were very important offensive and defensive strong points, well fortified with the small cannon called serpentines or falconets. In the later sixteenth century apparently topsails were first used, but these so-called topsails were small auxiliary, weak, square sails mounted upon flimsy small masts erected in the fighting tops, which would not interfere with combat and which were used casually in fair weather. We can assume that the *Sam Salvador* had six sails with a low, sloping prow much like the ramming beak of a galley, and that the sterncastle was a very high structure designed to be defended against boarders who might invade the low waist-deck.

Apparently the Dutch in the late sixteenth century were the first to reduce the size of the broad fortified wooden fighting top to make room for the spars and cordage necessary to hoist a large topmast which could be lowered to the deck at need and which had tackle descending to the deck. This was to become an important factor in the ship's motive force of six sails. However, this development of the topsail probably was later than the time of Jan's outward voyage to India, and the *Sam Salvador*'s six sails presumably included only the early version of the topsail. For purposes of comparison, it may be recalled that a nineteenth-century full-rigged ship had not less than twenty-four sails.

The *Sam Salvador*'s six sails included: the little, square spritsail mounted in the bowsprit or else slung under it, the square foresail and small topsail, the square mainsail and small topsail, and the lateen mizzen. The principal sails were large and heavy, made of two thicknesses of hempen or cotton cloth. To make more sail, additional horizontal strips called bonnets were lashed to lanyards through clews in the lower square mainsail or lower square foresail to extend their area. To reef sail, the bonnets were removed. There was not the variety of specialized gear, such as bunt lines on each sail, that was later used, and the sails were very hard to trim and brace in a gale.

In the sixteenth century the sails were dropped from the yard when they were to be set and were hoisted up to the yard and clewed when they were to be furled, but this was a dangerous method, since it took too much time in an emergency to reduce sail; therefore someone invented the quicker procedure of dropping the sail and yard, or, as we now say, lowering sail, and of hoisting it to make sail.

On the *Sam Salvador* the mainsail was raised or dropped by large wheels operated by special seamen often called *strinceros*. The ship's master had exclusive charge of the mainmast with the mainsail and its topsail, and the boatswain was responsible for the foremast and its two square sails. As there were no higher sails the sailors did not have to swarm aloft to furl the sails, as was necessary in later years. The hempen ropes, to be strong, had to be of large diameter, and when soggy they were heavy, swollen, and hard to draw through the wooden blocks, which had no pulleys in them. The ships built or rigged in India like the *Sam Salvador* had cordage of white coir made from coconut fibers. This was stronger than hempen ropes, but it grievously cut the hands of the sailors. Manila rope made of sisal had not then been adopted.

The large mizzen sail was of lateen cut and was mounted on a huge spar, tilted diagonally, which was made of several pieces of wood joined together. To tack or to come about it was necessary for the seamen to lay hold of this great diagonal yard and push or pull it around the mast, which was dangerous, difficult or impossible to do in a gale.

Officers and Seamen

THE SOLDIERS and passengers looked down on the sailors, except in times of storm or combat, when all depended upon them. If an enemy, by good gunnery, could cut the gear and top hamper with his grape shot, the ship became immobilized because of its inability to maneuver and was doomed unless the rigging could be repaired quickly. In such a desperate case the unprotected seamen had to go aloft under musket fire from the enemy's fighting tops and struggle to subdue the flapping, thrashing, torn sails, to secure the wildly whipping cordage, expertly to splice, reeve and repair the tackle, and perhaps even to haul up a new spar while the wallowing and plunging of the helpless vessel made their feverish efforts even more difficult. The enemy sharpshooters naturally concentrated their fire upon the laboring sailors, and the mortality was heavy, for even being grazed by a light musket ball would cause a man to fall to his death.

The responsibility for carrying on the ship's routine was divided between the officers. The captain had command of the soldiers, who might be compared to modern marines, except that they were proportionately much more numerous, since almost all naval battles were settled by short-range, small-arms fire, followed by hand-to-hand combat with a boarding force.

The pilot was responsible for the navigation, but transmitted his orders through the master. The master, besides being responsible for the main-mast and its tackle, also had command over all the lower officers, such as the boatswain, who was in charge of the foremast and the anchors, and the quartermaster, who controlled the pumps, the small boats, the repair of cordage and the cleaning of the decks and holds. The constable had charge of the gunners and drilled them in the practice of opening the ports, running out the guns and hauling them back again, and firing and reloading, which required much practice. The carpenter had, of course, important rank, for on a wooden ship his duties were manifold; and the caulker and cooper also were well paid and had their privileges. Since the ships were almost never quite watertight, the pumps had to be manned continuously, and slaves were generally carried for this arduous work, although soldiers were also often set to the pumps. In emergencies, when the pumping had to be desperately accelerated, all aboard, regardless of rank, were expected to lend a hand and work frantically in short shifts throughout day and night. Even so, once the seams had opened in a pounding sea and the hull began to fill, it generally was only a question of time before the efforts of the exhausted and terrified workers failed to keep pace with the increasing leakage. Finally, with a sudden foundering, the ship would be swamped and carry everybody to the bottom.

The average crew of a four-decked nao ranged from a maximum of two hundred to an average of a hundred and twenty men before the mast, usually consisting of sixty able seamen and sixty *grumetes*. These latter, generally boys in their teens, performed all the drudgery; they normally slept on the open waistdeck between the foremast and the mainmast, which usually was awash during heavy weather, and which in the latitudes below the Cape of Good Hope was often iced over or covered with snow.

In addition, the commissioned and petty officers numbered about eighteen, and there were four pages, or cabin boys, and twenty-six gunners.

Guns and Gunners

THE GUNNERS usually were Germans, Dutchmen or Lombards, and were well paid. Both the Spaniards and the Portuguese were inclined to employ Teutons as artillerymen, possibly because they were more phlegmatic than the high-strung Latins. With smooth-bore cannon of uncertain standards and no accurate sighting instruments, the gunners had to exercise their craft almost by intuition. Consequently the skill and quality of leadership of the constable, or chief gunner, was of primary importance.

The stately *Sam Salvador*, a great cargo ship built for peaceful traffic, was only lightly armed, having about twenty-four guns, many of them only eight-pounders. During the years since Vasco da Gama had made the first voyage to India, there had been no real naval challenge in the Atlantic Ocean to the Portuguese Indiamen. By government regulation the guns were required to be carried, largely as a matter of prudence, to be used against a stray pirate or in possible eventualities in some foreign port. Some captains did not even mount them on carriages, but negligently slung them in with the cargo in the hold; but even the most cursorily armed ships had at least a few very light serpentines, of an inch and a half bore, mounted on the fighting tops of the masts. In the early days, the guns of the broadside batteries were breech loaders, but as the cannon were made larger and the powder charge heavier, the cast-iron breech could not be tightly and precisely fitted to prevent a flareback, so muzzle loaders became standard. It took a great deal of time to reload one of these after it had been fired. Even a small cannon weighed a couple of tons. After it had been discharged, and before the match could be applied again to the touch hole, the ropes that held it against recoil had to be unloosened, the gun carriage hauled back into the ship, the bore swabbed out, the charge inserted and tamped into position, the stone or iron round shot rammed into place, the gun again moved forward by hackles and the carriage lashed safely, and finally the gun levelled and sighted on the moving target by screws operated by hand cranks, with allowance for the roll and pitch of the ship.

To obtain a lateral movement of the gun's muzzle to right or left, the order was "Two handspikes, muzzle right"; the handspike men would get their spikes under the rear of the gun truck on the right hand side and joggle the breech of the gun across the deck to the left, while at the same time other gunners would haul the rope tackle on the left hand side of the carriage until the muzzle pointed through the gun port toward the right at the desired angle.

Gun muzzles were depressed to fire at the enemy's hull below the water line or raised to discharge grape shot or a shower of broken bits of iron and gravel at the enemy's sails and rigging. The muzzle was lowered by the use of handspikes under the breech and then by shoving wooden wedges under the gun to hold its position. In a like manner the muzzle was raised by levering it up and wedging it. The gun-handling was laborious and slow and could be done effectively only by an expert and practiced gun crew. Even on a well-disciplined man of war, the effective range was only a few hundred yards, and most actions were broadside to broadside before grappling and boarding.

A well-drilled gun crew of six to nine men required nearly an hour after firing to make a second shot. On a merchant ship like the *Sam Salvador*, with a gun crew of landlubbers who had been drafted from prisons and who had never been drilled in naval artillery, it must have been extremely difficult to act quickly and get together a half-dozen veteran sailors and a few petty officers to man a gun. Since there was no sighting apparatus, the effective range of a cannon was only a few hundred yards; yet even at that short distance, the gun layer or aimer had great difficulty in fixing his sight because of the pitching, rolling deck that made his gun's muzzle describe circles before his eyes. In maneuvering before action, each ship of course tried to get to the windward of its foe, because this gave a decided tactical advantage in battle. This position was also advantageous for the gunner, because when his ship lay to windward of its target he could see the white splash in the water of a missed cannon ball and from it gauge his range. But when his ship lay to leeward, he faced the white-caps of breaking waves, and it was impossible to distinguish the white splash of the missed projectile. Another consideration in maneuvering was so to place one's ship that the enemy gunner would have the dazzling sun in his eyes when sighting the carronades.

However, on a peaceable merchant ship like the *Sam Salvador* it is probable that none of these technical artillery questions was given a thought by many of the crew.

Passengers—and Accommodations

HIGH-BORN PASSENGERS, accustomed to every luxury, had to submit to most of the trials of the lowest *grumete*. In fact, the superior passengers suffered more from illness than the lowly seamen who, because of being compelled to live and work outdoors under all conditions, were tougher and more resistant to sickness. Records show that the mortality of the ship's officers, artistocratic passengers, and well-to-do merchants was much greater on long voyages than it was among the part of the crew that was able-bodied, that is, not already diseased, when they came aboard.

Because of the light cargo on the outward voyage, there was always room for a good many passengers. The superior personages among them were government officials, churchmen, and some factors or merchants; they were usually in good health when they came aboard, although with the country generally plague-ridden this could not be counted upon. The great majority of the passengers, however, were poor devils of soldiers who, like the men before the mast, were largely drawn from the prisons or slums. They were at the outset in poor physical condition, and on the voyage were crowded together between decks with no comfort or sanitary accommodations.

The only toilet facilities on any ship were makeshift stools perched upon the bulwarks, without privacy, or privies mounted on the outside of the ship's stern and accessible only by an unsafe gallery hanging precariously over the sea. Neither was such as a seasick, diseased, or weak person would be inclined to use on a tossing, rolling, plunging craft at sea. Only the few privileged persons having separate cabins and body servants could utilize utensils in private.

The Outward Voyage

Encounter with a Privateer

ON MAY 15, 1583, when about fifty miles north of the equator off the West African coast, the *Sam Salvador* sighted a strange sail, yacht-rigged in the Dutch sense, which speedily overhauled the nao and broke out the French colors. Jan wrote that the decks of his ship were immediately in an uproar of confusion and terror. Most of the crew were sick, either from scurvy or the intense heat, and the majority had never been to sea before nor had any experience in firing naval artillery. However, the officers managed to discharge several of the large guns, and although the shots fell far short, the corsair drew off and sailed away, to the great relief of all aboard.

Jan later published his account of this episode in his *Itinerario*. The northern Protestant nations seized upon it with delight, contrasting the pusillanimous performance of the crew with the bellicose threats of the Portuguese government against interloping vessels on the West African coast. They jeeringly quoted the high-flown title which had been assumed by the Portuguese Crown, with papal approval, ever since the days of Dom Manuel the Fortunate—"Lords of Guinea and of the Conquest, Navigation and Commerce of Ethiopia, Arabia and India."

However, it is only fair to say that, even if they had been better sailors and under better discipline, the crew of the *Sam Salvador* could hardly have taken lightly the danger of capture by a privateer. The fear which these intrepid corsairs inspired in the Dutch and English merchantmen in the Narrow Seas has already been noted. However, in the incident Jan related, the pirate ship turned tail and withdrew; it is probable that its crew was so weakened by scurvy and tropical fever that an attack on a nao six or seven times its size did not look very inviting, even though such an attack would have been quite feasible under normal conditions.

In any case, a ship on the outward voyage was not such an attractive prey. Its cargo was by no means as desirable to capture as the oriental treasure and spices on a homeward-bound Indiaman, and the chances were that the casks of silver pieces of eight would be jettisoned before they could be taken. In addition, outward-bound vessels were not overloaded, and therefore were more maneuverable in combat; and they were put into good navigating condition before sailing. The corsair might have had a combination of reasons for sheering off from the attack. However, Jan's description of the panic aboard the nao was seized upon by Portugal's enemies because up to this time the Portuguese had been considered, with good reason, to be nearly invincible at sea. Jan mentioned with disdain

[61]

the kind of crews that manned the *Carreira da India*, comparing them unfavorably with the expert, war-hardened adventurers on the Dutch privateers, who at that period had been trained in the turbulent North Sea from boyhood, and because of their fighting experience with the Sea Beggars were adept gunners.

Actually, the Portuguese seamen, and also the soldiers, for that matter, were more to be pitied than condemned, for, as we have said, they were often merely bewildered peasants seized by the ruthless press gang while at the plow or while grazing their master's sheep, hustled aboard ship, and put in irons until the vessel cleared, without even a chance to send word to their wives and families. They had no incentive to fight desperately, while the Dutch adventurers with whom Jan proudly compared them had immense plunder to gain if they were victorious.

However, even these sullen peasant landlubbers were preferred by the ship's officers to their city-bred shipmates, because they at least had health and strength. The men drafted from the prisons were generally diseased and often broken in spirit as well, for they had been confined for varying lengths of time, on starvation rations, in crowded, filthy, vermin-infested jails. Many of these convicts were not guilty of any crime, but, lacking the protection of habeas corpus or trial by jury, had been thrown into prison for some trivial offense, or even because of spite or village feuds. At times an official request was sent to magistrates for their help in providing crews or soldiers for India. Then any poor victim of the law was given a choice of the galleys or the Indiamen, and soon found himself on the high seas.

There were, of course, also a few fugitives from justice and ne'er-do-wells who volunteered for the naos to escape home conditions. However, many opportunities for well paid employment existed in Portugal, where there were many more jobs than workers, and it was rare indeed for a good man willingly to sign up for the *Carreira da India*. The frightful mortality on these long voyages and, for the soldiers, the lack of freedom ever to return home to Portugal were but too well known. If a lad ever wanted to get away and go to sea, he could choose a far better berth on one of the numerous ships in Lisbon harbor with a shorter and more tolerable run, either along the coast, or to Brazil or West Africa.

The sailors in the *Carreira da India* were not ill fed nor badly treated; the work was not anywhere near as onerous as it became a century later, when masts were much higher and the sails, tophamper and rigging were multiplied and complicated. However, the noisome quarters were so unsanitary, infected and reeking with excrement, and the drinking water so unwholesome, that life aboard an Indiaman was a purgatory. The already diseased recruits from the jails made contagion for the rest practically unavoidable. If the voyage was at all delayed, scurvy became general, and many deaths resulted. For all these reasons, it is not surprising that many persons who survived the voyage, both passengers and crewmen, decided to remain in exile in the Orient rather than go through the prolonged trials of a return trip. Even Jan himself, young, vigorous, and unaccustomed to a life of ease, quailed at the thought of submitting himself again to the horror of at least five months of acute boredom, mental tension, and extreme physical discomfort.

The New Archbishop

JAN'S NEW MASTER was a very important dignitary, and the twenty-year-old, mainly self-educated Dutchman was fortunate to be thrown into close relationship with a personage of such intellectual and moral caliber. The Dominican friar, Brother Vicentius, who had been born in Lisbon as Vicente da Fonseca, was a member of one of the distinguished families of Portugal. Choosing at a very early age to enter the order of Saint Dominic, and devoting himself to study, he soon attained distinction both as a scholar and as a speaker of unusual eloquence. Humble and unassuming, he was persuaded to accept the post of court preacher by King Sebastian; because of the common sense and inspiring fervor of his sermons, he soon gained widespread recognition and spiritual leadership among all classes.

Brother Vicentius did what he could to curb the fantasies of the headstrong, visionary, half-mad, young sovereign, and he was at his side in the Moroccan debacle in 1578. Herded among the thousands of prisoners, he discreetly concealed his identity from the Moors; anxious to get back to Portugal to aid in restoring balance to the shattered country, he managed to be ransomed early as an unimportant and undistinguished monk. He at once attempted to exercise a moderating influence on Sebastian's successor, the senescent and irresolute King-Cardinal, and was recognized as one of the wiser leaders of the confused and distracted kingdom.

Upon assuming the throne, Philip II asked Brother Vicentius to accept again the post of court preacher and showered him with attentions, apparently because of the respect and confidence accorded to him by all elements of the nation. Philip seems to have felt confident he had won the Dominican's loyalty (as indeed he had), for he offered him the Archbishopric of Goa, one of the most munificent benefices in all his empire. When Brother Vicentius declined the nomination, the King enlisted papal support to try to get an acceptance from the reluctant cleric, and he was appointed Archbishop by a Papal Bull dated at Rome, January 31, 1582. He had demurred ostensibly because of the perils and hardships of the long sea voyage, but finally yielded reluctantly to the royal blandishments. These were backed by Philip's promise to bestow upon him an even more glittering churchly rank upon his return, after five years of service in the East. An eventual cardinalate must have been the promised reward, for there was in Portugal no further ecclesiastical promotion beyond the Archbishopric of Goa except to be made Archbishop of Lisbon, with the rank of Cardinal-Primate.

Some students of the subtly devious maneuvers of Philip have deduced that the King feared the influence of the popular patriot Fonseca in Portugal and wished to remove him from the local scene. However, it is known that Philip was very much concerned about the possibility of a revolt in favor of Dom Antonio in the faraway colonies of *Asia Portuguesa:* for this reason he had taken pains to send as Viceroy Francisco Mascarenhas, Count of Vera Cruz, whose fidelity he felt confident he had won by many favors, to hold India for him. It must be assumed that he would not have appointed to the Archbishopric of Goa, an office whose power was on a par with that of the Viceroy, any person in whom he did not have the most complete trust. Because of the proselytizing aims of the Portuguese in Asia and East Africa, the ecclesiastical establishment in Goa was of unusual size and wealth, and the Archbishop was endowed with very broad powers. It was essential for Philip to have a supporter in that key position. The fact that Brother Vicentius, as a Dominican, would also have authority over the Inquisition at Goa gave his appointment an added significance. Because of his sincerity and sense of dedication, it may be believed that he accepted the position, albeit reluctantly, in the expectation that he could restore the earlier ideals of Christian administration of the opulent colony and purge it of some of the corruption, materialism and sensuality into which its prosperity had caused it to drift. The exemplary manner in which he executed his duties while in Goa confirms this belief.

Jan wrote that during his five years in the service of the Archbishop he observed that his master followed a rigid rule of not accepting a gift from any person whatsoever. This was a remarkable attitude in a period when all public officeholders were expected to get compensation for their services in the form of gratuities from those they served. It was all the more extraordinary in view of the immense patronage at the disposal of the Archbishop. He could of course confer substantial favors upon his subordinate monks, priests and prelates. He held great power in dealing with the high Portuguese officials, as well as with many Indian, Malay and Arabian potentates. He also dealt with the hierarchies of dozens of native sects, many of whom could not understand that a public official could be incorruptible.

A retinue of forty staff members accompanied the Archbishop on the *Sam Salvador;* without doubt they had been assembled with great care by the astute prelate, who coupled his high aims with a realistic and worldly knowledge of politics and intrigue. During the long, tedious months of the passage to India, he no doubt took the measure of the men upon whom he would have to rely in the days ahead. It is likely, therefore, that he had probed into the character and capabilities of the energetic young Dutchman and decided upon his utility long before the end of the voyage. Jan had little Latin, was ignorant of canon law or theology, and did not have, then or later, a scholarly mastery of Portuguese or Spanish; so the Archbishop must at once have decided to use him in a bookkeeping and accounting capacity. Both at home and in the colonies, the Church and the Crown divided temporal authority and revenues on an almost equal basis, and even a minor Portuguese prelacy enjoyed substantial revenues and had need of reliable bailiffs and bookkeepers. How much more, then, did the enormous fiscal responsibilities of the Archbishop of Goa, which had been expanded at this time by a substantial increase in the tax to raise funds for the release of Christian captives held for ransom by the Moslems, require an efficient accounting staff to fill this important role in his official household.

Jan described one incident on the voyage in which the great prelate had to intervene in a brawl between the *Sam Salvador*'s commissioned officers and the military adventurers aboard, at a traditional Portuguese banquet held at the feast of Whitsuntide, May 29, 1583. The affray developed into a serious affair; tables were overthrown, the ship's commander knocked down and trampled upon, and the very safety of the ship itself imperilled. The wild anarchy reached so dangerous a point that the Archbishop emerged from his cabin and threatened to excommunicate the rioters before they could be brought to order. To prevent a further outbreak, the Archbishop made the tense and excited disputants surrender their rapiers and daggers and deposited them in his own cabin for the sake of safety. This outbreak was a symptom of the intolerable strain upon the nerves of the voyagers imposed by the almost insupportable conditions aboard ship in the *Carreira da India*, though such strained nerves were by no means confined exclusively to Portuguese ships. Similar riotous outbreaks are recorded later in both the Dutch and English East Indiamen, whose crews also were driven nearly mad by the same discomforts, deprivations and boredom.

Jan reported that when they were nearing the Cape of Good Hope the Archbishop asked the captain to steer close to land so that the famous promontory might be visible from the ship. Wishing to gratify this fancy of his distinguished passenger, the commander asked the pilot to change to a more easterly course. There was as yet no expectation of a landfall, but suddenly they sighted, through the dusky evening, a surf-pounded coast looming directly ahead. Everyone was thrown into deep terror, for the coast was only about two miles away, and they had their hearts in their mouths until the clumsy ship was able to come about and claw off the rocks into the open sea. Since there was no accurate means of calculating east-west position, the navigators of the *Sam Salvador* had not realized their real position. Later they found it convenient to lay the blame for this close escape upon the whim of the Archbishop.

Navigation

S I N C E they lacked any reliable method of ascertaining longitude, had no definite knowledge of the magnetic variation of the compass, nor of ocean currents, had no reliable nautical timepieces, and had only inaccurate, small-scale maps, it is remarkable that the naos made voyages of two hundred days from Lisbon to Mozambique, in East Africa, without once making port, and yet generally arrived safely and on time. A perhaps cynical description of their methods was: "God takes them out and God brings them back." Since the captain of a nao generally was an aristocratic landsman, the pilot, by royal decree, had sole charge of the ship's navigation; indeed, he had much more authority than contemporary English, Dutch and French pilots, who are generally known to have given high praise to the proficiency of the pilots of the *Carreira da India*. These seasoned steersmen had for instruments only a compass, an astrolabe, a cross-staff, a quadrant and hourglass, none accurately calibrated. They relied largely upon empirical observations, such as the types of seabirds observed, the color of the sea, the abundance of sargasso or other floating seaweed, the kind of marine life detected, and the sort of bottom they dredged up in soundings. They also observed and interpreted, as much as possible, the drifts and currents of the sea and the prevailing winds. All these indices varied with the seasons. Their particular reliance was upon the *roteiros* (rutters) or sailing directions compiled by their predecessors for the guidance of their successors. Considering these methods, it is no wonder that even the most experienced pilot sometimes found himself as much as a hundred miles off in his reckoning.

The route of the *Carreira da India* had changed very little in a century. After Bartholomeu Dias had blundered around the Cape of Good Hope, the Portuguese under John II, during the next decade, made many secret experimental voyages, learning the winds and currents, before the course was finally laid out for Vasco da Gama to follow. After a few further trials, the route was firmly fixed. A nao sailed south from Lisbon past Madeira, the Canaries and Cape Verdes, and then southwest well off the Brazilian coast until opposite the Abrolhos Shoals, between modern Bahia and modern Rio de Janeiro, and then southeasterly until the Cape of Good Hope was rounded.

The Outward Voyage

If the Cape was passed before July 20th, the route then was northerly in the Madagascar Channel to Mozambique and, after a rest, north-northeast to the mouth of the Red Sea and easterly to Goa. If the Cape was rounded after July 20th, the Madagascar Channel and Mozambique were avoided and the course lay first easterly and then northerly to Cochin (Portuguese Cochim), on the west coast of India.

Academic as this may appear on the map, the Mozambique route was a skillfully drawn course whereby the Portuguese naos got the full benefit of wind and current, provided, however, Lisbon was cleared about March 1st. Barring storms, a nao had fair winds and favorable currents all the way from Lisbon to Goa. However, the slightest deviation meant trials and troubles; for example, if the ship kept too easterly, the penalty was to be becalmed indefinitely in the doldrums off Sierra Leone. If the course was set too northwesterly, the ship met headwinds and adverse currents north of Cape São Agostinho which required it to return to Lisbon; if it bore too far to the west, it ran aground on the reefs which extended seventy miles off the coast of Brazil. After the Cape of Good Hope was rounded, there was risk of grounding on sandbanks or reefs in the Madagascar Channel. Any one of these disasters could happen as the result of a miscalculation by the pilot in figuring the east-west position of the ship. This was a problem which the pilots had great difficulty in solving, not only because of the lack of any means of calculating longitude, but because they had too little information as to the direction and strength of ocean currents.

With good luck, a nao could make the run to Goa in six or eight months. One ship, in 1645, did it in a little less than four months. However, if luck was bad the voyage from Lisbon to Goa could take a year, and involve catastrophic losses of personnel. If an outward-bound vessel did not cross the bar of the Tagus by March 1st, then everything went wrong; the ship might even "lose its voyage," and either have to winter in Brazil or return to Lisbon and try again in the following February, a year later.

Though the duration of the voyage from Lisbon to Goa was commonly six to eight months each way, a record round-trip voyage was made many years after Jan's time, in 1651, with a total time out and back of nine and a half months. These runs were on the usual schedule, leaving Lisbon before March 1st and rounding the Cape of Good Hope in time to catch the end of the southwest monsoon off the East African coast north of the equator. Thus they reached Goa in September or October after the abating of the monsoon permitted the surf to subside at the harbor mouth. Returning, they left Goa or Cochin with the northeast monsoon about Christmas, so as to round the Cape before the dangerous winter tempests set in there in May.

[67]

It was virtually impossible to ignore this schedule, and almost all deviations from it were unsuccessful. In emergencies, a dispatch boat might leave Lisbon in September, reach Mozambique in March, and Goa in May, eight months en route, but the need had to be great to warrant this risk.

While the loss of some naos was due to the stubborn obstinacy of the pilots or to the inexperience of the aristocratic captains, the records of the Portuguese in Jan's day compared favorably with the operation of the later Dutch East India Company.

Before the development of an accurate chronometer in the mid-eighteenth century, it was admitted that on a long voyage even the ablest and most careful navigator might be off course from five to fifteen degrees. As late as 1803, British warships sailing for the West Indies from Gibraltar were three hundred and four hundred miles out of their longitude.

The records of the British East India Company, even in the days when nautical instruments were much improved, show that between 1750 and 1800 more than one hundred and sixty valuable British East Indiamen were missing or were lost by wreck, fire or capture. It is almost unbelievable that, a century and a half after Linschoten's day, they only averaged six knots in speed, that at night they furled sail, and that at signs of threatening weather they took in most of their canvas and reefed what was left standing. Consequently, a great British Indiaman would take as much as nine months to sail from London to Calcutta.

In 1804, the Indiaman *Prince of Wales* hove to off the pitch of the Cape upon a black night in June and simply disappeared from the face of the sea. Not so much as a stick from it was ever found, though it was the Admiral's ship and had been in the middle of the fleet, surrounded by its mates. Likewise, in 1808, three great Indiamen—the *Glory*, the *Lord Nelson* and the *Experiment*—similarly went missing. And in the homeward passage in March, 1809, four Indiamen—the *Lady Jane Douglas*, the *Calcutta*, the *Bengal*, and the *Jane, Duchess of Gordon*—all went missing, and they all could not have been grossly overloaded. They were last seen off Mauritius, and nothing from any one of them was ever found. The Cape took them without a doubt. There was no disaster more sweeping than these modern British catastrophes in all the earlier tragic history of the Portuguese *Carreira da India*.

Even in the twentieth century, when navigators of great steam liners were prevented by fog from taking observations and had to proceed by dead reckoning, the ships went off their courses. The efficiently run British Union Castle Line alone lost off the Cape five fine modern steamers for this reason in a period of forty years—the S.S. *Drummond Castle*, 1896; S.S. *Tantallon Castle*, 1902; S.S. *Newark Castle*, 1908; S.S. *Cawdor Castle*, 1926; and S.S. *Winchester Castle*, 1936.

The Outward Voyage

A modern British hydrographer writes: "All over the surface of the sea are currents of unknown strength and direction. The British Board of Trade and Admiralty shows on its charts that in scarcely any part of the ocean are there less than ten miles of surface current in twenty-four hours and they show as much as forty to fifty miles current in many places. Unless these currents are taken into effect then the place of a ship by dead reckoning may be wrong by from ten to fifty miles (in a day) and the best information that we have of them is only approximate.

"There are in fact certain currents of ten miles and upwards per day due to wind (it may be wind in a distant part of the ocean) which the navigator cannot possibly know at the time he is affected by them. I believe it would not be unsafe to say that, even if the steerage and speed through the water were reckoned with absolute accuracy in the account, the ship's place could in general be reasonably trusted to be within fifteen to twenty miles of dead reckoning. And besides neither the speed through the water nor the steerage can be reckoned without allowing a considerable margin for error."

In sailing from the Straits of Magellan to the Philippines by dead reckoning in 1521, the pilot of Magellan's armada, Francisco Alba, was out in his reckoning no less than ninety-three degrees, or nearly a thousand miles.

The Dutch in the seventeenth century, having rounded the Cape, "ran their easting down" in approximately forty degrees south latitude before turning north to the Straits of Sunda. Nevertheless they found their dead reckoning to be but "a blind and stupid pilot." It was due to their uncertainty as to the course and distance that so many Dutch East Indiamen were shipwrecked and lost on the coasts of West Australia or Southeast New Guinea. In many cases they found themselves in the breakers when they thought they were three hundred or three hundred and fifty miles from any land. Even as late as the eighteenth century, both Lord Anson (1740) and Captain Cook (1770) made enormous errors in their position because of the impossibility of figuring longitude.

"Until the chronometer was perfected the only safe navigation was to steer to the known parallel of latitude of one's destination, which could be ascertained by observation of the sun by astrolabe or sextant and then alter course to the eastward or westward, as the case might be, until the land was made."

The very earliest navigators, such as the Vikings and the Portuguese brothers Miguel and Gaspar Corte Real in their voyages to Greenland and Newfoundland, had to rely entirely on dead reckoning for their courses in the most difficult waters in the world. Many of the Vikings were lost because of what they called *hafvilla*, a complete loss of knowledge of their whereabouts, and of course the Corte Real brothers never found their way back home.

The *Sam Salvador* safely ran the gauntlet of the Atlantic leg of its outward voyage, skillfully, and no doubt also luckily, navigating the narrowly hazardous course so as not to approach the Brazilian coast until well to the southeast of Cape São Agostinho. Had the ship taken its course to the north of that Cape, it could not have escaped being driven northwest by wind and current toward the St. Peter and St. Paul Rocks, in which case it could have been forced to sail back to Lisbon and to "lose its voyage" until the following year. This was what had happened in the previous year to the great *Sam Philip*, now the Admiral of the *Sam Salvador*'s fleet.

The *Sam Salvador* proceeded warily in a southerly direction down the Brazilian coast, favored by wind and current and taking care to keep east of the so-called Brazilian shelves, the reefs which extended seventy miles into the Atlantic, terminating in the much feared Abrolhos Shoals north of Rio de Janeiro. Then keeping to the west of Trinidad Island (not to be confused with the West Indian one) and to the north of the island of Tristan da Cunha, the ship sailed almost due easterly along the latitude of the Cape of Good Hope, and since the pilot was ignorant of its longitudinal position, as we have seen, the *Sam Salvador* nearly crashed on the misty South African coast near False Cape, which lies about fifteen miles west of the Cape of Good Hope.

Although this Atlantic stretch of the route of the *Carreira da India* was first plotted by Bartholomeu Dias and followed by Vasco da Gama in 1497, it was still, a century later, difficult to follow. The *Sam Philip*, the newest and finest nao in the squadron, the Admiral of the fleet and bearing the name of the King himself, had perhaps been rendered somewhat timid by its experience in the previous year, when it had lost its voyage and had to turn back to Lisbon. On the present voyage, it kept too far to the east, and as a result was becalmed so long south of Sierra Leone, on the African coast, that it arrived too late off the Cape of Good Hope to escape the wintry storms of that dread region; hence it was terribly buffeted and driven back. Being afraid, then, to try to sail up the tempestuous Mozambique Channel, the *Sam Philip* had to follow the outside course, which ran from the Cape of Good Hope until far east of Madagascar and then due north in the Indian Ocean, through the dangerous typhoon waters between Mauritius and Diogo Rodrigues Island. It then made port at Cochin, because the strong southerly current prevented its reaching Goa.

Jan reported that the *Sam Philip* came into Cochin about two months after the other four ships of the squadron had anchored at Goa, it "having passed and endured much misery and foule weather with sicknes and diseases, as swellings of the legs, and the scorbuike and paine in their bellies and so forth."

The Outward Voyage

Eastward Around the Cape

THE EASTWARD PASSAGE of the Cape of Good Hope by the other four ships in the squadron was relatively easy. On June 20, 1583, the *Sam Salvador*, after escaping the breakers at False Cape, was becalmed for half a day while the crew fished successfully and luckily with hook and line at about ten or twelve fathoms, where they struck a run of the large, haddock-like fish called *pescados* by the Portuguese. Then, sailing for two days in company with the *Sam Francisco*, they apparently had rounded the Cape when a heavy gale blew up, and they were tossed about under bare poles for two days. Like Bartoloméo Dias, when the storm had abated they did not know where they were, but fortunately found that they were safely past the Cape, to the east of the African mainland off Natal, in the Mozambique Channel.

All four naos had been fortunate in finally getting past the Agulhas Bank off the southeastern tip of Africa, where the warm, southward-flowing equatorial currents meet the cold waters from the antarctic ice fields. There the various disturbed meteorological and other influences create crushing, mountainous seas and irresistible, unpredictably shifting gales which are often fatal even to powerful modern steamships. Against these hazards a frail wooden sailing ship was almost helpless unless it was lucky as well as sound in hull, tight in tackle, and with its cargo properly stowed, as Jan was to learn on his homeward passage in 1588.

However, even though they were safely past the Cape and in the two hundred and fifty mile wide Mozambique Channel, which separates the great island of Madagascar from the South African mainland, the pilot of the *Sam Salvador* could by no means relax. There still was a likelihood of violent tempests off Natal, which had a grim record of many shipwrecks.

As they breasted the strong southward-flowing Agulhas current, the next danger lay in the Baixas da Judia (Sands of the Jewess), a perilous north and south stretch of reefs that obstruct navigation for many miles. These had been the cause of numerous wrecks, especially of ships outward bound from Lisbon to Mozambique. Indeed, the fine new *Santiago*, the Vice-Admiral of their armada, now sailing up the channel with the *Sam Salvador*, would the next year suffer a tragic shipwreck on those same Baixas da Judia, because of the carelessness of its pilot.

Mozambique

ON AUGUST 4, 1583, the look-out at the foremasthead of the *Sam Salvador* hailed the sight of Mozambique, the Portuguese capital of the

The Outward Voyage

East African coast. The town was the historic naval base where the naos of the *Carreira da India,* from the time of the first voyage of da Gama, had made port and secured water and fresh supplies on both outward and inward voyages. An unhealthy, fever-stricken haven, the burying place of many Portuguese mariners, Mozambique stubbornly retained its political primacy, although the Crown often considered moving its local headquarters to Mombasa, a healthful northern port which had many advantages. The much denounced old capital not only defeated the attempts of the reformers to supersede it, but later successfully beat off several efforts by the Dutch and English to capture it. In his delineation of the city, Jan displayed for the first time his unique reportorial and descriptive powers. During the *Sam Salvador's* fortnight there, he surveyed the place and reported upon its physical characteristics and its botanical, zoological, ethnic, social and governmental aspects. For a lad of about twenty years, with a limited background and experience, he showed remarkable talent in his verbal description as well as in his drawing. Already he was the possessor of the keen eye and agile pen that were to earn him a reputation as a writer of geographical travelogues and as a talented artist-cartographer. Even though the account and the map were published a decade later, and no doubt reflect some subsequent editing and polishing, nevertheless there is great freshness in the observations. A vivid impression had been made upon the naive young Northerner by his first contact with a wholly exotic and ancient civilization.

Nothing could have been more different from the plain and puritanical life of Enkhuizen than the unchanged customs of the vast, brooding, barbaric economy of the East African coast. The superficial rule of the Portuguese Catholic power over its colonies, precariously lodged in fortified ports, was obviously only a passing phase in that strange and timeless community. Before them the eras of occupation by the trading settlements of the Greeks, the Romans, the Moslem Arabs, the Persians and the Egyptians, had left only a few laconic parchments and a few mute stone ruins. But changelessly the gold, the ivory, the ebony, and above all the black slaves, continued to be drawn from the dark, mysterious interior, bartered for cheap trifles, and exported in lateen-sailed craft to whatever was then the ephemeral, luxury-loving metropolis of the civilizations that successively rose and fell in the outside world.

The squadron of four ships stayed at Mozambique for two weeks, giving the scurvy-ridden complement a chance to restore its health with an abundance of fresh fruit, meat and vegetables, before undertaking the month-long voyage across the Indian Ocean and Arabian Sea to Goa. As usual, however, many of the sufferers aboard were too far gone to recover, and a number of those who had kept in reasonable health at sea now succumbed to diseases endemic in the seaport, including cholera, the plague

[72]

and what was then known as the flux (now called dysentery). According to the medical thinking of the time, these maladies were to be ascribed to the "unwholesome aire" and to the "foggie mistes."

Jan wrote: "We stayed at Mossambique for the space of fifteen dayes to provide fresh water and victuails for the supplying of our wants, in which time divers of our men fel sicke and died, by reason of the unaccustomed ayre of the place, which of itself is an unwholesome land, and an evill aire by means of the great and immeasurable heat."

A stopover at Mozambique always proved costly in mortality, though continuing at sea without stopping was even worse. Today the four-centuries-old graveyard tells a pathetic story of adventurous Europeans who sought careers in the alluring Orient, but were stopped by death at the very threshold of their goal.

Much anxiety was felt for the *Sam Philip* because of its failure to arrive during their two-weeks stay in Mozambique. However, as we know, the *Sam Philip* was unable to make Mozambique at all, and it was a floating charnel-house when it finally limped into port at Cochin a good two months behind the rest of the fleet.

The Indian Ocean and the Arabian Sea

THE FLOTILLA remained in Mozambique as long as it did in order to await the abatement of the southwest monsoon, for the passage northeastward across the Indian Ocean was unsafe as long as the monsoon lashed it to turbulence, and their destination, the harbor of Goa, was quite inaccessible during the time that the monsoon-driven breakers foamed upon the sandbar at the mouth of the Mondavi River.

This immobilization of ship traffic in the Indian Ocean north of the equator for half of each year was later to have a profoundly unfavorable effect upon the interests of Portugal. The Dutch, who utilized favorable winds in both directions for year-round navigation to and from the East Indies, and who had had the advantage of being nautically guided by Jan's advice, were strategically based south of the equator in order to outmaneuver and to contain the Portuguese in Goa, who were held in port during the long period of the southwest monsoon.

The word "monsoon" was derived from the Arabic *mausim* (season). The summer season north of the equator, on the west side of the Indian Ocean down as far as the Mozambique Channel and in the Arabian Sea and the Bay of Bengal and nearby waters, is dominated by the southwest monsoon, which begins in May and ends in October. During this often unbearably hot period there is almost continuous rain, and a steady, violent wind from the southwest makes navigation almost impossible for small sailing craft, particularly as the visibility also is bad. Therefore the Goa-bound naos of the *Carreira da India* used to lie over in Mozambique until late in August, when the southwest gales were losing their force.

The winter monsoon in the same area, called the northeast monsoon, is beneficial to shipping; it begins in October and ends in May, although the demarcation on the calendar between the two monsoons is not precise.

The commonly held idea that the centuries-old, established Indian Ocean traffic of Arabia and Persia with India and East Africa is alternately wafted southward by the gentle northeast monsoon and northward by the brisk and rough southwest monsoon is not correct. Navigation by sailing vessels is carried in any direction in this area only during the season of the northeast monsoon, which is a balmy, steady trade wind. Therefore, sailings of the *Carreira da India* in the Indian Ocean, both to and from Goa, had to be timed for the six-month season of the northeast monsoon, as also did Portuguese naval and military operations based on Goa.

By August 20, 1583, the force of the southwest monsoon had abated sufficiently so that the squadron of four ships could weigh anchor and sail out of the harbor of Mozambique northward along the East African coast, passing to the west of the Comoro Islands. (Generations later these islands were to become pirate strongholds, and still later a rendezvous for American and European whalers.)

The flotilla kept northward along the coast, passing a succession of historic little Arab ports, each of which was a city-state and had enjoyed a fiercely independent sovereignty for many centuries until reduced to vassalage by the Portuguese. This chain of prosperous Arab maritime principalities extended for about a thousand miles up the coast, rich, powerful, and enjoying a high degree of Moslem culture. Because of considerations of defense, each was generally located on an islet a few hundred yards from the mainland and protected by stone battlements. Each had originally been founded by a refugee contingent from Egypt, Persia or Arabia, fleeing defeat in civil strife in their galleys or dhows with their families and retainers, and seeking a new home on the East African littoral. Had a leader arisen to weld them together into a strong Arab league they would have made a formidable confederacy, but jealousies and racial and sectarian differences had kept them apart. After centuries of independence and prosperity, they fell easily beneath the yoke of crusading Portugal.

One of the Portuguese strongpoints past which the *Sam Salvador* sailed was Kilwa, located at eight degrees south latitude. It had been founded centuries before by an aristocratic dissident religious cult from Persia whose sheik, when Vasco da Gama reached there, was the forty-fifth ruler in direct descent from the founder. It was called by Arab chroniclers in the fourteenth century "the most nobly built city in the Moslem world."

As the *Sam Salvador* passed Kilwa and proceeded up the coast, Jan could see the buildings of Malinde, the city most favored by the Portuguese because of the invaluable help given by its sheik to da Gama on his initial voyage. Next along the shore were visible the spars of shipping in the busy port of Mombasa, center of the immense slave trade. Here flourished a very profitable specialty of converting young African boy slaves into eunuchs, and also, by surgery, making four-year-old girls into so-called "sealed virgins"; both these types of human being were trained and educated for harem service, and were exported at very high prices when they had gained their teens.

Continuing northeasterly up the coast past Mogadishu, a formerly independent city-state of importance, the *Sam Salvador* rounded Cape Gardafui at the edge of the Red Sea and, passing by the large island of Socotra, famed for its aloes, a prune-like, medicinal, astringent fruit, continued across the Gulf of Aden, which Jan called the Strait of Mecca; then they changed course to the east, steering directly toward Goa.

By then the squadron had become separated, as each ship tried to outsail its mates in a race to be first to reach Goa's market. This rivalry between captains was a source of loss in case of maritime disaster, but it was rare indeed that a captain-general was able to hold together the units under his command. Such weakness of organization was responsible for serious mishaps, not only in the mercantile *Carreira da India*, but in Portuguese naval forces as well. Insubordination of sea captains was common not only in the Portuguese marine, but also in the fifteenth and sixteenth century Dutch, French and English merchant marines and navies. It stemmed partly from an anachronistic survival at sea of old European feudal feelings and jealous disunity, and partly also from the real difficulty of maintaining contact and communication between ships at that stage of maritime development. Even very strong captains-general like Ferdinand Magellan and Affonso de Albuquerque, and the great seventeenth century Dutch admirals, could not always hold their slippery captains in line.

Hence it was that the *Sam Salvador* had lost sight of its consorts on August 24th, four days after clearing the harbor of Mozambique, and made its way alone until it picked up the *Sam Francisco* on September 4th and kept with it until September 7th, when it disappeared in the night. Not until a week later did they see another consort, the *Santiago*, which, however, at once sailed away without pausing for any communication.

After they had passed north of the equator, the North Star again became a guide for latitude, and now, with the passing of the rains, night visibility was good once more. Also, in clear weather the distant outlines of the African coast supplied the needed longitudinal check, so that until they had to turn eastward from the island of Socotra the pilots of the *Sam Salvador* felt free to relax in safe waters. At the mouth of the Red Sea and along Socotra, the constable kept his gunners on the alert, with gun ports open and the muzzles of the cannon run out, because there was a real risk of Turkish raiding galleys darting out from Aden and the Red Sea ports, particularly at the time of the slackening of the southwest monsoon before the Portuguese naval patrols could be re-established. On this last fortnight of the long five-month voyage, the *Sam Salvador* had to be navigated by dead reckoning along the dangerous and still stormy Arabian coast, swarming with wreckers ashore and infested with the ubiquitous horde of pirate dhows from Oman. Although able to keep its easting along the general line of the known latitude of Goa, the pilot was now quite uncertain of the ship's longitudinal position, and kept an eager look-out for the expected appearance of swarms of snake-like sea creatures swimming and diving on the surface, their scales glittering in the sun or luminous in the phosphorescent seas at night; this was a sure sign of proximity to the Indian coast. At dawn on September 20th, just a month after sailing from Mozambique, the look-out excitedly hailed the appearance of a glitter upon the sea, the reflection of the rising sun on the brilliant scales of the thousands of serpents swimming on the surface which were known as *vintens*, or silver half-pieces of eight.

There was a loud outburst of jubilation from the decks, and a salute was fired to signify their nearness to the land, which soon became visible and was delightedly recognized as the highland near the entrance to Goa. Before dusk the anchor was dropped at forty-seven fathoms about three miles from land.

Landfall

AT DAYBREAK the *Sam Salvador* was surrounded by small boats peddling food, fresh water and supplies. Pushing its way through them was a handsomely decorated rowing barge, hung with silks and tapestries, with a band of musicians playing. This was the welcoming vessel of the Jesuits of Goa, bringing the dignitaries of the Society discreetly hurrying out ahead of the local officials to meet the Monsenhor who was to rule them.

Then came a State galley bearing the Viceroy and his staff to kiss the ring of the new ecclesiastical lord. Shortly thereafter, a sumptuous galley came alongside to conduct Monsenhor to a suburban villa ashore where he could rest from the hardships of the voyage while preparations were being made to receive him formally and install him with due ceremony in the archepiscopal palace.

Presumably Jan was not among the attendants who accompanied Monsenhor ashore, for he wrote: "The same day in the afternoon we entered the River, into the roade under the land of Bardes, being the 21 of September 1583 being five monthes and 13 dayes after our putting forth of the River Lusbone (having stayed 15 daies at Mosambique) which was one of the speediest and shortest voyages that in many yeares that before and since that time was ever performed. There we founde the shippe named the Saint Laurence which arrived there a day before us. The 22nd day, the St. Jacob came thither and the next day after, arrived the Saint Francis.

"There dyed in our shippe 30 persons among which some were slaves, and one high Dutchman that had beene one of the King of Spaines garde: —every man of us had been sick once or twice and had been let bloode. This is commonly the number of men that ordinarily dyed in the ships, sometimes more, sometimes lesse. About ten or twelve years since, it chaunced that a Vice Roy (for the King) named Ruy Lorenso Detavora sayled for India, that had in his shippe 1100 men and there happened a sickness among them so that there dyed thereof to the number of 900 and all throwne over borde into the sea, before they came to Mosambique, the Vice Roy himself being one, which was an extraordinarie sicknesse and it is to be thought that the great number of men in the shippe were the cause of breeding the same, therefore in these dayes the shippes take no more so many men into them, for that with the number they carrie, they have stinking ayre and filth enough to clense within the ship."

And so Linschoten's long dreamed-of voyage to the wonderland of India was completed, and very felicitously in all respects. Contrary to his statement that the loss of thirty men on the *Sam Salvador* was about average, modern research in Portuguese statistics shows that the average loss by death at the time was about fifty percent of a ship's complement and passengers.

The remarkably fast trip of the *Sam Salvador* no doubt contributed to keeping the death rate low, for the ravages of disease multiplied greatly on prolonged voyages, as was evidenced by the condition of the men aboard the *Sam Philip* after seven months and twelve days under sail.

Well might Jan and his brother, Willem Tin, offer grateful thanks to Providence for their health and safety, for it had been a notable voyage, not only because of its record of speed and salubrity, but also because the entire squadron reached India safely—an unusual achievement.

Willem Tin

J A N had frequently mentioned his half brother, Willem Tin, in recounting how he secured his appointment in the Pepper Fleet and managed to be assigned to the *Sam Salvador* so that they could be together. Once this was accomplished, however, his log of the voyage makes no further mention of his brother, although the two must have been closely associated throughout the trials and distress of the long passage.

Willem Tin had an important and lucrative position aboard the *Sam*

Salvador, since he was not only the fiscal agent of the crown, but also represented the two German syndicates who controlled the voyage, the Pepper Farmers, who owned the trading cargo, which consisted mainly of numerous barrels of silver pieces of eight, and the Ship Farmers, who owned the vessel itself. His principal duty as ship's purser, however, was to act as personal agent of the commander, for whose private account he sold bedding, clothing, toilet articles, medicines and a variety of preserved foodstuffs to all aboard. It was the established custom, as it later became on both English and Dutch Indiamen, for the purser to charge the government for daily rations of food, wine and grog for all seamen, soldiers and passengers who died on the voyage, whose names were not removed from the ship's rolls. The proceeds of these fictitious charges were part of the captain's recognized perquisites, and the purser received his due share. It was also his duty to take possession for the captain's account of all the private effects of passengers or crewmen who died on the voyage.

Mozambique was the established exchange where the contents of the confiscated sea chests of deceased members of the ship's complement were traded, and the value of these transactions was substantial. The reason the ship's captains preferred to dispose of their accumulated loot in the efficiently conducted black market of Mozambique was to avoid the inspection of royal officials and factors at Goa, their port of destination. Other business in Mozambique was the purchase of food and supplies for the voyage to Goa, and the ship's commander and purser naturally reaped a rich harvest in commissions and gifts in this connection as well.

Later on, when they reached Goa, Willem Tin could look forward to selling the articles of rarity and fashion which he and the captain had brought to trade for their private account. Then, having disposed of these at a high price to the dealers of Goa, he would turn to the task of purchasing—of course at a commission—the steward's stores needed for the return voyage. He would also acquire choice Indian merchandise to import duty-free into Portugal, in accordance with the official privilege granted him. No doubt he kept his eye open in addition for a choice emerald or ruby to smuggle into Lisbon for quiet sale. All in all, the round trip voyage might be expected to make Willem Tin a rich man.

Jan made no reference in his diary to his brother's activities in Goa until it was time for him to take ship for the return voyage, but then Jan's emotion got the better of his reticence and he voiced his regret. It was to be a whole year before Jan received the good news of Willem's safe arrival in Lisbon—to be followed by the calamitous word that the ship upon which he was taking his treasure home from Lisbon had been lost off the coast of England with all aboard.

CHAPTER IV

Goa

JAN WATCHED HIS MASTER, the Archbishop, go ashore soon after the fleet arrived. The exalted person's progress as he climbed down into the smaller boat which was to convey him to shore lacked nothing in stateliness. Jan knew Monsenhor was not to enter the city at this time, but that he would retire to a comfortable suburban villa on the Panjin Highland overlooking the Mandovi River. The villa was reported to be a delightful place, surrounded by a palm garden with pools and fountains, and Jan no doubt wished he could accompany his master to so halcyon a spot. He knew the Archbishop would stay there in retirement until the city had had time to prepare for his reception, which would take place with the greatest ceremony and public celebration.

The Archbishopric had been vacant for several years after the death of the former primate, the Dominican Henrique de Tavora, in 1579, and there had been no one in the colony of sufficient knowledge and authority to interpret the ecclesiastical policies of the new Spanish King of Portugal. Consequently the induction of a new Primate of the Indies was an event of surpassing significance to Goa.

At first glance it may seem surprising that the capital was not prepared for the Archbishop's advent, especially since it was anticipated that he would arrive with that year's fleet from Lisbon. However, the arrival time of the ships could never be predicted more accurately than within a range of several months, and since the outward passage of 1583 was one of the quickest on record it is no wonder that the capital was taken by surprise on September 19th when the *Sam Lorenzo* appeared. There was great rejoicing in the port when the captain informed the officials who came to greet him that the *Sam Salvador*, carrying the new Archbishop, had left Mozambique on the same day as his ship, and therefore the new prelate might be expected at any moment. Not only the vice-regal court, but the whole town was thrown into a turmoil of excitement. It was hurriedly decided to put the villa outside the city in order for Monsenhor's reception until the sumptuous archepiscopal palace could be refurbished and all the necessary preparations made for his joyous entry into the capital.

Jan heard that no sooner had Monsenhor made himself at home in his temporary stopping place than all the officialdom of Goa, high and low, both spiritual and temporal, headed by the Viceroy, Dom Francisco Mascarenhas, Count of Ota, rushed to kiss his ring once more, even though most of them had already welcomed him aboard ship.

When Monsenhor was safely ashore and established, Jan and the other members of his retinue, with the exception of his personal servants and advisers who had accompanied him to the villa, were at once given pleasant lodgings elsewhere ashore. During the ten days interval between their unexpected arrival and Monsenhor's formal entry into the city, it may be assumed that Jan, with his eager interest in everything new and exotic, took advantage of the opportunity to become acquainted with the renowned metropolis. "He who has seen Goa need not see Lisbon" was a Portuguese proverb, and Jan must have soon agreed that the two cities were equally beautiful, magnificent—and Portuguese. However, Goa's large buildings and Portuguese atmosphere were superimposed upon a background more exotic than anything he had ever seen. Maurice Collis described Goa as "the most sumptuous city ever built by Europeans in the East"; Camoëns called it "the lady of all the Orient," as well as "the mother of knaves and the stepmother of honest men." Other historians have called it the "Indian Rome" and "the Sodom and Gomorrah of the East." Jan was doubtless familiar with the city's reputation at that time, but his taste for firsthand observation must soon have sent him exploring it for himself.

When Jan landed there, Goa had an estimated population of over 225,000 people and was one of the largest cities in the world, ranking with Antwerp and London. After his glimpse of the busy harbor, with its exotic shipping, Jan's attention was doubtless drawn to the adjacent naval dockyard, where many large vessels were moored alongside the docks or lying ashore for careening. Stern security regulations were enforced there, so he could not be admitted for a closer look at the royal dockyards or the neighboring Ribeira Arsenal and Gun Foundry; in strict modern style, all entrants to these places had to carry personal identification and submit to having their clothing searched before admission. However, even from a distance one could see that carpenters, blacksmiths, caulkers and gun founders, mainly native artisans under European foremen, swarmed over the dockyard.

Next Jan must have come to that interesting institution, the royal elephant stables. Possibly he had already seen an elephant in Portugal, since from time to time one was successfully imported; King Emanuel, for example, had had one procured as a gift for Pope Leo X. Jan was no doubt delighted to see dozens of the great beasts penned together in their corral, and in the *Itinerario* he devoted a long and readable chapter to describing their characteristics and instincts. He explained their economic use in the colony, and related several sentimental folk tales and anecdotes about them.

After leaving the elephant stables, he next must have come to the Mint and to the office of the Comptroller of the Treasury, who ranked second to the Viceroy in the colonial administration. Beyond these was a substantial Custom House with a busy clerical staff largely composed of Hindu clerks under Eurasion or Portuguese department heads. Adjoining it was the Weigh House, with ample premises where both incoming and outgoing cargoes were taken to be evaluated and recorded under a careful system of registration.

Next Jan must have skirted the large garden which surrounded the imposing palace of the Viceroy. On this first visit he would not have dared try to pass the halberdiers of the guard, but he was later to know the palatial interior well. It was elaborately decorated and furnished for the reception of the many embassies from oriental powers with whom the Viceroy had to treat.

To be successful in oriental diplomacy, the Viceroy had to hold an ostentatious court, with a pretentious staff of functionaries, musicians and guards, the whole maintained with a lavish splendor designed to rival that of the Great Mogul or the Shah of Persia. Surrounded as it was on all sides by hostile military nations, the government at Goa had to preserve at any cost its prestige and the "face" so important in Asia. A unique feature of the palace, which was to catch Jan's fancy when he visited it later, and of which he wrote in the *Itinerario,* was the great hall of murals. These paintings depicted every ship of the *Carreira da India* which had reached port there since the first voyage of da Gama, together with the name of its commander and the date of arrival. There were also various commemorative murals showing historic happenings, as well as decorative representations of strange zoological or piscatorial curiosities and other natural phenomena.

Even if Jan had been accompanied by a competent guide, it would have taken him at least a week to make even a superficial survey of the great metropolis. It is certain that he must have been footsore at the end of each day's sightseeing, for the city covered a large area, having long ago grown beyond the walls and moats that originally enclosed it. There were more than fifty churches, convents and religious buildings in Goa, many of which were surrounded by groves and gardens and thus not visible from the public roads. Although he could not see them all during his first period of viewing the city, Jan's curiosity was to keep him busy learning more of Goa throughout his five years' stay there, and by the time he was ready to leave he was so thoroughly acquainted with the town that he drew a detailed map of it which was published in the *Itinerario*.

Next among the outstanding edifices of which he certainly took notice during his first week were the Misericordia, a large orphange run by a pious association of laymen, and the Royal Hospital, conducted by the Jesuits, a clean and sanitary building with airy terraces and facilities for three hundred to five hundred patients. The hospital's inmates were given every attention and comfort, but nonetheless the mortality rate was high, at least in part because European doctors had had little experience with tropical diseases.

Jan also saw the College of St. Paul, which had been founded by St. Francis Xavier himself. This fine group of buildings housed a seminary where native converts were trained and graduated in theology, ready to preach the tenets of Catholicism to their own countrymen in their own native tongue. There were three thousand undergraduates in the college who came from every part of the Far East, and there were eighty-eight Jesuits on the faculty. Besides theology, the students were taught astronomy, mechanical sciences, and the liberal arts—in fact, the university curriculum was one that no modern college would be ashamed of teaching. The learned members of the faculty, as might have been expected, also took a leading part in the cultural circles of the city. The college celebrated the holy day of its patron saint, January 25th, with a great annual celebration which Jan's acquaintances told him was traditionally attended by the Viceroy himself, followed by a suite of two hundred or three hundred gentlemen dressed in holiday costume and riding gaily caparisoned horses. The official visitors were welcomed by the students, witnessed their theatricals, and afterwards were their guests at a colorful banquet. The great Church of Bom Jesus, recognized as one of the finest in architecture in the world, had not yet been built by the dynamic, young order of Jesuits, but it was to be erected during Jan's stay in Goa, and plans for it were already discussed.

The Convent of St. Augustine, a magnificent palace with a notable botanical garden and a noble library, was probably the next building Jan encountered. Then came the Convent of St. Francis of Assisi, headquarters of the Franciscans in the Orient, and next the imposing Church and Convent of St. Dominic, famous for pomp and ritual.

He did not fail to view the renowned Cathedral of Goa, which was said to compare in grandeur with any church in Europe. It contained the original Chapel of St. Catherine built by Affonso de Albuquerque, which was visited in state every year on November 25th by the Viceroy in a solemn procession made up of the leaders of all elements of the city's populace.

It was natural for Jan to seek out the building which was to be his home in Goa, the Archepiscopal Palace. This was a relatively modest but dignified edifice, two hundred and thirty feet long and a hundred feet wide, situated in a large garden, and, at the moment Jan viewed it, crowded with workmen who were busily renovating and preparing it for the new Archbishop.

In Jan's walks about the city he was no doubt struck by its steady, burgher-like element, which was as apparent as its bizarre and oriental aspects. Blocks of modest, two-storied houses were built of cement and painted red, yellow or white; they had window panes of thin, highly polished shells, large porticos on the second floor with jalousies and lattice work to give privacy to the ladies, and secluded gardens in the rear. He must also have been struck by the abundance of good retail shops. There were wide sidewalks along the sides of the streets which he doubtless appreciated as he strolled along, and he must have compared them favorably with the narrow, cobbled walks of the streets of Holland. At that time Goa had another advantage which Dutch cities lacked, and a most important one—an abundant supply of pure, fresh water. Though Jan did not know it, this most precious asset was soon to be lost because of a feckless lack of sanitary practices in the city. He reported that a large and inexhaustible well called "Banganiin" in the center of the city supplied the purest water, and slaves went about selling its water for drinking. The water of the household wells was used "to dresse meat, wash and doe other things withall." After general contamination of the soil later set in, in the seventeenth century, all these thousands of household wells were to become infected.

The Auction Place

J A N must have lingered in the great public square at the end of Straight Street (as the Portuguese called the main street in most of their towns) to watch the open-air auctions held there every morning, except Sundays and holidays, from seven to nine o'clock. Evidently he never tired of this spectacle, for he described it vividly in the *Itinerario* and illustrated it with a more than double-page engraving. Jan called it the Leylon (*leilão* in Portuguese), and it was held early in the morning so as to escape the heat of the day. Jan likened it to the famous daily business meeting at the

Bourse in Antwerp, but at Goa it was a social event as well as a great international exchange. It was attended by the principal persons in town, both men and women, as well as by important merchants from all the trading centers of the Orient, Venice, and Germany. The society people of Goa came there fashionably dressed and attended by their slaves and servants, the women in palanquins and the men on horseback. Although not commercially involved, these fashionable folk took great interest in the proceedings and also used the occasion to exchange all the most up-to-date gossip and news.

Most of the vast commerce of Goa was conducted at these auctions. Besides the merchants and traders, among those present were notaries, clerks of court, lawyers and probate officers, as well as bankers and money-changers. They operated from outdoor counters and carried official books of record of all transactions which were subject to inspection and audit by the authorities or by the officials of any merchant guild whose commodities might be involved. All goods were presented for personal examination, including fine Arabian horses and slaves of both sexes and of many nationalities. These latter, like the horses, were scrutinized and tested from every angle, particularly those who had any special talents or skills, for many Portuguese men of capital lived upon the earnings of slaves who were artisans or craftsmen. Here also were auctioned off the finest of precious stones, diamonds and rubies, amber and pearls, and also antique Chinese porcelains, embroideries, paintings, and carved jade and ivory. Some merchants who had booths sent trained and trusted African slaves through the plaza carrying precious necklaces, strings of pearls and other treasures, calling them to the attention of prospective purchasers. Many traders sold individual items of high value, including *objets d'art*. Jan reported also that the probate court of Goa held routine official auctions here of the completely inventoried estates of Europeans who had died in Goa. Such estates were handled by the court in this way in order to protect the interests of the widows and heirs; because of the high death rate in India, the volume and value of such transactions were very large. In addition, mass lots of commodities such as spices, pharmaceutical-botanical items, and scented woods and dyes were freely auctioned, except for the Crown monopolies—which were pepper, ginger, cinnamon, mace, cloves, nutmeg, wormwood, borax, camphor, aloes, musk, civet spikewood, mastic, some precious stones, silks, porcelain, and fine raiment.

A striking fact which Jan no doubt noticed at once, and which he later brought out in his description, was that a group of Venetian merchants were always present at the auctions as buyers. They freely purchased the offerings, in particular, spices, dyes and pharmaceuticals; their purchases were then shipped by sea to Ormuz on the Persian Gulf, and thence overland by semiannual caravan to Aleppo in Syria, and from its seaport

Alexandretta across the Mediterranean to Venice. Jan's testimony on this subject has been overlooked by most historians, who have in general not recognized that the Venetians under Portuguese surveillance still continued to use their ancient overland caravan route and still retained a substantial share of their original oriental spice trade. Jan's statement showed that the development by the Portuguese of the ocean route to the Indies had not superseded and displaced the old Venetian caravans, and that the Italians were still carrying on as usual, but only with goods supplied by Portugal at Goa and under strict Portuguese clearance at Ormuz. This is logical when one reflects that the maximum of five shiploads which Portugal imported annually could not possibly have met the enormous European demand for oriental goods, although it did monopolize the importation of pepper into Europe.

The Grand Entry

T o J A N , the ten days between Monsenhor's landing and the triumphal entry into Goa must have seemed very brief, so busy was he getting acquainted with that fascinating city. His job may have called for attention once or twice, but it must be presumed that there was not much work to be done until the Archbishop was settled in the city. Jan did not mention in the *Itinerario* whether or not he himself walked in the great procession with the rest of his master's retinue, so we can only guess that he must have been in a bustle of personal preparation for the great day.

On September 30th the grand entrance was at last made in accordance with ancient tradition. It was a gala day for the whole town, and the balconies of the houses along its route were hung with tapestries, carpets and Chinese silks of the richest description, and crowded with enthusiastic viewers. Children strewed flowers in the path of Monsenhor's palanquin. The atmosphere was electric, and many of the people in the crowd had taken their places hours before the parade was to start.

First of all, riding four abreast on handsomely bedecked horses, appeared the members of the great military orders of the Knights of Christ, the Knights of Santiago, and the Knights of Avis. Then came the Viceroy with his bodyguard, followed by the Chancellor, the members of the King's Council, the Royal Treasurer, the Justices of the newly established Court of Chancery, and about a hundred other members of the civil administration, also on horseback. Next came the ecclesiastical part of the parade, led by the various religious brotherhoods in their distinctive robes —the Dominicans, the Franciscans, the Augustinians, the Jesuits, and the Grand Inquisitor with his familiars of the Holy Office. A silence came over the masses of people as the holy orders passed solemnly along, but as the high point of the procession drew near a murmur of anticipation was heard. Under an embroidered silk canopy, seated in an open palanquin and robed in gold and silver cloth, came the Archbishop himself. After him marched the members of his household, priests first and then civilians. Then came the Bishop of Cochin and the Bishop of Malacca in their palanquins.

Next came the faculty and students of the College of St. Paul and the functionaries of the older Catholic institutions. Following them came the guilds, represented by delegations in gorgeous regalia, each with its banners and symbols, the statue of its patron saint, and sometimes with floats, either wheeled or carried on the shoulders of the marchers. Always there was the sound of music, as bands of musicians and choristers came by.

Then came the crews of ships in the harbor, the shipwrights and dockyard workers, and various fraternities and social orders with banners and floats.

Finally, in the rear, came the Ambassadors of the great native states accredited to Goa, each riding a ceremonial elephant and accompanied by members of his household mounted on handsome Arabian horses.

The procession came to the Cathedral and entered it. The Archbishop took his seat upon his throne; alongside him was seated the Viceroy, while the two Bishops filled chairs slightly lower on the dais. The music of the organ and of several well-trained choirs, the smoke of the incense, and the chanting of many priests made a moving ritual. Finally, when the Archbishop was formally robed in his cloak of office, the trumpets rang out, the organ intoned the *Laudate Dominum*, and the cannon of the fortress loosed a twenty-one gun salute to the new Primate of the Indies. He was then conducted with due ceremony to his archepiscopal palace.

It may be conjectured that all this made a strong impression on young Jan of Holland, although he continued to nurse his general bias against the Portuguese people as compared with his own. Whatever he thought about them in other connections, and whatever his prejudices, he still had to admit that they knew how to fill a solemn ceremony with depth and meaning.

The Archbishop's Supremacy

N o w Jan took up his duties in the office of the Archbishopric, which controlled lands and fortunes as important as those of the government of the colony. In that period, it must be remembered, Catholic bishops and archbishops in Europe not only had broad spiritual powers and authority, but were also great feudal noblemen and princes with all their temporal attributes. In some cases they exercised sovereign powers, and some even were reckoned as potentates and commanded their own formidably armed forces.

In the sixteenth century, although Portugal had become a benevolent despotism, with the power of the king untempered by a parliament or a strong nobility, it was also to a certain degree a theocracy. The revenues and lands of the clergy exceeded those of the crown, the prelates had many inalienable privileges and monopolies, and they could, in case of need, appeal to Rome against any royal impositions. In *Asia Portuguesa*, where the propagation of the faith was a fixed royal policy, churchmen exercised even greater influence than in the homeland.

Prince Henry, Grand Master of the rich and politically powerful monastic Military Order of the Knights of Christ, had initiated his pioneering explorations by sea in the early fifteenth century. As a monastic ascetic, Prince Henry was actuated chiefly by crusading fervor, and was granted many ecclesiastical privileges for his proselyting order by the Pope. By the time the fleet of Vasco da Gama had established the *Carreira da India* along the route laid out by Prince Henry, who had died nearly four decades earlier, the undertaking had come to be practically under papal auspices. King Manuel the Fortunate, in laying down the form of government of *Asia Portuguesa*, made the propagation of Christianity a goal equal to acquiring control of the oriental spice trade. Consequently, in setting up the system of rule of the Indies, ecclesiastical perquisites and revenues that rivalled those of the lay government were freely conceded by the Crown. Likewise the canon law of the Church had an unchallenged place in the colonial courts.

These priestly fiscal and commercial powers had gradually expanded during the sixteenth century, and by Jan's time, his master's financial position was in many respects stronger than that of the Viceroy. Since the Archbishop had no military power, he was perhaps at a disadvantage in case of a conflict of authority with the Viceroy, but in actual fact the lay authority could not have relied upon the soldiers and sailors to take action against him, for they stood in dread of his power of excommunication. As to finances, the Archbishop legally had first call upon many of the revenues of the colonies. In political matters, he could depend upon strong factional allies about the throne in Lisbon and upon his clergy in almost every port and province throughout the colonies.

The Archbishop was appointed by the King, with Papal consent, and his tenure of office was for life. The term of office of the Viceroy was only three years, and since it would take him at least two years to get an answer from the King to any complaint or appeal against ecclesiastical encroachment, it is obvious that even a Viceroy of strong character and great ability would find it judicious to conciliate the Archbishop.

A concrete example of the Archbishop's power was the famous Archbishop's Prison in Goa, which was larger than the prison belonging to the civil government of the city. Looming up larger still was the imposing three-story black stone building of the Inquisition, under the direction of the Dominican Order, which was the original palace of the former Moslem ruler of Goa. It had walls with outer casings five feet thick and contained two hundred cells, in which were immured "heretics, apostates, bigamists, sodomists and sorcerers." These poor creatures were held for a great *auto da fé* which took place every two or three years. At this time, any natives who had become Christians and later had abjured the faith were generally put through a gruesome ritual and then, as so-called penitents, burned alive. The populace swarmed to view the spectacle, just as crowds in every European capital turned out to witness capital punishments of all kinds. Usually convicted Christians were condemned to the oars of the royal galleys, a form of slow death hardly better than the stake. The barbarity of this whole proceeding appears incredible, especially as it was conducted by clergymen in the name of Christian justice, even though they left the final execution of sentences to the lay officials. The political authority of the Inquisition in the Portuguese homeland, where it had fastened itself with despotic and paralyzing power upon society, had assured that its branch in Goa was well equipped and well manned, but, fortunately for the colony, in reality its scope and jurisdiction were quite restricted. The Jesuits were opposed to the Inquisition as a matter of practical common sense, as were the Franciscans and other orders, partly through jealousy, because it was directed by the Dominicans. Hence, the activities of the Inquisition at Goa were very limited, and for all practical purposes there was nearly full freedom of conscience there.

Although public religious observances were restricted to the Portuguese state religion of Roman Catholicism, the numerous Moslems, Buddhists, Jews and members of other sects were in no way molested in their private beliefs or non-public services. It could not have been otherwise, because the rule of Portugal in Asia was limited to the confines of its fortified seaports. Many Portuguese traders and priests lived and worked in areas which were under the jurisdiction of native rulers, and a persecution of non-Catholics in Goa would have brought about quick retaliation. Many of the Portuguese officials were themselves Eurasians with numerous relatives and friends who were non-Catholics, for it had been the policy of Portugal since the days of Affonso de Albuquerque to encourage the marriage of the Portuguese gentry in the colonies with high-caste native women, and particularly with those of Arab blood and noble descent.

An illustration of the high temporal position of the Archbishop of Goa in the government of *India Portuguesa* occurred when a new Viceroy arrived in Cochin from Lisbon in November, 1584, on the ship *As Chagas*

(Five Wounds). After seven months at sea, the ship had arrived at the Cape too late to go to Mozambique and had sailed direct to Cochin. Aboard was the new Viceroy, fully prepared to take over the government, but not yet arrived in Goa. Jan wrote: "Being landed he sent presently to the olde Viceroye to certifie him of his arrivall and that hee should commit the government of the countrie unto the Archbishoppe to govern it in his absence, specially because the Archbishoppe and he were verie good friends and old acquaintances having been prisoners together in Barbarie when Dom Sebastian King of Portugal was slaine, which the old viceroy presently did and went by sea unto Cochijn." For a period of ninety days, therefore, Monsenhor combined religious and worldly offices as acting Viceroy, and the new Viceroy did not arrive in Goa until February 5, 1585.

Once the Archbishop was in residence in the city, Jan must have found himself much tied down to the routine of his position as clerk for that official. However, he doubtless found occasional reasons to do errands about the town, and to continue his explorations in his free time. As he observed the busy life of the colony, he obviously began to feel at home in it and to know his way around.

The City

ON THE SURFACE, the city appeared orderly compared to others of its size. Practically no drunkenness was to be seen, largely because of the habitual sobriety of the Portuguese people. There were no public brothels, which is the more remarkable because, for six months of every year, during the southwest monsoon which made it impossible to send ships across the bar into the stormy Indian Ocean, all the soldiers and sailors were at large in the city without employment. A number of luxurious gambling casinos were licensed by the muncipality and operated under strict supervision, offering floor shows and concerts. However, as usual "the devil found mischief for idle hands to doe," and Jan happily made it clear that there was no lack of human weakness and vice in all its various forms in Goa. On balance, the tolerant city seemed really better behaved than many other great seaports, in Europe and elsewhere, especially since its practices could not be judged only by rigid Christian standards.

The Island of Goa was a triangle ten miles long and three to seven miles wide, ending in a cape where its western extremity projected into the Indian Ocean between two rivers. The city itself was shaped like a half moon. Originally it was a Mohammedan city-state ruled by a rajah, and already in those days it enjoyed a monopoly of the importation of Arabian and Persian horses into India. Since the Indian climate is very unfavorable to horses, there was a steady demand for replacements of cavalry mounts, as well as of horses for the boar-hunting and polo-playing knightly classes; this large and profitable trade was continued by the Portuguese after the fortified port was conquered in the early sixteenth century by Affonso de Albuquerque.

Before the coming of the Portuguese, Goa already had been a shipbuilding and shipping center. Besides horses, it had imported and distributed, throughout the nearby area, gold from Sofala, textiles from industrial Gujarat, ivory and ebony from Mozambique, slaves from Mombassa, cinnamon from Ceylon, and pepper from the neighboring Malabar Coast. Goa also had imported, for resale in the cities of East Africa, Arabia, and Northern India, spices, Chinese silks and wares and Japanese silver, all brought from Malacca by Arab dhows.

After Albuquerque captured Goa, he moved the capital of *Asia Portuguesa* there from Cochin, lower down on the Malabar Coast. The Portuguese *feitores*, or factors, as the merchants were called, not only retained Goa's established Moslem trade, but greatly expanded it. Soon, using native crews and pilots with Portuguese officers, the city became the home port for a wide network of coastwise shipping, which extended from Japan and China to Mozambique. Goa monopolized the heavier maritime traffic in the Arabian Sea and Indian Ocean and in much of the South China Sea, and before long its intercoastal commerce produced an even greater revenue than its famed annual pepper fleet. The richness of this Indian coastal trade was a well-kept secret which Jan was the first to make public; it was not fully comprehended by the English and Dutch until after their own competitive entry into the Far Eastern markets. This traffic was regulated in accordance with the general commercial practices of sixteenth-century Europe; therefore monopolies were licensed by the Portuguese Crown which permitted one annual sailing out and back to Goa, exclusively to each of the market areas now known as Bombay, Calcutta, Burma, Siam, Mozambique, Ormuz, Malacca and Macao. Each of these licensed voyages had a one-year royal franchise subject to renewal, the last named being the most lucrative.

Daily Life

J A N was much impressed by the comfort and grace of the home life of the colonists, and wrote of it vividly in the *Itinerario*. "The Portingals, Mesticos and Christians keepe worshipfull and bountiful houses, having commonly (as it is said before) five, sixe, ten, twentie, some more, some lesse slaves, both men and women in their houses every man according to his estate and qualitie, I meane married men. They are very cleanly and sweet in all things belonging to their houses specially in their linnen, for that every day they change shirtes and smockes both men and women, and [their slaves and servants] likewise with other thinges that they weare which they doe because of the great heat of that land. The Portingals are commonly served with great gravitie without any difference betweene the Gentlemen and the common citizen [townsmen] or soldier, and in their going curtesies, and conversations, common in all thinges when they go in the streetes they steppe very [softly and] slowly forwards, with a great pride and vainglorious maiestie with a slave that carrieth a great hat or vaile over their heads, to keepe the sunne and rain from them. Also when it raineth they commonly have a boy that beareth a cloke of scarlet or of some other [cloth] after them, to cast over them, and if it bee before noone hee carrieth a cushion [for his maister] to kneele on when he heareth Masse and their Rapier is most commonly carried after them by a boy, that it may not trouble them as they walke, nor hinder their gravities. When they meete in the streetes a good space before they come together they beginne with a great Besolas Manos ['I kiss your hands'] to stoope [with] their bodies, and to thrust forth their foot to salute, either with their hattes [in their hands] almost touching the ground: likewise when they come into the church [where] they have their stooles ready, which their slaves have prepared for them: all with the same manner of bowing [of their bodies] doe him great reverence."

Jan then described how quick to take offense and seek revenge for any slight these punctilious *fidalgos* were. "When any man goeth to visite the other in his house, although he which is visited be one of the principal gentlemen [of the Citie], and the visitor but a simple soldier, or some other man it is the manner that hee which is visited commeth unto the doore of his house, with his hatte in his hand, and with great curtesie to receyve him that commeth to visite him, and so leadeth him up into his hall or chamber, wherein he will speake with him, where he offereth him a chaire to sette down, and then hee himselfe sitteth [by him], then he asketh him what hee woulde have, which having understoode hee bringeth him down againe to the dore in the like sort, and so with a Besolas manos biddeth him farewel, and if he should not doe so, [when hee giveth him a stoole] shold give him one unlined, or one yt his lesse or lower than he taketh for himselfe, he that visiteth him woulde take it in evil parte, esteeming it a great scorne, and seeke to be revenged on him for the same."

The manner of life and the attitudes of extreme politeness were quite different from those to which Jan had been accustomed at home, but he realized that they were no mere surface manifestations. A half century later, Count Johann Maurits of Nassau, who had governed the Dutch colony in Brazil for many years, was to observe: "The secret of ruling Pernambuco is to remember that the Dutch merchants attach more importance to their money and goods than to their lives, while the Portuguese inhabitants value courtesy and politeness more than property or self."

The Ecclesiastical Establishment

J A N probably thought it extraordinary that so great a part of the capital was dominated by ecclesiastical organizations; doubtless it did not occur to him that this showed the Portuguese people and their government practicing what they preached. He must have noted what great emphasis was put on ritual and the outward, conventionalized forms of worship, but also he must have acknowledged that there were few major moral scandals in the Goan religious community. The natural human rivalry between the monkish organizations (there were no nunneries because so few Portuguese women came to India) was to a degree a contest in ostentation, but there was also a contest in zealous Christian practices in which the more institutionalized and easy-going older brotherhoods were stung into activity by the gadfly Jesuits, who set the pace for reform and for intense missionary work, instead of placid chanting and drowsy censer swinging.

The great cost of the elaborate Church Department of the government of *Asia Portuguesa* was not too heavy a fiscal burden as long as the Crown held its lucrative monopoly of intra-Indian coastal trade; and the expense could be justified as being for the spiritual, moral and intellectual benefit of the realm. However, partly because of the dissemination of Jan's information, Goa later lost its control of the intra-Indian trade to the English and Dutch, and its revenues were thereby sharply cut. Then indeed the priority allowed the Church in allotting much of the income of the colony, its freedom from taxes on its vast properties, and the exemption from military service of so many able-bodied monks and priests, put the situation in a different light. When the colony was, financially speaking, gasping for its breath, and when every *milreis* was needed for defense, there is no doubt that the expense of the ecclesiastical side of the government caused it to be looked upon as a parasite.

However, the state church was an inherent, if not actually preponderant, element in the life of the Portuguese nation. The proportion of churchly participation in the government of Goa was perhaps above the home average because of the early crusading commitment to the propagation of the faith. However, Goa was fairly typical of the structure of Portuguese colonialism, which was conducted everywhere by three basic elements: the priest, the factor, and the soldier. To these three was added a fourth which was also important, though not representing a major segment of the population—the judge, for the lay courts had high jurisdiction and acted as moderators which zealously safeguarded the inherent interests of the Crown.

The Four English Prisoners

J A N related a story in detail in the *Itinerario* as having occurred in 1584, in which he himself played an important part; it was about four English merchants who were brought to Goa from Ormuz as suspected spies of Dom Antonio of Crato, the pretender to the Portuguese throne. In his book, Jan presented the humanity and kindliness with which they were treated by Portuguese officials in a refreshingly favorable light.

These prisoners could speak no Portuguese and were in a desperate situation. Two of them, however, John Newbury and John Fitch, could speak some Dutch, since they had traded with Holland in the past. They managed to get in touch with a Dutch-speaking Jesuit from Flanders, to whom they appealed for help. They told him that they had been sent from Aleppo to Ormuz by the English "companie," or colony of merchants, with a caravan of trade goods. Once in Ormuz, they were to probe the possibility of establishing an English agency there, and also to purchase diamonds, pearls and rubies, for which they secretly carried a large sum in gold which they displayed to him. They related that they had opened a shop in Ormuz and had done so well that the Venetian traders became alarmed. The jealous Venetians concocted the story of their being spies and accused them to the Portuguese governor of Ormuz, alleging also that they were heretics and subversive to the Church. The Governor felt it his duty to arrest them and send them to Goa for examination, but did so in a very humane manner, safeguarding all their belongings, which he allowed them to take with them. (The historic friendship between Portugal and England undoubtedly influenced the attitude of the Governor in this case.) At all events, the Flemish Jesuit, convinced of their innocence, brought an English Jesuit named Stevens, who was the first Englishman ever to live there, to interrogate them; it was Father Stevens who asked Jan, together with a German named Bernard Burcherts, of Hamburg, who was also on Monsenhor's staff, to talk to them.

Jan also became assured of their innocence, and therefore he brought the case to the attention of his master, the Archbishop. This dignitary being, as Jan wrote, a "kind and good man," persuaded the Viceroy to release the Englishmen and allow them to open a shop in Goa. Monsenhor then gave them his patronage, which of course was enough to assure their success. Jan said that the Englishmen offered Monsenhor many presents, but "hee would not receive them, neither would he ever take a gift or present at any man's hands." The four Englishmen were received into

Goa's society, were very well treated, and became personally popular. However, the report of the spy scare at Ormuz reached Lisbon overland via Aleppo, and as a result the Viceroy received a letter from King Philip, also by overland dispatch, asking for a report on the incident. This was secretly revealed to the Englishmen. They were then allowed to take a hasty leave, carrying their fortune with them, but it is certain their flight could never have been effected without the connivance of the Viceroy. A bit later, official orders were received from Lisbon to transport them to Portugal for examination, so it was lucky for them that they had been allowed to get away. No doubt the Viceroy was well aware of what they could expect at the hands of Philip II. However, although it is natural for American sympathies to be with the bold English adventurers, it must in all fairness be admitted that, as a matter of statecraft and in the interest of their own governments, the Venetians and Philip II were justified in their adherence to the old policy of excluding other nations from their oriental preserves, especially since both France and England were at war with Spain and supporting Dom Antonio, the Portuguese Pretender.

A strange aspect of the case is that one of the four Englishmen, an artist named Story who was interested in ecclesiastical painting, elected not to join his partners in their flight. He stayed in Goa without molestation, either married a Eurasion woman or became a Jesuit, according to various contemporary reports, and in any case lived there until the end of his life, enjoying the patronage of the Jesuits in the embellishment of their churches.

Jan reported that no more English traders came to Goa, but that the Venetian merchants continued to be very active there, coming and going constantly.

A further surprising fact is that the three English refugees, after escaping from Goa safely, made a trading trip into the interior of India. One of them, Leeds, died en route, but Newbury returned in 1585 to England via Persia, while Fitch continued through India and did not get back to London until 1591, via Basra and Aleppo. An account of "Fitch's Voyage," published by Hakluyt in London, revealed the humanity and benevolence with which the Portuguese authorities treated the English adventurers. The ease with which they managed to travel freely and safely throughout the various Indian Kingdoms and through Persia and Turkey, with a fortune in gold and jewels in their possession, is amazing.

Jan said in the *Itinerario* that Story, the English painter who remained in Goa, "instructed him of al the waies, trades and viages of the countrie between Aleppo and Ormus and of all the ordinances and common customs which they usually hold during their viage over land, as also of the places and townes where they passed." Surprisingly enough, Jan ascribed the part the Jesuits played in freeing the Englishmen entirely to greed; he thought they expected through intrigue to get hold of the Englishmen's gold. In making this accusation he no doubt reflected the jealous hostility of his employers, the Dominicans, to the aggressive and expanding young Jesuit order. He also may have been influenced by the attitude prevalent in Holland at the time when he was preparing his manuscript for publication.

To indict the Jesuits for avarice then was common. However, much later, in the eighteenth century, when the religious order was banned by the Portuguese government under the Marquis of Pombal, all its secret records and accounts were seized, impounded, and later scrutinized by anticlerical researchers. It was discovered that, while the Jesuits, lacking established foundations, had indeed been zealous to secure funds, such sums as were acquired (largely by trade) had been, on the whole, prudently expended to maintain their schools and to finance their missionary efforts. The Jesuit order never had been opulent, but was always in pressing need of revenue to carry on its dedicated work. As to Jan's accusation, it was, apparently, completely without foundation.

However, any reflection at this time on the integrity of the Society of Jesus was well received by Dutch and English readers, because these ubiquitous papal soldiers of the Counter Reformation were heartily hated as well as feared in the northern Protestant countries. Jan and Cornelis Claeszoon, the publisher of the *Itinerario*, could make no mistake in ascribing any villainy to them, for when the book was published they were officially outlawed and subject to torture and death if captured in England or Holland.

A Report to Enkhuizen

J A N had been in India for a little over a year when in 1584 an opportunity arose for him to send a long letter to his family at Enkhuizen in the care of a Dutchman returning to Europe. Such personal channels were the only ones available for the sending of letters, though it is hard for a modern individual to imagine a complete lack of any postal service. Jan, of course, had no means of knowing that his beloved father, to whom he addressed his comments on life in Goa, was already dead. The original of this letter was discovered in the Dutch Archives only in 1882. It casts much light on the economic conditions of the period, being much more illuminating and informative in this respect than his account in the *Itinerario*—indeed, certain scholars refer to the letter as a "little *Itinerario*."

Jan gave many details in his letter home concerning the climate, the natural products, and the people and their customs, as well as considerable geographical data, all of which was new and fascinating information in Holland. Of particular interest to modern historians is his plan to return home overland, for he mentioned the specific stopping places proposed and gave the distances and routes between them. The details, he said, had been furnished him in writing by the above-mentioned four English merchants while they were prisoners in Goa.

In the letter to his family in 1584, Jan explained that what he had learned from the English traders had awakened in him a keen desire to see the Middle Eastern lands which they described. Three hundred or four hundred merchants left Goa annually bound for Venice and Mediterranean centers, he said, going first by sea to Ormuz and then by caravan to Aleppo, in Syria, where about four hundred Christian merchants, Italian, French, English and German, were domiciled, and where there were many Christian churches of various sects. As previously quoted, he wrote that from Aleppo's seaport, Alexandretta, goods from India were shipped not only to Venice but to a number of other Mediterranean ports, which he named.

Surprisingly enough, he told his parents that travel was safer and more free in Turkey than in Holland itself. He went on to say that he was studying Italian, which was more useful in Asia Minor than English or French because of the centuries-old Venetian and Genoan trade there. Obviously, at the time of this letter Jan had made up his mind to leave Goa and return home via the Middle East, and it is probable that his voyage was to be made in the company of Bernard Burcherts, his German fellow worker, who had been engaged with him in helping the English merchants. Jan then changed his mind and decided to stay in Goa; he wrote in the *Itinerario:* "In the month of April the same year [1585] my fellow [and servant to the Archbishop] called Bernard Burcherts, borne in Hamborough, travelled from Goa into Ormus and from thence to Bossora and from thence by land through Babilon Jerusalem Damasco and Aleppo from whence he sent me two letters by an Armenian wherein he certified me of all his viage which he performed with small charges and lesse danger in good fellowship and verie merrie in the company of the caffyles [caravans]. From Aleppo he went to Tripoli in Suria and there he found certaine shippes for England wherein he sayled to London and thence to Hamborough which by letters from him written out of Hamborough I understoode." This account in the *Itinerario* confirmed what he had written home in the preceding year.

Jan showed incidentally in this letter the fallacy in the general belief still current among historians that the water route via the Cape of Good Hope, as established by Vasco da Gama, was shorter and safer than the former Arabian caravan route. He calculated the distance from Goa by land to Venice as 2,389 Dutch miles, compared to an ocean voyage from Goa to Lisbon of 6,000 miles. He pointed out that a voyage by sea to

Portugal took eight months, at a cost of about two hundred ducats, while the overland caravan route took five or six months at a cost of only one hundred ducats, with opportunities for trade all along the way.

The Intra-Indian Traffic

THESE CONSIDERATIONS again brought out the little understood fact previously mentioned that the oriental trade of Portugal, and later of the Netherlands, was by no means confined to spice and pepper imports by sea into Europe; its profits in reality depended upon the coastal traffic between oriental ports. The Portuguese at Goa profited greatly from the purchase of Indian textiles from the cottage industries of the Gujarati, in Northern India, and on the Malabar and Coromandel coasts, which they resold in all the principal Asian ports. They also had a thriving business all through the Indian Ocean and Arabian Sea reselling imported Chinese silks and wares. We now know that this reciprocal west-east flow of commerce through the Indian Ocean from Ormuz to Canton had existed for uncounted centuries; as late as the sixteenth century, great dhows from Muscat and booms from Kuwait sailed to China, there was an important Arab trading colony at Canton, and until nearly the end of the fifteenth century fleets of Chinese junks sailed along the East African coast and to Ormuz on the Persian Gulf.

In his letter home Jan also mentioned the profitable trade of Goa with China and Japan. He said that Japan was no farther from Goa than Portugal was, and told how tempted he was to go on the annual "Great Ship of Goa," which had a monopoly of the trade between India and Nagasaki, Japan, with Macao and Canton as side stops. A fellow townsman from Enkhuizen, Dirck Gerritszoon Pomp, was the constable, or head gunner, on the Great Goa ship *Santa Cruz* (of about 1,400 tons) which had been built in Cochin, he said, and Dirck had urged him to come along on the three-year round trip. If he had only had a hundred ducats in capital, Jan told his parents, he would have accompanied his friend, for he could easily make two or three hundred ducats profit, and possibly as much as seven hundred, on an original capital of one hundred ducats. A realistic Dutchman, he reflected that there was no justification for going into any such operation without gaining a profit. It is perhaps interesting to note that, after having been active in a governmental-ecclesiastical position in which he handled goodly sums of money for over a year in Goa, where bribe-taking was alleged to be the rule, Jan had not been able to accumulate even so modest a capital fund as a hundred ducats. This is evidence of the honesty of Jan himself and of Monsenhor's staff.

Although he did not sail with Dirck, the inquisitive and fact-hungry Jan learned a great deal from him, upon his return, about the routes in the Indian Ocean and the China Sea, as well as about Chinese and Japanese trade and navigation; all this information was completely unknown at this time in both England and Holland.

Dirck Gerritszoon of Enkhuizen

DIRCK GERRITSZOON was born in Enkhuizen about 1544 and, therefore, was about twenty years older than Jan. His parents were Gerrit Maertenszoon and Elizabeth Dircksdochter, and his father had two sisters who were married to prosperous Dutch merchants domiciled in Lisbon. When Dirck was twenty years old he left home to seek adventure and sailed to visit his relatives in Lisbon. His uncles saw to it that young Dirck was given a good education, and after he had learned to speak Portuguese they got him a job as clerk and interpreter on a Dutch ship in the Lisbon run. When he was twenty-four, Dirck was qualified for a post in the *Carreira da India* and shipped on the *Santa Clara*, one of a squadron of five vessels that cleared the Tagus on Good Friday, 1568.

Although he had gone to India to seek his fortune, he did not enter trade there, but enlisted in the royal naval service, becoming a marine artilleryman and eventually a master gunner. This was a logical career for him to enter, for, as we have seen, in both the Spanish and Portuguese services naval gunnery was somewhat contemptuously left in the hands of the phlegmatic northerners. The Portuguese naval commanders were, as we know, of noble rank, and despised the Dutch tactics of relying upon gunfire to disable an enemy ship before closing in; being aristocrats, they favored the knightly practice of boarding and fighting at sword's length. Students of naval warfare ascribe many Portuguese defeats at sea to this unrealistic and stubborn adherence to tradition. The cool and deliberate gunners of Dutch ships crippled their Portuguese enemies, disabling their rudders and rigging, then raking the decks of the helpless hulks and decimating their crews, before boarding for the final hand-to-hand combat.

Dirck Gerritszoon took to wife in 1582 a Netherlands woman, Johanna Willemsdochter, born in Brussels. European women were extremely scarce in Goa, and it would be interesting to know Johanna's history. Soon after their marriage, Dirck sailed on his second voyage to Japan, and upon his return three years later found himself a widower. It may be assumed that his unfortunate wife met her death in childbirth, for the death rate of European women in childbirth in India very much exceeded even that of Europe, which, however, was also very high.

Goa

The Alien European Group

I T I S usually stated in accounts of life in Goa that the Portuguese government maintained a policy of forbidding the immigration of foreigners into the Indian State. This is another legend that Jan contradicted in his famous letter home, for he stated that there were a number of Netherlanders then in Goa, including a prominent merchant, Pieter Janszoon de Wit, of Rotterdam. He said that there were also in Goa five or six Jesuit priests from the Netherlands; however, he could not have been on very friendly terms with the Jesuits because of his identification with the Archbishop, who was a Dominican. He and Dirck Gerritszoon were intimate with a Frenchman of Dieppe who served as a drummer aboard the royal galleys. The position of trumpeter on a sailing ship or drummer on a galley was well paid and was, like that of gunner, often held by foreigners.

Jan apparently never succeeded in establishing himself socially in Goa with any of the Portuguese of rank. From both his published *Itinerario* and his private letters it is clear that he held only the social status of a modest foreign clerk. There is no evidence of his having achieved the slightest recognition as a person of any importance, and apparently all his friends were in the foreign colony of Europeans of secondary station. However, because of his great industry in reading all available Portuguese historical, geographical and navigational books about India and his zeal in map making and sketching, he must have stood out individually. No doubt he was patronized as an eccentric by the easy-going mediocrities of his circle. However, perhaps if his master had lived, Jan might have made noteworthy advances in Goan official circles.

The Goan Intellectuals

I T I S E V I D E N T, however, that Jan never, during his five years in Goa, received any recognition or encouragement from the group of scholars and writers who were domiciled there. Indeed, it would have been most unusual if he had, since he was in the main self-taught and of a pragmatic bent rather far removed from the theological and classical studies of his day. He had never attended a university and possessed none of the ordinary titles of scholarship.

It is interesting to note that in his *Itinerario*, although he claimed to describe every aspect of life in Goa, Jan never even mentioned the existence of the brilliant circle of historians and poets who made the colonial

Goa

capital superior in scholarship to the leading cultural centers of the mother country. In a century when literary genius was ablaze in Spain, Italy, France and England, there was but little reflection of the flame either in Portugal or Holland. Keen reporter though he was, Jan betrayed no awareness of Goa's intellectual life, which was relatively free of the deadening hand of the Inquisition. Some of the outstanding histories of the age were written there. *The Lusiads,* the only great epic of Portugal, was composed in Goa by Luiz de Camoëns, who lived there from 1561 to 1567 as one of a circle of scholars and poets. Among them was Garcia da Orta, whose outstanding botanical work, *Simples y Drogas da India,* was the result of thirty years of study in *Asia Portuguesa;* Camoens contributed a prefatory ode for this work when it was published locally, in 1563, by João de Emden, whose scholarly printshop also brought out several other notable works written in Goa. A great disciple of Garcia da Orta and a member of the Goan group of wits was Christovão da Costa, a Jewish *converso.* Born in Mozambique, Da Costa became the leading surgeon of Goa, and as a scientific student under Da Orta composed his celebrated *Tractado de las Drogas,* which was printed in Burgos, Spain, in 1578.

One of the most distinguished Goans was a renowned cartographer whose beautiful atlases are highly appreciated today, Fernão Vaz Dourado, a Portuguese Eurasian, possibly of Jewish blood, who worked in Goa from 1568 to 1580. Gaspar Correa, author of the immortal *Lendas da India,* lived long in Goa, and the renowned historian Diogo de Couto completed nine decades of Barros' *Asia* while he lived in Goa from 1559 to 1616.

It is probable that none of the polished literary group, with whom, no doubt, the erudite Archbishop was on close terms, even knew that the humble little Dutch accountant in Monsenhor's palace was then busily composing and illustrating a manuscript that was destined to be acclaimed as a geographical masterpiece. But although the historians, botanists and poets of Goa may have been unaware of the scholarship of the obscure young man, he was by no means ignorant of their works, and one wonders why, in publishing a minute description of life in Goa, he left out the literary aspect, one of the most glorious elements in the Portuguese colonial record. Was he, perhaps, hurt at being excluded from the circles where he would have been most at ease?

That during his stay in Goa Jan was immersed in reading the published works of the Goan scholars is indisputable, for modern Dutch historical scholars have established the fact that the *Itinerario,* in its botanical, geographical, historical and ethnical elements, is based very largely upon previously published works of the Portuguese authors above cited and of some of their predecessors. Of course, Jan used the printed material available at the time to confirm and supplement his own observations, readily drawing on whatever sources he considered reliable. It is not desired to minimize his scholarship in studying and summarizing the information available to him, nor to call him a plagiarist. It cannot be denied that his description of life in contemporary Goa is a masterpiece of reporting. Some of his accounts of outlying communities in East Africa and Southeast Asia were gleaned from his skillful interrogations of persons acquainted with areas unknown to him personally. Nevertheless, a goodly portion of his text in the *Itinerario* was lifted bodily from the published writings of the Portuguese in Goa without giving any credit to the authors. Even though he knew that the reading public in Holland was materialistic and had little appreciation or interest in foreign literary merit, little excuse for his failure to give credit to his sources can be found. There is something ungenerous in his suppression of any mention of this aspect of Portuguese colonial civilization; it seems part of a definite policy on his part to withhold credit for almost all the most commendable achievements of the Portuguese in the Orient. However, perhaps he never gave this aspect of the matter a thought, being avid for any information that came within his reach and blissfully unaware of modern standards of research.

The Defensive Heroism of Goa

ANOTHER FEATURE of Jan's description of life in Goa which is puzzling to any student who reads other authoritative contemporaneous accounts is the consistently prejudiced manner in which he dismissed the military and naval activities of the Portuguese scornfully or described them as inept and blundering, if not cowardly. In reality, effective and brilliant campaigns were annually conducted by the Viceroys during the trying years of Jan's stay in Goa, from September, 1583, until January, 1589.

We have shown how the Portuguese fatherland had been plunged into the depths of depression and disorganization first by the destruction of the national army in Morocco and the death of King Sebastian, then by the resultant furor of intrigue as to the succession to the throne, and finally by the war of defense against Spain and the conquest of the kingdom by Philip II. A sense of frustration and demoralization had understandably seized upon the colonial government, where the confusing dispatches from home arrived but once a year and were already six months old when received. In a period when conditions were changing overnight, the scanty additional news that arrived overland through Venetian and Turkish channels was unreliable, contradictory, and colored by the hostile interests of their sources.

Goa

Then the new King, Philip II, withheld the troop and naval reinforcements so desperately needed in *Asia Portuguesa* and conscripted all Portuguese resources at home for the creation of the Invincible Armada, which was being assembled at Lisbon to attempt the conquest of England. Of course, Philip's broad policy in this was not unwise, for had he successfully invaded England the colonial possessions of Spain would have been freed from any further harassment and an Augustan peace would have prevailed.

Unfortunately for the viceroys, never before had any colonial government had such need for consideration from the king, nor had there ever been before such a lack of ships, arms and men at Goa. At the very moment when the prestige of Goa had stood at its apogee with the various powerful native states of the Far East, an electric wave of doubt spread throughout the non-Christian world of the Orient. This was set off by the intoxicating news that mighty Portugal had been beaten to the ground by a Moslem army in North Africa and then subjugated at home by a neighboring Christian kingdom. Immediately all the East began to stir, and native rulers who had been paying tribute to Goa, or had been held in alliance or neutrality by the threat of the Portuguese sword, all began to prepare to assault the hated Christians in order to reclaim from them the cities, havens, strong points and trade routes which they had seized and exploited.

Asia Portuguesa was almost simultaneously assailed from every side, not only by its recognized enemies but also by those whom it had called friends and allies. Islam and Asia were on the move to drive the Portuguese from the Orient. The viceroys responded magnificently. Without aid from Lisbon, and able to wage war from Goa only for six months a year, they conscripted all the manpower available—not only clerks, traders and civil servants, but the black African slaves as well—and moulded them into a hastily mobilized fighting force. They requisitioned all the ships of the merchant marine, not only naos and galleons, but also caravels, bergantymes, fustas, and galleys, everything afloat, and converted them into warships of sorts.

When the Dutch became a serious threat to the Portuguese in the Far East, Philip sent urgent messages to Goa by the overland route in which he pointed out that the arrogant and overbearing attitude of the viceroys toward the Malay and Indian potentates, which had possibly been good strategy in its day, would inevitably lose their support now that they were being wooed by the Dutch. One reads so often in history that Philip was dilatory and out of touch with details that it is surprising and enlightening to note the incisive and practical tone of this advice.

When Philip II was crowned King of Portugal, he pledged himself to respect the individual rights of his new realm and made definite commitments to that effect which he carried out. However, he craftily avoided promising not to use Portugal's armed forces and its income from taxes to further the interests of Spain itself. Consequently, in Goa's hour of need, when reinforcements and ships were urgently called for, there were none to be had. In their deep bitterness at being neglected, the people of Goa complained that not only were Spain's national interests given preference over Portugal's, but that also the Portuguese colony of Brazil was favored over *Asia Portuguesa* because it lay in the zone of Spain's vast colonial realm in the western hemisphere, called the Spanish Indies. Hence it was said: "The Spanish Indies are Spain's wife, but the Portuguese Indies its concubine."

The hurriedly conscripted Portuguese civilians in India only numbered in the hundreds, and all told the army added up to but several thousand, while the Oriental armies which erupted on all frontiers of the colony were counted in the fifty thousands, with numerous cavalry elements and strong modern artillery.

When Jan reached India in 1583, the viceroy was Francisco Mascarenhas, Count of Santa Cruz, who had managed to defend Goa from an attack on the landward side by an army of 150,000 men under the command of Nyamaluco, the Hindu king. During the last year of his incumbency, Mascarenhas had recovered the important industrial province of Cambaya, in Northern India, from the invading troops of the Grand Mogul, and had forced the embittered hereditary enemy of Portugal, the Samorin of Calicut, to sue for peace. He had stamped out a rebellion in hitherto friendly Cochin, on the Malabar Coast, and had enlisted Persia in a defensive war against the Turks, whose galleys had emerged from the Red Sea to raid Portuguese merchant ships in the Arabian Sea, in which operation, however, the Portuguese were worsted. Also, thousands of miles to the east, the viceroy had managed to put down revolts in the important Spice Islands of Ternate and Tidor, and had been successful against an attack on Malacca by the King of Achin, from Sumatra.

Although Viceroy Mascarenhas had managed to stretch his slender resources and carry on defensive warfare in all parts of *Asia Portuguesa*, covering the whole vast area from the Red Sea to the Spice Islands, thousands of miles to the eastward, nevertheless his achievements received but scant mention in Jan's *Itinerario*—and that without the slightest praise or appreciation. However, Jan wrote in detail of a setback which was suffered by a minor Portuguese amphibious task force of fifteen small vessels in attacking a pirate squadron hiding in a river on the Malabar Coast. The boats of the landing party became stranded in the ebb tide and the ship of the admiral, the viceroy's nephew, a very gallant officer, was cut off; young Mascarenhas was killed and the squadron driven off by the exultant pirates. Jan, who had never in his career smelled gunpowder, gave a critical account of this petty operation and seemed to enjoy the discomfiture of the Portuguese, which he ascribed to a lack of discipline and of soldierly combativeness.

He could not avoid a certain dry and grudging reticence in mentioning the signally successful campaigns of the successor to Mascarenhas, the Viceroy Duarte de Meneses who, despite his lack of men and ships, also withstood violent attacks on all sides by strong native forces; he carried on what were really large-scale defensive wars by extending the drafting of civilian conscripts. He not only defeated an army of 50,000 which attempted to drive the Portuguese from their rich colony of Ceylon, but also, at the other extremity of *Asia Portuguesa*, successfully defended Malacca, key to the Spice Islands and to the trade with China and Japan.

Malacca was closely blockaded by the strong naval forces of the same Malay King of Achin, from Sumatra, who this time landed 90,000 soldiers to attack Malacca. The Portuguese at Malacca made a diversionary attack upon the enemy city of Johor, which they wholly destroyed, bringing to Malacca over 2,500 brass cannon captured there. After several fierce battles, the siege of Malacca was broken and the Sumatrans had to sue for peace.

At the same time Viceroy de Meneses fought a formidable Turkish force in East Africa and sent invading expeditions to put down rebellions in Madagascar and Mozambique. The strain of successfully carrying on these wars in such widely separated fields was immense, and, especially in view of the handicaps under which the Portuguese had to operate, they represented military exploits of the first rank.

It is interesting to note again that Jan confined himself to mentioning briefly that these operations were undertaken during his stay in Goa. However, he devoted much space to a scornful description of the one serious military setback which Viceroy de Meneses suffered. This occurred when a landing force which was sent to punish pirates on the Arabian Coast was cut to pieces, in much the same manner and for the same tactical faults which we described in the similar defeat by pirates suffered by the previous viceroy. Jan's bias showed clearly as he singled out this episode for stinging criticism—a criticism not undeserved in detail, but unbalanced in relation to the total picture, as well as in the spirit in which it was made. In this case, Jan succeeded in presenting the Portuguese as incompetent, unruly and cowardly soldiers, so that the general effect of his narrative was very misleading, and detrimental to Portuguese prestige. Of course, it was seized upon with alacrity by their enemies.

The gifted young Dutchman was both too young and too Dutch to be anything but partisan in such cases. In selecting the two debacles which he described in detail as evidence of the decadence of a haughty race—the thesis in which the Dutch wished to believe at that time—Jan ignored the general history of amphibious attacks. In such an operation, if the landing force is halted inland and its lifeline back to the boats threatened, it rarely makes an orderly retreat, and *sauve qui peut* usually becomes the order of the day. This was shown, among other cases in Jan's century, in the rout of Magellan at Mactan and of Affonso de Albuquerque at Calicut. Moreover, had Jan been able to read the future, it might have given him pause to see, in the seventeenth century, veteran Dutch infantrymen similarly demoralized and slaughtered in flight when their landing parties were repulsed by the Portuguese in Brazil, in West Africa and in China.

The early Portuguese paladins under Francisco de Almeida and Affonso de Albuquerque performed military miracles in taking by frontal attack strong, well-garrisoned forts with ample artillery defenses. The men under Albuquerque either were fearless adventurers hungry for fabulous spoils or else religious crusaders who made inspired, fanatical attacks against seemingly overwhelming odds. They were dare-devils fighting on the offensive, while the achievements of the Goans of Jan's day were defensive ones. Instead of being predatory raiders, most Goans were solid Portuguese burghers, of the second or third generation in India, or Christianized mestizos of half Arab or Indian lineage, who courageously fought to preserve the faith and the civilization of their Portuguese forebears.

Many readers of the *Itinerario* in Northern Europe gathered their first knowledge of Portuguese India from Jan's narrative and were misled into concluding that the once powerful *India Portuguesa* had decayed to the point of dissolution. In actual fact, the Portuguese settlements were to demonstrate a remarkably strong reserve of vitality and cohesion, and indeed, over the centuries, to outlast the Dutch, French and English Oriental colonies.

The Archbishop Departs

IN JANUARY, 1587, occurred an event that was to change the course of Jan's life and ruin his promising career in the service of King Philip. In that month the nao *Nossa Senhora da Sancção* sailed from Cochin bearing Jan's master, the Archbishop, homeward bound to confer about conditions in *Asia Portuguesa* with both His Majesty the King and His Holiness the Pope. At the time this step seemed most propitious for Jan's advancement, but it was to prove far otherwise. He wrote of it: "My Lord the Archbishop sayled unto Portingall, by reason of certaine quarels newly begun betweene the Viceroy and other Councellors, and the Archbishop. And although by the Viceroy, all the Councell and Gentlemen, and communalitie of Goa, he was intreated not to leave them, yet hee would not be disswaded from his purpose, but went to ride unto the King, of whom he was well beloved, which the Viceroy and others liked not very well of, fearing hee should give some information to the King, which would be smally to their profit and in that minde he undertooke his Voyage."

The cause of the dissension is not clear. The conflict in jurisdiction between Church and State was perennial in all the Hispanic vice-royalties and governorships, because the authority was uneasily balanced between priest, factor, soldier and lawyer, with the local judges generally having the final word, subject to ultimate decision by the Crown. Consequently there was a constant stream of accusations, appeals and recriminations to Philip II from Manila, Mexico City, Lima and Santo Domingo, as well as from Goa and the Eastern Captaincies like Malacca, Ormuz and Mozambique. The king's mail was continuously clogged with these colonial controversies, and Philip attempted conscientiously to intervene in them, neglecting more important affairs to do so. Since the king was an incorrigible procrastinator, and also from policy often delayed making clear-cut decisions, the disputant who could obtain an audience was most likely to get a favorable ruling; it was universally believed in Goa that Monsenhor could, through personal contact, influence both king and Pope to give him their support.

The time-table of mail between Goa and Lisbon would have made it impossible for the Archbishop to get a royal judgment upon his complaint earlier than eighteen or twenty months after its dispatch. A letter to the king could only leave Goa once a year, in January, arriving in Lisbon any time between June and September if the vessel carrying the dispatches made a safe voyage. A royal decision, if made promptly, would be carried in the annual sailing of the fleet for India in the following March or April and received in Goa in September or even as late as November.

Whether a dispute was over a question of patronage or privilege, or concerned with the social precedence so important to the punctilious Portuguese nobility, there generally were two appeals to the king, one from each side. These were supported by lengthy testimonials and corroborative evidence by partisans. All this was invariably couched in the lengthy, prescribed style of formality and flattery used in addressing His Sacred Majesty. Naturally, each disputant also wrote to his political allies at home to enlist their personal interest at court to try to influence the king's decision as much as possible.

The harassed and plodding Philip habitually delayed reading dispatches, sometimes for months, even when they were of the utmost military or diplomatic importance. Therefore it was improbable that an early decision would be made on appeals regarding petty colonial questions, since

Philip jealously insisted on handling everything himself. Many of these prolix colonial appeals are extant in the archives, and have even been annotated and printed. As the modern student analyzes them, taking hours to read and study each one, he marvels at the time the meticulous King Philip must have spent over such minutiae.

Monsenhor knew the king and the court very well indeed, and realized that if he wanted a prompt and favorable royal response he had best take ship himself. Therefore he set forth personally to dispatch his business at the Escorial and at the Vatican, planning to get back to Goa around September, 1588, after an absence of about twenty months.

It will be remembered that in 1582, when Brother Vicentius allowed himself to be persuaded by the king to accept the archbishopric, despite his distaste for the voyage, the king promised to reward him, after five years in Goa, with an appointment to a still loftier post. Five years had now passed, during which Monsenhor had labored in his difficult office apparently to the complete satisfaction of both the monarch and the Holy Father. He had arrived in September, 1582, and now it was January, 1587. They had been difficult years. He had occupied the chair less than a year when he had to undergo the anguish of the loss of Japan to Christianity when in July, 1583, the great Jesuit Rodolfo Acquaviva and his associates were martyred. In the following year he convoked the notable Third Provincial Council of Goa, over which he presided with wisdom and vigor, which was attended by Catholic clergy from all the Orient. There were five lengthy sessions held between June, 1585, and November, 1585, wherein many reforms and advances were brought about in the parishes, colleges, hospitals and convents in the East.

Archbishop João Vicente da Fonseca was untiring in his zeal to correct the abuses in the lay government as well as in the church and did not hesitate to upbraid the viceroy and some of his ministers for condoning acts of corruption. On one occasion he imposed a severe penance upon a woman of influence and high rank who had given occasion of public scandal. He had been a capable administrator and an inspiring and stimulating leader, and by his high moral character and zeal he had made a great contribution to the purification of the Church.

Nevertheless now, instead of asking for the promised advancement in Portugal, Monsenhor seems to have felt an obligation to continue in office in Goa, and meant to ask for complete authority to reform certain unnamed abuses, apparently in the vice-regal lay administration. Being a man of action, he proceeded accordingly, despite his expressed abhorrence for the squalor, delay and distress of the voyage. He discharged all his staff, except a few who would serve him aboard ship, his steward and Jan, the last two being left in the palace. Jan had won his chief's confidence, and his duties would be "to receive his rents and keepe his house and because as then the golden Iubeleo or pardon of Roome was newly brought into the Indies [called *La Santa Crusada*] being granted to the end, that with the mony that should bee gathered by vertue thereof, the Captives in Africa or Barbara that had been taken prisoners in the bataille, wherein Dom Sebastian, King of Portugal was slaine, should be redeemed, which was sent unto the Archbishop, being appointed the Romane Apostolicke Commissarie and for the same made me general clarke [*Schryverschap van de cobransa, Klerk der belastingen*] throughout al India [to keep account of the said receits] and gave me one of the Keyes of the chest, wherein the monie lay, with a good stipend, and other profits belonging to the same, during the time of his absence; thereby the rather to bind mee that I should remaine in his house, and keep the same till his returne againe, as I had promised unto him."

This promotion to a post of distinction in which he would have independent authority in dealing with fiscal officials throughout *Asia Portuguesa*, with an aura of delegated Papal sanction, was indeed a great step upward for the young man from Enkhuizen, who was then only twenty-five years old. He now could look forward to a serene lay career in the strongly entrenched and influential ecclesiastical establishment of Portuguese Asia. Since his master stood so high in the favor of both king and Pope, it was certain that he would return to Goa with some professional preferment for his young protégé. No doubt all Goa recognized this and smiled upon the serious, hard-working young Collector of Taxes, except perhaps the entourage of the viceroy, against whom Monsenhor intended to lay charges before the throne.

The nature of the proposed indictment is unknown, nor is there anywhere suggested any inkling of the causes of disagreement between Monsenhor and his formerly warm friend and colleague, Dom Duarte de Meneses, the viceroy. Both were men of high ideals and noble character who, as members of the ancient feudal aristocracy, had accepted Philip as the rightful heir to the Portuguese throne and had transferred to him the loyal service they had previously rendered to Dom Sebastian and to the Cardinal-King. Meneses should have been congenial to Monsenhor in the field of scholarship, as he was a good Latinist and accomplished in writing Italian verse. His military record as Governor of Tangier, in Morocco, had earned his appointment to the vice-royalty, where, as we have seen, he had won glory in several campaigns, particularly in the relief of Malacca. As governor, he showed himself a lover of justice and was said to have been completely free of personal avarice. However, like so many other good soldiers who have been placed in top civil posts, he was guileless in his trust of the bureaucrats who headed governmental departments, and he made favorites of career politicians who betrayed his confidence

Bramenes cum mortuus est, secundum eorum legem crematur, uxor autem ejus, præ amore, sese vivam in ignem cum illo conjicit.

De Bramene doot wesende wort nae haer wet verbrant, en zyn vrouwe wt liefde haers mans, verbrant haer levendich met hem.

SUTTEE. *In the ceremony of suttee the widow, dressed for a festival, is cremated along with her husband's corpse. Here she flings herself into the pyre to the sound of music and drumming; she was probably heavily drugged for the ordeal. Linschoten notes that the custom of suttee was instituted as a deterrent to the prevalent crime of husband-poisoning, rather than as a sign of wifely devotion.*

Nuptiarum ritus. et epulæ in Provincia
Ballagatę fupra Goam.

Maniere van bruyloft int Lant van
Ballagatę achter Goa gelegen.

A WEDDING PROCESSION *in the Malabar village of Ballagate,
near Goa. Musicians lead the way with pipe and drum, followed by
the bride and groom, while friends and family members bring up the
rear.*

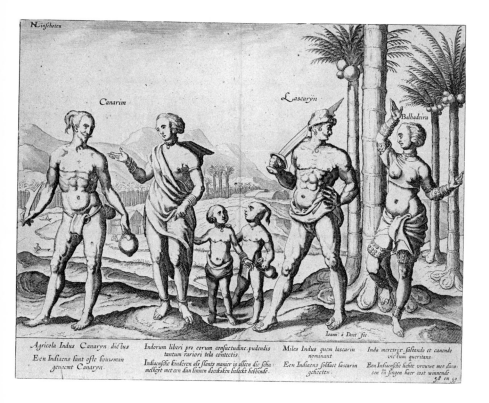

TYPES OF INHABITANTS OF INDIA. *At the left is a family
of farmers from Canaryn, including two children; Linschoten carefully
shows how their garments are worn. At the right are a dancing girl,
described by Linschoten as a light woman, and a lascar whom she
seems to be beguiling; the latter is a tough soldier native to the region
of Goa.*

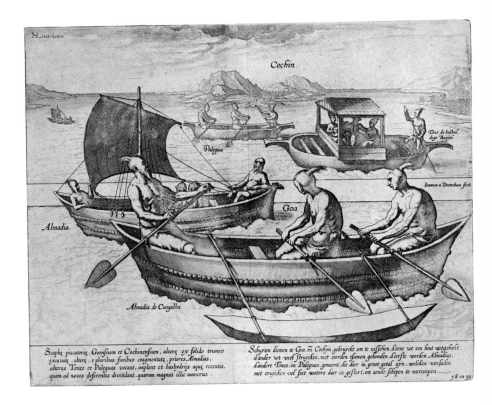

THE KING OF COCHIN ON AN ELEPHANT. *The King of Cochin was the most important and loyal Indian ally of the Portuguese. Here he is shown on a remarkably human-looking royal elephant, with his bodyguard of Nairs, who were first-class fighting men.*

SHRINE AND MOSQUE. *A Brahman shrine, at the left, which Linschoten called a pagoda, complete with a holy bull and worshipers, was a striking aspect of the Indian landscape then as now. The followers of Mohammed were also very numerous, and on the right Linschoten shows a solid mosque, with a railed cupola at the top instead of a minaret.*

Lectuli, et ratio, quibus Chinę proceres primarij (Mandorinos vocant) gestantur, cymbęq̃, quibus ad oblectationem per fluvios vehuntur.

Maniere als haer die Mandoryns van China welcke het princepael gouvernement hebben laten draegen en op die revieren vermeyen vaeren.

32 en 33

CHINESE MANDARINS. *This scene shows a mandarin with his retinue traveling by river boat throughout his province, while on shore another mandarin receives a petition from a merchant, abacus in hand. Linschoten must have drawn this picture from hearsay and imagination, for the Chinese Empire was totally unknown to Europeans.*

Naves e China et Iava velis ex arundine
contextis et anchoris ligneis.

Schepen van China eñ Iava met rietten
fejlen eñ houten anckers

A CHINESE JUNK *with two steering oars, the most efficient and seaworthy of Oriental sea craft. For centuries junks have been known in the harbors of all the Orient, from the Arabian Sea and Persian Gulf throughout the Indian Ocean to Oceania and the Philippines. In his caption, Linschoten called attention to the rattan sails and wooden anchor.*

and who engaged in corrupt transactions of which they kept him in ignorance.

It is also probable that some members of the viceroy's cabinet were, without his knowledge, partisans of Dom Antonio, and even in the secret pay of England and France. Just as Philip had his aristocratic spies behind every throne, so also the French and English monarchs, as well as the Prince of Orange, suborned trusted officials of the Spanish court and received copies of the king's most secret correspondence. Meneses would listen to no criticism of his favorites, and it was this blind loyalty to his subordinates that perhaps caused his break with his old friend Monsenhor. Presumably, the Archbishop had attacked members of the viceroy's council and some of the highly placed ecclesiastics identified with them, and Meneses was drawn into the dispute in their defense.

At all events, after the departure of the primate those whom he had threatened to denounce showed no great apprehension and continued in the activities which Monsenhor had so vigorously condemned. Then suddenly, on May 11, 1588, a report arrived from the Governor of Ormuz that a Venetian trader there had received an overland dispatch from Venice which told of the safe arrival of the Archbishop in Spain, where he had been received with the highest honors by the king. This good news, which indeed was only what might have been expected, elated Jan and all the other friends of Monsenhor, who could now be sure of preferment; but it was received with incredulous surprise and obvious terror by the viceroy. It was as if a bomb had been exploded under the table when the Cabinet was assembled about it. The shock of the news to the viceroy was so dramatic as to awaken a suspicion that the cabal had plotted to prevent Monsenhor's arrival at Court, and their panic was almost prima-facie evidence of guilt. Viceroy de Meneses had just enjoyed a triumphant celebration of the victory at Malacca, and up to the moment of reading the dispatch from Ormuz had been serenely complacent, but the news came like a dagger thrust. He collapsed, and within four days he died in a state of acute fright and depression which was ascribed to fear of the vengeance which the relentless Philip would visit not only upon him, but upon his family and his estate, and to the eternal dishonor of his noble name.

The conspirators who had implicated the poor viceroy in their plot must have awaited with apprehension the arrival of the annual fleet, which was sure to carry a royal summons to bring them to justice. It was common in *Asia Portuguesa* for a Christian who had run afoul of the law, if he could not obtain immunity through bribery, to seek asylum in one of the nearby native kingdoms, where a European refugee was welcomed and given remunerative employment for whatever skills he possessed. If he became an apostate from Christianity, he was all the more honored and advanced.

Therefore, having received this ominous warning, the enemies of the Archbishop no doubt were planning to escape when the expected blow should fall in the shape of a royal condemnation, which would arrive with the Spice Fleet in four months' time. To their tremendous relief and delight, nothing of the kind happened. On September 16, 1588, the *Sam Thomas*, the first of the five ships of that year's *Carreira da India*, brought the news that the Archbishop had died suddenly at sea, apparently from poison, over a year earlier, on August 4, 1587, only eight days out of Lisbon.

The art of discreetly poisoning a political rival had been highly developed in Italy in the Renaissance, had been brought from there to France and Spain, and was in widespread use as a weapon of court intrigue. Jan reported that such poisoning was also widely practiced in Goa, so the suspicion in this case was a natural one. (He remarked incidentally that Portuguese husbands were often poisoned by their native wives. Long before Portuguese days in India, the rite of suttee, in which the wife had to perish on the funeral pyre of her husband, had been originally introduced as a deterrent to husband-poisoning.)

Jan genuinely mourned his master's loss, and sadly wrote: "An houre before his death he seemed to be as well as ever he was in all his life and sodainly he was taken so sick yt he had not the leasure to make his will, but dyed presently, and voyded at the least a quart of poyson out of his body.

"To be short, he was cloathed in his Bishop's apparell, with his Myter on his heade and rings upon his fingers and put into a coffin, and so throwne unto the sea.

"These newes made many sorrowful hartes in India, of such as were his welwillers and friendes; and to the contrarie such as hated him were glad and reioyced for he had beene earnest to reprehend and correct them for their faultes; but none lost more by it than we that were his servantes, which looked for great preferment by him, as without doubt hee ment to have obtained it of the King, as being one of the principallest occasions of his going into Portingal, but death altred all.

"And although at that time my meaning and intent was to stay the comming of my Lord Archbishop and to continue longer there, yea possible while I lived; yet upon these newes I was wholly altered in my purpose. And that which perswaded me most thereunto was the losse of my brother William Tin that had beene with me in India, who sailing from Setúbal in Portingal towards Hamborough taking their course on the back side of England, was cast away and never could be heard of neyther ship nor men."

Goa

Jan's Political Downfall

JAN'S COMFORTABLY SECURE Indian world, with its promise of a brilliant career, had suddenly turned to ashes and sorrow. He was now tasting the bitterness inherent in political office, when the inevitable turn of Fortune's wheel strips an incumbent of his livelihood and of the support of his associates. Overnight he found himself an alien in an indifferent and hostile land. The news received from Enkhuizen through Dutch cannoniers on the newly arrived fleet made him homesick. His father and both his half-brothers were dead, and his mother was trying to operate the *Haarlem Arms*, back home in Enkhuizen, with the help of his younger brother and sister, who had now grown to maturity.

In Goa all seemed changed, and no one thought of the former rulers of the colony. A new viceroy, Emanuel Sousa Coutinho, had arrived, as well as a new Archbishop with new subordinates. Jan had to vacate his snug quarters in the palace, turn over to cold and patronizing successors his key to the money chest, and render an accounting to them of his stewardship. His importance was gone; he was a shrunken personage.

Moreover, the newly arrived officeholders reflected the new, less tolerant attitude of Lisbon toward the rebels and heretics in His Majesty's disobedient provinces in the Northern Netherlands, of which Enkhuizen was a center of defiance. The contumacious William of Orange was dead, as was also the so-called King of the Netherlands, the French Duke of Anjou. Things were looking much better for King Philip, who had seized all Dutch ships in Portuguese harbors and closed the port of Lisbon to Dutch trade. Jan's personal safety might be in jeopardy if this trend continued. An invincible armada was reported poised to descend upon England and strike down Elizabeth, the excommunicated sister-in-law of Philip. After that, Enkhuizen and all North Holland would be brought to a cruel justice.

Jan's position was now uncomfortable, for the foes of his late master had retained power in Goa; after the voice of their accuser had been stilled, no charges whatsoever had been made against them in Portugal. Jan had no proof concerning the identity of the murderer of the kindly man whom he had loved and revered, but it was logical to place the blame upon those whom Monsenhor had intended to expose. These were the same men to whom he now had to report as his masters. He realized it would be prudent to get back to Europe, but he dissembled and made an apparent effort to secure a permanent governmental position in Goa. He was afraid that he would not be officially licensed to leave for home if he asked permission, as it was now quite well known that he had acquired an intimate knowledge of the economy of *Asia Portuguesa* and also had accumulated much data on the political and military situation there. So, as he said in the *Itinerario*, he took care to be identified as a permanent member of the community and to appear to want to stay there for life. In any event, all passages had been taken on the fleet now making ready to sail, and at best he might plan to get away with the next overland caravan of foreign traders which would leave within half a year by ship to Ormuz and thence by land to Aleppo. He could work toward getting a limited passport for a temporary absence, along with the other aliens who regularly left Goa with an outgoing caravan and returned with the subsequent incoming one.

A Chance to Escape

T H E N, suddenly, a God-given opportunity arose for him to escape with the annual pepper fleet after all; the fleet was still at Goa and ready to clear for Lisbon. An unusual situation had arisen, and, with his insight into underlying conditions, Jan recognized an opportunity to get official license to sail at once. There had been a very heavy pepper crop that season, and more bulk in pepper was being offered for export than could be accommodated by the five naos then loading for Europe. The treasury at Goa was heavily burdened with debt, as a result of the costs of several recent wars, and was anxious to convert this commodity surplus into silver *reales* from the hoard of the German pepper factors at Cochin. Also, there were political reasons for allaying the unrest among the Malabar native states by relieving them of their glut of pepper.

The viceroy's Council therefore invoked some long-unused provisions in the royal contract with the pepper trust, which was made up of German bankers known as the "Pepper Farmers." These clauses gave the viceroy the option of purchasing any surplus of the pepper crop and re-selling it for the royal account after first giving the Pepper Farmers the refusal of it.

There was, however, an obstacle to overcome before the pepper surplus could be exported to Europe; another German monopoly, known as the "Ship Farmers," had a contract with the Crown limiting the annual *Carreira da India* to five naos in all. However, an escape clause existed in this charter whereby the Crown, in case of a pepper glut, could purchase an additional nao if one were available, after giving the Ship Farmers the refusal of it.

The Council now began to think of acquiring the fine fourteen-hundred-ton nao *Santa Cruz*, built of teak by the Rajah of Cochin who had sold it to the Captain of the Japan Voyage. It had just returned from that three-year cruise, on which Jan's friend, Dirck Gerritszoon of Enkhuizen, had served as constable. After some negotiating, the Council purchased the vessel for ten thousand ducats, with the German banking syndicate of the Fuggers and Welsers financing the transaction. The seller made it a condition of the sale that the master and the constable should be retained in their posts on the ship, thus assuring for his friends their passage back to Europe.

Jan watched these negotiations very closely and anxiously, for he was on friendly terms with the German factors, and had secured their promise that if the deal was successfully consummated they would employ him as the factor for the Pepper Farmers on the *Santa Cruz*. This position was somewhat similar to that of the supercargo on an ordinary ship; it was an enviable post, for it carried with it not only transportation home, but the use of a cabin with daily rations provided, and certain other perquisites, all at the expense of the Crown.

Jan's Social Life in Goa

THEREFORE when the transactions were completed Jan was overjoyed, particularly since he would have his fellow townsman, Dirck Gerritszoon, as a shipmate. Yet at the same time he felt a very understandable wave of sadness, and what he wrote upon that occasion incidentally betrayed that perhaps many of his later published criticisms of life in Goa should not be taken literally. He wrote that, having obtained his passport and secured the various other required certificates, "I tooke my leave of all my friends and acquaintances not without great griefe, as hee that was to depart out of his second naturall dwelling place or second fatherland by reason of the great and long continuance that I had made in those countries, so that I was in a manner halfe disswaded from my pretended voyage. But in the end the remembrance and affection of my true natural countrie got the upper hand and over-ruled me, making me wholy to forget my conceipt unto the contrarie; and so committing myselfe and my affaires unto God, who onely can direct and help us and give good success to all endivours I entred into my new pretended course."

This circumspect, rather sentimental conclusion was a politic one to publish in Holland five years later, when Portugal was an avowed enemy, but there can be little doubt that Jan left Golden Goa very reluctantly and only for safety's sake.

Although we have no knowledge of any such affair, the pangs of parting from a beloved mistress may well have been one cause of his indecision. Indeed, it would have been highly unlikely for a healthy young man of twenty-five to have refrained from forming such a tie, and we know from a subsequent incident in Enkhuizen that Jan was hardly strait-laced where such matters were concerned. In the *Itinerario*, he wrote that the climate, the diet, and the way of life in Goa developed female sensuality to the point of a consuming appetite. Where polygamy and concubinage were the established and religiously approved rule and the harem a cherished institution, and where most Christians owned female slaves who were legally subject to their owner's wishes, it could not have been expected that conventional Dutch standards would apply. Indeed, when the Dutch themselves later began to colonize the Indies, their practices in matters of sex and sobriety gave rise to much scandal. There were not many Portuguese women in the colonies, but they found the hot climate of India much more supportable than did the Dutch women, who arrived later. Jan's social circle appears to have been made up entirely of aliens, and doubtless included few if any European women. In this convivial, happy-go-lucky group, which had so many picnics, boating parties, music festivals, and dances in the lush gardens to which they were all devoted, there was doubtless for the European men the delightful companionship of the complaisant and charming native women.

The foreign colony to which Jan belonged in Goa lived and acted in the same manner as, much later, European colonists did everywhere in the nineteenth and early twentieth centuries. They revelled in their superior social and economic status as a lordly race, with many cheap and willing servants, an abundant and inexpensive table, and no need to perform manual labor of any kind. In all colonies, even in our own age, it has been the practice for people of the lower middle class, being far from home, to pretend to an elevated social standing. This was particularly true of the Portuguese in sixteenth century Goa, since they have as a race always held such matters as escutcheons and lofty lineage to be of very great importance.

Jan Huyghen becomes van Linschoten

IN THE ORIENT, where "face" has such value, the natural ceremoniousness of the Portuguese was particularly accentuated. Jan satirized their pretentious swagger and pomp, their airs of nobility, and he was equally biting and even humorous in describing the jealous punctilio of persons of exalted rank who were prickly about any slight upon their dignity. Yet in spite of all his disdain for false pretensions, Jan Huyghen himself came home from India bearing the assumed patronym "van Linschoten," which modern historical research has never been able to explain. It has been suggested that, having begun to rise in Portuguese officialdom, he probably saw fit to adopt the name van Linschoten to indicate that he belonged to the gentry in his own country. The particle "van" in Dutch, like "de" or "da" in Portuguese, was then (as now) part of many noble Dutch names. It might well, therefore, have been impressive to the highly rank-conscious Portuguese with whom he needed to advance himself.

At Liberty

W H E N he secured his passport, Jan discreetly pledged that he was only taking a leave of absence and would return to Goa. However, in granting him his leave the government of *Asia Portuguesa* made an egregious error, for they let slip out of their grasp the man who, more than any other, was destined to strike a fatal blow against their safety and continued prosperity.

On November 23, 1588, the *Santa Cruz* crossed the bar of the Mandovi River and put out to sea from Goa; Jan rejoiced to have escaped from his enemies and to be homeward bound. On November 28th, the ship anchored at the fortified port of Honor, on the Malabar Coast, and by December 6th, 6,700 quintals of first-grade pepper had all been very carefully stowed in bags in sealed compartments. The *Santa Cruz* then sailed south, keeping well inshore because daily, then as now, from midnight until noon there was a powerful wind offshore, and then for the next twelve hours there was a steady west wind blowing landward. However, as the offshore, seaward wind had the greater force, it was necessary for the *Santa Cruz* to hug the coast; otherwise, if it was blown out to sea, it would not have been able to get back to the coast again and, as Jan said, "the ship would lose its voyage to Portugal as has often happened." It is occasional phrases such as this, cropping up as they do in the maritime records of the fifteenth and early sixteenth centuries, that remind us how lubberly the best ships of those days were, and how little able to sail closely into the wind.

The alongshore course was a highly scenic one, and Jan wrote: "All the coast of Malabar is verie pleasant to behold: for that they sayle so close unto it that a man may tell everie hill valley and tree that is therein, being very greene and fair land."

On December 11th they made port at the important fortified city of Cananore, where they lay for a day and a half shipping reserve spars, cordage and other marine supplies; then, leaving Cananore, they sailed down the coast past unfriendly Calicut, where Vasco da Gama had made his entry almost a century earlier. Finally, on Christmas Eve, they anchored at Cochin, the former capital of *Asia Portuguesa*, where they completed vitualling and watering the ship and stowing cargo, much of which was excess and therefore had to be lashed on deck. Indeed, such excess cargo constituted a great hazard, and it should by no means have been taken aboard.

The other five ships of the fleet were already in Cochin when the *Santa Cruz* arrived, and they planned to sail out at intervals in due order. The oldest and least seaworthy, the *Santa Maria*, was given precedence in order to get past the dreaded Cape of Good Hope as early as possible, because the stormy season was now developing and every day's delay meant that much greater hazard.

The Manuscript

As FINAL preparations were made to sail out into the Indian Ocean, Jan reflected that he had now passed five years and four months in *Asia Portuguesa*. He was carrying back with him a profound and extensive knowledge of all aspects of that hitherto mystery-shrouded wonderland, whose secrets he was to unveil to his countrymen to their immense advantage.

It is indicative of the general civil freedom of the Portuguese community that Jan was allowed to carry aboard with him not only his voluminous notes, but also a number of botanical and zoological specimens which he later displayed in Enkhuizen. It is questionable whether he would have been permitted such liberty in the days before the rebellious discontent in the Indian government due to the Spanish rule in Portugal. Perhaps, however, he had greased the palm of some government inspector. In any case, if the truth had been known, the export of the manuscripts in his chest was far more dangerous to *Asia Portuguesa* than a mere pouch of diamonds or rubies, which he would have had to register and upon which the King would have levied heavy duties. The port authorities at Cochin were generally meticulous in their examination and recording of the contents of all chests, but Jan doubtless convinced the unimaginative inspectors that written notes were harmless. He would not have passed the scrutiny in his Dutch homeland so easily, for we know that later, upon his return to Texel from his two polar voyages, his ship was not allowed to dock nor were any of the crew allowed to land for several days, until all logs, maps and notes descriptive of the areas visited were looked into and carried away by the representatives of the Admiralty. Such procedure had also been the invariable rule in the port of Lisbon in the reigns of Dom Manuel and of Dom John III.

It is not known exactly whether the bulk of the text of the *Itinerario* was actually written in Goa, but it probably was revised during this return voyage on the *Santa Cruz* to the Azores and during Jan's two years' stay at Terceira Island, where he had ample leisure to study and write, and many opportunities to check the accuracy of his facts.

His description of Goa, which was based on personal experience, is a remarkable work; in it he described, down to the minutest details, the domestic life of the lower middle-class Portuguese, mestizos and alien Europeans with whom he was thrown. Sometimes his biased attitude toward the Portuguese calls for rectification and perhaps allowance for a political or nationalistic motive, but this is to be expected. It is somewhat disappointing to the modern reader, used to personal confessions, that he maintained such complete objectivity about his subject that he did not reveal much concerning his own personal activities and experiences, although it is easy from what he has written to get to know his character and manner of thinking.

Jan made a valuable contribution to economic history by giving complete data on the prices, wages, weights, measures, currency, and foreign exchange in *Asia Portuguesa* at that time, as well as in his businesslike exposition of the flow of intra-Indian commerce, which included a listing of markets, commodities and products. His ethnographic and botanical descriptions are surpassingly well illustrated by his own remarkable sketches, and his superior charts drawn on the spot explain with great explicitness the geographical relationships of the places and regions about which he wrote, which were then quite unknown to his Dutch and North European readers.

At first glance, it is evident that Jan Huyghen van Linschoten failed to touch upon various salient and important aspects of life in Golden Goa at the peak of its prosperity, but careful reading of the *Itinerario* reveals the depth and comprehensiveness of his book. It is impossible not to pay homage to it as one of the monumental geographical works of the Western World.

CHAPTER V

The Homeward Voyage

ON JANUARY 20, 1589, after the complement of the *Santa Cruz* had received Holy Communion in a body at High Mass in the Cathedral at Cochin, the ship's trumpeter, accompanied by a standard bearer and an honor guard, took position in the Cathedral Plaza and sounded the alert. It was a warning that the great nao was about to sail, the last of that year's fleet of six pepper ships bound for Lisbon.

Three weeks earlier, on January 1st, the *Santa Maria* had weighed anchor and set sail for the squadron's rendezvous at the Atlantic Island of St. Helena. The others had followed at intervals of several days, the latest having been the large new ship, the *Sam Tomé*, which had cleared on the 15th with much formality and ceremony, for it had a group of notable personages aboard. One of its distinguished passengers was Dom Paulo de Lima Pereira, the hero of Malacca, who with his family and entourage was returning home with a rich fortune, to be honored by the king for his brilliant services during his career of thirty years in India.

The *Santa Cruz* now lay anchored in the calm sea about a mile offshore, and as Jan and others of the crew were rowed out, they made way for a shore-bound flotilla of heavy barges carrying the stevedores and porters who had just completed the lading. Numerous small boats clustered about the nao, full of friends and relatives bringing bon voyage gifts and making weeping farewells.

The Homeward Voyage

The Ship's Complement

T H E *Santa Cruz* was particularly popular with the people of Cochin, who were proud that so magnificent a nao had been designed and built there by their own Rajah. Indeed, it was named for the city, for the official Western name of Cochin was Santa Cruz. The record of achievement of the sturdy, teak-built vessel during its recent three-year cruise to Japan had enhanced its local prestige. However, most of the veteran sailors who had learned to handle the bulky, fourteen-hundred-ton craft in the typhoon seas were not now aboard to help navigate it on its perilous passage around the Cape of Good Hope. Only two of the wardroom personnel had been retained, the boatswain and the constable, Dirck Gerritszoon of Enkhuizen. These two officers had prevailed upon the former owner, as we have seen, to stipulate that they should keep their berths.

Jan wrote that, of the fifty sailors signed aboard the *Santa Cruz*, not ten knew how to handle the tiller and hardly more than that had ever been sailors. In view of the maritime hazards to which the *Santa Cruz* could expect to be exposed during the voyage to Portugal, this should have been a cause of uneasiness, if it was known, to the relatives of the passengers who came to wish them Godspeed, for certainly the inexperience of the crew entailed an even greater risk than usual. The cause of this disturbing situation was that, when it was known the additional nao would be added to the usual pepper fleet of five and therefore a full crew for it would be recruited, a great demand arose for positions aboard ship on the part of persons who wanted to get back to Europe but had been unable to secure passage, some because of the lack of a license or passport, some because no space had been available, and probably even more because they could not afford to pay for the passage.

Many persons were stranded in *India Portuguesa* for lack of funds for a return ticket. Among these were a number of soldiers who had been conscripted for the Indian army, who had, of course, received free passage and rations on the outward voyage, but who, having completed the required minimum of three years of service, found that the Crown only provided rations on the homeward trip for about a month, that is, about as far as Mozambique, or well east of the Cape of Good Hope. This meant that almost all the fifteen hundred so-called soldiers who were brought out annually against their will had to spend the rest of their lives in India, marry native women (if they married at all), and never see the homeland again. This was, of course, a matter of established crown policy designed to provide permanent Portuguese settlers, and it should be added that the

Crown did provide certain substantial economic privileges to honorably discharged soldiers who married and settled down in the colony.

About the only way, therefore, for the average subaltern or common soldier to get back home, unless he was lucky enough to win prize money, was to become attached to the household of some wealthy *fidalgo* who might take him back to Portugal in his retinue. The rich aristocrats in Goa generally maintained ostentatious establishments of retainers and slaves and supported a bodyguard of halberdiers or musketeers drawn from the army. As most of the *fidalgos* participated in the annual summer military campaigns of the viceroy, it was their custom to employ these feudal retainers at the king's expense, except during the monsoon season, when they supported them in their households, displaying the general pomp with which the vice-regal court was conducted. (Such colonial pretentiousness was then, as later, partly a matter of policy, and meant to impress the natives.) The prominent Portuguese who sailed for home used to depart with great ceremony and éclat, and for this reason generally took a squad of pikemen or arquebusiers aboard with them.

This system of aristocratic patronage was an effective one. The most far-sighted and ambitious soldiers sought to become attached to an influential noble, not only because they thereby gained preferment, promotion, and the chance of an eventual return to Portugal, but also because a small private army might in an engagement become the spearhead of attack, and its members sometimes, if the attack succeeded, could lay hands on immensely rich booty. However, the ordinary soldiers, who did not belong to such elite corps, barely managed to eke out their idle existence in Goa during the unfavorable monsoon season, and it was these men who were most eager to disguise themselves as sailors and try to get employment in the crew of the homeward bound nao *Santa Cruz*.

Acceptance as a crew member meant not only free passage with rations and a pittance in pay, but also the privilege of carrying back two "chests" to Lisbon, one small chest upon which the seaman had to pay neither freight nor customs duties, and a second, similar one, called a "liberty chest," upon which no freight was charged but whose contents were subject to full customs duty at Lisbon. The sailors, who had no money to invest in the contents of such chests of their own, therefore agreed to carry their chests for the account of others; these rights found a regular market in Goa and Cochin and were eagerly bought up by merchants for cash sums—money which in reality represented the sailor's wages for the return voyage.

The privilege of hiring seamen for the return voyage was one of the legal perquisites of the admiralty officer at Goa. He charged a fee for licensing an applicant and signing him on as a foremast hand. The amount of the fee was as much as the traffic would bear; often it was very high indeed, if some poor, trapped man desperately wanted to get back to Europe.

The conditions of life before the mast on the return voyage were much more tolerable than on the outward run, because returning ships were not overcrowded with steerage passengers and hence sanitary conditions were better. Also, the holds had to be cleaned out before storing the king's pepper, and the presence of many aromatic spices was thought to have a purifying effect upon the air in the ship. At that time much weight was given by the medical profession to the "purity of the ayre" in one's environment, and therefore this benefit was emphasized aboard a pepper ship.

Moreover, the homeward bound ship's complement was made up of healthy men, instead of the wretched, diseased jailbirds who formed so large a part of the personnel of an outgoing nao. Instead of wearing polluted rags, as did the poor conscripts from Lisbon, the crew from India had a supply of clean linen clothing, which could be bought for a trifle in Goa; and, above all, there were always aboard a number of muscular and healthy Kaffir slaves from East Africa, acquired at small cost in India and fed inexpensively en route, who would become very valuable merchandise at the quayside in Lisbon. These slaves were kept busy policing and swabbing down the decks and, being men of great stamina, were detailed to man the pumps, which in all Indiamen were kept going continually. The greatest attraction of the homeward voyage, however, lay in the prospect that, after three months of travail at sea, the nao could expect to come to anchor at the Atlantic Island of St. Helena. They would tarry in this earthly paradise for a fortnight, while the scurvy sufferers and other sick or weakened members of the complement rested ashore in a balmy climate and refreshed themselves with all manner of fresh fruits, vegetables, game and seafood. Should their recovery be delayed, the sick would be left ashore with every comfort to await the arrival of next year's fleet. Even the unfortunate slaves, who were shackled in the hold while the nao lay in port, at least had a good rest and the benefit of the refreshing diet. Great care was taken to guard the slaves, however; the king had issued strict orders to prevent their escaping ashore, for once in the fastnesses of the high mountains they could not be caught. It was crown policy to keep St. Helena unpopulated, left only to the immense herds of edible game and myriads of wild hogs and sheep and cattle that easily subsisted there; all its amenities existed solely for the benefit of the annual visit of the homeward bound fleets of the *Carreira da India*, as the outward bound ships did not touch there.

However, it was somewhat too soon to anticipate at Cochin the delectable aspects of the Eden that was St. Helena, for many a man who sailed from Cochin would fail ever to set foot on its restful beaches. The dread-

The Homeward Voyage

ful casualties suffered in the *Carreira da India* on the outward voyages were generally in individual men, but even more terrifying losses on the homeward voyages were in terms of whole ships; and that meant that crews, passengers and treasure were lost as well. From almost every annual homeward bound fleet of five, the black tempests of the Cape inexorably swallowed up at least one without a trace.

The Overloading of Cargo

So when the family farewell parties came alongside the *Santa Cruz* in Cochin harbor and saw the overladen ship sunk so low in the water that its hawseholes and closed gunports were nearly awash even in that calm sea, they had misgivings indeed. When they clambered aboard and found the top deck and hatches piled seven layers high with chests, bales and bundles, the longboat and the skiff both filled with merchandise, and bundles even lashed to the shrouds and ratlines, they wondered with dismay how the crew could possibly haul on the sheets and braces, or quickly find their way forward or aft in an emergency. Any seafaring man among them could realize that it would be utterly impossible to put out the customary sweeps in a crisis, for each huge ashen oar required seven strong rowers to tug at it, and a great arc of the deck would have had to be kept free for them to tramp back and forth with their stroke.

To a practiced eye it was evident at once that, in the first gale, the roaring seas would soon sweep clean all the dunnage now piled so high. The even more fearsome question was whether, in one of those swift, sudden blows off Natal, the burdened *Santa Cruz* would be able to keep afloat until the cleansing rollers had washed away its heavy excess baggage. Could the laboring nao stay upright long enough to permit the frightened crew to jettison the deck cargo?

One did not have to be a marine expert to appraise the risk of disaster, for all in the port of Cochin remembered that, three years previously, in the fleet in which Monsenhor (of blessed memory) had sailed for home, the fine nao, *As Reliquias*, had suddenly foundered and been lost. This occurred because the factors had secretly and stupidly withdrawn the ballast, and substituted precious cinnamon for it. When the anchor was weighed and the sails dropped, the great nao, made top-heavy by an inordinate deck cargo, capsized and went down right there at Cochin, before the very eyes of hundreds who had come out in small boats to see off their friends and relatives. Fortunately, they were on the spot and were able to save the passengers and crew from drowning, but the ship with its precious cargo was a total loss. Jan was well aware of the risks he was facing, for he mentioned at length the needless loss of the *Reliquias* and apprehensively drew a parallel with the situation aboard the *Santa Cruz;* no one knew for sure, not even the captain or the pilot, how the cargo was stowed beneath the hatches. Jan wrote that they would be a month at sea before they were really in possession of all the facts about the stowage.

The *Itinerario* painted a bitterly critical picture of the abuses in the lading of the pepper naos, abuses which Jan correctly exposed with an acid pen. From the perspective of several centuries later, one can see that these failures in governmental regulation and, indeed, in the most elementary common sense in handling cargo, were by no means confined to the Portuguese in history. One by one, the colonial powers fell a prey to them. This fact, of course, does not excuse Portuguese weaknesses—but the reader must suspend his judgment until the whole situation is set forth. Jan erred in simply ascribing this lamentable and shocking breach of trust to the venality of Portuguese port officials and to the avarice and greed of Portuguese shippers, which he took to be inherent in the race and at the same time evidence of the corruption and decadence into which they had descended. In reality, the malpractices of longshoremen which he described still occur, to a greater or lesser degree, in many major ports in the modern world.

He might well have denounced the culpability, under given conditions, of most seafaring peoples, as well as the nearsighted economic policy of nations; instead, he indicted the Portuguese as the sole transgressors in an otherwise righteous world. Anyone at all familiar with stevedoring, wharfing, freighting and stowing will recognize practices which no doubt already prevailed on the piers of Tyre and Sidon.

What intensified the flagrancy of these abuses in *Asia Portuguesa* was the agonizing pressure that was felt by both shippers and passengers, squeezed not only by predatory stevedores and rapacious harbormasters, but by implacable urgencies created by the economic situation of the day. As so clearly described in the *Itinerario*, the situation was that, to get a consignment of merchandise or of personal effects safely stowed in an outgoing pepper nao, a shipper or passenger had to bribe the dockmaster or head stevedore; otherwise the goods would be left on deck at the mercy of the elements. The scathing manner in which Jan so tellingly described this practice not only makes the fee of the longshoreman appear to be a predatory extortion, but the legal fee of the Crown official a corrupt bribe. All payment exacted of the harassed shipper was ascribed by Jan to sheer commercial greed. In view of the tragic and heart-rending disasters which resulted from this overloading of the naos, the narrator took a somewhat smug satisfaction in placing the blame first upon a criminal and callous attitude on the part of the stevedore, who was exempt from any penalties and could safely wash his hands of guilt while pocketing the fruits of his

The Homeward Voyage

rapacity, the second upon the shoulders of the Admiralty, whose bureaucrats were implicit partners of the predatory longshoremen.

Looking at these deplorable excesses from a present-day perspective, one can first of all brush aside the prejudiced Dutch indictment of the Portuguese in the *Itinerario*. When one weighs objectively the sixteenth-century European economic theory of colonial monopoly, one arrives at the following conclusions. First, the stevedores were not so much extorting bribes from the shippers, but to a degree were being suborned by them. Second, the shippers were victims of a vicious economic system, which drove them frantically to seek escape from disaster by offering bribes in excess of the normal fees of the stevedores' guild, so as to obtain not primarily a special advantage over their fellow shippers, but rather the particular safety of their own shipments. The basic guilt for this unrealistic abuse of good marine practice may be laid at the door of the prevailing and then universally accepted theory of monopoly, of demand created by artificial scarcities. This was preached as gospel by the economists of the age and widely practiced by the Hanseatic fiscal advisers of the Portuguese. It was later adopted in regard to India by both the English and the Dutch trading corporations which succeeded to the trade of *Asia Portuguesa*, who both later suffered unexplained losses of their overloaded ships just as the Portuguese before them had done.

It was in accordance with the economic theory of maintaining scarcity that the sailing of freighters from Lisbon to Goa was rigidly restricted by royal order to five naos a year; because of the vicissitudes of the seas, this averaged out to only three or four.

When these naos were loaded in India for the return trip, the two lowest decks were reserved exclusively for the king's pepper crop, which was sealed off in compartments intended to be waterproof. Space on the third deck was first held for the several other royal monopolies, such as saltpeter, indigo and cinnamon. Then came the substantial space held for the religious foundations, such as the Jesuit Hospital of the Misericordia, or poor house, and for other charitable institutions of the various orders. All these had important industrial, commercial or agricultural properties in India which had been bequeathed or donated to them, the products of which were converted into needed cash through export to Europe.

Much room was also needed to store the water, wine, food and wood necessary for an eight months' voyage, as well as the considerable supply of powder, cannonballs, small arms and armor for defense, and the sails, rope, spare canvas, spars, anchors, and reserve timbers for repairs. Then there were the sections for storage of the liberty chests of the captain, the officers and crew. There were a number of cubicles, or cabins, occupied by the officers of the ship, by the superior passengers and the clergy, and also for special use, such as the chapel and the sick bay. Then came sleeping quarters for the crew. Only at the end of the list was consideration given to space for the baggage of passengers and for the commercial exports of merchants.

These commercial exports represented the entire mass carriage of all commodities moving from the immensely productive peoples of South Asia and East Africa to the large consuming market of all Christendom. The only supplementary or competitive traffic was that of smuggled cargoes of dhows and booms via the Arabian and Red Seas, and the movement of goods by camelback and packtrain via Persia, Turkey and Syria, and much of this land-borne merchandise was siphoned off into Asia Minor and did not reach Europe.

The residual cargo space available in the hull for the immensely valuable bulk of ivory, silks, fine textiles, lacquerware, porcelains, dyes, pharmaceuticals and spices could not possibly have exceeded four hundred tons in cubic capacity on a ship like the *Santa Cruz*, one of the largest cargo carriers then afloat. Inasmuch as there were by law only five naos allowed to ply in the cross-Atlantic route in a whole year, it will be seen that the total maximum cargo space available for this whole mercantile exchange between the teeming continents amounted to only about two thousand tons, a pitifully inadequate capacity. It was less than what is offered today by a single medium-sized freighter—and there are thousands of such cargo carriers that now engage in the same east-west traffic. The stored-up pressure of the choked, mammoth volume of merchandise seeking an outlet was therefore irresistible and explosive.

Viewed from this perspective, one can see how blind and baneful were the efforts of the German and Italian monopolists who controlled this inter-continental trade to dam the mighty forces of international commerce. Any indictment of special cases of greed and corruption is shallow and superfical, as compared to the immense economic forces at play as titanic demand struggled against pigmy supply.

At that time there was no workable medium of foreign exchange between Europe and the Indies. Merchandise and gold or silver had to be personally transported by the merchant, and precious stones represented the only other convenient medium of transfer. Even a great noble like Paulo de Lima Pereira, who sailed on the *Sām Tomé* in company with the *Santa Cruz*, had physically to carry with him the fruits of his thirty years' struggle in the Portuguese Indian service. One could not simply ship one's possessions, one had to carry them in person. With Pereira's great influence, his bailiff perhaps did not have to bribe the stevedores to get space for the impedimenta, household slaves and retinue of his eminent and prestigious master, but the accommodation of such a large party necessitated the displacement of cargo capacity below decks needed to house the personal belongings of many lesser men. These others, too, were attempting to carry out their long dreamed-of plan of retirement to the home-land, and their whole fortunes were represented by their few cases of precious Indian products, the distillation of all their gains after years of struggle, plodding and sacrifice.

It is no wonder that any such man returning to the homeland would, in a frenzy of apprehension, offer the head stevedore an inordinate fee. At all costs he wished to avoid having his entire estate irretrievably left behind on the pier, at the mercy of dock thieves and wharf rats, or stored on the upper deck of the ship exposed to the elements and liable to jettison.

In those feverish hours before sailing in which all was in jeopardy, men worked in a frenzy. One can understand the ludicrous expedient of one desperate passenger, who paid the ship's commander to let him put his precious belongings in a skiff to be towed in the wake of the great nao, in the mad hope that it could miraculously be brought safely across the raging seas to the safe haven of Lisbon, so many leagues and so many months away. One can imagine the superstitious prayers and vows which he, poor man, must have muttered as he haunted the high stern of the nao and anxiously watched his stout little skiff wallowing briefly in the wake. In an atmosphere such as this, the extravagances of delirious men passed all bounds, and so-called greed and corruption took on a pitifully human aspect.

There was another motive for a shrewd shipper to pay a premium to the head stevedore to have his cargo stowed advantageously, and that was the terms of marine insurance. During some centuries, the Portuguese had developed a system of "general average insurance," probably derived from Genoa, whereby any loss or damage to any lot or part of the cargo was assessed against the whole freighting of the ship. General average has been described as "the extraordinary sacrifice or expenditure which must be contributed by all in the time of emergency or disaster in order to preserve a common venture." This had been in effect for Portuguese ships in the Atlantic traffic to Southampton and Bruges and to West African ports from Lisbon and Porto long before the initiation of the sixteenth century *Carreira da India*, but this system of general average insurance was never applied to the Indian run. Because the risk was so great, it was, of course, impossible to get any insurance coverage on deck cargo. The cost of insurance on the contents of the hold was very high, because there was no spreading of the loss against undamaged cargo, as under general average insurance. In a heavy gale off the Cape, it was customary, after throwing overboard the deck cargo and even the longboat and any other weighty material on deck, to open the hatches and to pull out and jettison whatever material came to hand. Therefore many a long-headed shipper paid the head stevedore a good bonus not only to stow his shipment below decks, but also to place it in an inaccessible part of the hull where it would not be sacrificed for the good of the ship. In such a case, neither rapacity nor greed could reasonably be charged.

A nao was supposed to have been put into first class shape before clearing for the homeward trip, and the royal regulations required that before the port authorities could give clearance papers, the captain, pilot and master should certify under oath that the ship was fully seaworthy. However, this became a perfunctory matter, because a nao often had to set sail with considerable bilge already in the hold, due to leakage in the hull caused by slovenly reconditioning in the Arsenal at Goa.

Seaworthiness—A Suicidal Gamble

THE ODDS against a safe westward passage around the Cape of Good Hope in the sub-equatorial winter were due to the size and weight of the waves and to the unpredictable shifting of the gales. Even a modern steamer has a difficult time combatting these furious tempests. The returning sixteenth century Indiamen entered this severe trial under foolhardy handicaps which could have been avoided by prudence.

The first of these risks, which caused the loss of many fine ships, was negligence at the great royal shipyard at Goa, the largest industrial enterprise in the Orient. As soon as a nao reached Goa from Lisbon, it was the practice to anchor it for some days in the fresh water of the Mondavi River in order to clear the unsheathed wooden hull of the myriad barnacles and the mass of seaweed which had become attached to it during the extended ocean passage. As these parasites were saltwater creatures and growths, they were unable to survive in fresh water and soon dropped off and died. The dangerous *teredos*, or sea worms, whose boring could riddle a rudder post, also were driven off by the fresh water. Once these parasites were disposed of, it was necessary to make an inspection of the unsheathed hull to see what timbers had been honeycombed or what seams had been opened by the washing away of the caulking between the planks.

In the early days of the *Carreira da India* a ship at Goa recently in from Lisbon was always put into drydock and its hull was gone over very carefully, but toward the middle of the sixteenth century a much more superficial system of checking was adopted. This was copied from the procedure customary in Italy, in which a ship was tipped over at low tide by pulling upon ropes attached to the mastheads, and then held in that position while the still-wet hull was examined and treated. This easy method was perhaps satisfactory in the Mediterranean, where the voyages of the relatively light ships were not protracted and the hammering of the waves was not so strong as to be weakening to the planking of the hull.

The Homeward Voyage

However, this method was not sufficiently painstaking to meet the severe conditions of the *Carreira da India*, partly because the waterlogged timbers were not allowed to dry before inspection, but mainly because the careening of a ponderous nao in this manner, as if it were a coasting lugger or fishing boat, subjected the mighty hull to an intense strain which could either weaken some members or spring some seams. Such damage would not be manifest until the ship was heavily pounded in a Cape storm, but then serious, hidden leaks often developed somewhere beneath the cargo which the carpenter could not locate in time to prevent the seepage from outstripping the pumping. An overburdened and carelessly stowed nao, already staggering under the hammering impact of the giant seas, would suddenly fill, become waterlogged and unmanageable, and go down with all aboard. The disappearance of many a fine ship without a trace is thus ascribable to slovenly careening in the Indian shipyards.

Although improper stowing, overloading, poorly caulked and carelessly reconditioned hulls, and lubberly crews all greatly handicapped the naos in their struggle against the fiendish seas off Natal and around the Cape, a basic fact is that the naos were built too large in the first place to meet the conditions under which they operated. To design a durable hull made of many small wooden parts, pieced together and rendered waterproof only by caulking with bits of oakum, was difficult enough. But such a vessel could not be maneuvered, through the use of its sails, into a position that would lessen the impact of the waves, because its sails themselves were rendered completely unusable by the same gales whose strength it was desired to mitigate through their use. To survive the blows of a storm and maneuver against it, the ship required to be handily guided, and a huge sailing ship wholly lost its defensive mobility in a gale because the sails had to be furled.

When, at a later period, the British followed this same route around the Cape, they were reasonably successful as long as they kept their sailing ships to a size of less than five-hundred-tons burden; but once they began to make their Indiamen comparable in size to the naos of the *Carreira da India*, their losses began to approximate those of the Portuguese. Indeed, the test of rounding the Cape is so severe that, even with today's improvements in navigation, many modern steel-hulled steamers are lost in the black gales off that dreaded promontory.

Jan did not mention the grossly oversized hulls as an important cause of losses off the Cape. However, another chronicler, Faria y Sousa, when describing the period in which Jan was living at Goa, recorded that in the twelve years between 1579 and 1591, "because of overloading and of making them too big," twenty-two ships were lost. On the basis of five naos making the round trip annually, or sixty in twelve years, it is evident that over a third of the vessels of the *Carreira da India* went to the bottom with all their crews and treasure because of faulty design and operation during the very time of which Jan wrote.

This was a costly drain upon the manpower and wealth of Portugal, and occurred just at the juncture when the realm needed ships and seamen as never before. It was not only prostrate under the heel of Philip and weakened by the losses suffered in its forced participation in the great Spanish Armada against England, but it was on the very eve of naval war with Holland in the Orient.

Much of the alleged deterioration of Portuguese seamanship that Jan attacked in the *Itinerario* was due to the change in the design of the ships. Formerly the Portuguese had sailed warships, but now they operated capacious, peaceful freighters, manned not by picked seamen but by inferior, conscripted landsmen. The great voyage of Vasco da Gama from Lisbon to Calicut and back in 1499 took two years and two days and was a masterly feat. In accomplishing it he lost only one of his four ships. In the succeeding three-quarters of a century, from 1500 to 1579, only thirty-five ships were lost, about one in eleven, or less than nine percent. In the twenty-one years between 1589 and 1610, when the naos had become much larger (after Jan had returned to Enkhuizen and the harrying of the *Carreira da India* was in full cry) thirty-five naos were lost, about one in three, or thirty-three percent. In the entire century from 1550 to 1650, one hundred and twelve naos failed to return to Lisbon, or about twenty-two percent. After 1650, when galleons were used instead of the larger naos, casualties were sharply reduced. However, even in the period of the greatest losses, certain competent commanders suffered no mishaps and also had little sickness aboard their ships, so it is apparent that the quality of the command under which the naos were handled was an important factor.

Many sixteenth century Portuguese realized, of course, that the time-honored practice of paying only nominal salaries to the crews of the *Carreira da India* and letting them compensate themselves by so-called "ventures" contributed to the dangerous overloading of the naos. Therefore many suggestions were made that adequate salaries should be paid without any speculative bonus, but all such proposals failed of permanent adoption, despite the efforts of the government, largely because of the resistance of the officers and seamen themselves who preferred to speculate.

At the time of Jan's homeward voyage, the harrying by the English of the naos of the *Carreira da India* had just begun, and from then on the clumsiness of the naos became a greater handicap than ever. By 1622, the disadvantages of the huge, four-decked naos, of a thousand tons or over, was so strongly emphasized by many naval officers that, as previously stated, the king issued a decree that only galleons of three-hundred or four-hundred-tons burden, with only three decks, could be built. These were considered safer, faster, and able to be more effectively handled in combat than the naos; also, they could enter shallow harbors and be protected by the shore guns if pursued, while a nao of deep draught would have to lie outside and risk capture. One officer argued: "Five galleons only cost as much as three naos, and whereas five galleons sailing in company amount to a powerful fleet, three naos are but three helpless carracks which, after two voyages, have to be broken up in the yard—whereas the galleons can be used for many years in the coast-guard fleets. When five galleons leave India they all reach Portugal safely, except on occasions when God obviously wishes to punish, whereas when three naos leave Goa they cannot all arrive safely without a miracle, since they leave as doomed ships owing to their huge size and heavy lading, as may be seen from the case of the nao *Reliquias,* which foundered on setting sail without actually leaving port."

All Aboard!

O N T H E *Santa Cruz,* however, on January 20, 1589, few were thinking of all these considerations as the ship cast off the lines of the cluster of small boats carrying their farewell parties and the anchor was pulled up by the chanting members of the watch as they trod about the capstan. After the anchor had been catted and the nao had drifted clear of the shore boats, a twenty-one gun salute was fired from the ship in honor of the Rajah of Cochin and was answered from the citadel, as the foresail and spritsail caught the land breeze and the nao headed south-southeast out to sea. The great mainsail was then dropped, for in those days sail was made by dropping the course from the upper yard and was furled by being hoisted, just the reverse of the present-day method; it was a much slower and more awkward procedure, and a dangerous one when it was desired to take in sail in an emergency.

Jan said that, as they got under way, the sailors found it difficult to carry out the commands of the master because the deck "was piled so high with great pots and chests and hennes cages and such like that it seemeth rather a Labyrinth or a maze than a ship and so they committed themselves to the grace of God and set sayle."

Instead of sailing from Cochin southwest as ships always hitherto had done, they steered south-southeast, to avoid the Maldive Islands and the surrounding congeries of bars and reefs, upon which so many ships had been lost in the past, including the caravel in which Ferdinand Magellan had tried to sail homeward from Cochin as a passenger three-quarters of a century earlier.

By sailing in this direction at the command of the chief pilot of the flotilla, the pepper fleet officially blazed a new course. The chief pilot had first tried it on his previous voyage, and for his experiment he had been imprisoned upon his arrival at Lisbon. However, he had succeeded in convincing the Admiralty of the wisdom of his deviation, and the new course was thereafter adopted as the official route. The *Santa Cruz* held this course for a hundred and fifty Spanish miles, until the equator was crossed, and then at seven degrees south latitude the direction was changed to southwest by west to carry the nao directly to the Cape of Good Hope.

Because of the confusion and difficulty of getting about the cluttered deck, one of the ship's boys fell overboard. The *Santa Cruz* was immediately thrown into the wind to drift while the skiff was lowered, but the small boat was found loaded up with the liberty chests of the master; before these could be cleared out and the skiff brought to the bulwarks, the nao had drifted two miles and the child had long since been lost from view. This was a good example not only of the state of affairs aboardship, but also of the inability of the square-rigged naos to come about and sail into the wind.

On February 3rd, having been at sea for a fortnight, the *Santa Cruz* overhauled the great new ship, the *Sam Tomé*, which had sailed from Cochin five days earlier. As the ships converged and the pilot of the *Sam Tomé* identified the *Santa Cruz* by the whiteness of its rigging, which was of Indian coir instead of hemp, he evidently was chagrined; he had thought it to be one of the naos which had left Cochin earlier than his vessel. When he realized that he was being outstripped, he sheered away without speaking to the *Santa Cruz* and made all sail to leave it in his wake. Jan criticized this as childish rivalry, and said that because the Lisbon-bound naos engaged in a race to be the first to arrive at St. Helena, they took undue risks and jeopardized their safety. He stated that it was the false pride of the pilot of the *Sam Tomé* which led to the loss of that magnificent nao, all because he was pushing on to get to St. Helena first. He wrote that the big nao encountered a great gale off the Cape, and instead of running before it with reduced sail and thus being driven back eastward, the pilot stubbornly struck all sail and attempted to outride the storm with bare poles. Jan wrote: "He trusted over much in her strength so by the great force of the seas, together with the overlading, it was stricken in pieces and swallowed in the sea both men and all that was within her, as wee well might perceive comming onto the Cape, by the swimming of whole chests, pieces of masts and dead men tied unto bords and such like fearfull tokens. The other ships also that arived in the Iland of Saint Helena told us likewise that they had seene the like most pittiful sights, which was so small loss of so great treasure and so many men; so that wee which beheld it, thought ourselves not free from the like danger. Therefore it is manifestly seene that all the works and navigations of men are but meer vanities and that wee must onely put our trust in God, for that if God be not with us in our actions all our labor is in vain." Actually, we now know that the ship had run upon a reef before being pounded to pieces by the waves; some survivors of the *Sam Tomé* managed to land on the African coast, and after great suffering, a few reached Mozambique.

Heavy Weather

ON FEBRUARY 17, 1589, after having been at sea a month, the *Santa Cruz* ran into a heavy gale with enormous seas, and the yard of the main topsail was shattered. A continual north and northwest gale raged for a week. Then, after a week of fair wind, probably the southeast trade, the nao encountered a terrific east wind with heavy rain, and the seas were so great that the tiller broke in pieces, as likewise in quick succession did the two spare tillers with which they replaced it. In addition, the upper part of the rudder was splintered and washed away, and the loose rudder constantly thumped against the stern and was in danger of being wholly broken away. For two days the huge, rudderless hulk rolled and plunged and was flung about helplessly by the seas, which constantly rushed over the hatches and waist deck. On the second night the electrical phenomenon called the lights of St. Elmo appeared, crackling and glowing luminously like five candles set on the main yard; this was an omen of good weather, and heartened the sailors.

Jan crept with difficulty, as he said, "from under the hatches to note it," and to join in singing a misericordia as the master blew his silver whistle and commanded every man to salute it with "Salve Corpo Santo!" —"and therewithall our men being all in great feare and heaviness and almost out of hope began again to revive and be glad, as if thereby they had been fully assured of better comfort—and so wee had better weather."

Then a ship's council was held to decide whether to sail for Mozambique, steering the clumsy, huge *Santa Cruz* by means of two ropes fastened to the broken rudder, or to try to mend it. The carpenter extracted some suitable pieces of timber from a part of the inner hull and they tried in vain to fasten them together and fashion a new rudder, but this attempt was not successful. Then they made an anvil out of the breech block of a cannon and a bellows from two ox-hides, took a piece of iron from a broken small kedge anchor, and hammered out a steel strap; after two days' work they managed to bind together the broken rudder and to hang it in position. Sail was once more made, and as Jan piously said, "wee set forwards in the name of God and gave divers almes to Our Lady and the Saints with many promises of a pilgrimage and of a better life, as being in misery men commonly do."

The next day the pilot was able to shoot the sun and learned that the ship was in the latitude of Natal. Of course he could not tell the longitude, but guessed it to be about 400 Spanish miles to seaward. Jan said all were disturbed at their position, as apparently they were in the most treacherous waters of the whole voyage, waters which most thought more dangerous than at the Cape. Therefore, in accordance with the superstitious seafaring custom of the time, they threw overboard a treasured article which they hoped would propitiate the tutelary deity or devil of that place.

When the pilot learned their whereabouts, he ordered the ship made ready for a gale; the men inspected and tightened the cordage, checked the lashings on the gun carriages and the battens on the hatches, and jettisoned any cases and bundles of cargo which remained on deck, in spite of the protests of their unfortunate owners. For, as Jan wrote, "In this coast they have but one hour fayre weather, and another houre stormie weather, in such manner as if heaven and earth should waste and be consumed . . . In that place likewise with a cleare and fayre weather there cometh a certayne cloude, which in shew seemeth no bigger than a man's fist and therefore by the Portingals it is called *Olho do Boy* or ox-eye and although as then it is cleare and calme weather and that the sailes, for want of wind, do beat against the mastes, yet as soon as they perceyve that cloude, they must presently strike all their sayles, for that commonly it is upon the ships before they perceyve it and with such a storm and noyse that without al doubt it would strike a shippe into the water, if there be not great care had to looke into it, as it chaunced to the second fleete after the Portingalles had discovered the Indies." He then went on to describe the disaster that in 1500 befell the ill-starred fleet of Pedro Alvares Cabral in this part of the ocean. The flotilla of a dozen ships, most of them caravels of lateen rig, was lying becalmed with all sails set. Suddenly, without warning, an incredibly furious blast struck them; it immediately sank at least four ships, and some accounts say eight, with all hands. Among those who thus perished was Bartholomeu Dias, who had discovered the Cape.

Off Treacherous Natal

ON MARCH 12, 1589, the *Santa Cruz* lay in a calm at thirty-one degrees south latitude, with all sails furled as a precaution; without any wind at all, the sea suddenly rose tumultuously, with waves as high and violent as in a tempest. These unnatural-seeming seas drove upon the nao from all points of the compass, tossed and flung the vessel in every direction, and, worse yet, sometimes crashed against it simultaneously on all sides and "clasped the shippe in such manner betwixt them, that they made all her ribbes to cracke and in a manner to open so that it is very dangerous for the shippes."

As previously stated, this phenomenon is supposed to be caused by the conflict between the southward-flowing, warm Algulhas Current and the northerly Antarctic Current, but some geographers ascribe it to atmospheric or astronomic influences and others to seismic disturbances. It is at times almost as hazardous to power-driven craft as to sailing ships, and has caused the foundering of steel steamers when heavy caroges shifted, even though they were supposedly well stowed.

The *Santa Cruz* was buffeted in these wild seas for a period of four days in which everyone aboard lived in terror that some of the seams would open under the pounding of the tons of water that dashed against them with all the force of great iron hammers. The foremast began to show signs of strain, so it was tightly wrapped about with heavy cable, and later the mainmast and mizzen were also reinforced. The nao still lay storm-tossed with sails furled, presumably at the same latitude, thirty-one degrees south, on March 20th; it had been held without progress in all that raging sea for eight days of terror and distress. On that day, they took the risk of setting sail in a brisk breeze in order to escape what appeared to be nearly a maelstrom. The gale soon became a storm and, after striking all sails, they rigged the bonnet (a strip of canvas designed to be clewed to the bottom of the mainsail to extend its area) upon the forecastle and sailed with this tiny improvised sail before the wind, so as to reduce the impact of the crushing waves. To add to the buoyancy of the heavily laden ship, the crew now threw over the side everything that could be reached, and finally, in desperation, even sacrificed the heavy longboat, their only means of salvation if the nao had to be abandoned. After a purgatory of two days and three nights, the storm abated. It was the feast of the Annunciation; "all aboard gave Almes to our Blessed Lady of the Annunciation," the weather turned fair, and sail was made again. Now, however, a strange malady struck everyone on the ship, and "ye disease tooke us in ye mouth, lippes, throate and Tongue which tooke off the skin and made them swell whereby they could not eate but with great paine, and not one in the ship but had it."

Then for fifteen days they had a fair wind and sailed south by southeast for the Cape; on April 9th they had reached thirty-three and a half degrees south latitude, but had no idea what longitude they were in, except that the sea was somewhat greener and they saw a number of whitish birds with black-tipped wings called *Mangas de Velludo* (Velvet Sleeves). The pilot said these birds came from the neighborhood of Delagoa Bay, and he guessed they were about forty miles offshore; but although they sounded continually they got no bottom.

Then for five days they were lashed by a howling gale and fled before it with only a half of the foresail up. Jan apologized for their running back before the wind, when it was the general Portuguese custom to try to hold what westing they had gained by simply lying with all sail struck and drifting out the storm. He wrote: "This oftentimes is the cause of their casting away, by reason of the great force and strength of the waves that runne there, so that it seemeth almost impossible for a ship to beare out so great a force, though it were of iron." How astonished the little Dutchman would have been could he have foreseen that within two and a half centuries there would be ships fashioned wholly of iron struggling against those same dread billows, just as he had pictured them in his vivid imagination. He found that even running before the gale was by no means safe, for the nao several times was pooped by following seas. He wrote, "Yet wee had danger enough, for that the sea came behinde and over our shippe and filled all the hatches whereby we were compelled to binde our Mastes, Cables, and all the ship round about with Ropes, that with the great force of the Sea it might not stirre and flye in pieces." This is the second time he explicitly stated that in a heavy storm they passed a cable under the keel and about the hull of the big nao to help keep it from buckling. He then proceeded to give a realistic account of the feelings and actions of the crew during this storm, and it is not only the most vivid of his writings but also ranks well in the forefront of dramatic sea stories.

He told how they had to pump night and day, every moment. It was as cold there off the South African coast as in Holland in the winter, just above the freezing point, "whereby wee were all sore toyled and out of hart . . . Wee esteemed ourseves clean cast away." They were forced by turns to go to the tiller and then to the pumps, so that they "had no time to sleepe, rest late nor cloath ourselves; to help us better the tiller shaft broke into pieces and nearly killed two or three of the men . . . God had pittie on us, so that there happened no other hurt."

The pilot organized a squad of thirty of the passengers, whom he divided into port and starboard watches of fifteen each, stationed upon both sides of his chair; he entrusted to each group a rope attached to the port or starboard end of the great yard of the square foresail. Then he assigned to twelve of the strongest sailors the holding of the long wooden tiller-shaft, and he also placed the boatswain with twelve men on the main hatch with ropes reaching to another yard, presumably of the main topsail. The deputy pilot then took a position behind the pilot's chair, but higher up in the stern, so that he could discern the approach of threatening rollers in time to meet them. He would shout his observations to the pilot, who would then signal the steersman and indicate to the two groups of men at the sheets how to haul or loosen their ropes to veer the bow toward the onrushing wall of water before it struck the hull so that when "the waves came and covered the ship the men at the rudder could hold Stiffe, and the ropes on the Fourke-yard and the boatswains ropes to bee pulled Stiffe to keep the ship right in the waves, for if the waves had once gotten us about, that they had entred on the sides of the Shippe, it had certainely beene said of us Requiescat in Pace."

The exhausted men at the sheets and tiller were relieved from time to time from their tense stations on deck by being shifted to the alternate but equally fatiguing chore of operating the pumps, some of which worked by cranking wheels, others by lifting rocker arms up and down. After five days of this unending toil without any let-up in the storm, a council of the officers and of some principal passengers was called to decide what should be done. The decision was that the *Santa Cruz* had been so buffeted that it was now too weak to try to pass the Cape; it should try to make port at Mozambique, 500 Spanish miles away. They would winter there and repair and reprovision the ship. The decision was unanimous, was put into writing, and was signed by all present. Jan said that this "greatly grieved the common sort," because they felt it would be as hazardous to try to navigate back again past dangerous Natal and up the Mozambique Channel as to continue to try to get beyond the Cape. Besides, they would have to stay at Mozambique a whole year and sell everything they possessed at half value in order to live, especially since everything for European sustenance there was imported from India and was as dear as gold itself.

The Mutiny

THIS DECISION brought about a near mutiny among the sailors, who cursed the captain and officers because of the shortages in spare spars, tillers and rudders, and the lack of suitable reserve timber from which replacements could be made. Their greatest indignation was at the lack of sufficient cordage, which was, in fact, inexcusable. The men were exhausted, terrified and desperate, and evidently were on the verge of a bloody outbreak. Moreover, as we have seen, many of the foremast hands, although inexperienced as mariners, were men of capacity in other fields who were working their passage home. They knew full well that the shortages of such essential reserves were significant and could not be glossed over with shrugs and excuses. Discipline must have broken down, rank been ignored, and the officers put to the question, in danger of their lives. It must have been a dramatic situation, with the groaning and laboring *Santa Cruz* rolling nearly to its beam-ends, then pitching almost vertically thirty or forty feet down into the trough of waves masthead high. With the rollers sluicing through the waistdeck, and a dozen men struggling to hold the tiller, the mutinous group must have invaded the quarterdeck and pressed about the captain and the master, while the pilots and boatswain devoted all their attention to keeping the ship afloat. Fortunately, being Portuguese and not unduly addicted to alcohol, the demoralized men had not broken into the steward's stores, as northern seamen would probably have done in like circumstances. However, Jan's account showed that the sailors were quite out of hand, and it was touch and go whether the guilty officers would be heaved over the side. When they accused the captain of having embezzled the money appropriated for stores, the frightened man tried to lay the guilt upon the master, whom the captain blamed for not having requisitioned cordage while the ship was in Cochin, as was his duty. The master swore he had requested and been supplied with the needed quantity of coir, or coconut fiber suitable to be laid into ropes, and that he had delivered it to the captain, who had then sold half of it in the market and pocketed the proceeds; he swore that their present disastrous shortage was wholly due to the captain's thievery. The aristocratic commander, who after all was not needed to navigate the nao and was indeed quite useless in the crisis, was apparently a hair's breadth from death when, with subtle insight into the thinking of sailors, or else perhaps in a maudlin state of panic, he began to berate the Deity whom all had been loudly supplicating for salvation just a short time ago, and deftly turned the blame from himself and laid it upon an unheeding and ungrateful God!

What a dramatic, tragic, unforgettable scene it must have been! It was a nightmare to haunt Jan's memory forever—the knot of haggard, wild-eyed sailors, half mad with exhaustion, lack of sleep and fear of death, and righteously vindictive against the cringing, terrified aristocrat, all his dignity washed away, and whimpering his frightened denials, hardly audible against the screaming gale and the savagely roaring waves—his blasphemies startling the blood-hungry mutineers. The cluster of menacing avengers were hardly able to hold their balance as the huge barrel of a nao wallowed and plunged in the gigantic thundering combers like a seamonster in its last dreadful agonies. In the background the disciplined groups of stricken passengers stumbled in the sluicing torrent pouring over the deck; they were harnessed to the ropes and frantically responded to the half-heard shouted orders of the undaunted pilot, though they expected every moment to be engulfed in the watery mountains that rushed on every side against the groaning hulk.

Jan said: "The Captaine could not tell what to answere, seeing us in that trouble, but said that he marvelled at nothing so much as why our Lord God suffered them beeing so good Christians and Catholiques, as they were, to passe the Cape with so great torments and dangerous weather, having so great and strong shippes, and the Englishmen, beeing as he said, Heretickes and Blasphemers of God, with so smal and weake vessels, and passed ye Cape so easilie. For they had received news in India

[137]

that an English shippe had passed the Cape with verie great ease." This adroit appeal to the men's prejudices evidently shocked and confused them and diverted their imagination, and his effrontery saved his skin. After all, it was an accepted thing for a captain to pilfer from the stores and food funds; indeed, this was habitually done also in the English ships. What did the sailors mean, to complain about such an accepted thing?

Jan remarked of the Portuguese that they brought about these "disorders" in administration and supplies "not once remembering what may after fall out, but when they are in danger, then ther is nothing els but crying Misercordia and calling to Our Lady for helpe."

In any case, murder was averted, and "so wee made backe againe toward Mosambique being in great despaire, for that no man cared for laying his hand to worke and hardlie would any man obay the Officers of the Shippe."

He wrote that they now again saw, tossing in the waves, the flotsam and jetsam of a wreck, with dead bodies lashed to spars "whereby we thought to have companie and that we alone were not unfortunate, for that is commonlie said that companions in miserie are a comfort to one another, and so it was to us." This indeed is eloquent evidence of the despairing mood of Jan and his shipmates.

But this time it was indeed darkest just before dawn, for when all had given up hope and expected the sorely stricken and already half water-filled nao to give up the struggle and plunge gurgling beneath the waves, suddenly a dead calm came which lasted for two days and enabled the pilots to take an observation and to ascertain, if not their location, at least their north and south position. To their incredulous delight they found the nao to be at thirty-seven degrees south latitude, so that with all the fury of wind and wave and their own surrender in steering north before the storm toward Mozambique, the mighty, unseen Algulhas Current had actually carried them south about a hundred miles and away from the dread coast of Natal.

Jan's frightening experiences aboard the *Santa Cruz* inevitably remind one of St. Paul's voyage from Jerusalem to Rome, as described in Acts 27. "But before very long, a fierce wind, the 'North-easter' as they call it, tore down from the landward side. It caught the ship and, as it was impossible to keep head to wind, we had to give way and run before it. . . . Next day, as we were making very heavy weather, they began to lighten the ship; and on the third day they jettisoned the ship's gear with their own hands. For days on end there was no sign of either sun or stars, a great storm was raging, and our last hopes of coming through alive began to fade."

A near mutiny took place on Paul's ship as well. "In the middle of the night the sailors felt that land was getting nearer. They sounded and found twenty fathoms. Sounding again after a short interval they found fifteen fathoms; and fearing that we might be cast ashore on a rugged coast they dropped four anchors from the stern and prayed for daylight to come. The sailors tried to abandon ship; they had already lowered the ship's boat, pretending they were going to lay out anchors from the bows, when Paul said to the centurion and the soldiers, 'Unless these men stay on board you can none of you come off safely.' So the soldiers cut the ropes of the boat and let her drop away.

"When day broke they could not recognize the land, but they noticed a bay with a sandy beach, on which they planned, if possible, to run the ship ashore . . . they found themselves caught between cross currents and ran the ship aground, so that the bow stuck fast and remained immovable, while the stern was being pounded to pieces by the breakers." [1]

All the sailors and passengers on Paul's ship got safely to shore, and they found themselves on the island of Malta. After three months spent on the island, they set out again in a ship that had also wintered there, and finally they reached Rome. It is amazing to realize how little the conditions of seafaring had changed between the first century after Christ and February, 1589!

Around the Cape!

J A N S A W that the water now was green, the Cape birds appeared in the air, and "about evening a swallow flew into our shippe, wherat they much reioixed, saying that it was a sign and foreshowing that Our Lady had sent the swallow on bord to comfort us and that we should passe the Cape . . . So as it seemed that God miraculouslie against al mens' reason and judgement and all the force of the wind and storms would have us passe the Cape when we were least in hope therof, whereby we may plainlie perceive that all men's actions without the hand of God, are of no moment."

Therefore the ship's council was again assembled. They voted to rescind the previous decision to make for Mozambique and once more to try to pass the Cape, "seeing we had such signes and tokens to put us in good comfort that God would help us. . . . This being concluded, we sung the Letany with *Ora Pro Nobis* and gave many almes with promises of pilgrimages and visitations and such like things, which was our dayly worke."

With that, the crew regained their morale, became "lustie," and worked willingly despite another great storm and high waves; for they were glad

[1] *The New English Bible, New Testament.* © The Delegates of the Oxford University Press and The Syndics of the Cambridge University Press 1961. Reprinted by permission.

to risk life and fortune to get around the Cape, rather than to seek safety by retreating to Mozambique.

It was now April 28th, and three months since they had left Cochin, but the peak of the terrible wintry season was now approaching; every day the weird gusts not only screeched more malevolently and with more fiendish force, but also more unpredictably in their sudden changes of direction, so that the tortured sea was in chaotic turmoil and seemed to take out its raging resentment upon the helpless and bewildered *Santa Cruz*.

Jan wrote, "Wee thought verily wee should have been cast away for that at everie minute the sea covered our shippe with water." To lighten it they cast overboard many chests from below hatches, including much costly cinnamon, a monopoly of the Crown, and whatever came first to hand.

"Everie man made account to die and began to confess themselves and to aske each other's forgiveness, thinking without more hope, that our last day was come." After twenty-four hours of this dull agony, "great almes were given in our shippe to many Virgin Maries and other saintes, with great devotion and promise of many things when they came to land, at last God comforted us and sent us better weather."

On April 20, 1589, just three months after leaving India, they once more managed to shoot the sun, and found themselves at thirty-six degrees south latitude; again they saw green water, albatrosses, and many sea-wolves (seals). On April 22nd they cast the lead twice and found no ground, which was a good sign that they had probably passed Cape Algulhas, where a ship finds ground at least thirty or forty miles from land. Soon more Cape pigeons and other land birds appeared, and the water was green and without the fearful rollers that had pursued them. Then "we seemed to come out of Hell into Paradice with so great joy that we thought we were born anew."

Safe in the Atlantic

THERE WAS a good, fresh wind, although "somewhat cold," and they encountered much floating seaweed which was like reeds or canes in thickness and which the pilot said was a sign that land was at most fifteen or twenty Spanish miles away. They also saw many large, spotted sea mews, called feysoins (Portuguese *faisões*, meaning pheasants), which are indigenous to the Cape. So the pilot called everyone on deck to wish a joyful farewell to the Cape; the *Santa Cruz* then changed course to north-west and northwest by west and headed for St. Helena.

Jan here made an interesting comment which confirms what can be gathered from other contemporary sea journals, that the naos and galleons, despite their seaworthy qualities, were not yet rigged in 1589 to be able to sail into the wind, although they could approach within some degrees of doing so and thus were not entirely dependent upon a fair wind, as Magellan seems to have been.

Jan wrote that when they changed course for St. Helena the pilot reckoned he was already fifty miles beyond the Cape, although he had not actually seen land. He said it was very unusual for a pilot to steer for St. Helena from the Cape without first skirting the African coast to reassure himself as to his actual position. Pilots were always in doubt as to their longitude, and needed to see land in order better "to set their course unto St. Helena, wherein they must alwaies keep on the left hand otherwise it were impossible for them to come at it if they leave that course; for if they once passe it they cannot come to it again because there bloweth continually but one kind of wind, which is southeast and thus having passed the Cape we got before the wind."

For the next fortnight the voyage was most pleasant, as they bowled along happily in the steady southeast trade wind. He said, "They may well let their sayles stand and lay them down to sleep for in ye greatest wind yt bloweth there, they need not strike their maine yard above half the mast." To decrease sail was hard work, as we have already had occasion to remark, for the sails had to be hauled up instead of being dropped down easily, as now.

St. Helena

ON MAY 12 TH at dawn they saw the island of St. Helena lying about two Spanish miles ahead of them, "whereat there was so great joy in the ship, as if we had bene in heaven."

Then came the problem of rounding the northeast promontory so as to get into the haven on the north without being blown past; Jan said, "but if they chance to put further out or to passe beyond it, they must go forward for they can get no more unto ye land." The inability of the great naos to go about and tack into the wind was a grave handicap. Consequently, by hugging the shore, they got around the promontory and could see before them the snug harbor in which at good anchorage lay five Portuguese ships. Still keeping close to the shore, for fear of being blown helplessly north and thus losing any chance of making the harbor, the Santa Cruz suddenly lost headway because the high peaks had cut off the southeast wind from their sails; the big nao failed to answer the rudder and began to drift in a current toward the shore, so it looked as if the ship must strike on the rocks and be a total loss. Since the longboat had been jettisoned, all they could do was try to tow with the skiff and put out sweeps from the top deck. There was no use dropping anchor, as the pilot knew how immensely deep were the soundings at that point. Their "row and tow" efforts, puny as they were, delayed the crash while emergency crews from the other five ships in the harbor came racing down in their longboats and got lines aboard the *Santa Cruz*, just as the nao's long bowsprit touched the great cliffs rising from the sea. The rescuing boats managed to haul the nao away from the rocks and alongside its sister ships of the armada, where it anchored in the very safe and comfortable haven.

CHAPTER VI

The Atlantic Islands

Reunion in St. Helena

W H E N the boats from the other ships in the harbor of St. Helena came alongside to tow the *Santa Cruz* from its perilous position, all aboard wanted to learn what the strange fifth ship that was anchored there could be. Five pepper naos had sailed from Cochin ahead of the *Santa Cruz*, but Jan and his shipmates had seen what they were certain was the wreckage of the *Sam Tomé*, the fifth to leave India; they were sure it could not have arrived at St. Helena. In its stead was a much older, more weather-beaten nao. They were surprised to hear that this was a trader owned by the German bankers of the House of Welser. It had gone directly from Lisbon to Malacca to get Chinese silks and porcelain, Japanese silver, spices from the Moluccas, tin from Banka, and rubies from Pegu (now Burma). Although Jan had occasion, as we shall see, to speak of this nao many times in the *Itinerario*, he never mentioned its name, but always referred to it as "The Ship from Malacca."

Its voyage out had been satisfactory, but, before the return lading could be completed, the harbor of Malacca was blockaded by the King of Achin, from Sumatra, and the nao had had to lie there for fourteen months, until the siege was broken by a relieving army under Dom Paulo de Lima. By that time only eighteen or twenty of the original crew of two hundred men were left alive because of the disease that was rampant in the besieged city. One of the survivors was the factor, or supercargo, an Antwerp man named Gerrit van Afhuysen, who hailed Jan happily; he was an old friend from the days Jan had spent in Lisbon. During his enforced stay in Malacca he had gathered much information about trade and commerce in the East Indian economic area of which Malacca was the metropolis, and he therefore was able to supply Jan with invaluable geographical and business data regarding all of Oceania and the markets in the China Sea. This supplemented the important navigational and mercantile facts about the Far East which Jan had already gathered from his friend Dirck Gerritszoon of Enkhuizen, the constable of the *Santa Cruz*. This word-of-mouth data was the basis of Jan's enlightening chapters describing the little known Far Orient, which proved to be of such utility to the merchants and navigators of the Netherlands and of England.

Jan departed from his usual impersonal, objective style when he wrote of his delight in encountering Van Afhuysen, with whom he evidently had been on close terms of friendship in Lisbon. He spoke of their mutual pleasure in the reunion and of their reminiscences of the old days, and he also emphasized his indebtedness to Gerrit for the information he acquired from him. It must have been a special delight to run into another Dutch-speaking crony, for he and Dirck had been the only ones to speak his native language on the whole long voyage. Jan's friendship for Van Afhuysen was a durable one, and it was soon to influence his career.

The Outsiders' Group

A L M O S T the only other time that Jan displayed any personal warmth of comradely feeling in all his Indian experience was when he referred to his relationship with Dirck Gerritszoon of Enkhuizen and with Bernard Burcherts of Hamburg. The only Portuguese person for whom he seemed to have felt any affection was Monsenhor, his master, for whom he had a respectful regard. There seemed to be a gulf between him and the Hispanic persons with whom he was associated; his social life in Goa was apparently limited to a circle of Nordic Europeans. He wrote of his Netherlands friend Frans Coningh, the gem cutter, of Goa: "Strangers of what nation soever they be, use to take acquaintance one of the other, being out of their owne countries (speciallie in India) where there are very few and do hold together as brethren, which to them is a great comfort."

Later, in the Azores, he showed a greater affinity for the English prisoners he met than for the Portuguese, although he had friendly relations with the pro-Spanish governor, Dom Cristóbal de Moura, Knight Commander of Alcántara. In writing of the various Portuguese military and naval actions that occurred during his stay in India, several of which were signalized by feats of valor, Jan paid tribute to only one act of personal heroism, that of the trumpeter in the landing operation against the Arabian pirates at their lair at Nicola—and the praise of his gallantry was no doubt influenced by the fact that the trumpeter was a Netherlander.

Recuperation in the Haven

As the fleet lay at St. Helena, there was still a faint hope that the missing Sam Tomé might, after all, reach port. The exhausted crews rested and restored their strength, for every ship of the flotilla had been storm-tossed and wracked at the Cape as cruelly as had the Santa Cruz. Each crew had their own story of misery and privation. The Admiral of the squadron, the Sam Christovão, had had such a difficult time that fully half of all the cargo had to be thrown overboard, and all the passengers had been put to the pumps night and day without rest. It had reached St. Helena in a sinking condition, with its hold full of water; it would have gone down in the harbor had not the crews of the other ships helped pump, while the carpenters and caulkers partially stopped the leaks. The carpenters discovered, much to their surprise, that the hull, and especially the rudder, were riddled with wormholes of the teredo, or saltwater wood-worm. As the ship was new and on its maiden voyage, the Royal Arsenal at Goa, which was supposed to recondition every newly arrived ship of the Carreira da India, had probably assumed it to be in good condition; perhaps they charged for careening, inspecting and reconditioning it without making any inspection at all.

As soon as the Santa Cruz anchored in the safe and snug harbor, the boatswain was sent ashore with a detail of men on an important mission; they set up a number of small tents in a grove near a brook. Then they took the sick men ashore and assigned a single tent to each individual. The other ships had previously done the same, and there was already a substantial encampment. All this ferrying from the Santa Cruz had to be done with a single skiff, since the longboat had been jettisoned off Natal, and now its lack was sorely felt.

The balmy, temperate air, clean water, and abundance of fruit, vegetables and fresh meat, as well as plentiful seafood, quickly restored the health of many of the sick. However, several of the invalids had not recovered when the Santa Cruz was ready to sail nine days later, and these men had to be provisioned with certain staple supplies and left behind. A total of fifteen sick men in all, from the whole fleet, would have to spend the year at St. Helena, and would be able to sail home with next year's fleet.

The rest of the crew had had much delight in fishing, hunting, and bathing on the shores of the bay. Every day in a body they attended the services of thanksgiving which were held in the little chapel dedicated to St. Helena, and many carried out the vows which they had made in their hours of fear during the tempests. This small church was a veritable shrine, and was treated with singular devotion and reverence by the crews of the *Carreira da India*, probably because of the terrors and emotional experiences through which they had passed just before reaching the asylum of safety. The pepper fleet of the previous year had found, upon their arrival, that the altar and church had been defiled by unknown vandals during the long months between the visits by the Portuguese, and a feeling of great shock and indignation had shaken the men at this unpleasant discovery. It was later found that this sacrilegious act had been committed by the crew of the English corsair Cavendish on his celebrated voyage of circumnavigation.

The Island Paradise

J A N described St. Helena as an earthly paradise, as indeed it must have been in his time. The island consists of a cluster of volcanic peaks, rising so high that they tear open the many rain-laden clouds that are blown westward across the Atlantic from Africa; there are several showers daily, and hence a number of little streams flow down the mountainsides and irrigate the valleys. When the Portuguese discovered the island, in about 1502, it held no animals nor any fruit-bearing trees. However, the sea in that region was thick with fish, on which vast numbers of seabirds subsisted. The early Portuguese ships, which used to stop at St. Helena to fill their water barrels, began to leave domestic and game animals there; they also planted figs, bananas, and many other fruit and nut bearing trees, as well as a large number of useful vegetables. At the time Jan visited the island there were thousands of hogs, sheep, cattle, poultry and pigeons, which were so tame they could be caught by hand.

The Portuguese Crown had decreed that the island should not be settled, but should be kept in its virgin condition to serve as a rest haven for the ships returning from India. In all other newly discovered lands the Portuguese had established colonies and erected forts, but St. Helena was left as a delightful exception to this rule. The creation of this refreshing and recuperative station was only one of the many sensible and civilized arrangements in the well organized realm of *Asia Portuguesa* in the sixteenth century, all of which were based on a peaceful, harmonious regime. This was soon to be destroyed by the Dutch and English invasions.

Jan wrote that there had been one exception to the rule of allowing no settlers on St. Helena. There was an ancient hermit who lived in a grotto, where he prayed for those at sea and took care of the small chapel of the saint. He was looked upon as a man of sanctity, and each fleet customarily gave him a supply of staples to supplement the native food that was his for the gathering. However, it was finally discovered that this supposedly holy man had a long-standing agreement with a merchant in Lisbon to smuggle to him, in each annual pepper fleet, five hundred or six hundred prime goatskins. After this revelation the old hypocrite was, by royal order, transported back to Lisbon. On another occasion, several slaves of both sexes escaped from a ship and settled in the mountains. Their numbers, of course, multiplied, until they were a small tribe; they began to destroy the cherished wild life of the little island. It required the effort of a large armed force finally to round them up and deport them—a sad story for the little band of refugees, but a necessity for the great flotillas which depended on the unspoiled island for its life-restoring supplies.

Jan appreciated the idyllic aspect of this ocean paradise. He said it had been discovered miraculously, through Divine Providence, for the refreshment of the Portuguese ships, "for if this Iland were not, it were impossible for the shippes to make any good and prosperous viage for it hath often fallen out that some shippes which have missed thereof have indured the greatest miseries in ye world and came half dead and spoyled into Portugal." He himself, however, was soon to have a part in wrecking this oceanic Eden. When the *Itinerario* was published, the Dutch corsairs learned for the first time the location and halcyon conditions of the tiny island, hidden as it was in the wastes of the Atlantic and never even visited by the outbound Portuguese fleets from Lisbon. Apparently there had been no foreign intruders on the island before Cavendish. He had forced a Portuguese pilot, whom he had taken prisoner in the Straits of Sunda, to navigate his ship around the Cape of Good Hope and then take it to St. Helena for water and fresh food.

Some of the Dutch marauders had suffered extreme hardships in their early voyages in the unknown South Atlantic because of lack of drinking water and had made desperate appeals for aid at the Portuguese equatorial islands of Sam Tomé, Annobom and Príncipe, off West Africa, and at the Cape Verde Islands, but had been rebuffed. They then had even sailed frantically across the South Atlantic to Buenos Aires and Rio de Janeiro to try to obtain fresh water, but all without success.

After the publication of the *Itinerario*, however, the Dutch predators swarmed about St. Helena, made it a pirate base, and lay in wait there to trap the weary Portuguese freighters homeward bound from the Indies. Thereafter the naos no longer dared to stop there, but gave it a wide berth, so that the return voyage from Goa to Lisbon became much more difficult and more racked with privation. This, however, did not happen until early in the seventeenth century.

It was customary, when ships visited St. Helena, to carve the date and the name of the vessel, as well as individual names, on the large trees near the landing place. Jan commented that there were hundreds of these carvings on living trees, some of which went back over three-quarters of a century to the year 1510, and with the growth of the trunk or limbs of the trees the letters and numerals had expanded to giant size.

To illustrate his description of St. Helena in the *Itinerario*, Jan added a skillfully drawn map of the island. He drew its elevation from all four directions, including the view of the harbor; he noted that he sketched these while the *Santa Cruz* partially circled the island in its coming and going. The charts are extremely well made, in the projection that was then customary, with hills and cliffs standing up vertically as though seen from the deck of the ship sailing by. As on all Jan's charts, there is a picture of a ship; this is not for decorative purposes, but is drawn in the exact location of the vessel from whose deck the sketch was made, thus giving the correct angle of the point of view.

After the *Santa Cruz* had lain at St. Helena nine days, had cleaned and replenished the water butts, procured an ample supply of fresh fruits and vegetables, and given everyone a good rest and as much healthful food as any of them had ever eaten before, the Admiral displayed the signal flag for sailing. Anchors were weighed and catted and, with cheers for their fifteen sick shipmates left behind, the fleet stood out in the Atlantic to the northwest. The prows were at last headed for Europe and home.

Spiritual Protection

A L L , of course, had attended Mass that morning to give thanks again to Divine Providence and to the Virgin, each man to his own guardian angel, and each to whatever saint he recognized as his personal patron, for having carried them safely through the recent dangers; and for their further protection they earnestly prayed with many vows. These intrepid, resourceful men of fortitude believed literally that all natural phenomena were controlled and directed by supernatural beings, former humans canonized by the Church who, having achieved immortality, now concerned themselves with the fortunes and the fate of living men. It was the firm and pious belief of all aboard that the attention of the saints could be attracted and their miraculous aid and protection could be gained by gifts to their shrines and by acts of devotion. Self-denials, penances, and self-inflicted chastisements were helpful in securing this intervention. From the captain-general of the armada down to the smallest cabin boy, all prayed openly and unashamedly for a safe conduct through the dangers that lay ahead. Every man carried his amulet, a blessed medal or cross, an effigy, or a miraculous bit of bone, wood or stone, a holy relic that would protect him.

Everyone aboard, including the most erudite and gifted priests, recognized that there were persons, perhaps even among their messmates, who secretly practiced sorcery, black magic and witchcraft to enlist the services of evil spirits and of the personal but invisible devils that were all about. At every dawn there were long matin services, litanies and hymns, and every half hour, when the ship's sandglasses were turned, the cabin boys chanted prescribed prayers. At sundown the ships' companies, led by their captains, chanted the *Salve Regina* and asked God's care for the night. The presence of priests as passengers on all the naos resulted in a more conventional and ritualistic form of religious exercise than otherwise would have been used. The mariners' extreme need for help of some kind was evident, and it was natural that they should implore supernatural assistance both to survive the rigors and dangers of wind and ocean currents and to withstand the debilitating, insidious diseases and pestilences that beset their leaky, cranky, frail sailing ships, whose pilots could not possibly ascertain their position at sea within hundreds of miles of where they actually were. It was more in genuine piety than in grim mockery that men then said, "If you would learn to pray, go to sea!"

The Ruined Adventurers

M A N Y of Jan's fellow voyagers, although humbly grateful to be still alive, had little to be thankful for otherwise. After years of hard work, privations, scheming and conniving, and after finally succeeding in carrying aboard the *Santa Cruz* their hard-won gains, they had been taught by the hungry seas "that riches has wings," and that "the worldly hope men set their hearts upon, turns ashes," as they watched their precious chests of treasure heaved over the sides of the ship during one of the terrifying storms.

For these poor men it would be a bleak and bitter homecoming; no man was more scorned in opulent, purse-proud Lisbon than a penniless returned adventurer from *India Portuguesa*, broken in health and spirits and ill fitted to adapt himself to an altered society and economy. The stay-at-home friends and relatives, who had expected to profit from his riches, gave him a scant welcome if his treasure had all been tossed overboard.

Even those fortunate ones aboard the *Santa Cruz* whose cherished possessions were still intact could not be sure what trials might still lie ahead of them. They would certainly have been apprehensive had they known that the shield upon which they relied, the navy of Portugal, their invincible defense for a century, could no longer protect them against new and ruthless predators.

However, all were now physically rested and in health, their quarters on the ships had been cleaned, and good drinking water and fresh provisions were aboard; once the sails were set, the unfailing southeast trade wind made their progress smooth and comfortable. On the fifth day out from St. Helena, however, a sad incident occurred; a slave fell overboard from the *Santa Cruz*. The sails were immediately struck and the skiff dropped alongside, but the nao had drifted so far that it was impossible even to locate the unfortunate man. The ship had been sailing before the wind at a fair speed, and of course was unable to come about and tack, as a more modern sailing ship would have done.

Every Ship for Itself

T H E   S I X   N A O S were now well spread out; the *Santa Cruz* had managed to come within hailing distance of the *Santa Maria* and later of the Ship of Malacca, but without incident. It was obvious that there was no effort to keep the ships together. This was typical of fleet operations in the *Carreira da India*, and it has never been clear why such convoys could not be held more closely in hand. Probably the discipline was practically nonexistent because they were merchant freighters, rather than war ships, and despite their high-sounding titles, the captain-general and the admiral had little control over the individual captains. The naos were so vulnerable to disaster and so lacking in life-saving equipment that on almost every voyage some of the units of a fleet failed to reach their destination, as we have seen; there is no question but that, had the fleets kept together, many losses could have been avoided.

That it really was possible to hold the ships of a fleet in hand was demonstrated when convoys passed in well-knit array through areas threatened by corsairs or enemy warships. The otherwise general laxity in this respect was not confined to Portuguese fleets, but was a problem with the English and Dutch merchant fleets as well.

The benefit of keeping together was now demonstrated when the admiral, the *Sam Christovão*, overhauled the *Santa Cruz* and ordered it to keep its sister ships company to Ascension Island, which lay one hundred and ninety Spanish miles northwest of St. Helena. Although this was not in the direct route of the fleet, and customarily was by-passed, it could easily be reached, as it lay in the path of both the trade winds and the ocean current. The *Santa Cruz* was informed that, despite the repair work and extensive patching done at St. Helena on the *Sam Christovão*, the big nao was still taking water faster than the pumps could eject it. The crew, not in open mutiny, but in fear for their lives, had unanimously asked the commander to anchor at the desert island of Ascension and discharge the cargo there, so that the leaking nao could be sailed in ballast to Portugal. Their argument was that, since not one vessel in twenty years ever visited waterless Ascension, a small detail with casks of water and provisions could guard the valuable cargo ashore until a relief nao could be sent for it from Lisbon. The ship's officers had felt it would be possible to keep the ship afloat for the rest of the voyage, and had themselves, from the admiral down, been working in twenty-four hour shifts at the pumps. However, in view of the temper of the men, they felt it best to accede to their request, and hence asked the other ships to stand by to assure their safety.

The Desert Isle

THE SQUADRON reached Ascension on May 28th. With a strong, fair wind, a favorable current, and a quiet sea, it had taken them seven days to cover the one hundred and ninety Spanish miles, or about seven hundred modern nautical miles, more or less; in other words, aided by the current and under the most favorable conditions, the speed of the naos under full sail possibly was about four knots.

Upon arrival at Ascension, the admiral-ship sailed around the island sounding diligently, but was unable to get bottom. The crew urged that the ship approach closer to the shore and sound again, but the pilot refused to do so because he was afraid of reefs. The captain-general than persuaded the *Santa Maria* to lend him an extra pump; he asked the same favor of the *Santa Cruz*, but they were reluctant to give one up in spite of his plea. Then, after a half-promise by the captain-general that he would transfer to the *Santa Cruz*, when they reached the calm zone which lay ahead, some of his lading which might otherwise have to be jettisoned, the captain of Jan's ship grudgingly parted with the pump. The greater safety assured by the possession of two more pumps had the effect of pacifying the crew of the admiral.

Jan took advantage of this incident to make a vividly graphic chart of Ascension Island which later was published in the *Itinerario*, along with those of St. Helena, which the volcanic island resembled in its general geographical contours; however, its peaks were too low to pierce the rain-carrying clouds, as did those of St. Helena, so it had no rainfall whatsoever. The island was utterly barren, without a single species of fauna or flora, although it was literally swarming with great flocks of seabirds, which drew an easy subsistence from the plentiful marine life about the coast. The aquatic birds, the size of young geese, showed no fear at all of the ships, but alighted on the decks and spars and even upon the heads and shoulders of the men with no hesitation. Here was an easy and plentiful source of food, the crews thought. They tried the birds cooked in various styles, but the flesh was so fishy and unpalatable that they gave up the attempt in disgust.

The swarming fish were almost equally easy to catch; and there were even many large flying fish which obligingly fell upon the decks. The crews were able to salt down a supply of the fish for future consumption, and only their lack of cargo space limited the quantity of tasty preserved fish they prepared.

In the Doldrums

T H E N , sailing with the good southeast trade wind, the Santa Cruz steered northwest by west, past the dreary St. Peter and Paul Rocks just north of the equator. They soon sighted the North Star for the first time since leaving India, and at the same time the Southern Cross faded from their view. On June 8th, a fortnight out from St. Helena and about four degrees north latitude, the southeast trade wind which had made the voyage so pleasant was left behind. Now the naos entered the equatorial counter current and drifted into the doldrums, where they encountered a dead calm with frequent showers and violent thunder storms. The Santa Cruz drifted without any headway, and the bow swung in erratically aimless circles. The wet sails hung slack, and the spars slatted and banged against the masts. The nao rolled continually in the heavy, windless swells as it spun languidly in the invisible current. The intense equatorial sun burned savagely upon the unshaded deck crowded with squirming, jostling men, who were kept topside from the shaded quarters below by the overpowering stench from the fetid bilge, the stifling effluvia of which shimmered in the heat as it rose visibly above the hatch. The deck was burning hot to the touch, and the tarry, greasy packing bubbled and oozed from between the dirty, slimy planks. Sleep at night was fitful, and heat rash and hives tormented the unhappy crew. Men were irritable, snarled and cursed at one another, and laid hands on knives without cause. Scattered among them were the scurvy-stricken and those suffering from the flux, or dysentery, rolling in their own fecal matter and vomit. Those still in comparative health and on duty were too listless to clean up the squalid mess, and all depended upon the frequent heavy showers to wash some of the filth into the scuppers. The rain was warm and did not cool the torrid air, nor did the frequent mighty thunderbolts relieve the oppressive sultriness. Utter boredom and discontent lay heavily upon all who were not in actual physical torment, and nothing mattered to anybody. Men counted the hours and the slowly gliding days until the sluggish drift of the current might be expected to carry them into the blessed northeast wind. That deliverance was still unpredictable, and perhaps as much as another tedious fortnight of discomfort and depression lay ahead.

The few women aboard were particularly afflicted by the oppressive humidity and the nauseating odors and squalor. In Goa they had become accustomed to bathing and changing their linen several times daily, and to living at their ease behind latticed blinds in harem-like privacy, waited upon hand and foot by household slaves. On the *Santa Cruz* they collected rain water for their laundry, but the ever-present dampness prevented the wash from drying. The children were fretful, sick, ill-nourished, and quarrelsome among themselves, which put an additional strain on their mothers and led to tension between them and sometimes outright hysteria. The ladies were ordered to keep to their narrow, stifling quarters by their jealous and autocratic husbands, who wished to shield them from the wolfish eyes of a hundred sex-hungry, desperately lonely men. The few who came on deck had no privacy, and in the wretched conditions that prevailed were deprived of the feminine dignity, delicacy and elegance to which they aspired.

The Privileged Few

THE PRESENCE of the priests afforded the ladies some protection; but the privileged facilities of the ship's officers gave them uncontested opportunities to make amorous advances and assignations in their cabins, and was often cause for scandal. For a woman, a passage on the *Carreira da India* was a time of torment. The officers were in a position not only to alleviate their distress, but to offer them much luxury and relaxation. In the *Carreira da India*, just as later in the British East India Company, the ship's officers had a very different position in relation to the passengers than that on ordinary ocean liners. Because of the absolute monopoly in shipping and the enormous profits to be made by anyone who could get even a little cargo space in this exclusive annual voyage, the officers, who had ample space allotments themselves, were men of income and were in a position to grant important favors. Considering the vicissitudes and hardships of a voyage lasting from five to eight months, during which the regulations gave the captain and the pilot not only complete authority, but rare perquisites as well, it was only natural that there should be rivalry among some of the women to attract their attention and favor; sometimes the officers, instead of pursuing the women passengers, were themselves pursued, and had to be very much on the defensive. Jan said that on the *Santa Cruz* the captain, the pilot, the master and the boatswain, the four ranking commissioned officers, each had two or three cabins at his disposal, of which the captain's quarters were the most sumptuous.

He added that each of these four officers was served his meals separately, in his own quarters and by his own slaves; each dined off a silver service "with silver lampes, beakers, cups and bowles." Their tables were supplied with fine viands and delicacies, while some of the poor passengers literally starved to death. A cruel social and economic inequality then was, of course, the rule ashore as well as at sea, much more commonly than in the modern Western world; but the contrast was particularly sharp on an Indiaman, where so many deep discomforts and privations were suffered by all but the chief officers and the wealthier passengers.

A Breeze at Last

T H E   F R I E N D L Y trade wind had died down and the calm had fallen on June 8th, when the astrolabe showed that the *Santa Cruz* was in four degrees north latitude; twelve days later, at eleven degrees north latitude, the look-out at the mast-top suddenly sang out "Gale Ho!" Everyone ran to a vantage point and gazed with delight at the few ripples on the sea which foretold their deliverance from inaction. The master blew his silver whistle and ordered the rudder—which had hung idle for almost a fortnight—to be manned. Soon the limp sails began to fill fitfully, then really to billow out. There was a sighing in the air and then a slight humming in the rigging, the canvas tightened and began to pull, and the master whistled once again, this time to have the sheets manned. The nao heeled over slightly and began to move; a wake was perceptible astern, and faint white-caps began to show to windward. The breeze was from the northeast and brought a refreshing coolness that changed the expressions and feelings of everyone; almost immediately all apathy disappeared, there were smiles, gaiety and horseplay on deck, and all expressed their relief in feeling once more the caress of the wind on their cheeks. Before dusk the other ships of the armada appeared on the horizon, and the fleet began to unite after having been carried in different directions by the currents during the calm.

Setting the course to northwest by north, the armada passed the point of Cape Verde on the West African coast on June 23rd and three days later saw the Portuguese Cape Verde Islands, ten in number. They had no reason to make port there at that time, and Jan did not devote any space to a description of them. In any case, they were scarcely visible, and only appeared in faint outline from the masthead.

Soon they found themselves in the brownish-yellow seaweed that covers the Sargasso Sea, which Jan found of great interest. He wrote that the weed got its name from a plant that grew in freshwater wells in Portugal. In spite of all his scientific interest in this strange vegetation on the surface of the sea, he did not observe the swarming sea-life that throve in it, for he would certainly have commented upon it if it had caught his attention and aroused his curiosity. There is no doubt, however, that he gathered a good-sized bundle of it to dry and put in his sea chest as a sample to take back to Enkhuizen; for he brought home many natural curios, botanical, geological, and zoological, which the learned Doctor Paludanus later exhibited in his museum there.

The northeast trade wind, occasionally interrupted by brief calms, blew on the starboard quarter, and they sailed across the imaginary division line on the charts of the Tropic of Cancer, through the Horse Latitude—so-called because, when becalmed there for long periods, the outward bound fleets of the *Carreira da India,* in order to conserve water, had had to push the horses they were carrying overboard. Then they sailed past the Spanish Canary Islands and Portuguese Madeira. Jan devoted a chapter in the *Itinerario* to an interesting description of the Canary Islands, but could make no map. He did not devote any attention to the important island of Madeira, perhaps thinking it already sufficiently well known to his readers.

Land Ho!

THE SQUADRON made its European landfall at the Azores at noon on July 22nd, when the lookout picked up the islands of Flores and Corvo. The cry of "Terra! Terra!" resounded through the ship. The nimbler passengers ran up the ratlines, while the rest clambered on to the high poop to try to distinguish two vague, low shapes on the horizon which looked no different, at first, from clouds.

It was six months since the *Santa Cruz* had cleared Cochin, and it was high time both passengers and crew should have relief, for scurvy was raging through the ship, with twenty-four already dead and many others nearly so. Jan told of the victims "which many times were found under the fore deck that had laine dead two or three days, no man knowing it, which was a pittiful sight to behold, considering the miserie they endure aboard these shippes."

The Corsairs

AT DUSK, out from between the two islands came three small ships, no one being above sixty tons in size. They approached the admiral, the crippled *Sam Christovão,* and suddenly opened fire, at the same time hoisting the English flag.

However, it became dark before any real action developed; the six great Indiamen crowded on all sail, heading for the island of Terceira, where they expected to find the naval escort which always awaited the Pepper Fleet to convoy it to Lisbon. The three English corsairs followed them, keeping together and having their large stern signal lights burning, even though there was moonlight. Throughout the night the Portuguese watched them exchange signals by lanterns from the fighting tops on their mastheads.

In the morning, one of the pursuers turned back and sailed out of sight, presumably to see if there was another Indiaman struggling behind which they might cut off and capture. Later in the forenoon this scout returned. The three corsairs drew together to take counsel, and then all converged upon the *Santa Cruz*, the hindmost in the flotilla and therefore the easiest to isolate. The ship now was in a dangerous position. They were passing between the islands of Graciosa and St. George and quite near the latter, which lay upon their lee side. The strategy of the corsairs was to force the big nao upon the rocky lee shore, for then they could easily take it. The scene must have been a stirring one—the sparkling blue sea with the verdant islands, the six heavily laden Indiamen with all their white canvas spread, strung out in mad flight like a herd of elk harassed by three wolves, and the three little corsairs which followed the ancient law of the hunter in endeavoring to cut off the straggler of the group. The English, in their handy, swift little craft, with pennants flying, drums beating, and trumpets sounding, three times circled the fleeing *Santa Cruz;* they discharged heavy cannon into its hull and succeeded in cutting the rigging and sails by sustained fire from small guns called calavers and by heavy musket fire.

Constable Dirck Gerritszoon unfortunately had not been supplied with trained gunners nor with the facilities necessary for defense. Despite his own ability as an artilleryman, he managed to fire only a single heavy gun at the raiders, and it then took an hour to reload. There was so much clamor and shouting on deck by the short-handed and demoralized crew that the English, who were only a few hundred yards away, began to mock them and to shout a variety of insults across the narrow space that separated the two ships, so that it seemed they were as occupied in jeering as in shooting. Fortunately, although the small-arms fire from the English corsairs cut much of the rigging, it did not succeed in severing any of the essential stays, supports or other critical cordage; the heavier cannon neither managed to smash the rudder of the *Santa Cruz*, nor to cause a dangerous leak in the thick teak planking of the India-built hull. Jan said that the enemy fire was so "well laid on" that the Portuguese fighting men did not dare to show their heads over the bulwark. One reason the Portuguese were demoralized was their fear that the fortified harbor of Angra, on the island of Terceira, which was their destination and which was known to be disaffected toward Philip, might have been occupied by the English. Otherwise they could not explain how three puny corsairs could dare to attack the Pepper Fleet in waters where for a century death had been the penalty for any such trespassers. Before they had left Lisbon, in early 1588, the Invincible Armada was being assembled there to operate in the Narrow Seas about England and the Netherlands; now, although they had received no word of the results of that campaign, the audacity of the raiders made them fear that all was not well with Spain.

By good piloting, and thanks to a favorable breeze, the *Santa Cruz* managed to escape being driven upon the rocks of St. George by the privateers, who for some reason kept their distance, instead of attempting to grapple and board, "little knowing in what case and feare we were." The encounter developed into a chase, with the English easily keeping their position on the stern of the harassed *Santa Cruz*.

Meanwhile, the other five naos had sailed ahead in safety, leaving the *Santa Cruz* to grapple alone with the corsairs, and the men on the harassed ship felt abandoned indeed. Jan was bitterly critical of the other Indiamen for leaving their sister ship at such a juncture and trying only to save themselves. However, faced with small, fast, well-armed privateers the naos were easy targets, and their only hope was for the main body to get away while one of their number was sacrificed to the rapacious sea raiders. Their unwieldy size made it difficult for them to maneuver, and the corsairs could and did sail circles around them. Their armament was light, while the English ships were fighters, sufficiently armed for combat and manned by crews of daredevils avid for adventure and plunder. Jan himself wrote that the naos were "so overloaded that they were hard to steer." In addition, their untrained crews were sick, exhausted, and debilitated; and the admiral ship of the flotilla was so crippled as to be barely able to keep afloat. Under those circumstances, it seemed only sensible that the fleet should cut its losses. The duty of the captains was to save their immensely rich cargoes, upon which the exchequer of Portugal so largely depended, as well as their ships and crews; it would have been foolhardy to expose themselves unnecessarily to the enemy guns, when one lucky shot might mean the loss of the nao. Therefore, the *Santa Cruz* found itself alone to bear the brunt of the battle. The seemingly heartless policy of cutting losses has been followed both on land and sea by every power, even down to the wars of the twentieth century. In modern terms, the *Santa Cruz* was, perforce, expendable.

Now, instead of continuing to fire at the rudder, foremast or rigging of the *Santa Cruz*, the three raiders lowered their colors and sailed along as if they were part of the flotilla. The fleeing squadron was nearing the city of Angra, the port of the *Insula de Iesus Christus de Terceira* and capital of the Archipelago of the Flemish Isles (the Azores), where the Pepper Fleet expected a rendezvous with their naval escort. Instead of finding their protective war galleons awaiting them, they saw two small despatch boats put out from the harbor, and they were horrified to see these two craft trustingly make for the three smaller ships, thinking them part of the fleet. The naos desperately fired cannon and waved warning signals in time to divert the two caravels, which sheered away from the raiders.

At this point, inexplicably, the three English ships abandoned the fleet and sailed away. The officers of the naos barely had time to feel relief before the skippers of the despatch boats came aboard the Admiral, the *Sam Christovão*, with orders from Lisbon. The news they bore was grave for all. The Admiralty at Lisbon commanded the Indiamen to anchor under the batteries at the harbor of Angra, and under no circumstances to leave the harbor, but to await further orders there. The black news was that the previous year's invasion of England had failed and many of the Spanish and Portuguese warships had been lost. Not only was there an English squadron under the Earl of Cumberland somewhere in the offing, but Sir Francis Drake, with a mighty fleet, had raided the coast of Portugal itself and blockaded Lisbon. He was expected at any moment to attempt a landing at Angra; the entire population of the island of Terceira had been conscripted and was under arms. Probably this explained the puzzling tactics of the three English ships; instead of being privateers, they were undoubtedly Drake's scouts. They were no doubt satisfied to see the Pepper Fleet imprisoned in Angra harbor, where they could capture it at their leisure.

Perhaps the English expected that the native Portuguese in Terceira would welcome them as deliverers and gladly surrender the hated Spanish garrison to them. In this event the enormously rich Pepper Fleet might fall into Drake's hands intact, without damage to ships or cargo; the ruin of the Portuguese merchants would not matter to the English. Jan and his two compatriots, Afhuysen and Gerritszoon, did not fear death at the hands of the English, but they would of course lose their personal belongings and their merchandise and savings like everybody else if captured. The prospect was a dismal one, and the dejection was all the greater because, after so many hardships and dangers, everyone had been counting on a final happy homecoming.

A Hazardous Anchorage

THE PROSPECT of remaining long at anchor in Angra harbor before being convoyed safely to Lisbon was disquieting in itself. This was because the crescent-shaped haven, although protected by high hills on three sides, lay open to the south and southeast; in late July, August and September furious storms were likely to come without warning and sweep violently into the anchorage there. Consequently during those months any ships lying there had to be on the alert to slip their cables and make for the open sea at any instant, to avoid being trapped in the harbor and dashed against the shore.

This danger was so acute that the homecoming Pepper Fleets never anchored at Angra, in the ordinary course of their voyages, but merely sent small boats ashore to deliver the mail or to pick up supplies while the naos beat about outside the harbor to await their return. Since Jan's fleet arrived on St. James Day, July 24, 1589, the stormy season was due to begin at any time; the big, lubberly naos would find it hard to extricate themselves from the harbor if a southeaster should suddenly blow up. However, their orders from Lisbon were explicit; they were told not even to anchor in the roadstead, but to go as far as possible into the harbor and take up a position directly under the walls of the castle. They had been lucky enough to avoid capture by the Earl of Cumberland's English fleet, which was known to be cruising about the Azores to intercept them. Since he had missed them on the high seas, he might be expected to follow the English practice of sending the boats of his fleet into the harbor to "cut them out," even under the guns of the land batteries—that is, if Sir Francis Drake did not get there first!

As soon as the anchors splashed into the good holding bottom at Angra, there was an exodus from the fleet, everyone passing through the barrier of keenly watchful customs men. Only a few cabin boys were left on the ships to provide for the manacled slaves. A delegation of monks and nuns had been the first aboard, to carry the sick to the hospital; all the able-bodied were frantic to set foot once more on solid earth, to get fresh food and especially fresh water, and in most cases to seek the company of the many prostitutes who crowded the pier. A few passengers and crew members did make their way to the Cathedral to render thanks for their safe deliverance from the elements and to ask divine guidance in the threatening days ahead. There were nearly two thousand souls on the naos, and there was much merrymaking and relaxation ashore for them. However, the air was tense with anxiety in all the city as fishing boats and coastal caravels brought continuous news of the depredations of Cumberland's ships in nearby Madeira, the Canaries, and their own group of islands— and equally disturbing accounts came in of the uncontested raids of the mighty Drake on the mainland. It was something new for the haughty Portuguese and Spaniards to be threatened by hostile navies in their own home waters.

The weather continued fair, despite the season. In the general atmosphere of mixed dread and holiday, no one in authority in the *Carreira da India* took into consideration the ever-present risk to the precious ships in Angra harbor, despite the fact that they contained all their personal fortunes. The most prudent step might have been to unload the cargo and transport it all, including the king's pepper and spices, to some place among the hills of the interior where it would be safe from the English.

The customs regulations at Angra were rigid, and the private ventures on the Indiamen would have had to be put under bond if they were unloaded. Because of the rapacity of the local staff, no doubt the owners of the cargo would have had serious misgivings about the safety of their goods; they might almost have preferred to risk an English raid or a south-easter.

Jan's scornful criticism of the heedless lack of responsibility of the Portuguese officials was fully justified in this case. Although there was much discussion in official circles about the risks to the naos and their valuable cargoes, the ships continued to be left with only cabin boys and slaves aboard, and not a single ship's officer or seaman on hand to meet emergencies.

Disaster Strikes

AFTER twelve days of thus tempting fate, suddenly a howling south wind blew up in the middle of the night. Someone on one of the ships fired a warning gun, all the many church bells in town started ringing, and everyone turned out with a great hue and cry, thinking the English were upon them. When the ships' officers reached the piers the high waves made it impossible to embark in small boats to go out to the naos, and the cabin boys and slaves who were aboard could not launch a skiff to get ashore.

The anchors of the *Santa Cruz* began to drag toward a sand bank, but they finally held. The cables of the Malacca ship gave way, and although there was a heavy spare anchor catted in place, those aboard did not know how to let it go. The ship keeled over so badly that they cut away the masts, but in spite of this measure it was driven up on the rocks at the foot of a cliff and sank. The top deck remained above the surface of the water, but it was swept by the raging seas and all aboard were lost. The other ships, including the *Santa Cruz*, began to drive up on the shore, and in some of them the men decided in desperation to cut the masts. Then, as suddenly as it had come, the wind veered to the northwest, the seas became calm, and the five remaining pepper ships were saved.

The Predators

JAN WROTE, "It was a great pittie to see what costly thinges from the shippe from Malacca as silkes, damaskes, clothes of gold and silver and such like wares fleeted upon the sea and were torne in peeces." The unfortunate owners hired divers to salvage much cargo from the sunken hull, although a considerable portion of it was spoiled by the salt water. Many costly items were retrieved, but as soon as anything was brought ashore it was seized by the local customs agents, who were not unhappy that valuables destined for their brethren in Lisbon should fall into their clutches instead. The owners begged to be allowed to send their shipwrecked property in caravels and fishing smacks to Lisbon, and offered to put up bonds to insure its delivery to the customs authorities there. They gave many presents to the officials, but they were all to no avail, for these worthies appropriated whatever caught their fancy, promising to pay for it later—which Jan said they never did. No consideration was given to the hardships and the expense which the merchants had undergone during the cruel siege of Malacca and later in the hazardous rounding of the Cape. Jan said that the pleas of the ruined traders were pitiful, but they had not the slightest effect upon the hard-hearted bureaucrats.

An Important Appointment

EVIDENTLY Gerrit van Afhuysen, who probably was not fluent in Portuguese, nor familiar with their predatory customs bureau, was unable to cope with this problem and turned to Jan for advice—indeed, more than advice, for he enlisted him as a go-between. As it happened, the pepper on the *Santa Cruz*, for which Jan was the king's factor, and the spices and other goods on the Malacca ship, both were for the account of the same "farmers," the German firm of Welser. Word came from them by caravel from Lisbon, no doubt at Afhuysen's request, assigning to Jan the task of negotiating with the royal tariff examiners at Angra. Apparently because of his extensive experience with similar bureaucrats in India, Jan was given seniority over his friend. He accepted this employment, and through some secret arrangement by his powerful employers he had his own goods and ventures quietly taken from the *Santa Cruz* and sent "by other shippes" to Lisbon for his private account; in the meanwhile he went ashore to salvage as much as possible of the shipwrecked treasures, not only from the sunken ship in the harbor, but more pressingly still, from the avaricious officials.

His new position as a king's functionary was one of some prestige, having been astutely arranged by the Welsers, whose position at court was very strong. At all events, the twenty-six-year-old Netherlander was treated with unusual attention by Dom Cristóbal de Moura, the Governor of the Azores; he established himself on such friendly terms with the Governor that he not only received permission to go anywhere that he wished in Terceira, but actually twice was lent the Governor's own horses to make exploring trips with his friend Afhuysen. Jan wrote: "And [he] gave us leave to see all the fortes, which at this time is not permitted to the naturall borne Ilanders . . . We road twice about the Iland, which he granted us leave to doe by meanes of certaine particular friendship we had with him, neyther could the Portingales hinder us therein, because wee were in the King's service, as Factors for the King's pepper." Of course, Jan's status as a loyal subject of Philip II from Spanish-held Haarlem, and Afhuysen's citizenship in Spanish Antwerp, gave them as good a claim to acceptance as any Spaniard.

"The Governor would willinglie have had mee to have drawn a plot of the whole Iland that he might have sent it to the King; wherein I excused myself; yet I made him the town with the Haven coming in and the Fortes of Angra which he sent unto the King, the like whereof you may in this Booke behold for the which the Governor was greatlie affected unto mee and showed mee much friendship.

"Wee had in our lodging a French merchant and a Scot, that willinglie would have gone with us to see the Iland, but could not be suffered." At that time the Scots, as alert as the Dutchmen to turn a penny wherever possible, were active traders in Hispanic markets; the Kingdom of Scotland was neutral in the struggle between England and Spain, and Scotchmen often were sought as go-betweens by both sides.

Jan's advancement in the service of the Welsers and in the favor of the Spaniards came somewhat later than the actual disaster. However, he must have stepped forward immediately after August 4th, the date of the loss of the ship in the storm, to help his harassed friend Afhuysen. On August 8, 1589, the officers of the pepper fleet had a conference with the Governor and asked permission to ignore the order of the Lisbon Admiralty to wait in Angra until a fleet could be sent to convoy them to Lisbon. A strong war galleon had just arrived in Angra en route to Lisbon, from Pernambuco, Brazil, with the Governor of Brazil aboard. The captains of the pepper ships, rightfully fearful of the hazards of their Angra haven, were willing to run the gauntlet to Lisbon if accompanied by the galleon.

The Fleet Escapes

THE GOVERNOR was in a difficult position. He could have played safe by merely acknowledging his lack of authority to overrule the Admiralty, but in view of the great need of the crown for the pepper revenues, and also because of the peril of their anchorage, he patriotically made a bold decision. Undoubtedly at the risk of his head, Dom Cristóbal took it upon himself to override the Admiralty. His boldness was rewarded, for on August 12, 1589, two days after the naos had sailed, an English squadron of six ships of the line under Cumberland appeared off Angra and drew close in to survey the harbor, but sailed off upon ascertaining that the birds had flown. The boldness and initiative of the governor stands out in refreshing contrast to the inertia and general paralysis which then plagued the Spanish bureaucracy and handicapped the Spanish administration at all levels.

The very next day, the five pepper naos and the Brazilian galleon reappeared at Angra, having been driven back by contrary winds. They hastily took on fresh water, were reinforced by the governor with four hundred Spanish soldiers from the fort, and quickly made sail again, for fear of the return of Cumberland. Their luck held, and in eleven days they passed over the bar of the Tagus, just a day before Sir Francis Drake appeared there with forty men of war, seeking them. The elusive pepper fleet had been almost eight months en route; the *Santa Maria* had weighed anchor at Cochin on January 1, 1589, and dropped anchor at Lisbon on July 24th. The five Indiamen hastily moved far up the river, where they were protected by royal war galleys; the English did not dare try to force the harbor defenses and risk being trapped in the Tagus.

The pepper fleet's safe arrival was celebrated with "great gladness and triumph." It was indeed a lucky thing for Portugal, for, as Jan wrote, "you may sufficientlie perceive how that onely by the grace and special favor of God, the Indian ships do performe their voiages, yet with great miserie, paine and labour, losse and hinderance. . . . This present voiage may be considered a happy and prosperous voiage, for oftentimes it chanceth that but one or two of the five that yearely sail to India come safe home, as of late it hath bin seene."

These concluding remarks summed up Jan's account of the pepper ships' round trip to India. They reaffirmed what he wrote his parents in 1584 concerning his personal distaste for the discomforts of the *Carreira da India,* which he found so repugnant that he would have preferred to take the overland caravan route home. This was probably one reason why he later declined to participate in the pioneer Dutch ocean voyage to the East, in 1594, despite his exceptional qualifications. It also no doubt explained his dedicated interest in persistently trying to find a shorter, safer route to the Orient via the North Pole.

However, all that was in the future. Although the *Santa Cruz,* with Constable Dirck Gerritszoon aboard, lay safely moored in what Jan always called "the River of Lisbon," he and Gerrit van Afhuysen were still far from Lisbon in the Flemish Isles, guarding the shipwrecked treasure from the Malacca ship. Although Dirck Gerritszoon had left the Flemish Isles on the *Santa Cruz* in August, 1589, expecting his two friends to follow soon, it was not until two and a half years later that they were finally able to reach Lisbon. Dirck by that time was back home in Enkhuizen, where the neighbors nicknamed him "China" because he was the first Dutchman to come back with a first-hand report of that fabled land.

On Guard at Angra

FOR THE TWO who remained in Angra to direct the work, the labor of sending divers down to bring up the valuable cargo, salvaging and re-conditioning it, and its inventorying and valuing, was soon completed. After that, all that Jan and Afhuysen had to do was guard the merchandise as well as they could from the constant pilfering of the Azorean customs officials. They also supported the individual and collective efforts of the shipwrecked merchants to get official permission locally to withdraw their consignments, upon the posting of a bond for the putative amount of tariff in Lisbon; if such permission were granted, the merchants then would be free to convey their cargo, at their own risk and expense, in caravels or fishing boats, to Lisbon. However, despite pleas, bribes and political pressure the desired release was not granted, although it was always dangled just beyond the reach of the distressed petitioners.

Since most of the king's pepper from the Malacca ship had been re-stored to a marketable condition, the Welsers, with all their court influ-ence, were continually being promised that a well-armed galleon would be sent promptly to bring the pepper to Lisbon. However, the eagerly awaited ship never came, despite the pledges with which Jan and Afhuysen were regularly beguiled. Exporters and importers were accustomed to being patient in the days of sailing ships and pack trains, whose routes were often cut off by the far-flung events of the constant warfare of the period. Therefore the phlegmatic young Netherlanders adapted them-selves, as a matter of course, to delays that would exasperate a modern merchant to a point of extreme frustration. In fact, with all their procras-tination and bureaucratic bumbling, the Hispanic officials could have been matched and even surpassed in slowness by the dawdling Dutch func-tionaries of Jan's own homeland. The young Netherlander was later to learn this to his great cost, when he was commissioned to outfit a Dutch fleet speedily and encountered nothing but official delay, inertia, and empty promises.

Jan complained acidly, in the *Itinerario*, of the unconscionable delays to which he and Afhuysen were subjected by the customs administration at Angra, and he wrote feelingly of the distress suffered by the unfortunate merchant venturers who had gone through many privations and risks in foreign lands and at sea and were now being barbarously misused by their own countrymen, from whom they should have received sympathetic assistance.

Jan, held idle by red tape and delays, set an example to any man by the truly admirable manner in which he adapted himself to the situation and converted his personal frustration into benefit. He developed and expanded notably in knowledge, savoir faire, and penetration during his two and a half years' ordeal in Angra. It was a period of ripening and maturing for his personality, a respite during which he was able to digest and master all the knowledge and experience he had gained up to that time. When he landed at Lisbon at last, after nine years of absence, his mature assurance and attitude of responsibility had probably largely been developed and polished at Angra.

His position as Royal Pepper Factor, with its accompanying perquisites and privileges, gave him a position of authority in the colonial society of the little port. It was a period of great uncertainty, and naturally Angra seethed with discontent and anxieties. Jan, however, instead of seeking distraction in recreation and idle pastimes, as most men would have done, turned his attention to the notes and drawings he had compiled during his travels, and it seems probable that a great part of the text of the *Itinerario* was written during this enforced pause in his activities. Moreover, in Angra he no doubt had access to the great Portuguese chronicles and geographical and botanical works from which he drew so copiously.

The Azores lay at the ocean crossroads of the world, and had a floating population including many stranded or retired Portuguese masters and pilots; therefore Jan was able to acquire here much of the priceless sea lore which he later put into the pages of his maritime handbook, the *Reysgeschrift*. It seems reasonable to surmise that these top secret rutters, or sea journals, of the royal navy and of the *Carreira da India* would not have been available to Jan had not the ill-used Azorean pilots and masters hated the mainland administration of their Spanish conquerors.

When the Reverend Petrus Plancius and his associates in Amsterdam later set out to obtain Spanish and Portuguese sea charts and *roteiros* in preparation for the invasion of the preserves of the *Carreira da India*, their secret agents and the Dutch diplomats used bribery to try to achieve their ends, and their underground activities had the tacit support of the Dutch authorities. However, when Jan gathered the nautical information which was printed verbatim in the *Reysgeschrift*, he did it without any suggestion or subsidy from the Netherlands government. His effort was apparently made because of his interest in the subject and his patriotism—as well as his personal ambition. He acquired all his indispensable navigational data through personal enthusiasm and zeal in pursuing what may have begun almost as a hobby.

The Atlantic Islands

The Flemish Isles

T H E *Itinerario* devoted considerable space to the Azores. One chapter, headed "Description of the Islands of Açores or the Flemmish Islands," covered the seven principal islands, while a second chapter described the secondary and outlying islands of Corvo and Flores, and a third, the longest, was "Devoted to certaine notable accidents that happened during my continuance in Tercera." The comprehensive description of the archipelago was done in Jan's usual painstaking and thorough manner, and fully covered all the natural aspects of the islands, as well as their social and historical features. He somewhat apologized for devoting space to the portrayal of the economy of what was really a European community by saying: "This shall suffice for the description of the Flemmish Islands, called the Azores, which by dayly traveling unto them are sufficiently knowne; for that at this time many of our nation doe sayle thether so that everie marchant knoweth them. This briefe description therefore is by me set down for the instruction of such as deale not in the trade of Marchandise, and know them not, whereby they may see what manner of countries they are."

Be that as it may, the modern historian is grateful to him for having so minutely depicted the economy of the time. As he said, "ships come there not only from the maritime countries of Europe but also from the Spanish Indies and Brasilia and Cape Verde and Guinea and the Portingall Indies and all the East." It is apparent that the colonial life of this insular crossroads which he so carefully described reflected much of the atmosphere of a wider world.

The Azores were at that moment a center of warfare between the principal naval powers of Europe, and almost his every page, though he was only describing life in petty, obscure settlements, contains some echo of noteworthy events that were taking place in the influential chancelleries, courts, bourses, and banking houses of Europe.

He wrote: "They are also called the Flemmish Islands, that is of the Neatherlanders, because the first that inhabited the same were Neatherlanders, whereof till this time there is a great number and offspring remaining that in manner and behaviour are altogether like Neatherlanders." In writing of the Island of Fayal he said: "In that Iland are the most part of the Neatherlanders offspring, yet they use the Portingales language, by reason they have beene so long conversant among them, and those that used the Dutch tongue are all dead: they are greatly affected to the Neatherlanders and strangers." It is not surprising, given Jan's objective attitude toward his own part in his narrative, that after his remarks about these kinsmen who were so "greatly affected" to his race, he added no personal touch, though he must have received a warm welcome from them. It would have been out of character for him to write about the personal interest he must have felt in these descendants of a colony of Flemish gentlemen and their vassals. It had been founded there nearly two centuries earlier by the sister of Henry the Navigator, a Duchess of Burgundy who had agreed to help her brother by settling the new-found archipelago with her sturdy and prosperous subjects. The Flemings, aristocrats and peasants, gladly came with their livestock and tools to enrich themselves by developing the islands.

The Paradoxical War

IT IS INTERESTING to note that the years of Jan's stay in the Azores, from 1589 to 1591, were just after the defeat of the Invincible Armada, in which decisive action the Netherlands navy, while guarding the home coast, did not directly participate. Dutch merchant ships still continued to serve as freight carriers for Spain, and even as chartered fighting ships to King Philip, and no Dutch corsairs or naval vessels yet raided the Spanish-Portuguese sea lanes about the Azores. Jan referred to Dutch ships being pressed into Spanish service as freighters in an emergency; however, such ships were not confiscated, but conscripted, and presumably their owners were satisfactorily compensated for them.

Those same two years in the Netherlands saw the liberation of many fortresses and cities from the Spaniards, who had withdrawn their armies into France to attack Paris. With the hatred between the Dutch and Spaniards fighting in the Netherlands then at its very height, we see in Jan's book how very dependent Spain was, nevertheless, upon Dutch merchant vessels to supply not only foodstuffs for the Spanish people, but also to bring to Spain essential naval stores from the Baltic. The same Dutch yachts and flyboats that fed the civil populace of Spain were allowed to take back to the Netherlands the vast volume of salt needed for the herring industry, upon which the Dutch economy relied. This paradoxical situation has, of course, been commented upon at length by political economists, yet nowhere is it demonstrated so strikingly and so unconsciously as in Jan's narrative of the events during his stay in the Azores. He himself never perceived this incongruity, and he only incidentally and unintentionally brought out the fact that Spain and Portugal would have been even more at the mercy of the British cruisers had England dared at that time to violate the flag of Dutch merchant shipping. However, the English were the principal allies of the Dutch army, and recognized, albeit reluctantly, that the sale of marine supplies from the Baltic to the Spanish Admiralty and the sale of food and munitions by the Dutch to the Spanish army quartermasters provided funds that kept the Dutch Republic afloat financially; therefore the English naval squadrons patrolling the Spanish coast respected blockade runners that flew the Dutch flag and which claimed the rights of neutrals.

It also is evident that many English merchantmen came to the Azores to get woad, an essential vegetable dye used in textile manufacturing; these merchantmen pretended to be of Scottish registry, although the sham appears to have been fairly transparent, and was winked at by the authorities.

Another point of interest incidentally disclosed in this narrative is the relative humanity displayed by English naval commanders toward the Spaniards they captured, both from merchant prizes and from war galleons. In the early part of the sixteenth century, no quarter had been shown by the Spaniards to passengers or crews of "Lutheran" ships intruding upon the waters about the Azores, and this savagery had been repaid with interest by the English and Dutch. Jan wrote, however, of several cases in which the English took pains to put ashore the complement of their prizes, instead of letting them "swim for it." Also he mentioned the courteous consideration shown by both sides to naval officers who were captured. War at sea was still piratical and brutal, but some slight measure of chivalry seems to have entered into it.

The Rivalry of the Sea Kings

PERHAPS the most important of the incidental contributions made to our interpretation of the period by Jan's account "of certaine notable and memorable accidents that happened during my continuance in Tercera" is the perspective which he had from the high cliffs of that sea-girt natural watchtower upon the struggle for the mastery of the seas which went on before his eyes in the critical years of 1589–1591. No chronicler of world events and trends was ever more marine-minded than the young Enkhuizer, no point of vantage was more suitable than Terceira, and no audience more sophisticated and understanding in nautical matters than the amphibious sixteenth-century Dutchmen for whom his story was written. What Jan was privileged to witness was the passing of the scepter of sea power, and hence of world power, from the sea-kings of the Iberian peninsula to the northern sailors who ruled the Narrow Seas. Jan did not see this as an epic drama being enacted before him, nor was he conscious of its enormous historical significance. Penetrating and broad as was his vision, his recital of nautical events was little more than the prosaic chronicle of sailings, entries, wrecks and disappearances, of storms and of captures, such as today would be read in the maritime columns of newspapers in any great seaport—though it would doubtless be withheld during a time of war and blockade. It is not naval history except incidentally, but is rather a collection of marine news items about sailing ships in a time of extreme stress. He was viewing the foundering of a great ocean realm, due not so much to the superiority of one contestant over the other as to the fact that one was so continually stricken by the natural elements that both grew to believe supernatural intervention was tipping the scales of victory. The consistent ill luck of the Spaniards and the almost universal good fortune of the English against them finally resulted in a spirit of fatalistic demoralization in the one and a confident sense of invincibility in the other.

Neptune Takes Sides

JAN SHOWED THIS as he described the good fortune of a fleet of nineteen galleons laden with silver which was bound for San Lucar and was diverted by contrary winds to Lisbon, thus avoiding an English fleet of twenty ships lying in wait for them outside their original destination. "For if the Englishmen had met with them, they had surely beene in great danger and possibly but few of them had escaped by reason of the feare wherewith they were possessed because fortune, or rather God, was wholly against them, which is a sufficient cause to make ye Spaniards out of hart; to the contrarie to give the Englishmen more courage, and to make them bolder for that they are victorious seeing al their enterprises doe take so good effect that thereby they are become Lordes and masters of the Sea and neede care for no man as it well appeareth."

Just a century had elapsed since the first voyage of Columbus, and during that period innumerable ships of Spain had crossed the Atlantic from the New World without fear of maritime foe and with a reasonable degree of safety from the perils of the sea. The art of building wooden sailing ships had advanced greatly, the Spanish galleons were masterpieces of naval architecture, and the Spanish navigators were rivalled only by the pilots of Portugal.

At the beginning of the sixteenth century, Spain was a great manufacturing nation, as well as an agricultural and pastoral one. However, by Jan's time, it had sent so many members of its population to its overseas colonies and into its European armies that the country was no longer so great a producer, and depended to a much greater degree on imports from its vast foreign possessions, including great quantities of precious metals for conversion into coinage. This meant that, to transport its cargoes, the Spanish ships, like the Portuguese, were built for freight capacity rather than for speed or combat, so that finally the size of the hulls became excessive in relation to safety. No matter how skillful their shipwrights were, it was impossible to procure timbers of sufficient length and diameter to make such immense hulls strong enough, when heavily laden, to withstand a tempest.

This same exaggeration in the size of their ships had been a problem for the Portuguese, and for the same reasons. However, the weather conditions encountered by the Spanish galleons in the Atlantic were much less trying than those which so harassed the Indiamen of the *Carreira da India*. The Atlantic run was much shorter and safer, and the Spanish galleons could choose favorable seasons in which to make their crossings. Consequently the maritime losses of Spain during the early sixteenth century do not appear to have been beyond tolerable limits, and on the whole fortune seemed to have smiled upon their transatlantic passages. However, in the latter part of the century, the luck of Spain changed. Ill fortune began with the disasters which beset the Invincible Armada on its distressed homeward passage after its setback in the English Channel. That great war fleet had gone into action against the English in their home waters with a very heavy sick list, and despite the fact that its supposedly ample supply of ammunition became exhausted it had conducted itself with great credit against the slightly larger armada of the defenders, which also had heavier armament and handier ships, with replenishment of ammunition available. The series of running battles through the English Channel were so nearly a draw that at the end the English winners were in doubt of their own victory, and were glad to break off the action, once they were sure that they had successfully defended their threatened homeland. But the badly battered Spaniards, on their long homeward retreat around the north of Scotland into the Atlantic, were harassed and stricken by storm after storm and received no mercy from the sea, although even so, two-thirds of the unsunk but damaged fighting ships eventually managed a safe return.

From that time on, in the subsequent years of which Jan wrote at Terceira, fate struck blow after blow at the Spanish merchant marine. Spain had risen gallantly after the beaten Armada had limped home. The shipyards, armories and arsenals kept working day and night, and new and better fleets of galleons were launched, only to be overwhelmed by the sea as never before. The English navy, jubilant after its victory, was mobilized more strongly than ever to raid the Spanish sea lanes. Strong fleets under Hawkins, Drake and Frobisher blockaded the Spanish and Portuguese ports and brought home prizes worth millions of ducats. But as soon as the Spaniards, at great cost, had assembled a force to meet the English raiders, it was scattered or destroyed by a violent storm. It seemed as though God scourged the Spanish seamen and protected the British raiders. The tenor of these events was so incredibly consistent that, as Jan said, both sides accepted the belief that the hand of the Almighty was raised against Spain and that He sent His tempests to chastise them! Sometimes, however, the Spanish took refuge in the belief that it was Satan, and not the Almighty, who was besetting them. For example, Jan wrote a stirring account of the capture and death of Sir Richard Grenville, of the *Revenge*, whose action against the Spaniards was immortalized by Tennyson in the poem beginning:

> At Flores in the Azores
> Sir Richard Grenville lay.

Soon thereafter, when a dreadful tempest sank much of the Spanish fleet, Jan wrote that "this fearful loss by storm was even greater than that inflicted upon the Ships of the Invincible Armada . . . It may well be thought and presumed that it was no other but a just plague purposely sent by God upon the Spaniards and that it truly might bee said, that the taking of the Revenge was justlie revenged uppon them, and not by the might and force of man but by the power of God as some of them openly said in the Island of Tercera that they believed verilie God would consume them and that Hee took part with Lutheranes and Heretickes saying further yt so soone as they had thrown the dead bodie of the Vice Admirall Sir Richard Grenville over borde they verilie thought that as he had a devilish faith and religion and therefore ye devils loved him, so hee presently sunke into the bottom of the sea and downe into Hell where he raysed up all the devilles to the revenge of his death and that they brought so great stormes and torments upon the Spaniardes because they maintained the Catholicke and Romish religion."

Accustomed as they had been for generations to the invincible naval might of the king of Spain, the people naturally could attribute his downfall at sea only to supernatural causes. Jan wrote further in the same vein, and this time, in the spirit of the Hebraic prophets, he ended by cautioning his own countrymen to beware lest they, like the Spaniards, be chastised. "Whereby it plainly appeareth, that in ye end God wil assuredly plague the Spaniards having wholly blinded them so that they have not the sence to perceive it, but still do remain in their obstinate opinions: but it is lost labour to strive against God and to trust in man, as being foundations erected uppon the sands which with the wind are blowne down and overthrown as we dayly see before our eyes and now in the best times have observed and therefor let every man but looke into his owne actions and take our Low Countries for an example, wherein we can blame our owne sinnes and wickednesse which doth so blind us that we wholly forget and reiect the benefites of God, continuing the servantes and yoke slaves of Sathan. God of his mercie open our eyes and hearts that wee may know our onely health and savior Jesus Christ who onely can help governe and preserve us and give us a happie ende in all our affaires." This quotation from the *Itinerario* is somewhat confusing in its last clauses, because Jan apparently commenced by ascribing the misadventures of the Spaniards to divine punishment for their blindness and ill doings, and then he wound up by chiding his own countrymen, although not the English, for their heedlessness toward divine direction. Perhaps he had a superstitious feeling that this should be added so that Dutch luck should not change. Walking humbly in the sight of the Lord, he may have felt, was to be recommended.

It was customary in those days for Calvinistic writers to tack onto whatever was written for publication, and especially if it was a printed government paper, a homily, admonition or jeremiad in scriptural terms. Though this was termed by their critics "puritanical cant," Jan and his publisher were careful to append such sanctimonious clauses to many of his general statements. However, assuming that Jan wrote this in Terceira, it was logical that he should have first expressed the general feeling there that the dreadful marine disasters which had recently afflicted Spain were a divine punishment for the sins of that nation. This was what was being preached from pulpits throughout Spain itself at that time, with the injunction to all Spaniards to mend their private lives in order to appease the divine wrath, and thus to say so was quite orthodox and unexceptionable. Then, after writing this, Jan may have reflected that, after all, the beneficiaries of these divine punishments upon the Spaniards were his own people, the heretic and rebellious Hollanders with whose cause he might perchance be officially identified by the Spanish authorities in Terceira. Another explanation of the passage, then, may have been that as a safety measure he denounced the Netherlanders for their own misdeeds, presumably against the Crown and the Tiara. When the *Itinerario* was published in the Netherlands five years later, such a saving clause was no longer necessary for self-protection, but perhaps through faulty editing it was not deleted. Or perhaps it may have been left in the book as a warning to that faction in the Dutch Reformed Church to which he was then opposed. In any event, it is only the first part of the quotation that need concern us, as it showed how the series of catastrophes that so weakened the Spanish marine was interpreted as a sign of the wrath of God. It was only natural that this should seriously undermine the morale of a dauntless and hitherto always victorious people whose motto had always been "God with *Us*." The élan of the English raiders and later of the Dutch was correspondingly so stimulated that they ignored great odds and confidently attacked the intimidated and previously invincible Spaniards at sea.

The Atlantic Islands

Spain's Marine Disasters

THE MARITIME RECORDS of that period give the following partial list of Spanish losses. In October, 1589, of a fleet of fifty treasure galleons sailing from Havana, thirty-five were lost in storms at sea and one by English attack. Of the fourteen storm-damaged surviving vessels, twelve were intercepted by the English off the Portuguese coast, so only two out of the original fifty finally reached Lisbon. In November, 1589, two very large treasure ships from the West Indies took on a reinforcement of soldiers from the Azores and sailed for Lisbon, but one foundered in a storm in mid-ocean and the other was wrecked on the Portuguese coast. Jan estimated that in 1589, out of two hundred and twenty Spanish galleons which sailed from Mexico, Santo Domingo, Brazil, Cuba, the Cape Verdes and the Guinea Coast of West Africa, only fourteen or fifteen arrived safely in Lisbon; of these great losses, except for a few taken by English raiders, all were sunk by storms in the Atlantic. In 1589 a fleet of fifty ships laden with silver and rich cargoes sailed from Mexico for the Azores; thirty-five of them were destroyed by a storm in the Gulf of Mexico. In the same year fourteen galleons from Santo Domingo were sunk by storms in the Atlantic. In September, 1589, there was assembled at Terceira a fleet of East Indian naos and West Indian galleons which, with an escort of thirty men of war and ten chartered armed Dutch flyboats to protect them against the English, totalled one hundred and forty large ships. "There sodainely rose so hard and cruell a storme that those of the Island did affirme that in man's memorie there was never any such seen or heard of before, for it seemed the sea would have swallowed up the island, the water mounting higher than the Cliffes, which are so high that it amaseth a man to beholde them, but the sea reached above them and living fishes were throwne upon the land."

Jan described the horror of this calamity through several pages of the *Itinerario*, giving the distressing particulars of a number of wrecks, and concluding that the loss to the Spanish marine in this one storm was greater in men and ships than the total of the losses in the Invincible Armada of 1588. "Of the whole Fleete and Armado being one hundred and forty ships in al but thirty-two or thirty-three arived in Spaine and Portugale, yea and these few without mastes all torn and rent, and with so great miserie paine and labor that not two of them arived there together, next day the third and so one after another to ye number aforesaid. All the rest were cast away upon the Islands and overwhelmed in the sea, whereby may bee considered what great losse and hinderance they receaved at that time for by many mens judgementes it was esteemed to be much more than was lost by their armie that came for England [the Invincible Armada], but it may be well thought and presumed that it was no other but a iust plague purposely sent by God upon the Spaniards." Disastrous as was the loss in ships, which rendered Spain unable to defend its coasts against the English raiders, yet worse still was the loss of silver and gold from America, upon which Philip depended to sustain his large armies in Italy, France and the Netherlands, and upon which the whole exchequer was based. Likewise, the loss of spices in wrecked naos from India beggared the government of Portugal and prevented it from effectively defending *Asia Portuguesa* against the Dutch. It was what insurance underwriters call "Acts of God" which finally ruined Philip II and forced his kingdom into formal bankruptcy. But before this occurred, the indomitable ruler, although sorely hurt by the repulse of the Armada, rallied his strength and by superhuman efforts actually assembled another Invincible Armada, as strong as that which had been lost. This second Armada was ready to sail, and had aboard all the flower of the gentry and grandees of Spain, when it was suddenly smitten by a gigantic tempest that sank it almost completely, drowning most of its complement, the irreplaceable young men who were the hope and promise of Spain.

Jan wrote: "The 30th of August we received very certaine newes out of Portingal, that ther were eighty ships put out of the Coruna laden with victuals munitions money and Souldiers to goe to Britaine [Brittany] to aide the Catholickes and Leaguers of France against the King of Navarre." And then word came that Sir John Hawkins, with a squadron of ships carrying eighty guns apiece, and a fleet of forty warships under Drake, and other squadrons, was awaiting this new Armada in the English Channel. Once again the Lord of Tempests smote the ships of Philip, and this latest fleet was utterly destroyed. Mighty Spain then became so defenseless on the ocean that Philip had to send word to the West Indian treasure fleet to lay up in Havana for the year; when the order was disobeyed, every galleon was snapped up by the English blockaders lying off Lisbon and Cadiz. Likewise Philip sent word to the naos of the pepper fleet to avoid the Azores and Cape St. Vincent and make a roundabout approach to Lisbon, but the English took most of them anyway.

The staggering losses that Philip suffered in ships and treasure could be, and were, time and again, replaced; but the brave Spanish and Portuguese admirals and captains, men who were as irreplaceable to Spain as Cavendish, Drake, Frobisher, and Hawkins were to England, were irretrievably gone; it was these human losses, too, that accelerated the decline of Spain on the seas.

The Atlantic Islands

Philip's Fiscal Error

PHILIP II, a great King, was one of the most fortunate of men in a worldly sense, and one of the most afflicted of men in his private life. A slave to duty, his virtues were overshadowed by his shortcomings. He nearly succeeded in carrying out what he conceived to be his destiny, to become the master of the Western world. His vast dream was defeated by his fiscal limitations, a defeat partly brought on by his dogged refusal to accept the reality of two palpable facts, one of finance and one of engineering. The first was his blind stubbornness in refusing to recognize that the financial backbone of his empire was the income derived from the taxation of the industrial and commercial provinces of the Netherlands, and not from metals from the mines of Mexico and Peru. He used the revenues from the New World to destroy utterly the real sources of the wealth of the Spanish Hapsburg dynasty—Bruges, Antwerp, Ghent and the other Flemish and Walloon commercial world centers, where burghers of great industrial and financial genius had created for him, as Duke of Burgundy and Count of Flanders, the reservoir of an immense source of revenue. His destruction of this rich inheritance brought about his bankruptcy.

His suicidal program of pouring the gold of Cortez and Pizarro into the bottomless pit of devastated but grimly resistant Flanders and Brabant depended upon the maintenance of the sea lanes established by Columbus. Philip's failure to maintain the uninterrupted operation of his Atlantic ferry, the life artery of the Spanish European Empire, was the final cause of the breakdown of his military and naval program in Europe. Jan correctly diagnosed the trouble: the great, unwieldy argosies, bringing to Lisbon and to Seville the wealth of both Indies, simply "burst to pieces," as he invariably described the foundering of the naos and galleons. They went down in the same seas through which their smaller, stouter predecessors had safely sailed.

Jan, initially a loyal subject of Philip II, continually protested in the *Itinerario* that it was the overconfidence of the Hispanic naval architects and engineers that led Philip to follow the fatal policy of his royal Portuguese relations (for he was part Portuguese) in risking his maritime dominance by creating larger and larger merchant ships. In his chapters written at Terceira, Jan analyzed what was then not perceptible to the diplomatic observers in the chancelleries of Europe in 1595. The *Itinerario* correctly set forth the fact that faulty naval architecture was leading to the mercantile discomfiture of Spain in its struggle to retain control over the foreign trade of Europe.

In the catastrophic years Jan so vividly described, the Hispanic peoples suffered immense setbacks and enormous maritime and fiscal losses. Yet enfeebled as they were by the waste of their manpower, through courage and fortitude they still tenaciously retained the bulk of their colonial empires for three long centuries, and Portugal finally survived as a colonial power longer than did its English and Dutch rivals.

Release at Last

A F T E R Jan had served two and a half years in Terceira Island in the post of Factor of the King's Pepper, permission finally came from the Admiralty licensing the various owners of the cargo of the shipwrecked Malacca nao to bring their sequestered property to Lisbon on their own initiative and at their own expense. It was stipulated, however, that all goods so shipped should be officially recorded, and that a surety bond be supplied guaranteeing that the merchandise would be delivered to the king's customhouse in Lisbon. Heartsick and despondent after their many disappointments and frustrations, and in many cases already ruined, the distressed traders banded together under the guidance of the Pepper Farmers and set up a mutual company. For some reason the order from Lisbon did not license shipment of the pepper, but ordered it to be transported to the interior and stored there. This may have been a stratagem to keep it off the market in order to maintain an artifically high price, as pepper was the general vehicle for speculation on the Lisbon bourse, and its price was very sensitive. However, the cloves, cinnamon, nutmegs, mace, Chinese porcelains and lacquerware and other valuable cargo held in escrow in the customhouse at Angra were now released and licensed for shipment.

It is to be assumed that Jan alone was put in charge of this joint venture, as he did not mention his associate, Afhuysen, in connection with it. A "Flushinger," that is, a Dutch merchant ship from the deep-water port of Flushing (Dutch Vlissingen), was chartered from the mainland, and it arrived in Angra in late November, 1591. Because of the lateness of the season the harbor was dangerous, and haste was made to load the ship and get away, particularly as the coast was at the moment free of English raiders.

Fortunately they cleared before it became stormy. No doubt few left the Azores with any regrets, although Jan himself, now twenty-eight, had put his stay to good use and presumably also had taken what opportunities there were to increase his capital. In any event he had become, under the tutelage of the Welsers, a mature man of business, and had filled the dignified role of a minor Spanish government functionary. Above all, apparently he had utilized the unique situation there to complete the draft of the *Itinerario* and to acquire, weigh and polish the nautical data upon which the *Reysgeschrift* was based. To him it could only have been an agreeable and profitable interlude.

The voyage was uneventful as the Flushinger rode through some slight storms, and to their relief they encountered no sail except a fleet of ten Hollanders carrying wheat to the Italian port of Leghorn—which again illustrates the neutral status of Dutch cargo ships in that time of war. "And so by God's helpe we arrived in the river of Lisbone, being nine yeares after my departure from thence."

Jan stayed in Lisbon until July "to dispatch such things as I had to doe"; then, on July 17, 1592, he went to Setúbal, the Portuguese salt-shipping port, where he was sure to find a Holland ship which would accept him as a passenger to the Netherlands.

Homeward Bound

ON JULY 22, 1592, he sailed homeward on the *Three Kings* in a fleet of twelve Dutch freighters. His account of the passage was succinct, because nothing could have been of less interest to the average Dutchman of his time than an account of a humdrum passage in a flyboat from Setúbal to Texel. Yet this brief journal illustrated the perils of any ocean voyage in the days of sail, when navigating instruments still were primitive.

There was no course better known to European sailors than the run in midsummer from Portugal to the Channel. The Phoenicians had made it regularly, sailing from the Pillars of Hercules to the tin-bearing Isles of the Britons. Thereafter each succeeding Mediterranean nation made Oporto or Lisbon a port of call en route from the Straits of Gibraltar to the English Channel. The Venetians and Genoans were followed by the Portuguese, all of them laying over for the winter in a northern port and returning the following summer.

By Jan's time perhaps a thousand Dutch freighters followed the route annually. It will be remembered that on his first voyage, as a boy in a fleet of eighty Dutch merchantmen, he sailed from Texel to San Lucar in a placid voyage of eleven days. Despite the fact that every detail of wind, current, shoals and shore was intimately known, no one could venture upon the voyage carelessly. Jan remembered that his half-brother, Willem Tin, after doubling the Cape to India and surviving all the dangers of that dreadful route, on the presumably easy trip home as a passenger from Portugal to Holland was lost at sea off England with all his shipmates.

Jan's passage home was anything but easy. After a perilous and difficult voyage, not of eleven but of forty-two days, seven of the twelve ships in the flotilla finally reached Texel, and his own ship, the *Three Kings,* narrowly escaped being wrecked on the very last day of the journey.

"The twenty second of Iulie wee set saile, being in all twelve ships and because we had a contrairie wind, we put out higher into the sea. The twenty seven of the same month wee had a lasting storme, whereby we ranne against another ship, being both in a hundred dangers to bee sunke, for we were within a spanne of touching one another; but God holp us and wee parted from each other which seemed almost impossible: for that the bore [bow] sprite of the ship that came against us, strake upon our Foukyard and therewith broke in peeces and presently thereupon his Fouke-maste fell over borde, whereby hee was forced to leave the fleete." Such collisions were then common in fleet operations, due to the difficulty of sailing into the wind, and just three years later Jan was to suffer a similar narrow escape when the yacht of Willem Barentsz almost collided with his own in a storm in the Arctic seas near the North Cape.

"Another also of our companie had a leake, so that he made towardes the coast againe, where to save the men hee ran the shippe on shore, as afterwards we understood, and so we remained but ten in companie. . . . The first of August, being ninety miles in the sea, because the wind held contrairie, so that wee could not hold our right course, wee spied three strange shippes but were not long before we lost the sight of them againe. . . . The fourth of August there came three other shippes among our fleete, which we perceived to bee Biscaines [Spanish corsairs] whereupon we made towardes them and shot certain peeces at them, and so they left us." This incident shows why it was advisable for the merchantmen to sail in company, for even though Philip's warships would not have molested Dutch cargo carriers on the North Atlantic run, the Viscayan pirates, who were the best sailors of Spain, and fully equal to the Dutch in seamanship, generally hesitated to attack them when they were in a flotilla; the dreaded Dunkirkers in the English Channel generally also refrained from attacking a large group of ships.

"The sixteenth of August the wind being yet contrairie and because we were about fifteen passengers aborde our shippe, our victuailes, specially our drinke beganne to faile, so that wee were constrained to keepe an order and to stint every man to his portion, being as then one hundred and twenty miles from Hessaint [Ushant] inwardes in the sea, under forty six degrees which is called the half sea." Although they calculated their position as being off Ushant, at the entrance to the English Channel, it is probable that at this point the skipper was feeling his way. It was possible that the Dutch captain had figured his latitude of forty-six degrees with sextant or astrolabe, and concluded from his chart that he must be off Ushant; but to calculate his actual distance from that point as one hundred and twenty miles he would have had to see the English Land's End, or some recognizable landmark on the French coast, and then measure the distances on his chart. As Jan proceeded with his story, it was evident that the skipper later could not locate his position either in the North Sea nor when near his home port of Texel, but had to hail local vessels to get his bearings. At all events, he was pointed into the English Channel, and not into the cul de sac of the Bristol Channel, into which so many inward bound vessels had blundered.

"The eighteenth of August we had a storme whereby three of our fleet were left behind because they could not follow us." This is not clear, except that perhaps the three could not sail as close hauled into the wind as the others in the flotilla. The original fleet of twelve ships was now reduced to seven.

"The twenty fourth of August we cast out the lead and found ground, wherewith wee were all glad for it was the entrance into the Channel betweene England and Fraunce." Obviously, the navigators of the *Three Kings* still had to depend upon soundings to guess their position.

"The twenty seventh of August, being in the Channel, there came two small English shippes to view our fleete, but presently put in againe to the coast of England." These must have been naval patrol or scout ships, on the watch for hostile raids on Channel shipping.

"The twenty eight of August we descried land, being looseward from us, which was Goutster and Dartmouth. The next day we put into the strait between Dover and Calleys [Calais] where there lay one of the Queen's Shippes but she hosited anker and sailed to the coast of England without lookinge after us, so wee set fower men on shore [evidently these were passengers for England] and then wee had a scant winde wherwith wee entred into the North Sea not seeing any bodie.

"The first of September being clowdie we had a storm out of the northwest, whereby we could not discerne land, but in the evening we met two ships that came out of the East Countries. They had seene land saying it was Texel, willing us to follow them and so we discovered lande, being the Vlie but wee thinking it to bee Texel would not follow the other ships but put so neare unto it that we were in great danger; and then we perceived we had deceived ourselves and saw the other ships take another course toward Texel but we had the wind so scant and were fallen so low that wee could hardly gette from the Shore, and withall we had a sodaine storm: Whereby our Fouke-maste brake, our maine mast being alreadie crackt where upon wee were fully determined to anker there and stand upon good comfort and hope in God: and sodainely the wind came better, so that with great paine and labour about Sunne setting wee entered the mouth of the Texel without any Pylot: for that by reason of the great winde they durst not come out: so that to conclude we got in, and there with thanks given unto God we ankered. In the morning being the second of September, our Gunner thinking to charge the peeces and for ioy to shoote them off before the towne, a ladle full of powder took fire and with the force thereof strake off his right hand and burnt him in many places of his bodie, wherewith our joy was wholly quailed and abated.

"The third of September we arrived in Enchuisen where I found my mother brother and sister all living and in good health, it being twelve years nine months and a halfe after my departure from thence. For the which God Almighty with his sonne Christ Jesus our Saviour be praised and blessed to whom belongeth al power honor and glorie now and for evermore. Amen."

Thus ended the *Itinerario* and commenced another phase of the life of Jan Huyghen van Linschoten. He was then twenty-nine years old.

CHAPTER VII

Home Is the Sailor

Once More, the Zuider Zee

THE STORM-BATTERED *Three Kings* was cleared by the watchful Admiralty's police boat at the harbor of Texel on September 2, 1592, and the next morning at dawn was allowed to proceed. With a flood tide and a favorable wind, it sailed down the Zuider Zee past the busy harbor of Medemblik, and in the early afternoon the lookout at the foretop sighted the misshapen, squat, brick tower-fortress, the impregnable *Drommedaris*, erected by Charles V to command the water approaches and to guard the entrance to the harbor of Enkhuizen.

The fortified seawalls loomed up. No doubt Jan surveyed the scene with keener interest than any other passenger aboard as they advanced past the sandbanks and shallows which had always helped hold off naval attackers. He saw with practiced eye the forest of masts clustered inside the breakwaters that sheltered the inner haven, and also the many yachts, flyboats and busses anchored in the outside roadstead, exposed to any change in the wind from the prevailing westerlies. He must have classed the city's outer harbor facilities with those of Angra, on Terceira Island of unhappy memory, rather than with the snug havens of Seville, Lisbon, Mozambique, Goa, or St. Helena, in whose anchorages he had felt so secure from any storm. Although Enkhuizen's original protected inner quays had been somewhat expanded by digging extensions to its channels, it had become overcrowded. It was really adequate only for sheltering the

[181]

herring fleet and the ocean-going yachts and flyboats that brought in the Portuguese salt from Setúbal, but it now was called upon to serve far more than these. The port had become the base for the overseas operations of the refugee Protestant merchants from Spanish-dominated Antwerp, as well as the headquarters for the corsairs. The docks were congested, and many ships had to anchor in the exposed roadstead.

The Home Harbor

T H E *Three Kings* seems to have been an Enkhuizer in the established salt-import run from Setúbal, and as it limped into its home harbor with damaged foremast and mainmast its skipper probably needed no pilot to con him in, although no doubt the harbormaster's boat indicated the pier alongside which he should tie up. The quays ran in front of various packing houses, and a salt ship generally moored alongside the fish packery to which its cargo was consigned.

As Jan sniffed the familiar fishy whiff and the pungent smoke from the pickling sheds that combined to produce the unmistakable scent of salted herring, his memory perhaps contrasted it to the fragrance of the spice ports, with their verdant, graceful background of silhouetted, nodding palms and lush tropical verdure. The little herring port was overtopped and dominated by its two high church towers, with the belfry of the South Gate Tower their only rival; these three lent the only architectural grace to the scene, for the impressive group of municipal buildings which later was to ornament the town had not yet been built. The tidy brick houses, with a horde of noisy gulls perched on their gabled roofs, and the congeries of noisome, dingy, rambling packing-sheds all along the harbor front, presented an unpretentious panorama compared to the golden city of Goa, imperial Lisbon, or monumental Seville, but it was home. He had written, when tempted by the possible rewards of a career in India, " . . . in the end the remembrance and affection of my true natural countrie got the upper hand and over ruled me, making me wholly to forget my concept unto the contrarie and so committing my selfe and my affaires unto God, who alone can direct and helpe us, I entered unto my new course."

Nothing Succeeds Like Success

A N D N O W , pious Christian that he was, he no doubt not only gave silent thanks for his safe homecoming, but also asked for help and guidance in steering his future course amid the obstacles that would confront an ambitious young man in the caste-ridden community to which he was returning. He came back not as the tavernkeeper's lad who had left home a dozen years before, but as a successful man of affairs who had made his mark in administrative posts of responsibility in those exotic wonderlands which had recently become a focus of intense curiosity to his fellow countrymen. It is to be assumed that, in his two years' regime as "General Clarke of the Romane Apostolicke Commissarie to raise the tax throughout India and to keep account of said receits and monie with a good stipend and other profits belonging to the same," the honest Dutch accountant had not neglected any legitimate opportunities for personal gain, though we know he had not got rich. As factor of the royal pepper consignment in the Azores and representative of the German bankers there he could not have missed adding considerably to whatever small fortune he had brought out of India aboard the *Santa Cruz*. In the eyes of the business oligarchs who ruled Enkhuizen, his standing would be gauged by his monetary success rather than by the considerable depth of scholarship and culture which he had attained in his foreign travels, for in booming, busy Enkhuizen, after the monasteries had been closed and thus the old connection with the Italian and humanist world severed, there remained but one measure of worth—the florin.

Fortunately for the lad who had left as plain Jan Huyghen and who now was returning as the nabob J. H. van Linschoten, no struggle was necessary to gain recognition; his fame had gone before him. Although there was no established postal service of any sort, his letters from Goa had all reached home, brought by Dutch cannoneers and trumpeters in the annual pepper fleets, or overland by Dutch or German traders in the Aleppo caravans. His fascinating accounts of the great unknown wonderland had been circulated throughout the community, and excerpts from them had even been published. Later, when Dirck Gerritszoon Pomp, the constable of the *Santa Cruz*, had triumphantly arrived home with his treasure in guilders, he had been lionized and affectionately nicknamed "China" because of his Marco Polo–like yarns of the unknown Celestial Kingdom. Dirck's halting and inadequate narrative had been included by Lucas Janszoon Waghenaer in his nautical publication, and although "China's" prose indicated that he must have been (one hoped) a better gunner than writer, nevertheless it had awakened intense local interest. And we may be sure that Jan's prestige was greatly enhanced in Enkhuizen by the reports of him given by this loyal friend and shipmate.

During the past two and a half years in which Jan had stayed in the Azores and in Lisbon, he had had easy contact by letter with home because of the frequent sailings of groups of Dutch merchantmen from Setúbal and other Portuguese ports. As we have previously noted, the Flushingers, Amsterdamers, and Enkhuizers frequently carried not only Portuguese salt for their home ports, but also supplies for the Spanish army in Flanders, just as on the outward trip from the Netherlands to Portugal they carried timbers, marine stores and even armaments for the Spanish navy. Although these yachts under the allegedly neutral Orange flag ran some risk of being taken by English, Sea Beggar, or Dunkirk cruisers, nevertheless they generally were unmolested, and as the freights were very profitable, the skippers and owners took the risks. Consequently, although discretion in what one wrote was advisable in case it should fall into hostile hands, men placed like Jan were able to keep in touch by letter with the homeland.

In view of the intense eagerness with which he noted down and described, in Angra, the international maritime drama which was being enacted before his very eyes, it is inconceivable that he should not have written home of his experiences in the Azores, particularly since by now he had both the urge and the facility to express himself with his pen. Jan had been excited and aroused by what he saw from the high cliffs of Terceira Island, whether or not he realized he was witnessing an epochal series of historic events in which the newly developed sea power of England was methodically breaking down the century-old Hispanic domination of the seas.

Because of his advantageous observation post and his unique and comprehensive knowledge of the Hispanic marine, Jan saw that, even weakened by the incredible series of nautical disasters which had undermined its defensive power, Spain well might hold off the English raiders—if the Dutch freighters could take over the burdens of the Spanish merchant marine and free Spain's galleons to concentrate on defensive naval action. The only question was whether the stubborn Philip could be brought to accept the inevitable, recognize the independence of the revolted provinces and make them allies. He would thus free the armies which were tied up in the Low Countries while retaining the navigation of the Scheldt River so essential to his treasury, for his real wealth had always come from Flanders. His galleons would then be free to protect his silver fleets arriving from the Spanish Indies and his pepper fleets coming from the Portuguese Indies.

This situation was confusedly seen by certain enlightened men in Enkhuizen and other centers of political and trade leadership, but soon they divided into two factions. One was the mercantile peace party that was willing to let Spain keep Antwerp and the South Netherlands in consideration of vast trade benefits that would accrue to the North Netherlands. They were astute enough to feel sure that they thus could enjoy the profits of all Spain's Flemish trade without the expense of fighting for them. Moreover they then would not lose the invaluable services and capital of the exiled Walloon and Flemish refugees from the South Netherlands. The other group, the Orangist war party, objected to giving up its strategic plan to free the South Netherlands and wanted to establish a genuine United Provinces; this party was itching to join with the English in profitably raiding the ocean routes from West Africa, *Asia Portuguesa*, and the Western Hemisphere in order to weaken Spain and enrich themselves.

To both these bitterly contending Dutch factions Jan's information was of fascinating interest. Since he had for some time been sending home reports of vital significance, it is not surprising that he was given a warmly cordial reception by the ordinarily snobbish and aloof ruling class of the city upon his return. The bold young adventurer's adoption of the aristocratic-seeming patronym "van Linschoten," presumably first formally used in Goa to gain face in that pretentious, artificial, and cut-throat society, was now swallowed without protest by the arrogant oligarchs of his home town, by whom he was welcomed as a valuable ally.

Jan was, of course, happily received by his mother and younger brother and sister at *The Arms of Haarlem*, where he again enjoyed good Dutch home cooking. He distributed the exotic gifts he had brought to members of his family, and he listened sadly to the details of his father's death and with unflagging attention to all the news of near and distant connections. In addition, he was overwhelmed by the attentions of the notables of the town. He was the focus of great social interest and curiosity, and became the man of the hour.

Burgomaster Semeyns

JAN HUYGHEN VAN LINSCHOTEN was at once sponsored by one of the most distinguished of the oligarchs who ruled the town not only politically, but socially and financially as well. Burgomaster Meinert Simonszoon Semeyns, Councillor for the Stadtholder Count Maurice of Nassau, held a foremost position in Enkhuizen, and this dignified ruler of the town at once sought out Jan and showed him many marks of consideration, making the young world-traveler welcome to his mansion; there his son and his married daughter, Reinu, became Jan's intimates. Having been recognized by the ruling clan, Jan established a residence on Breestraet, in the fashionable end of town. He had been socially accepted and now had his foot upon the first rung of the ladder of success.

With keen political insight, Meinert Simonszoon Semeyns foresaw at once that Jan could be utilized as a tool for the further entrenchment of his family's position. Events confirmed his judgment. In less than three years, his daughter Reinu, who had become a widow, was married to Jan Huyghen van Linschoten, who thus became a member of the ruling clan of Enkhuizen. We now, of course, hear no echoes of society's gossip, but the fact that Reinu presented Jan with a daughter five months after the nuptial ceremony could hardly have failed to cause comment. However, history only records the dates of the marriage and of the baptism.

Local and National Government

MEINERT SEMEYNS was much more than a local politician, being one of the regents who at that time ruled the northern Seven Provinces which constituted the Republic of the United Netherlands. The organization of the nation was complex. Until the revolt against the King of Spain in the sixteenth century, the government of the Seventeen Provinces, as they then were, was the same structure that had been set up in about 1470 by the Duke of Burgundy. This was gradually demolished during the early revolution, and by 1572 the hegemony of the nobility and prelates had, in the seven provinces of the North Netherlands, been succeeded by a popular government formed by the assemblies of the various States or Provinces, who all nominally accepted as chief of state an official called the Stadtholder.

After the assassination of William of Orange in 1584, the powers of the office of Stadtholder were largely curtailed, and William's eighteen-year-old second son, Count Maurice, was made Stadtholder and given command of the armed forces. Although Maurice was popularly called Prince of Orange, the title legally was held by his elder brother, who was in Spain, where he had originally been taken as a hostage and later stayed on supposedly as a supporter of Philip II. The Dutch Republic then, upon the death of William of Orange, became in fact ruled by an oligarchy of lawyers, merchants and bankers, in the interest of the commercial and capitalistic classes. The ostensible federal ruling body or parliament was the States General. Each seemingly independent member of this national legislative assembly was in reality subservient to the direction of the provincial assembly of whatever province he represented. These provincial assemblies were themselves completely under the thumb of the boards of aldermen or the burgomasters of the towns which had sent representatives to them. So the States General derived its authority from the provincial assemblies, which were in turn under the orders of the town bosses, the burgomasters, or aldermen.

The boards of burgomasters had originally been more or less democratically chosen from the leading citizens of the towns. However, as the members were all elected for life, or until removed by vote of their own board, and as all vacancies were filled by the appointment of the board itself, each city council became a self-perpetuating autocracy. Before long the government of each town became the prerogative of certain families, who saw to it that they kept all offices and posts in their own hands. Others in the community, no matter how able, well-born or wealthy, could not become members of the oligarchy, except by marriage. It was a closed corporation.

Soon these self-created oligarchs were given the popular name of regents. The regents were the political bosses of the towns whose machines controlled the provincial assemblies (or States, as they were called), which in turn controlled the States General; consequently the regents in reality ruled the United Netherlands. The leader of the regents, whose authority was loyally recognized by the Stadtholder, Maurice of Nassau, was the brave, alert, and very able Johan van Oldenbarnevelt, of Amersfoort, who, having acted previously as pensionary (something like town administrator) of Rotterdam, was now appointed Grand Advocate of the States of Holland. Then about forty-five years old, he became the savior of Holland and Zeeland when they were literally at their last ditch, and by his commercial genius he brought about the great economic expansion of Amsterdam and made it a world metropolis.

As a form of government, however, all this was very inefficient, and the great energy and ingenuity of the resurgent Dutch people were much crippled by it. They were clumsily governed by these stratified political bodies which naturally split into factions; important decisions of state policy, therefore, were delayed and hampered by compromises only reached after much debate and negotiation. This can be illustrated by the political position of Jan's patron, later his father-in-law, Meinert Semeyns. Although Enkhuizen was in West Friesland, which was a part of the Province of Holland, yet Semeyns did not work with the majority of the regents of Holland, but was a leader of a dissident minority in both the provincial assembly and in the States General. This minority was made up of the regents of the entity called the Northern Quarter of the Province of Holland, comprising the then important municipalities of Enkhuizen, Hoorn and Medemblik. They were politically associated with groups of regents from certain other provinces who were commercially, and hence politically, opposed to the predominance of Amsterdam in the government of the United Provinces.

Regents Versus Orangists

As OLDENBARNEVELT primarily represented Amsterdam, the members of this commercially jealous group were politically opposed to him. It naturally followed that, in seeking a rallying point, the Semeyns group advocated that the Stadtholder's supreme powers be restored to what they were prior to the death of William of Orange, to whom Enkhuizen had always been loyal. Soon two political parties took shape, called the "Regents" and the "Orangists," although the members of both factions were actually regents. Likewise, although all the regents were members of the Dutch Reformed Church, their factional rivalry created a bitter schism in the Church itself, and Oldenbarnevelt was forced to assume leadership of one church faction and Count Maurice of the other.

Jan, immediately upon his arrival, found it politic to align himself with his fellow townsmen as a partisan of the Orangists. Likewise, he at once saw that it would be prudent to become a member of the Dutch Reformed Church, for although the great majority of the people in the United Provinces still remained Catholics, they were of the poorer classes and without political importance. Philip II had seized control of the Catholic prelacy in the Netherlands, filled the offices with foreign clergy, and used the Church as an instrument to perpetuate his own despotism. Therefore all the regents had had to align themselves with the national faith of the Dutch Reformed Church. No sooner had Jan happily stepped down the gangplank of the *Three Kings* than he found it advisable to abjure his loyalty to the king and to the Church in whose service he had spent the whole of his career.

Doctor François Maelson

JAN SOON GAINED the support of another personage in Enkhuizen who, while not a regent, was of higher and broader political rank than even Meinert Semeyns, with whom he was a colleague on the council of Prince Maurice, the Stadtholder. This was Doctor François Maelson, a self-made man about a dozen years older than Jan, who, like him, had changed his patronym, and whose brilliant career would not have been possible in an exclusively aristocratic society like that of Portugal, but could happen only in a democracy like the Netherlands.

Doctor Maelson was the son of a poor cobbler in Enkhuizen named Pieter Maeckschoon. As a boy, he had somehow acquired a good education, no doubt in one of the local monasteries. He displayed great aptitude, was given the opportunity to study medicine, and managed to win a medical degree. Although he commenced to practice as a physician, and presently became the town doctor, he soon developed an interest in politics which made it seem desirable to him to change his last name to Maelson, rather than the plebeian Maeckschoon, which meant literally "make clean," and was the designation of an orderly or cleaning-man. When in 1572 Enkhuizen was the first town in the Netherlands to side with the Prince of Orange, François Maelson was appointed pensionary (town clerk), at the same time representing the municipality in the provincial assembly. In 1575 he was one of three delegates sent to ask aid for the insurgent provinces of Queen Elizabeth of England, and in 1578, when Amsterdam embraced the cause of liberty, he was sent there by the provincial government. This led to his taking an important part in the deliberations with William the Silent upon the question of conferring the countship of Holland on the House of Orange-Nassau.

When, in 1589, King Philip having been abjured, the West Frisians aspired to become an autonomous province, Dr. Maelson was appointed "syndic" of their common interests by the West Frisian cities. The provincial States and Stadtholder Maurice then called a meeting at Alkmaar where all claims and divergencies were peacefully settled. Dr. Maelson became a member of the newly created council of the Stadtholder instead of continuing to act as a syndic for purely local interests. He also served his country as Minister to Denmark when in 1596 diplomatic differences arose between the Dutch republic and the Danish court.

Since Maelson had retained his residence in Enkhuizen, he now enjoyed great prestige there. When he showed favor to Jan, it greatly helped the latter's standing, and his support later on was to be of signal assistance to the returned traveler.

Lucas Janszoon Waghenaer

ANOTHER MAN of local consequence who admitted Jan to his friendship was the renowned maritime cartographer Lucas Janszoon Waghenaer, an experienced practical navigator who had retired to Enkhuizen to design and publish coastal charts. In 1584 and 1585, while Jan was at Goa, he had brought out his famous *Spieghel der Zeevaerdt*, which was translated into English as *The Mariner's Mirror*. Waghenaer's translated sailing directions, or routiers, came into such general use in England that they generated the term "waggoners" as a synonym for "rutters." In his *Thresoor der Zeevaerdt*, of 1592, Waghenaer quoted copiously, in the section regarding the Orient, from Jan's letter home of 1584, but without giving due credit to his source. It seems obvious that writers and compilers of this period were by no means as scrupulous upon this point as modern authors, for Jan himself did not bother to credit his Portuguese sources in the *Itinerario*. However, Waghenaer, in one of his subsequent books of sailing directions, the *Enchuyser Zeecaertboeck*, did acknowledge the help given him by his friend Jan Huyghen van Linschoten, particularly in regard to Arctic navigation.

It now is in order to interrupt our biography of Jan Huyghen van

Linschoten to give a sketch of the life and character of the man who became the co-author of the *Itinerario* and of the *Beschryving* and who at the time of publication overshadowed in prestige the self-effacing and hard-working Jan.

Doctor Bernardus Paludanus

THE NOTABLE of Enkhuizen who particularly welcomed Jan was the Town Physician, the learned Doctor Bernardus Paludanus, graduate in medicine of the University of Padua, a humanist and scientific naturalist. Formerly a Knight of Malta, a Count of the Empire and a Papal Pronotary, he, like Jan, had adhered on his return home to the tenets of the Dutch Reformed Church. He too had changed his name, from Barent ten Broecke to the Latinized form Bernardus Paludanus.

Paludanus was born in 1550 in the town of Steenwijk in the province of Overijsel of an old, established burgher family, but he is in the main identified with his adopted home city of Enkhuizen. (Some decades after his death, a history published by the firm of Elzevier, in Leyden, was to call him "the apple of the eye of Enkhuizen.") He apparently received his early education in the Cathedral School at Steenwijk, which was known as a good school. Then he is believed to have attended the famous Latin School in nearby Zwolle which, until the University of Leyden was founded in 1575, was the leading school of humanistic learning in the Netherlands. From Zwolle, he went on to a German college, though it is not known which one; a note in his autograph album dated at Rome in 1579 makes reference to his collegiate career in Germany. At that time it was the custom of men of letters to keep such albums in which they asked the interesting persons with whom they came in contact to inscribe some apothegm, witty or otherwise. Because the *Album Amicorum* of Paludanus has been preserved, it has been possible to trace some details of his early years.

That Paludanus had already attained recognition as a scholar in his early manhood is established by an entry in the diary of the renowned Dr. Carolus Clusius, who referred to having encountered in 1577 in Vienna that "most learned man, Bernardus Paludanus, the Frisian." It was in that year, when he was twenty-seven years old, that Paludanus matriculated at the great University of Padua, which then shared with the universities of Salamanca, Bologna, Paris and Oxford the intellectual leadership of Europe. The University of Leyden had only just been founded, but not its offspring, the University of Edinburgh, in Scotland. Apparently Paludanus was, however, in no hurry to get to Padua, for after leaving Steenwijk he first toured Lithuania and Poland and then visited Vienna before crossing into Italy. In April, 1578, he entered the medical school at Padua, and was fortunate in securing as his master the renowned Doctor Hieronymus Mercurialis.

Undergraduate Life

ALTHOUGH the majority of the students at Padua were Italians, there were many from Hungary, Poland, England, Scotland, and Germany. The University segregated the undergraduates according to divisions known as "nations." At that time there was no Dutch nation, and Friesland was recognized only as one of the seventeen Netherlands Provinces of the King of Spain; Paludanus as a Frisian was enrolled in the German nation —perhaps because of the affinity of the German and Dutch languages and the contiguity of their countries. Although Paludanus was a Catholic, a number of the German students were Protestants and, as such, although given equal educational opportunities, had to put up with various restrictions; curiously enough, they were denied medical attention if they were sick. However, such was their eagerness for learning that this did not deter them from attending the great university.

Padua was the inheritor of the wisdom of Antonio of Lisbon, who later was canonized as Saint Anthony of Padua, and of Albertus Magnus, the teacher of Saint Thomas Aquinas. With its stirring memories of Giotto, Petrarch, Mantegna, Donatello and Titian, it was a magnet for aspiring young scholars. Only a few years after Paludanus' graduation, the University of Padua called the immortal Galileo to take the chair of mathematics, and to teach medicine it acquired the services of the great English doctor William Harvey, who had discovered the fact of blood circulation in the human body. The University received much patronage from neighboring Venice, under whose rule it lay, and Paludanus had every opportunity to enjoy the unparalleled facilities of that dynamic city, as well as of nearby Vicenza, a great book-publishing and typographical center.

Tour of the Levant

FROM the viewpoint of modern ideas of university life, it is puzzling to note that, soon after matriculating, Paludanus took ship from Venice for a voyage to the Levant. In July, 1578, he was in Tripoli, then a stronghold opposed to Christian Europe, and in August he was in Arab-ruled Jerusalem and Bethlehem. He then went to Alexandria and Damietta, and not only stayed in Cairo but was permitted to go out into the desert to visit some of the famous ruins. Both Egypt and Palestine were under the rule of the Turkish Sultan Murad, who was then at war with Western

Europe; however, during the last half of the year 1578, at the time when Paludanus was on his tour, it may have been a period of truce between Venice and the Turkish Empire. At all events, Paludanus was not a mere tourist, for he evidently studied attentively the flora, fauna and geology of these exotic lands, made many notes, and was allowed to bring home his papers and many specimens and samples.

The episode is one of the several unsolved mysteries of the early life of Paludanus, and it may be surmised that in the Near East, as elsewhere, he was under the guardianship of a potent patron, probably a German Catholic prelate who had sponsored him. In relation to his voyage, it must be remembered that at nearly this same time Jan was writing his parents from India that travel in the Turkish Empire was safer than in the Netherlands for a European businessman.

The Grand Tour

IN JANUARY, 1579, Paludanus was back at the university; he must have been given what in modern educational terms would be called "credits" for having made the tour through the Levant, for in April, 1579, he was chosen as one of the Student Councillors of the "German Nation." However, in the middle of June, 1579, he resigned that college post and again left the university, this time to make a trip to Rome. He no doubt thought that a trip through the gorgeous Renaissance cities of Central Italy would teach him more than he could learn from the lectures at Padua. From Rome he went to Naples, then under Spanish rule, and he was back again at Padua in the fall of 1579. However, in December, 1579, he went again to Rome and Naples, and then took ship to Malta. This island was at that time the headquarters of the Knights Hospitallers of Saint John of Jerusalem, who had been driven by the Turks from their old stronghold at Rhodes and were given a refuge on the island of Malta by the Emperor, Charles the Fifth. Letters have been found in the Dutch archives addressed to Paludanus as "Knight of Jerusalem," and he might have taken steps during his earlier stay in Palestine to qualify for this brotherhood. It is possible that he went to Malta in order to be formally invested in this heroic and influential order. He returned to Sicily from Malta for his third visit there, and at that time, as a student of geology, he ascended the slopes of Mount Etna.

In early May, 1580, he was again in Rome, and, surprisingly, was appointed by Pope Gregory to the coveted position of Papal Pronotary. Then, returning to his classes at Padua, he attended lectures for only a month before submitting his thesis, for which he won the high degree of Doctor of Philosophy and of Medicine. The subject of his thesis is unknown, but in the records of the graduation of ten scholars at Padua in 1579–80 we find at the bottom of the list the name Bernhardus Paludanus Frisius. His university curriculum had included the theory and practice of medicine, anatomy, chemisty, and in particular embraced botany, which was the basis of the *materia medica*, and concerned the ingredients and elements of simples, potions and nostrums. The authorities were the ancient Greek physicians Galen and Hippocrates.

Doctor of Medicine

AFTER his graduation, Paludanus set out for home, but in a leisurely and roundabout fashion. In August he was in Innsbruck, from which he went to the great cities of Augsburg and Nuremberg, and thence to Leipzig. He then accepted the post of court physician to the important princely family of Von Schonburg, but after successfully delivering the Countess of a son he resigned, and from there made his unhurried way to Dresden. Apparently he planned to go from Dresden to the great metropolis of Antwerp, and a mystifying record exists showing that he had reserved passage from Antwerp on a Spanish ship to sail, on March 5, 1581, to Santo Domingo, then a very important city in the Spanish West Indies, and the seat of the first university in the Western Hemisphere. However, he obviously abandoned this plan and continued his tour of Germany, visiting Stuttgart, Baden and Heidelberg, and finally reached Cologne. There he received a staggering blow: he learned that an epidemic of the plague had swept through Steenwijk and that his father, stepmother and seven brothers had all perished, along with his brothers-in-law and many of his other relatives and friends. He tried to hurry home at once, but found that the Spanish army had occupied Friesland and a direct return was thus blocked. He consequently made a detour to Hamburg and took ship to Amsterdam, and thence went by boat home to Steenwijk.

A Sad Homecoming

SOME LETTERS written after his homecoming have been preserved and reflect the spirit of dejection and sorrow which possessed him when he found himself once more in the city of which he had so many happy memories. It was to him indeed "the abomination of desolation." Physically, the town was a shambles as the result of the siege and sack by the Spaniards in 1580. The breached walls, the stark brick chimneys still standing mournfully above the piles of rubble, the defaced public buildings gutted by fire, the desecrated churches, the rubbish-filled plazas with the rows of shade trees chopped down for firewood—all was rack and ruin, disaster-stricken and tragic.

There were many social changes, many new faces, and strange men filling the public offices once held by the dignified burghers of the old order. Paludanus was filled with anguish by the memory of all his family and friends and their old, happy life—all now swept together into the trench of a single, common, unmarked grave. It was impossible to withstand the forlorn loneliness of his environment, and his sorrow was fast driving him into melancholia. He had no alternative but to flee the place.

Town Doctor of Zwolle

PALUDANUS sought refuge in Zwolle, where he had old friends from his school days; and in December, 1581, he was appointed town doctor of Zwolle for a two-year term at an annual salary of one hundred gold guilders, with rent-free quarters in the old Bethlehem monastery.

During his absence in Italy, the political situation in Friesland had changed, and the old Catholic burgher families which had governed the towns for so many generations had been unseated by Calvinist leaders. The monasteries and convents had been closed and the priests deprived of their pulpits. In the churches, the stained-glass windows, crucifixes and statues had been removed, and the vast interiors were reduced to the bleak, white-washed austerity demanded by the new Reformed Church. It had not been so much a question of theology, for many Catholic Frisian leaders were themselves supporters of the Prince of Orange against Spanish tyranny. However, both the Catholics and the Lutherans stood on slippery ground, for both had been taught that a subject must adopt the religious beliefs of his sovereign, who was the Lord's Anointed. The Calvinists allowed all men the freedom to worship according to their individual interpretation of the Scriptures. Therefore when the Catholic Church in Friesland had perforce to conform to the Spanish king's program of imprisonment of heretics, in many cases of their execution, and in all cases the confiscation of their property, it was only natural for the people to turn to Calvinism.

Tangled Religious Feelings

THE DILEMMA of the rebellious Stadtholder, William, Prince of Orange, illustrates the problem which had to be faced by many Protestants who, having relinquished Catholicism, might still hesitate before the choice between several Protestant denominations. William chose the

Lutheranism of his German relatives. Thus he found himself still at odds with his Calvinistic followers, who were almost as hostile to Lutheranism as to Catholicism. Many Dutchmen always distrusted their great leader for that reason.

When Bernardus Paludanus, Knight of Malta, Count of the Empire and Papal Pronotary, encountered the changed religious atmosphere of formerly humanist Zwolle, he lost little time in conforming to the new religious views of the community. Evidently the unknown rich and influential prelate who had so favored the career of the young Frisian throughout Catholic central and southern Europe no longer held a place of power in Friesland. Undoubtedly his shock and grief, together with his hatred of the Catholic Spaniards who had destroyed his home, were contributing reasons for his change; he must either have felt an active dislike of his old faith, or have felt that it no longer mattered. At any event it no longer would afford him a career.

In November, 1583, the parish register in Zwolle records his marriage in the Reformed Church to a local *juffrouw* (maiden or miss). His bride died very soon, and he then took, as second wife, a widow whom he married in the town of Edam. After four years of service as the town physician of Zwolle, Paludanus resigned and crossed the Zuider Zee to West Friesland. In February, 1586, he became the town physician of Enkhuizen, at a larger salary than he had received in Zwolle—one hundred and fifty guilders, but without free housing. He was to hold this post for almost half a century, until his death at the age of eighty-three.

The Enkhuizen Physician

I N 1591, seven years after he had settled in Enkhuizen, the University of Leyden made a strong effort to lure him away from his post by offering him a professorship of medicine at a salary of four hundred guilders a year and with attractive privileges and benefits. The University stipulated that he should bring with him to Leyden his already famous collection of curiosities and rarities. The burgomasters of Enkhuizen became much agitated at the thought of losing their *Stadtsdokter*, increased his pay by fifty guilders, and urged him to stay. In September, 1591, he wrote a somewhat whimsical letter to the University of Leyden and declined their handsome offer with the wry comment that he could not induce his wife to move away from Enkhuizen. At that, the University pressed him even more strongly; but in November, 1591, he wrote the Curators of Leyden a firm letter stating that, quite apart from the wishes of his wife, he felt he should not abandon the municipality which had shown him such consideration.

Home Is the Sailor

In 1592, the same year in which Jan Huyghen van Linschoten returned to Enkhuizen, Paludanus made a voyage to England, the purpose of which is unknown to us, but his autograph album shows the names of many scholarly and distinguished friends he made there, including the famous historian, the Dutch Consul Emanuel van Meteren.

Paludanus' Museum

W H E N, in his college days, Paludanus made his tour of the Levant, he collected many rarities and geological, zoological and botanical specimens. These were the beginnings of his collection, which started out merely as a curio cabinet, but developed into a museum of natural history of no mean size and importance. As a collector, Paludanus showed considerable talent, and his "Kabinet" soon became a magnet for natural scientists from many lands and a source of great pride to the citizenry of Enkhuizen.

Northern Europe was just beginning to throw off the shackles which had bound its scholars to the writings of ancient naturalists such as Pliny, and was also rejecting the myths and fables of medieval travelers. Men like Paludanus now began to investigate, compare and record their own observations, particularly in the new continents overseas which had been opened up to the Western World. Hispanic scholars already had published a number of pioneering works of natural history, many in Latin and hence easily read by northern students. Paludanus carried on a voluminous correspondence in Latin in which he sought information and exchanged speculations with other naturalists wherever he could learn of their existence.

As a practical collector, he had managed to arouse the interest and co-operation of officers of many of the ships that came to Enkhuizen from the far parts of the world. He taught them to search for and note the novelties in which he was particularly interested, and showed them methods of preserving specimens suitable for his collection. He thus built up a corps of enthusiastic volunteer helpers who contributed substantially to the enrichment of his museum (and incidentally started the craze for such collecting among seafarers that helped to fill many curio cabinets in dwellings all around the world until the early years of the twentieth century).

A Volunteer Collector

W H E N Jan's letters home received some attention in his home town and aroused the curiosity of its inhabitants, doubtless Paludanus took note of the existence of the young adventurer and found some means of reaching him by letter while he was still in the mystery-laden *Asia Portuguesa* and influencing him to become an ardent and painstaking collector, who sought out and acquired for preservation many items of zoological and botanical rarity. Some of these pieces were identified by Jan himself in the *Itinerario* as being available for inspection in the museum of Doctor Bernardus Paludanus, and his narrative made clear what care he devoted to bringing back in his sea chests these scientific treasures, despite the hardships and cost involved.

Consequently, no one in Enkhuizen could have awaited the return of the Argonaut more eagerly nor greeted him more warmly than the renowned man of science so respected by all his neighbors. The esteem in which Jan was held by the learned doctor, who accepted him as a co-worker in natural science, must have helped his local prestige greatly, and Paludanus himself must have found the intellectual companionship of the younger man a boon in the sterile cultural environment of Enkhuizen. To one who had known the social and intellectual interchanges of Padua, Bologna, Vienna, Venice and Rome, life in Enkhuizen, in all its early Calvinistic rigor, must have been barren indeed. The regents of the period gave less consideration to an artist or a writer than to a useful caulker or shipwright—an attitude that has not been unknown in more modern times and in lands much closer to home.

Paludanus and His Friends

JAN, like Paludanus himself, had been hitherto closely identified with the Catholic Church and accustomed to the comforts and privileges of the hierarchy, even though on a fiscal and administrative level rather than on the scholarly plane Paludanus had known in Padua. It was true that Jan was in the main a self-educated man, and probably knew little Latin, but he was a keen student of political economy and a reflective observer of the lives and customs of exotic races. Moreover, he was quite competent in cartography and geography, the two sciences that were engaging the intense study of constructive men at the time. Although he approached the humanist learning of Paludanus with the respectful awe of a disciple, his vigor and common sense more than offset the stilted and pedantic processes of the learned doctor, so that on balance it may be said that the contribution of the junior outweighed that of the senior member of the partnership that was formed between them.

A Scholarly Circle

PALUDANUS, in his isolation at Enkhuizen, had found comradeship in two fellow alumni of Padua who resided in nearby Hoorn. These kindred spirits whose interests and background were so congenial to him were Doctor Theodorus Velius and Doctor Petrus Hoogerbeets, both medical practitioners but, like Paludanus, devoted to higher learning, both being poets of some ability. Velius' history, *Chronijck van Hoorn*, is still the authoritative source of information on that great seaport in that period. These two had led him into association with a third member of their circle in Hoorn, Cornelis Taemszoon, a young man of good family who had travelled abroad and who, like them, was devoted to poetry; however, instead of writing in the orthodox Latin of the Paduans, he was a radical who expressed himself in his native Dutch tongue.

Paludanus drew his three friends from Hoorn into an informal Enkhuizen group that he headed, including Lucas Waghenaer, Dirck "China" and Jan. Although the latter trio were men of the sea rather than of the library, one may be sure that in the interchange of ideas the scholars got as much or more than they gave—though they doubtless patronized the men without degrees and titles to their names.

Cornelis Claeszoon

W A G H E N A E R soon brought into the little circle his own closest associate, Cornelis Claeszoon of Amsterdam, a scholarly but very realistic and successful man of business who was soon to dominate the group. A refugee from Brabant, he had come to Amsterdam in 1578, after the Calvinists had regained control; the city, between 1572 and 1578, had been under the unprogressive rule of a benevolent Catholic oligarchy mildly sympathetic to Spain and loyal to King Philip. With the return to Amsterdam in 1578 of the Calvinist exiles, and especially of the Belgian ones from the South Netherlands, Amsterdam was reborn.

Upon his arrival in Amsterdam, Cornelis Claeszoon started in business as a book dealer; he was employed to help set up the city library, which was formed by confiscating books from various Catholic cloisters. He then became a bookbinder, and later he began to operate a small printing shop, doing job work and producing handbills, almanacs and astrological prophecies.

His printing business had developed to substantial proportions by the time Philip II seized control of Portugal, later placing an embargo upon the Dutch import trade in East Indian products and forcing the desperate North Netherlanders to try to find ways of importing these essential commodities directly. When the Reverend Petrus Plancius secured for Amsterdam, through spies and bribery, priceless Spanish and Portuguese charts and sailing directions, he turned to his fellow Belgian refugee, Cornelis Claeszoon, to print the maps and navigational data, under license by the

States General. The two formed a close alliance. Claeszoon became the pioneer Dutch publisher of geographical maps and writings and soon dominated that field, employing skilled engravers and artists, and producing handsome atlases and geographies. Always at his elbow was the learned astronomer and geographer, the political and money-minded clergyman Petrus Plancius.

Claeszoon at times farmed out the printing of his books and even allowed other publishers to sponsor his productions, but he always kept control of what was published. Like Petrus Plancius, he nursed a deadly hatred of Spain, and therefore he introduced subtle anti-Hispanic insinuations and allegations into his many publications. This was a most effective kind of propaganda.

Publication of the "Itinerario"

CORNELIS CLAESZOON, always on the alert for publishable manuscripts in the field of navigation and discovery, quickly perceived the possibilities in Jan Huyghen van Linschoten as an author. Jan, on his side, apparently soon realized that his new friend could be useful in putting out his works concerning the little known wonders of the overseas world.

Because of the suddenly intensified interest of the Netherlands in the possibilities of a trade invasion of the Orient to help the depressed Dutch economy, both men were aware that it was a favorable moment to bring out such material. However, when the publisher broached the subject to Jan, although the project was truly dear to his heart, his modesty and lack of self-confidence caused him to demur because of his lack of education and his inability to express himself in the rhetorical style of other works of the period on such topics. Impressed as he was by the learning of his friend Paludanus, whom he looked to as his mentor, the diffident Jan suggested that his friend might consent to appear as a co-author with him. Claeszoon no doubt decided that the name of the scholarly celebrity would lend authority to such a work and augment its sales, so therefore, when Paludanus consented, the make-up of the book was decided. It was to be Jan's personal narrative of his voyage to the Indies, his experiences there and his impressions of the Portuguese colonies. It would also include the equally interesting details of his return trip, with the occurrences of his stay in the Azores. All this material he already had in manuscript form.

In addition to this travelogue of his nine years' journey, Jan had written a description of the cities and countries extending from Mozambique on the East Coast of Africa all along the shores of the Arabian Sea and Indian Ocean, and of the China Sea to China and Japan. As we know, he had compiled this geographical, economic and historical account from the published works of the Portuguese, supplemented by such hearsay information as he had been able to pick up from interviews with travelers. In addition, he had written many essays on the zoology and botany of the area, almost all of it based upon Portuguese books. Jan was an excellent draftsman and had made many detailed drawings of members of various native races and groups, with their arms and apparel, as well as of the types of Portuguese colonists. He had also drawn scenes showing various phases of the economy. Besides, he had very carefully pictured the botanical species that were imported into Europe for medical and pharmaceutical purposes; any plant, fruit or nut which was edible and used in the Orient was faithfully depicted as well.

Jan also had brought back his illustrative charts of the cities and havens he had visited on his voyage. Claeszoon must have realized even on first reading of the manuscript what a masterpiece he had in hand. It represented the intensive labor of nine years, interestingly written, well composed, and co-ordinated. The range of the *Itinerario* was comprehensive and it was penetrating in its depth. While it was in part a compendium of selected, previously published works, it also contained many original observations based upon the experiences of the author. It not only was one of the most dependable texts ever produced for research into Asian history, but also indirectly served, by reflection, to interpret some of the thinking of the Europe of that day concerning world problems.

An Author of Parts

F R O M the text of his journal, the sturdy Dutchman emerges today as a recognizable modern European, even seen, as he was, against the background of a polygamous, slave-supported, wholly artificial and exotic society in India, and also in the midst of his distressful accounts of the perils of sailing ships, and of plagues, scurvies, disasters, fiscal losses and frustrations. The reader of today feels that he knows this matter-of-fact narrator, and finds him understandable and congenial.

It is ironical today that the contributions of the learned Doctor Paludanus which were appended to the journal of the supposedly unsophisticated Jan to give it tone and literary distinction are totally lifeless and without charm. Jan's simple, unaffected and compelling narrative stands out vividly against the pedantic prose of the renowned doctor, who had received the best liberal education that Europe then afforded. Even though Doctor Paludanus was a widely travelled man whose erudition was acclaimed everywhere in the Low Countries, a man who could have been a professor at the Netherlands' only university but had refused this honor, nevertheless, with all his fame, he possessed no facility at all with the pen, while Jan was a naturally gifted reporter.

Fortunately, it was decided that the annotations of the doctor, in their joint publication, should be set in Roman type, while Jan's text was set in so-called black letter. The flow of Jan's journal can therefore be easily followed by the modern reader, without interruption.

Medicinal Botany

DOCTOR PALUDANUS, like most physicians of his time, was an herbalist and a botanist and himself cultivated many of the plants and roots that were the basis of the *materia medica* of the day. There were, of course, no reputable pharmaceutical manufacturers, professional distributors, nor licensed druggists, nor were any chemical derivatives used as drugs. Consequently, all practicing physicians had to raise botanical ingredients for their simples in their own yard, and had learned the technique of reducing flowers, leaves, stems or roots into nostrums. The various duchies and principalities at this time made grants of money to purchase formulae and prescriptions for general use of their subjects, but most of these were the concoctions of quacks.

A good proportion of the medicaments and physics then administered in Europe were based on forest and plant products imported by the Venetian-Oriental spice traders. Paludanus was well acquainted with these botanical elements and had samples of most of them in his museum. In the *Itinerario*, Jan generally devoted a whole chapter to the description of each important botanical item, such as ginger or rhubarb, perhaps accompanied by a sketch. When such a pharmaceutical item was one with which Paludanus was acquainted, he appended his own comment. Practically all Jan's technical descriptions of botanical drugs were copied from the published works of Portuguese authors; his own contributions were largely commercial, which was, of course, the aspect in which the Dutch were mostly interested.

Of rhubarb, he wrote: "The Rhubarbe of Venice is better because it cometh overland than that which is brought unto Portugal because it cometh over water, as also are all thinges and herbes that belong to Physicke because they are better preserved by land than by water, they are little brought by sea, but it is a marchandise that is most caryed by land unto Venice, as also because the Portingales deale not much therein." Once again, of course, he was emphasizing the interesting fact that Venice was still a major factor in Europe's spice trade with India almost a century after Vasco da Gama had established the ocean route from Portugal.

Jan's treatise on any plant of pharmaceutical value was generally factual, and he treated it largely as an article of commerce. He described its appearance, growth, conditions of cultivation and local use, and the details of its export; while the comment of Doctor Paludanus was largely concerned with the medical use of the item in question. The latter's dissertations reveal the appalling ignorance of the medical profession in a period when there was little knowledge of the human circulatory systems, very little acquaintance with anatomy, and no understanding of such elementary facts as the causes and effects of contagion or infection. The medical authorities whom Paludanus quoted with respect, if not actually the classical Roman or Greek physicians, were ancient Arab or Moorish writers who had derived their theories from them—the same authorities quoted all through the Middle Ages.

Materia Medica

To QUOTE an example of Paludanus' style and subject matter, the following passage is what he added to Jan's sensible layman's description of cloves, which were a costly article of commerce and hence of interest to the Dutch. "The water of greene cloves when distilled is very pleasant of Smel and strengtheneth the hart, likewise they procure sweating in men that have the Pox. Some lay the polder [powder] of Cloves upon a man's hand that hath a paine in it, that proceedeth of colde. They strengthen the Liver, the Maw and the Hart, they further digestion, they procure evacuation of the Urine and stop lascativenes and being put into the eyes strengthen the sight and four drammes being drunk with milk, doe procure lust."

Of nutmeg, the doctor wrote: "The Nutmeg comforteth the braine, sharpneth the memorie, warmeth and strengtheneth the maw, driveth wind out of the body, maketh a sweet breath, driveth downe Urine, stoppeth the Laske [diarrhea] and to conclude, is good against all colde diseases in the heade in the Braine, the Mawe, the Liver and the Matrice. The oyle thereof is better than the rest for all the aforesaid named infirmities."

He prescribed mace, saying: "for a colde and a weak Maw, it procureth digestion of the Meate, drieth up all evill humors and breaketh wind."

Scattered throughout the *Itinerario* is a great deal of similar advice by the pedantic doctor. That familiar fruit, the ordinary date, was prescribed against pestilent fever, and he testified, "I healed my selfe therewith of a pestilent fever being in Syria." He prescribed it against the Plague and against "heate in the Liver and Kidneyes." The leaves of the date were said to cure "wormes in children's bellies." Another fruit, the preserved berries called *myrobalanes* "purge the stomach from bile, are good against shaking of the limmes cause a fair color and drive away sadness." Among other benefits, they were said to cure "Dropsie and Agues, cleanse the body and especially the Braines, Kidnies, Stomake and strengthen the Hart, give an appetitie and ease belching."

When it is realized that these prescriptions were confidently published, without reservations, together with explicit reference to the authorities, and represented the practices not of a quack or charlatan, but of a highly respected member of the medical profession, one gains some idea of the primitive state of the *materia medica* in civilized Europe at the beginning of the seventeenth century. It should also be remembered that, just as in Chaucer's time and before, the practice of cupping or letting of blood was widely used, in addition to such nostrums as Paludanus prescribed; and astrological influences, religious rituals and the application of holy relics supplemented medical remedies.

Although Doctor Paludanus had matriculated in medicine at the University of Padua and had won his degree, it is probable that he actually took up practice as a means of livelihood only after the changing situation in the political world had blasted his hopes for a loftier career; unfortunately, the details of his political plans are not known. His avocation as a naturalist and collector must have absorbed most of his time and energies, for his activities in this field were intense and widespread, and the creation of such a museum as his was no mean accomplishment.

The Collaborators

DOCTOR PALUDANUS may well have edited and polished the prose of his younger colleague in the *Itinerario*, for it will be remembered that Jan had perhaps asked for his friend's assistance because he realized his own deficiencies. Indeed, it was remarkable that Jan was able to write Dutch of even minimum literary standards, for since the age of sixteen he had conversed, read and corresponded almost exclusively in Portuguese and Spanish. Until he boarded the *Three Kings* for his homeward passage, he had been in the company of not more than a handful of Dutch-speaking people during the whole twelve-year period.

It is an amazing thing that Jan, who had arrived in Enkhuizen only in September, 1592, had, in collaboration with Doctor Paludanus, prepared for publication three voluminous tomes in two years. The first book actually to be published was the *Reysgeschrift*, or Mariners' Handbook, including many *roteiros* or rutters of Portuguese pilots; it was to have great influence upon Dutch navigation and in 1595 to be carried in manuscript form by the Houtmans on the first Dutch voyage to the Indies. Jan apparently compiled this book without the aid of Doctor Paludanus. Then came the *Itinerario* proper, with the Doctor as co-author; both the

Reysgeschrift and the third book, the *Beschryving*, were included with the *Itinerario* when it was published.

In the composition of the last book of Jan's trilogy, the *Beschryving* (Description), Paludanus was an almost equal partner, for he is credited with having written the sections based upon his translations from the Italian. In composing this book, neither man wrote from personal experience, and the geographical descriptions had to be drawn from numerous foreign sources. The work was a general survey of the geography, natural history and botany of the lands of both hemispheres that were unknown in the Netherlands; it had been suggested by Cornelis Claeszoon to round out the *Itinerario* and *Reysgeschrift*. Paludanus took it upon himself to describe West Africa, relying largely upon Italian sources, especially on Philip Pigafetta and on several Latin works, but Jan translated the Spanish account of West Africa by Lopez for him.

Jan wrote most of the text regarding the Western Hemisphere, drawing on materials in Spanish and Portuguese, particularly on the works of José de Acosta, Oviedo and Pedro Martyr; Paludanus translated the French of Jean de Lery on Brazil for him. There was no scholar or authority to whom the two workers could turn for advice. The only books available were the ones they were translating, which fortunately were dependable sources. Nothing had as yet been published in their native Dutch on the subjects concerning which they were writing. Under the circumstances, they produced a most creditable work. Inasmuch as maps and charts were to play the most important part in their book, it was necessary for them to go to great lengths to co-ordinate and reconcile the sectional and partial charts composed by navigators and geographers of many nationalities and of different decades. To collect and to join together these conflicting maps called for intense study and expert mathematical calculations. There can be no doubt that the publisher, Cornelis Claeszoon, sought and received the advice of Petrus Plancius on many cartographical problems.

One reason for assuming that Paludanus did considerable amateur editorial work on the *Itinerario* is that Jan was otherwise occupied in 1594 and 1595, when the *Itinerario* was being printed; and also, the book exhibits some inconsistencies and errors that its author would have caught. In this connection, it must be remembered that in those days publishers did not require the author to correct the proofs of his book, and in fact reserved to themselves the right to change the text without reference to the author. The latter, unless he was already renowned, generally was in a position subservient to the publisher; at times, a publisher even insisted that a work be published anonymously, except for the name of the publishers. The reason why Jan might appear to have been neglectful in the final proof-reading of the work upon which he had labored so long and so lovingly was that he had again yielded to his incurable wanderlust, and once more was launched upon a maritime adventure.

Historians have invariably commented upon the perversity of circumstance which caused Jan Huyghen van Linschoten to refrain from taking part in the First Dutch Fleet to the Indies, after counseling its entrepreneurs, supplying to them the nautical secrets of the *Reysgeschrift*, and sagely advising them to steer their course to Java, instead of to the Malabar Coast of India, which would no doubt have been fatal to them. Indeed, had he cast his lot with the expedition to the East Indies and survived the voyage, he would have been far more successful and would have grown far richer. It was an extraordinary paradox that Jan, who was largely responsible for the initiation of the voyage, should have refrained from going along.

It is probable that part of Jan's reason for not joining was his distaste for the hardships, squalor and disease that were inescapable in the *Carreira da India*, and which he considered could not be avoided by the Dutch expedition. In this respect he was well advised, as there were few voyages from Europe to the Orient which endured such suffering and frustration as that encountered by the fleet that left Holland on March 10, 1595, with a crew of two hundred and eighty-four men in four ships, and returned with eighty-nine survivors in three ships after a veritable nightmare of two years and four months of bickering, murder, mutinies, poisonings, and constant internal strife—and with a spice cargo of disappointing value to cap the climax. In any case, however, even had Jan wished to go, it is probable that he would not have been welcome, since the undertaking was exclusively an Amsterdam speculation and no Enkhuizer would have felt at home in it.

However, when the First Fleet sailed for the Indies in 1595, Jan would not have considered embarking with them, for at that time he was at the very pinnacle of success, due to his having become a favorite disciple of a very great maritime Merchant Prince.

Balthasar de Moucheron

FOR THERE had entered upon the Enkhuizen scene the kinetic personality of Balthasar de Moucheron, the great Belgian entrepreneur, who had found it impossible, due to the Spanish war, to continue to conduct his wide-ranging international business from Antwerp. Therefore, about 1585, he had established his headquarters in the city of Veere, near Middelburg on the Island of Walcheren, in the Province of Zeeland.

The world famous "Wool Staple," or wool market, of Antwerp had already established itself in Veere, and for years previous to that, it had been the "wool staple" for Scotland, then a kingdom independent of England. (Under the medieval system, a certain market was given the monopoly of trade in a particular commodity, and this market was called the "staple.") Since De Moucheron had been there for a while as a boy, when his father had had a business office in Veere, he felt an attachment to the town. As it transpired, however, Amsterdam would have been a better choice for him, for there his great vision, creative imagination and inspiring leadership would have found appreciation and a wider scope.

However, before selecting little Zeeland for his new base of operations, he negotiated with several foreign governments, including Denmark; and his decision to make Veere his headquarters won the firm support of Prince Maurice, the Stadtholder, whose principal backing came from the Provinces of Zeeland and West Friesland. This alignment with the Orange party automatically put De Moucheron in competition with the Regents' party headed by Jan van Oldenbarnevelt.

It was a crucial time in the history of the North Netherlands. The Seven United Provinces had been literally at the last ditch when the repulse of Spain's great armada by the English gave the Dutch a respite. Then Philip imprudently withdrew the Duke of Parma, together with his victorious army, from the Netherlands to France; as was noted in the last chapter, he had, as part of his grandiose design, prepared a second Invincible Armada, even stronger than the first, which was to support Parma's invasion of France. As we know, a terrible tempest destroyed the Spanish fleet, sinking forty large galleons and drowning five thousand of the flower of Spain's youth. Parma was left tied down with his troops before Paris, and he was unable to protect his rear in the Netherlands.

The opportunity thus presented was seized by the Dutch, to whom the initiative had now passed. Young Maurice, who had been reared under the tutelage of Van Oldenbarnevelt, and who had ability as a soldier, led the Seven United Provinces in driving the unsupported Spanish garrisons from their key points, and thus freed the subjugated provinces. Now the new young nation was able to breathe freely and to plan for expansion and advancement. At last it could challenge its ally and benefactor, England, in a race to seize the lucrative Oriental commerce from the faltering grasp of Portugal, which had been ruthlessly weakened by their common enemy, the world-dominating Philip II of Spain.

A New Nation Is Born

THE DUTCH, a rising middle-class people in Jan's period, had only one interest and one goal—profit by trade. As their chief asset in their race against England they had the abounding vigor and indomitable boldness of an entirely new nation. They had few resources, but an overriding lust for gain and much innate shrewdness and daring. Although the Dutch were an amphibious people, they were almost wholly ignorant of celestial navigation except on the North Atlantic routes, where they had learned it from the Portuguese who employed them as carriers to West Africa and Brazil. They also knew little of world finance on a large scale. Both these skills were essential to attain their goals.

At this time they were supplied with the needed knowledge, funds and systems by the capitalists from the South Netherlands who had been dislodged from the world metropolis of Antwerp by the ruin which the Spaniards had brought to their industrial and commercial trade. The leaders in the explosive development of the Seven United Provinces were uprooted Flemings and Walloons who had migrated north with their assets, not so much for religious reasons, as is often alleged, as because of the favorable opportunities afforded them in the Northern Provinces for the continuance of their world commerce. These commercial refugees had first looked to England as their logical second home, but they had been rudely rebuffed by both English capital and the English guilds. They then turned to their northern brethren who, being in desperate fiscal straits, welcomed them, accepted their leadership, and, being apt pupils, soon took over the vast world trade which had been brought to them.

The Growth of Amsterdam

T H E M E N of Amsterdam were the most wide-awake and alert of all the Dutch merchants in seizing this opportunity, and they quickly took a lead that was never overcome by their rivals, who were led by the maritime Province of Zeeland. The burghers of Amsterdam worked hard to attain and retain their leadership. They realized the shortcomings of their harbor, and therefore deepened their narrow, winding channels, installed buoys, put up lighthouses, and provided spacious docks and piers. Over two hundred thousand refugees crossed the line from the Southern Provinces (modern Belgium) into Holland in 1585 alone, and Amsterdam made every effort to attract these paupers who brought with them only their skills, trade secrets, and lists of foreign customers. The city offered refugee weavers, for example, fifty florins for every loom erected; they also lent two hundred florins on long term loan to every qualified artisan to help him to establish a business.

The fecundity of Amsterdam was amazing. Under the initial leadership of the Belgians, it was soon to outstrip London and by 1609 to become the chief city of Europe. In 1622 the population was about 100,000, and by 1662 it had grown to 250,000. Amsterdam inherited the manufacturing supremacy of Ghent and of Florence and the financial leadership of Antwerp, and soon it also had seized the so-called Spice Trade of Venice. Before long, the tapestries of Holland equalled those of famous Arras, their glassworks rivaled those of Venice, and in sugar refining they led the world. Lagging at the beginning in the maritime race, with only their humble coastal freighters, the Dutch soon mastered the transoceanic routes and even held supremacy over England as a naval power for a very short while.

World economic conditions very much favored Amsterdam's growth, and for a time the Dutch merchants were looked upon as financial miracle workers and wizards. However, much of the rapid expansion of Dutch industry was due to the policy of England and France who, as allies of the struggling United Provinces, so lowered their tariffs upon Dutch goods as to cripple their own producers.

During Jan's life there were also debilitating civil wars in England, France and Italy, which greatly helped Dutch trade. Germany, perhaps Holland's most logical competitor, was suffering such devastation in the Thirty Years War that its population was reduced from eighteen million to only eight million souls.

Dutch Domestic Development

THE ABOUNDING ENERGY and ingenuity of the North Netherlanders led them to transform their soggy salt flats, skillfully draining off the salt water and creating pastures upon which, by scientific development of grasses and hay, they raised the world's best cattle. They improved their crops to support three times the population on the same acreage, and had a large surplus to export to the rest of the Western World. Since the Reformed Church expected every member to work out his own salvation by daily recourse to the Scriptures, most peasants perforce became literate, and the resultant general advancement in schools and education was reflected in all phases of the life of the Commonwealth.

When Jan had reached Enkhuizen on the *Three Kings* in September, 1592, Prince Maurice had already won most of his victories, and the great resurgence of the nation was under way. In that year the frustrated Duke of Parma died brokenhearted, Spain ceased to be a threat, and the economic boom in the North Netherlands gathered force, with the Belgian leaders in Amsterdam reaping a good deal of its benefits, much to the chagrin of their fellow exiles in Zeeland and West Friesland.

Home Is the Sailor

Zeeland to Outflank Holland

BALTHASAR DE MOUCHERON, as fiscal leader of the Orange faction, conceived a plan to outflank the Amsterdammers and to assume the leadership which they had taken. He long had enjoyed a very substantial trade in Russia through the port of Narva, in the Gulf of Finland, going from there by land to the great annual fair at Novgorod; this trade was directed by his brother Melchior in the Moscow branch of the House of De Moucheron. After he had moved to Veere, his brother Pieter, who was the head of the London House of De Moucheron, reported to him that the Muscovy Company of London was doing a very active Russian business by sailing directly to the White Sea, north of the Arctic Circle.

The Muscovy Company of London had already experienced some competition from Dutch interlopers. Some Netherlanders had for a long time been quietly trading to Lapland via the White Sea. As early as 1557 they had reached Kegor, which is farther east than Vardo, and in 1562–64 they had continued to visit Lapland. In 1565 Johan Westerman, the Burgomaster of Enkhuizen, and his son Willem Jansen Westerman, had sailed to the White Sea with some Flemings from Bruges. Thus the route was already known to the Netherlanders before De Moucheron took it.

In 1587, Balthasar de Moucheron sent several ships to the White Sea, to compete with England, under a license from the King of Denmark, who at that time was also ruler of Norway; the results were so profitable that he switched his operations from Narva, on the Gulf of Finland, to the White Sea, although he left his brother Melchior to continue to handle trade and diplomatic relations at the Court of the Grand Duke of Moscow, the ruler of Russia. De Moucheron's principal early partner in the Arctic had been Oliver Brunel, who himself had long traded in the White Sea and who had established financial relations in Enkhuizen. Brunel had long been obsessed with the idea that it would be possible to sail during the summer season through the White Sea eastward to the Kara Sea and thence either up the River Ob straight into China, or else past mythical Cape Tabin to the legendary Strait of Anian (now called Bering Strait), and thence to China and Japan. It was the old theory of the Northeast Passage to China, proposed by Cabot a century earlier and abandoned by the English only after several tragic failures. Brunel secured financial support from De Moucheron and others in Enkhuizen to try out his theory, and sailed along the west coast of Nova Zembla; he secured a good cargo of furs and "mountain crystals," but his ship capsized at the mouth of the Petchora River, not far from Waygats Strait. He then went in search of a new commission, which he is said to have found in Greenland.

Home Is the Sailor

The English Pioneers

IT WAS EXTRAORDINARY that neither Oliver Brunel, Petrus Plancius, Balthasar de Moucheron nor François Maelson knew that in 1556 Stephen Burrough, captain of the pinnace *Searchthrift*, had been sent by the Russia Company of London to sail eastward from the White Sea to Cathay, had discovered Waygats Strait, thereafter named Burrough's Strait, and because of approaching winter had returned home. In 1568 another expedition was sent by the Russia Company to find the northeast route to China. The commission given to these adventurers by the English Ambassador to Russia, dated August, 1568, shows a greater familiarity with the Strait of Waygats (in Russian Waigatch, corrupted by the Dutch into Waaigat, or Windy Hole), the Kara Sea, and the River Ob than was ever later acquired either by Jan or by Petrus Plancius. Further records of the Russia Company show that before 1584 the English not only had passed through Waygats Strait and the Sea of Kara, but actually had sailed up the Ob River into the heart of Russia. Apparently all this detailed information was in the possession of the impecunious Reverend Richard Hakluyt, whom Petrus Plancius was paying through the Dutch Consul, Van Meteren, in London, to disclose some of the secret navigational information of the English; and yet Plancius learned nothing at all of these important facts. The Dutch, alas, were to spend much in lives and fortunes in a fruitless attempt to find the Northeast Passage, as we shall see in Jan's reports to the States General.

The Northeast Passage

GEOGRAPHICALLY, the idea of the Northeast Passage had merit, but it would have been feasible only if it could have been completed during the warm season, which lasts about three months. This same Northeast Passage has recently been effected by specially constructed, fast motor ships, aided by ice breakers, wireless, aircraft, sonar and radar, and along a route well surveyed, marked, and provided with supply depots; it will no doubt soon be monopolized by atomic powered merchant submarines.

Brunel, though an able and practical man, had underestimated the distance to the Bering Strait by several thousand miles, just as Columbus had underestimated the distance from Spain to India and Magellan the miles across the Pacific from Chile to the Moluccas. In his fanatical enthusiasm Brunel had gathered much corroborative evidence, mostly based on myth and legends, and finally had convinced the hard-headed De

Moucheron of the practicability of the scheme. So many incredible geographical paradoxes had been demonstrated to be true in that century that only the ignorant were skeptical and only the wise were gullible. To a man of De Moucheron's great imaginative powers and vast concepts, the plan seemed not impossible; and if he could establish such a quick, safe, economical route to the Orient, the Zeelanders would easily become the undisputed masters of Oriental commerce, bring England and Spain to their knees, and incidentally teach Amsterdam a lesson!

The Arctic Adventure of De Moucheron

H O W E V E R, even after conceding that the project would be at least a good gamble, De Moucheron submitted it to several judicious and responsible individuals in whose judgment he trusted. One of these was Jacob Valcke, the Treasurer of the Province of Zeeland, and another was Dr. François Maelson, who in turn took it to the Stadtholder. He approved of the venture, but said it ought not to be exclusively a Zeeland and West Friesland undertaking; he counselled that Jan van Oldenbarnevelt should be consulted and that it should be a national rather than a provincial enterprise. De Moucheron was not entirely happy about acquainting the Amsterdammers with the proposition, as he placed no trust in these relentless competitors. However, of course he acquiesced. When the plan was laid before the Grand Pensionary, Oldenbarnevelt, he called in the celebrated mathematician and geographer, the Reverend Petrus Plancius, who was known to be much interested in the Arctic, to give his advice.

Petrus Plancius

P E T R U S P L A N C I U S, born in 1552 in a border village of West Flanders as Pieter Platevoet (Peter Flatfoot in English—Plancius being the Latin version of the name which he took in accord with the learned fad of the period), studied in Germany and England, and possibly in Antwerp under the great geographer-cartographer Mercator, before taking a theological degree in Flanders. Ordained a Calvinist minister in 1576, at the age of twenty-four, he spent the next seven years preaching in the Calvinist centers about Brussels. When the Spanish Catholic overlords once more tightened their repressionist policy, he escaped to the North Netherlands (together with a large and dynamic group of his countrymen) and accepted a call to preach in Amsterdam, where he was to remain until his death in 1622.

Known far and wide as the *Predikant,* or preacher, Plancius attained a position of power and influence in Dutch life. The theology and internal politics of the Dutch Reformed Church, national politics, and maritime adventure were his passions. As an outstanding cartographer and geographer he had his finger in the expansionist maritime policy of the country, running his own spy system to obtain the maps and navigational secrets of other nations. He founded a school for ocean pilots through which he controlled the licensing of ship's officers, thus combining his educational aims with his compulsive grasping for personal power. In addition to his obsession about reaching China via the Northeast Passage, he was one of the main financial backers of the first Dutch expeditions to the Orient, a fact which he carefully kept secret; he never showed any public evidence of wealth. His seven sons, for example, were all educated at the University of Leyden at church expense, and with the exception of one who died, all became ordained ministers with official church posts. There is no probate record of the disposition of Petrus Plancius's estate after his death, and his financial affairs and undoubted wealth remain a mystery to this day, nor is there any knowledge about what became of the many precious secret charts of which he was the custodian.

To De Moucheron's gratification, Petrus Plancius expressed complete confidence in the plan of voyaging to China via the Northeast Passage as laid out, except that he believed the route to the Strait of Anian should be laid out north by northeast to the northern tip of Nova Zembla Island and then northerly across the polar sector to the Strait of Anian. He did not accept the plan of sailing due east along the coast through the Strait of Waygats to the Kara Sea, which he described as an inland lake with no eastern outlet. This difference of opinion, however, was a mere detail, and Plancius expressed complete concordance with the general theory.

As Plancius was the most eminent cartographer and exponent of the theory of celestial navigation in all the Netherlands, the Grand Pensionary Oldenbarnevelt accepted his endorsement of the enterprise without hesitation, and demanded immediately that the city of Amsterdam should be allowed to participate in the expedition.

The Predikant's Theory

DE MOUCHERON was relieved that Plancius had given the weight of his great prestige to the adventure. The masterful men of Amsterdam now wanted, as usual, to run the show, and a very sharp dispute arose at once, since De Moucheron was not willing to be imposed upon. The Amsterdammers quite ignored the years of arctic experience of the original organizers of the project, and did not hesitate to reject their carefully thought out plans of operation, proposing to abandon entirely the voyage in the White Sea by the east, along the coast. They suggested, instead, following Plancius's theory, that the fleet steer due north, if need be straight across the Pole and over the top of the world, and thus reach China by a direct line—following the Euclidean doctrine that a straight line is the shortest distance between two points. According to their theory, the expedition would find open, ice-free, warm seas at the North Pole, which would make the proposed course navigable.

Aside from climatic considerations, the direct course looked feasible to a theoretical geographer, who plotted a curved line on his globe as the shortest distance between North Cape in Norway and the arctic coast of China. This course is now followed by modern airplanes flying above a stretch of thousands of miles of the frozen Arctic Ocean, encumbered with mountainous masses of ice and snow, gale-swept and shaken by titanic terrestrial forces. To imagine that a frail wooden ship could possibly sail through this terrible region showed a complete ignorance of actual conditions. The practical and able men of Amsterdam, themselves successful ship owners and shipmasters, were in this matter completely obsessed by a nautical theory conceived in a secluded library by a clergyman who was also a mathematician and student of geography, but who had never been to sea.

However, De Moucheron was secretly very much pleased that intruding Amsterdam, following Plancius's plan, intended to diverge almost at right angles from the route planned by the Orangists. This was because he had stipulated, in submitting the charter to the States of Zeeland for approval, that he should be given exclusive title to the small island of Dolgoi, lying near the entrance to Waygats Strait. It was his intention to fortify and garrison it and to establish a trading post there for his own company. Consequently, when the Amsterdammers announced their intention of following a course almost at right angles to the coastal course of the Zeelanders, De Moucheron was relieved that they would not be with him at Dolgoi, although of course he pretended to object violently to the proposed deviation.

The Rival Units

AFTER considerable wrangling, it was arranged that the flotilla should be made up of three ships, one from Veere, one from Amsterdam, and one from Enkhuizen; the latter was at the insistence of Dr. François Maelson. Johan van Oldenbarnevelt personally signed instructions to Willem Barentsz, the commander of the Amsterdam ship, in the Hague on May 16, 1594, ensuring co-operation between the Amsterdam and Zeeland elements. He ordered that the squadron keep together past North Cape until near Nova Zembla; then Barentsz was to follow the Plancius route northward along the west coast of Nova Zembla, while Cornelis Corneliszoon Nay, "Superintendent" of the Zeeland and Enkhuizen ships, was to keep easterly along the coast to the Strait of Waygats. If Barentsz was held up by ice in the north, he was to sail back and join the Zeeland and Enkhuizen contingent. In any event, he was to return to the rendezvous at Colgoyen (Russian Kolgúyev) Island and wait there for the other two, so that they could return home in company. Similar orders were issued by the Zeeland State to Cornelis Corneliszoon Nay and the other De Moucheron officers, including Linschoten, in regard to their squadron, which was to return and join Barentsz if they were held up at Waygats.

In the instructions, which called for explicit reports on all navigational, geographical, and ethnological features, there was included a promise of liberal compensation for carrying out orders and an implication that those responsible for any deviation would be held sternly to account. Upon their return to the Netherlands, for reasons of secrecy, no one was to be allowed ashore, and no person from land was to be allowed aboard, until permission was given after reporting to the provincial authorities.

The Project Takes Form

ALTHOUGH the city of Amsterdam had won its point and had been allowed to participate in the adventure, it was recognized that De Moucheron was the father of the undertaking and that he should direct the fitting out of the expedition and the appointing of personnel. As it was necessary to take advantage of the short summer season in the Arctic, the preparations were rushed as much as possible.

Jacob Valcke, the Zeeland Treasurer, took responsibility for finding a vessel to represent his province. The city of Zeeland, however, only furnished a third of the cost of fitting out the *vlieboot* (or flyboat) *Zwaan* of Veere, the other two-thirds being paid by Balthasar de Moucheron and Jacob Valcke, who also supplied most of the cargo for trading purposes.

In the same manner, the Northern Quarter, or West Friesland, made up principally by the municipalities of Enkhuizen and Hoorn, fitted out in partnership with Dr. François Maelson a *vlieboot* of the same size called the *Mercurius*.

De Moucheron named as *Commies*, or supercargo, to be responsible for the commercial and diplomatic interests of the squadron, his nephew, François de la Dalle, who had already travelled in the White Sea and knew Russian. Dr. Maelson named Jan Huyghen van Linschoten to be supercargo for the *Mercurius*, but he was to be subordinate to De la Dalle. All the complement were picked with the greatest care for their suitability for their duties, and it was greatly to Jan's credit to be selected. Moreover, he was ordered by the States General to serve as general clerk for the voyage, and to keep a careful official log and journal. Dr. Maelson had probably seen the manuscript or the galley proofs of the *Itinerario* and therefore knew that Jan was particularly well qualified for this important post. Amsterdam supplied a flyboat named the *Messenger* under the command of Willem Barentsz of Ter Schelling, who brought along as tender, to use in sounding and for work in shallow waters, a rugged fishing smack from his home port.

It was typical of Amsterdam, and explains one reason why that city was so successful in forging ahead against competition, that they selected as skipper a mariner without peer, for Willem Barentsz was not only renowned as an intrepid navigator and steersman, but also was recognized as a very competent astronomer and cartographer. He was destined to become one of the greatest heroes in the history of the Netherlands. Unfortunately, because he came as the representative of Amsterdam, he was not wholly compatible with Jan and the Zeelanders and West Frieslanders. The longheaded Balthasar de Moucheron had won to the support of his plan Stadtholder Maurice, Treasurer Valcke, Dr. Maelson, and the admiralties of Zeeland and West Friesland early in 1593, with the intention of getting a fleet away and in the White Sea by May 1, 1594, which was the beginning of the short summer season in the Arctic. When the admiralty of Amsterdam insisted upon participating in the expedition, the resultant negotiations and typical Dutch bargaining delayed the project. Nothing positive could be done until the agreement was finally signed between the three admiralties, on May 11, 1594; De Moucheron had expected to have his ships well on their way to Waygats Strait by that date. There had been much to do in a hurry, including the preparation of diplomatic credentials and letters of greeting from the Stadtholder to unknown Oriental personages who might understand no European tongue. Regal presents were entrusted to Superintendent Nay as gifts to such potentates as might be encountered. The Dutch had yet made no very distant contacts, and no one who was qualified as an interpreter could be found. However, a Slavic student at the University of Leyden named Christoffel Splindler or Spindler, who understood Russian, was hired as interpreter. He would be useful if the squadron, instead of reaching the Strait of Anian, should go down south through Siberia on the long River Ob and try to reach the Orient in that direction, as had been once envisioned by Brunel. Another possible interpreter was a lower-class Russian named Michiel who had settled in Enkhuizen and married there, who served as a seaman on the *Mercurius*.

Many other special preparations for the Arctic were made, including large stores of candles, a supply of anthracite coal for a stove on each ship, an extra supply of brandy, and many woolen clothes, boots and gloves.

The general food supply was calculated for a voyage of eight months. All three ships had a double sheathing of planks added to the hulls, together with a second, or false, keel and an outer cutwater to serve as an ice breaker. Extra anchors and cables also were supplied. In spite of a great effort to make haste, a whole month was lost. This was to prove costly indeed, for much later grief might have been avoided had the expedition not been forced, because of the late start, to discontinue its exploration in the Kara Sea, and therefore to return home elated with false impressions.

Jan had been very busy on the manuscript of the *Reysgeschrift*, which Claeszoon had decided to print before the *Itinerario* because of the pressing demand which he knew existed for it. The expedition to the Far East which was even then secretly being prepared by a group of Amsterdam merchants in the hope of breaking the Portuguese spice monopoly had been coached by Jan concerning navigational and commercial details, and as he was anxious to have at least galley proofs of the *Reysgeschrift* available for their pilots, he had been concentrating on this book.

However, when Jan received his official commission for the polar expedition from the States General via the admiralty of the Northern Quarter, he had to leave the editorial work on the *Reysgeschrift* with Claeszoon, the publisher, so that he could work day and night at his new duties aboard the *Mercurius*. Every day's delay in sailing was costly and hazardous, and torches on the pier and candles and walrus-oil lamps on the *Mercurius* lighted a busy scene from dusk until dawn. Everyone was exhausted when, on June 1, 1594, the mooring lines were cast off and, with an ebb tide, and using only a foresail, the *Mercurius* worked its way through the crowded haven into the Zuider Zee to meet its consorts at the Helder.

After lying off Texel for several days to receive final orders and to fill some last-minute needs for supplies, wind and tide now being favorable, Jan Huyghen van Linschoten on June 4, 1594, again put to sea. Fifteen years had passed since as a lad he had sailed from this same port to seek his fortune. Now, already a successful and honored gentleman, the holder of a commission from the Stadtholder and an assignment from the States General, he was sailing from Texel once more, this time on a mission that might bring him great honor and perhaps a fortune such as he had never dared dream of possessing.

CHAPTER VIII

To the North

Down to the Seas Again

ON SUNDAY, June 5th, 1594, the *Mercurius* raised anchor at midday, made sail, and with a fresh easterly wind set its course. Jan must have experienced a lift of heart to be under way again, off on a new adventure which he could never have foreseen as he voyaged home from distant Goa, or consolidated his position in Enkhuizen upon his return. The riches of the East! His imagination was still possessed with those fabled lands, and this was the real reason he had had no hesitation in undertaking a voyage to the frozen north which might provide an easier passage to the Indies than he had known in the service of the Portuguese Archbishop.

Before they set forth from Texel, a conference had been held aboard the *Swan* at which the Superintendent, C. C. Nay, had given the regulations for the cruise. He had stipulated that Kilduyn Island, off the coast of Lapland, should be the rendezvous in case the ships should become separated by fog or storm. Even then, the Amsterdam contingent had shown little spirit of co-operation, and the next day, when the superintendent had sailed his ships out of Texel into the North Sea and signalled to the Amsterdam vessels to follow, the *Messenger* and its little companion had delayed doing so.

Jan began at once to keep his daily record of the voyage, recording the directions of the wind, the currents of the ocean, the conditions of the weather, which included much snow, hail and mist, and the position of the ship, when this was ascertainable. He also was careful to record what sails were carried by the *Mercurius* as it met the varying weather conditions.

As early as June 14th, they had progressed far enough north to be struck by the length of the days; the longest day of the year was at hand, and even at home in Enkhuizen, the days were long. Jan, in his log, spoke of the "perpetual daylight," for they were now approaching the regions of the midnight sun. Large numbers of whales were visible as they sailed along, and as Jan commented upon them in his diary he thought of them merely as curiosities; he could hardly imagine the great profits the Netherlanders were to draw from the whaling industry after they had learned the secrets of the whaler's trade from the Basques.

The waves slapped against the hull, the wind sang in the rigging, and the ship reeled over, creaking and groaning as it rose and fell in the seas. Jan was again where he had longed to be, on a lively ship in the ocean at the best season of the year, in good quarters, with ample, homelike rations, and with able and congenial Dutch messmates. In rank, as *commis*, or supercargo, he was officially next to the skipper himself, and in many situations superior to all his colleagues except François de la Dalle, the *Opper Commis*. However, in the plunging, rolling, brisk little ship, with the bracing north winds and the tossing arctic seas, his dreams were no longer of literary or social recognition, nor even wholly of profit, although no Dutchman would overlook that. Instead, he imagined establishing a short, quick route to China that would not only give his homeland a monopoly of Oriental trade and make it supreme in Europe, but would also abolish the frightful toll of human life which was exacted by the dreadful Cape passage of which he had such bitter memories. He no doubt expected that, when he found the Strait of Anian, he would, with Balthasar de Moucheron's help, become a merchant prince, and through the influence of François Maelson and Meinert Semeyns perhaps an exalted *Jonkheer*, a member of the Dutch nobility. However, with conscientious precision he addressed himself to the keeping of the records of the trip, as ordered by the High and Mighty Lords of the States General of the United Provinces. In this official log he could express none of the exuberance and gusto with which he began his voyage; but he was not accustomed to giving way to his personal feelings in his writings in any case. Written accounts were far too serious for any such personal considerations as how Jan Huyghen van Linschoten felt on a certain day! Indeed, he was too dignified a citizen to give way to such frivolity in writing.

After two weeks at sea, at last they saw a sail in the distance, but it was too far away to be identified. They saw the coast of Trondhjem, in Norway, and the Lofoten Islands; then they rounded the North Cape, where they had to steer cautiously through mist and snow. They had now entered the Arctic, and the coast of Europe lay to the south. They skirted Lapland, but did not pause at Wardhuis (Dutch corruption of Norwegian Vardöhus), the Danish-controlled island that was a general rendezvous for Dutch trading ships. Off Wardhuis, they were boarded by some English fishermen with fresh codfish for sale, a welcome change in their diet of the past three weeks.

Challenge at Kilduyn Island

THEY NOW CAME to Kilduyn Island, which, although only about two Dutch miles long and one Dutch mile wide, had a safe harbor which could eventually be fortified to provide an effective halfway station for a Dutch fleet. This was to be their rendezvous with the Amsterdam ship, the *Messenger*, commanded by Willem Barentsz. As soon as they had entered the harbor, the *Swan* was boarded by the captain of a Danish ship, who demanded to see their Danish license for sailing into these waters. Denmark then comprised most of Scandinavia, and as a strong naval power had long dominated the Arctic seas. However, Superintendent Nay gave temporizing answers when the Dane demanded the fleet's destination and purpose. Soon another Danish ship entered the harbor, and its captain also came aboard; however, he got no more information than the first Dane had. The next arrival was an armed Russian trading ship, which had come there to buy stockfish. Its captain also came aboard, and in the name of the Grand Duke of Muscovy aggressively protested their fishing in the sea about Kilduyn without a Russian license. Although Superintendent Nay knew that his ships were strong enough to defy the Russian captain, he thought it best to placate the Muscovite.

Indeed, the officers were surprised to learn that the island had already been claimed by the Russians. They had every intention of taking possession of it themselves eventually, but through diplomatic maneuvers if possible, and it was for this reason that the Russian captain was not ignored as the Danes had been. The Dutch officers probably gave the Russian a good bribe, no doubt using the Russian-speaking François de la Dalle as their intermediary. The Russian commander was apparently quite won over by the Dutch officers, probably by the personable young De la Dalle in particular. The latter immediately sent off a cautionary report to his uncle, Melchior de Moucheron, who was then in Moscow intriguing against the local English agent, and at the same time sedulously laying the foundation for a Dutch-Russian alliance which he planned to conclude as soon as he got word of the success of the fleet's mission to discover the Strait of Anian and the Northeast Passage to China.

Indeed, the far-sighted Balthasar de Moucheron's urgent demand for the immediate fortification of Waygats Strait (also called Jugor Strait, and then Nassau Strait) had been based upon his fear that the English would seize it first. He feared also that the English would enter into alliance with the Muscovites, who had already assumed sovereignty over the coasts of Lapland and Siberia. It was for that reason that he visualized the creation of a stronghold comparable to Gibraltar, Ormuz or Aden there in the north. The strait would be frozen for the greater part of every year, and hence vulnerable to attack across the ice; it would therefore be necessary to construct a strong fortress, with warm, spacious barracks and large storage facilities, which could repel attack during the long winter and hold out until the Dutch could relieve it during the summer months. However, De Moucheron could not get the slow-moving Zeelanders to make any advance preparations for his program. All this was doubtless in the back of the minds of the Dutch officers as they made friends with the Russian commander who had challenged them so aggressively at their first meeting.

Checking the Instruments

IN KILDUYN, with the ships quietly at anchor, the officers decided they would check their instruments by the sun. They calculated their location to be 69 degrees 40 minutes, which modern observations show to have been twenty minutes too high. In fact, a modern check has shown that all the calculations of north latitude in Jan's journal in the Norwegian Sea were erroneous by as much as a degree and a half. The officers of the *Mercurius* were careful navigators, and no doubt took readings which were as accurate as possible; however, it is obvious that the nautical instruments of the day left much to be desired in precision. It is interesting in this connection to observe that the calculations of Willem Barentsz, who was a veritable genius as a navigator, have been rechecked and have proved to be amazingly accurate.

Jan's Account of Kilduyn

WHILE they were anchored at Kilduyn, Jan drew two detailed pictorial maps of the island and illustrated them with sketches of the pastoral Finns and Lapps who spent the summer there, but every winter retired to the mainland forests where shelter and firewood were available. Jan was, as always, interested in the people of the region in which he found himself, and his excellent drawings showed the costumes they wore, their huts, their fishing boats and *lodkas*, or luggers, their reindeer and sleds, their dogs, and their method of drying fish. He also drew the omnipresent wild geese, ducks and other water fowl, which were a staple of their diet. His text described the geography of the island, with its heights and geological structure, its vegetation, and its freshwater springs. Indeed, Jan's brief stay at Kilduyn initiated him into an entirely new world. In the *Itinerario* he had shown, in engravings, the various types of natives in India, with their clothing, arms, and some details of their domestic background; these were the people he had observed in the back country around Goa and Cochin, on the Malabar Coast. He had also made drawings of the indigenous people around Mozambique, in East Africa. Now he found himself among a mongoloid, migrant, pastoral yet amphibious people who were of a type entirely new to him, and he displayed his keen interest in his drawings. Their houses, made of logs, caulked with dung, and flanked with banks of earth, had windows of thin, translucent deerskin or sheets of thin ice, while the chimneys were made of wood, covered with clay for protection against the fires. Their staple food was fish, which they caught through the ice in winter. The fish were mainly salmon and herring, which they dried in the sun, smoked, or ate raw, cut into slices with a sharp knife and salted.

Reindeer supplied meat, milk, furs and leather for the Finns. The sinews were made into thread, and the antlers into knife handles. The women scraped the skins until they were soft enough to be fashioned into leggings and other garments; it was the women, too, who smoked the venison and made sausages of the meat. Each man identified his own herd of deer by notches on the ears, and any unidentified strays were sold and the proceeds put into a fund which each tribe maintained for its aged members. Rustlers or reindeer thieves were treated as public enemies, and each family had a dog to help protect the herd against wolves. Although Jan had seen many other animals used as beasts of burden, among them elephants and camels, he thought that the reindeer was ideal for that purpose. It could draw a sled over the snow-covered ground as far as a hundred miles in a day, its spreading hooves serving as snowshoes; it had uniquely waterproof, and even buoyant, fur.

Jan noted that the *marta*, or sledge, used by the Finns was about nine to fourteen feet long; it had a hood to protect the driver against falling snow, and runners made of birch poles which slid equally well over the moss and tundra in summer and the snow in winter. He reported seeing a Finn riding a reindeer, seated well up on the withers and balancing himself with a pole. He was also intrigued by the highly practical portable cradle which a Finnish woman carried on her back; it was made of a hollowed log stuffed with moss, and the infant it contained was completely covered with a cloth which protected him from insects and served as a sun shade.

On his homeward voyage from India, Jan had seen large flocks of aquatic birds at Ascension and St. Helena Islands, but the immense flocks of migratory birds that were arriving on the White Sea Islands at the time the *Mercurius* was there surpassed them by far. Uncountable clouds of geese, cranes, ducks, gulls and snipe filled the sky with their screeching and piping. The geese flew in V-formations or in long chains, the swans in solid flocks, and all species of ducks in irregular masses. A certain type of big goose which arrived in large swarms moulted all its feathers in July; in their featherless state, these geese could not fly and were easily caught in great numbers, smoked, and preserved for winter consumption.

Jan also admired the enormous walruses, with their huge ivory tusks, and he was excited to see an immense polar bear swim through the sea, climb upon an ice floe, and pounce upon a huge walrus who was sleeping in the sun. Such sights as these filled his days with interest and novelty.

Leavetaking at Kilduyn

ON JUNE 29, 1594, the Amsterdam vessels sailed north from Kilduyn. Before their departure, the skippers agreed that, in accordance with the instructions of the States General, the two squadrons would meet again in the harbor there in September if neither had reached its distant objective. The first to return to Kilduyn was to wait for the other's arrival, and they would then sail home in company.

Several days later, on July 3rd, in clear, sunny weather with a fair wind west by south, the *Swan* and the *Mercurius* weighed anchor and steered for Waygats. They were sailing every day through twenty-four hours of light, as Jan duly reported. Whales disported themselves alongside the ships without fear, and schools of porpoises played around them. Jan saw herds of seals sunning themselves on the ice floes which floated everywhere, and there were abundant flocks of the fat geese that made such toothsome eating.

Navigational Records

BEARING IN MIND that his report was largely for the benefit of Dutch pilots who would follow their course in later voyages, Jan carefully recorded each casting of the lead, making notes concerning the color and composition of the specimens brought up from the floor of the sea; a tallow base was used to assure that material from the bottom would adhere. Sometimes it was found to be sandy, sometimes composed of clay, or of mud with pebbles or shells; at times there was no deposit at all on the lead, which indicated that the bottom was rocky and might not be good holding ground for anchors. All this was of great importance, for in those days navigators had to rely to a great extent on the lead to locate their position, in particular their longitude, through measuring the depth in fathoms and ascertaining the kind of bottom, then comparing these data with the records of previous voyages. The use of anchors was of the utmost importance. The rig and hull of a ship were so clumsy that in a heavy gale it was the practice to take in sail and drift, but if the ship were sailing off a lee shore or in shallow or narrow seas, great reliance had to be placed upon the anchors. However, in the waters which they were now entering, it was safer in a gale to get into the lee of a slowly drifting icefield or berg and hang onto it with a kedge anchor. Because of the great difficulties of sailing in these seas, Jan noted every variation of the wind in direction and intensity, as well as the degree of visibility in the rain, snow, hail or mist which was their frequent weather.

The half-hour glass was their only timepiece; they had, of course, no thermometer or barometer; and there was no patent log to record speed. Everything depended on the pilot's ability and alertness. The crude astrolabes or sextants were quite inaccurate on the unstable deck, and even when the pilot was rowed ashore to take an observation on firm land, his results were only approximate.

As chartmaker, Jan was pioneering, for there were no previous maps to follow; to guide them there were only the rough rutters from Balthasar de Moucheron's former expeditions. The two skippers and their mates had had experience in the waters to the west of Kilduyn, but now they were entering unknown seas. Therefore they had to be constantly on the lookout for hidden reefs, and tried, if possible, to detect any currents or trends. There were thus special hazards in the close quarters into which they now were steering. Their compass was peculiarly unreliable because of deviations due to their nearness to the magnetic pole as well as to the North Pole itself; at that time there was no clear realization of the magnetic pole's existence, though Spanish geographers had an inkling of it. Hence, with their gaze turned trustfully to the Polar Star—when they could see it—the pilots wondered exceedingly at the strange gyrations of their formerly trustworthy compasses.

Jan was conscious that his was no routine task of making entries in a log, for he was recording and mapping the future passage of an imperial route to be followed by great Netherlands argosies which would in the years to come bring back countless treasures from fabled Cathay. Every day during the voyage he faithfully sat down to his desk, his goose-quill pen in hand, with a crock of ink made of the juice of gall nuts, and wrote his report for the States of Zeeland and for West Friesland on handmade flax paper. His desk swung on gimbals and was lighted by a swinging, pendant pewter lamp which burned walrus oil, and the stool upon which he sat was lashed to the deck. Oblivious to the plunging, rolling, lurching *Mercurius*, he made his entries regularly, lost in the work of reproducing the scene about him in text and in drawings. He was also aware of the possible future military utility of his work, for upon the faithfulness of his charting of these waters was to depend the success of some Dutch war fleet of the future, sailing to defend the vital ramparts to be constructed at Waygats Strait—or the Straat Nassau, as he later rechristened it.

The fleet was now sailing constantly in a foggy or a snowy atmosphere, past floating icefields and vast icebergs, and by various reefs and shallows. In such circumstances, the clumsy functioning of their navigating instruments placed a great strain upon the pilots, who realized that their "guesses," as they frankly called them, were likely to be faulty.

Jan was on deck much of the time, busy with the drawing of his charts from nature. He had already painstakingly drawn, in great detail, the outline of the entire coast of Lapland, as he was now to do the coast of Samoyedsland and Siberia, all along the littoral, through Waygats Strait and far into the Kara Sea, up to a river delta which he was to identify, mistakenly, as the mouth of the River Ob. Out in the open in bitter weather, he no doubt regretted the warmth of the tropic seas where he had drawn other portolan charts. It was too cold to remain long without moving, so he had to do his sketching of the coast in quick, brief snatches of time. In all, he was to make thirty-six charts, which he would later develop fully in the cartographic style of the time, including a picture of a ship to show the point from which the view was drawn. He was also careful to jot down sufficient indications for his later annotations in both Dutch and Latin.

Captain Nay and his entire staff well knew the significance of their undertaking. If they were successful in reaching the distant and perhaps mythical Strait of Anian, they would obtain the mastery of Europe's oriental commerce for the United Netherlands. However, such mastery would not be meekly accepted by their rivals. It would undoubtedly involve a violent struggle with England, which would probably be aided by Denmark, the Hanseatic Cities and Venice, and perhaps even by Spain. The Dutch were realistically aware that the position of Russia in such a struggle might be decisive, for although the Russians lacked good warships, they had as a naval base the newly established city of Archangel, the only ice-free port in the White Sea, and might hold the strategic islands of Kilduyn and Wardhuis to flank the Dutch route, while massing land forces on the continental shores of Waygats Strait.

Therefore, as we know, Balthasar de Moucheron had laid plans, with the approval of the Province of Zeeland and of the Stadtholder, to seize and fortify for his own account the island of Dolgoi, which well might, he thought, be the strategic key to the Northeast Passage. He had also provided, as we have seen, that as soon as the squadron could send back word to Middelburg that the first objective, Cape Tabin, had been reached, the States General would immediately and with all despatch send the necessary forces (which were even now being prepared) to fortify the entrance to Waygats (or Jugor) Strait, which separates Waygats Island from the Siberian mainland. The plan also, apparently, included taking Kilduyn Island.

In addition to seizing Dolgoi Island, De Moucheron also entertained an alternate project of taking the much larger Colgoyen Island. Therefore Jan doubtless took careful note of the latter, insofar as the mist and snow allowed him to do so. Colgoyen could provide a larger, defensible base, and was near enough to the proposed fortress at Waygats Strait to receive protection from it; it was also within possible trading distance of Nova Zembla and the commercially important Russian estuary of Petchora. It is amusing to note that, although Jan drew much of the outline of Colgoyen Island explicitly, there are two places on the chart where thick, bulbous clouds are drawn obscuring the shore; these are the very snow clouds which kept him from seeing more at these two spots, as he notes ingenuously on his map.

A Lucky Encounter

GENERALLY the *Mercurius* sailed close enough to the Samoyedan shore to permit Jan to draw its coast faithfully, as it appeared in silhouette, just as he saw it from the deck of the ship. When icefields began to fill up the open sea, they sent the light-draft pinnace to take soundings and explore the coast; it returned with a report that alongshore the water was around twelve feet deep, and thus was quite navigable for the two ships. At about that time, they saw a sail approaching from the west. It proved to be a Russian *lodka* from the White Sea, bound for Petchora. The Dutch watched it go into a harbor on the mainland and anchor, then followed it in, anchored alongside, and invited the Russians aboard. After a friendly meeting, they submitted their proposed course to the Russians, who generously examined it, pointed out many errors, corrected their route, and helpfully informed them of islands and reefs of which they had had no previous knowledge. They were grateful that the Russians, even though ignorant of celestial navigation, were able to sketch for them the entire coastline, with its capes, peninsulas and bays, and to point out the safe route to their objective, Waygats Strait. This information was priceless to the Dutch, for it represented the accumulated knowledge of generations of native navigators; and the irregular route which the Russians indicated could not possibly have been worked out by newcomers without hardship and losses.

To the North

In all the logs of early Dutch and English voyages in the north, mention is made of the consistent friendliness and sympathy of the Finns, Laplanders and Samoyeds to visitors to their coasts. Their friendliness may have been due to the fact that visitors to those lonely and uninviting shores were very few, and had given the indigenous peoples no reason to fear them. It is in marked contrast to the hostile attitude of the natives in the Orient and in the Far Pacific who, even though armed only with bows and arrows, ambushed and slaughtered many European explorers. The friendliness of these northern peoples to the Dutch expedition of 1594 was certainly increased by the fact that François de la Dalle knew their language and their manner of thinking, at least up to a point.

Hopes Confirmed

THE DUTCH MARINERS, in their conversation with the Russian officers of the *lodka*, were overjoyed when they understood that, once past Waygats Strait, they would find the Kara Sea warm and ice-free. The Russians explained that the immense floes that now impeded their progress came down from Nova Zembla, and were not met farther east. Alas, historians have observed that, in all ages and in all lands, explorers seeking a certain goal have deluded themselves by unconsciously suggesting the answers which they desired to get from the aborigines whom they have interrogated. All François de la Dalle's knowledge of the language had not prevented his betraying to the amiable Muscovites the answers which he hoped to hear, and these were accommodatingly fed back to him. The Dutch officers were exhilarated by this confirmation of their fondest hopes by local mariners of whose competence and experience they already had received convincing proof.

Unwelcome Advice

THE NEXT DAY, a squadron of three other *lodkas* came sailing down the coast and likewise were hailed and questioned, but they proved to be more surly and secretive than their friendly predecessors. They emphasized the dangers and difficulties of the route through Waygats Strait, but De la Dalle believed they were intentionally trying to discourage him. In view of the difficulties which the Dutch encountered in the following year, however, it seems that the unpromising advice of the second group of Russians was the more realistic.

To the North

A Practicable Course

THE ROUGH CHART they were now following gave a course which appeared to wind erratically past reefs and sandbanks, and it seemed so impracticable that they sent the little pinnace ahead to make constant soundings. They found that, eccentric and winding though it seemed, the route did develop a navigable channel free from ice, along which they made steady progress eastward.

A Blundering Kill

ONCE they found a young whale floundering in a narrow, shallow cove. Excitedly they put out their boats and attempted to kill the whale, but at first they only succeeded in turning or bending the heads of the lances or harpoons that they inexpertly thrust against him. Evidently Dutch steel at that time must have been of an inferior quality, for there are other accounts of Dutch swords and axes proving too soft to penetrate the hides of polar bears, or of spears being twisted and bent when used against those thick-hided animals. In any case, they continued their attempts to kill the whale, and one spear finally penetrated a vital spot and brought forth a spouting geyser of blood; the whale soon expired. None of the crew had had any whaling experience, but they had learned how to boil down walrus blubber to extract train oil. Therefore, they hauled the carcass ashore and successfully rendered a number of casks of good oil from it. This was a unique experience for Jan to relate in his journal, and he told the story with obvious enjoyment.

Hugging the Shore

THEIR VOYAGE along the coast was frequently anxious, especially when a gale drove great masses of floating ice toward the land, threatening to trap them on a lee shore. The ice fields were composed of great jumbles of piled-up blocks, many of them larger than the ship. The motion of the ocean currents and tides kept the ice churning, toppling and crashing with a continuous rattle and clatter, and at times a roar like thunder. Jan noted that sometimes whole trees and masses of rock, earth and vegetation were carried on the surface of a floe, evidently having been pushed into the sea by glacial action or having toppled from some icy cliff. They were now navigating at around sixty-seven degrees north latitude, and were not far north of the Arctic Circle. The summer temperature here was generally above the freezing point, and, with the frequent sunshine and mild breezes, the bergs and floes were doubtless not as menacing in size and solidity as those encountered by the squadron under Barentsz which had separated from them at Kilduyn to proceed directly north toward the Pole.

The fitfully changing weather was disconcerting, for while the temperature averaged about forty degrees, a sudden gale from the north would whirl upon them with snow and hail which would blot out all visibility. The alternations of weather and the evaporation from the melting ice caused much fog, and because of their nearness to the shore it was often necessary to haul in sail and anchor until the fog cleared. Jan mentioned one inexplicable experience when they were suddenly struck by a blast of hot air blowing offshore; he compared it to a draft of blazing heat from the suddenly opened door of an oven. This passed by so quickly that it left them unharmed, though they were mystified and frightened.

Mysterious Fires

IN THE BRIEF periods of dimness (it could hardly be called darkness) at night, Jan could occasionally make out the glow of distant fires, but in daylight no habitations were visible, and no human beings were seen. However, at last they were hailed by two Samoyeds who asked to be ferried across from the mainland to a nearby island, where they said they wanted to trap animals for their furs. In the winter, they would be able to cross back again over the frozen sea. François de la Dalle asked them about the fires that were seen at night, and they replied that they were from the camps of wandering hunters like themselves, who kept out of sight for fear of the strangers. They asserted that there were no permanent settlements in these desolate wastelands.

A Near Disaster

WHENEVER the atmosphere was free enough from fog at noon to permit them to make an observation of the sun, the two skippers tried to calculate their latitude, but the crude astrolabes could be used efficiently only if the sea was quiet and the deck stable, a rare occurrence. None of the navigators had had any experience in the waters east of the White Sea in which they were now sailing. Although it was the warm season, with almost perpetual daylight, and with much open, ice-free water, the skippers

were tense and uneasy. The strong, capricious currents, the sudden gales
with snow, the frequent fogs, and the wind-driven icebergs and tumbling,
crunching floes, were all nerve wracking. The fact that they had no charts
and that their course was dotted with reefs, rocks, sandbanks and shallows caused them constant apprehension. The pinnace and the ships' boats
were sent ahead regularly to test currents and to take soundings. However, in spite of all their caution they were at last involved in a near
disaster. In a driving rain and poor visibility, the *Swan* was sailing a little
ahead of the *Mercurius* one day when she suddenly ran aground—and
in another moment the second ship did likewise. Before the sails could
be set back or any adjustment made, both ships were hard aground, stem
and stern.

Nothing that the crews could do was of any avail, neither kedging,
towing, nor shifting of weight. In this extremity, all were frightened and
prayed aloud for deliverance. Jan described what happened next as a
miracle, and it must have seemed like one; the wind shifted, the tide rose,
and the two ships floated free. Jan devoted a long passage in his official report to expressions of gratitude to the Almighty for their salvation, and
it is impossible as one reads not to recall his scorn in the *Itinerario* when
he described how the Portuguese sailors, in a like instance, abandoned reliance on their own seamanship and looked heavenward for succor. However, perhaps it is too much to expect emotional consistency when feelings
of national pride are involved.

Cryptic Crosses

SEVERAL TIMES in their progress the little squadron sent landing
parties ashore to investigate the meaning of crosses erected on small islands,
but François de la Dalle was unable to interpret the cryptic Russian in-
scriptions carved on them. Jan made a careful copy of a rather elaborate
cross which stood on the island they named Mauritius, after the Stadtholder, Prince Maurice. They also erected more than one cross themselves, upon prominent high spots on islands where they landed; they
carved messages for the Amsterdam boat which they expected would follow them, for they were confident that Barentsz would find his own proposed northern route impracticable.

Waygats Island

EVERY DAY there was some small happening of interest for Jan to
describe. One day it was thousands of waterfowl of a dozen kinds nesting

on an island, while the next it was a pest of gnats that assailed the crew. He described a high wooden cross on a barren, desolate island, thousands of seals sunning themselves on a rocky shore, or the great fright of the mariners when they ran aground on the hidden reef. On another day, he described the light and color effects of the sun's rays on the glistening ice-fields. At last he told of making their landfall at the goal of their voyage, Waygats Island, which lies between Nova Zembla and the Siberian Coast, and which blocks the passage between the Arctic Sea and the Kara Sea except for two narrow straits to the north and south of it.

Mindful of the proposal to fortify Waygats in the near future, the Dutch pioneers devoted careful attention to exploring the interior of that island, to charting its coast and havens, and to recording its climate and possible fertility. There was no evidence of any permanent habitation; in a few valleys they saw some green growth, but in general the surface of the ground was covered with the same moss as the tundra of the mainland. There were many freshwater ponds and some swamps. One day when they were exploring along the coast in a boat they sighted a man waving a white deerskin to them, but when they landed to speak to him he ran away. They observed that he looked much like the Laplanders in dress and general appearance, and they were sorry not to have had a chance to talk with him. On the west coast of the island they saw many dangerous reefs and rocks on which sea fowl congregated. There were a number of hillocks inland, and Jan and the others were extremely puzzled to find windrows of driftwood, large trees complete with their roots, and even the wreckage of a large *lodka*. Since these were on high land far from the shore, and had obviously been deposited there by the ocean, disconcerting hypotheses came to mind. Were there at times great floods or tidal waves that swept over the island? Were there mountainous masses of drift ice piled skyward by Arctic storms? These were not merely academic questions, for if Waygats Island was to become the Dutch stronghold of the north, with an impregnable fort, a harbor, and quarters for a garrison, it must above all be safe and secure against Arctic storms. The uncertainty on this score troubled Jan greatly. One theory which he considered was that the island might have been suddenly thrust upward from the earth's surface by some seismic disturbance. This might possibly explain the presence of the large trees, but it could hardly account for the driftwood and the hull of the *lodka*.

On July 23rd, the sun disappeared briefly and a short night set in for the first time since June 17th. Jan was reminded by this that only about a month remained during which they could get past the Strait of Waygats and find the warm, ice-free sea to the east which would lead to China. However, they still had to complete their study of Waygats Island before pushing eastward, so they continued surveying and charting all its aspects; they recorded the bottoms, the swift currents and the strong tides, and in one place they even found a maelstrom. This work was both exciting and profoundly serious to all of them.

As Jan meticulously mapped and charted the various features of the island, he carefully and impartially gave them the names of all the prominent men back home, who would be pleased and flattered to be so honored, as well as of the home places. He recorded a Nova Hollandia, a Nova Walcheren, a new West Friesland, Moucheron Cape, Maelson Island, and Staten Island (so named in honor of the States General). The names Mauritius, Orange and Nassau were used in honor of the Stadtholder and the Princely House. Two small rivers were named in honor of their two ships, the *Mercurius* and the *Swan*, and even his own name, Van Linschoten, was not omitted. It is pathetic today to see the handsomely engraved maps on which this proud nomenclature is marked, to understand the atmosphere of national optimism which engendered them, and to realize that not a single one survives on any modern chart. It was truly "such stuff as dreams are made on."

Jan did not forget Doctor Paludanus as he went about his important business of exploring and charting, for he collected specimens as eagerly as he did everything else. The tusked skulls of walruses, the antlered skulls of reindeer, and many other curiosities for his friend's museum were stowed away upon the ship.

The Isle of Idols

ONE DAY, on a small island off Waygats, they came upon a little hut that seemed to be a shrine of some kind, for it contained three hundred to four hundred carved wooden idols in human form. Were these idols, perhaps, carried in a religious procession at some time of the year? There were no indications of their use, only the silent, crude, stiff figures. There were no houses or any traces of inhabitants upon this eerie island, and the only clue to what it might signify lay in the piles of reindeer horns which lay about and which must have had some ceremonial significance. There was no fresh water on the islet, so any visits there must have been of a brief and ritualistic nature. The Dutch explorers were glad to leave the place.

Friendly Samoyeds

SHORTLY THEREAFTER they ran into a group of Samoyeds who were using sleds, each pulled by three reindeer, to draw them over the moss and tundra of the summer season. At first the natives seemed belligerent, and Jan noticed that their bows and arrows resembled those of the Persians which he had seen in the Far East. François de la Dalle advanced to parley with them, speaking in Russian, and made them presents of bread, cheese and brandy. They grew more friendly, but suddenly the ship's trumpeter sounded a routine call that shattered the quietness of that savage place. The natives were startled and mistrustful again, and were hard to soothe. François de la Dalle continued questioning them, but their answers were of little interest or help to the Dutch. They apparently did no fishing and had no boats, but lived entirely upon their herds of reindeer, which supplied them with everything—food, caps, gloves, boots, and other clothing, as well as transportation. During the winter they migrated southward, and lived in the pine forests which furnished them with shelter and fuel. No matter how closely he questioned them, François de la Dalle could learn nothing of the great warm sea to the east. One point of some political significance was that they had never heard of the Grand Duke of Muscovy, so at least for the moment the Dutch did not have to worry about any Russian action to block them at Waygats.

A little farther, as they sailed down the strait, they encountered some other Samoyeds on the shore, and they were able to communicate with them through their Russian-born crewman, Michiel, who proved to be more familiar with their dialect than was François de la Dalle. Michiel was able to quiet their distrust somewhat, but he could not elicit any useful information from them about the warm, open sea for which the Dutch mariners were so anxiously groping.

They continued their work of mapping, sketching, sounding, making observations, and setting up such navigational markers as a barrel on top of a pole. The shifting gales, the fogs, snow flurries, and hail storms, as well as the rushing tides and the strong currents, kept the skippers under great strain. There were sandbanks, reefs or submerged rocks on every side, and worse than these, floating icebergs and floes, so the navigators had to be continually on the alert.

The New North Sea!

ONE MORNING, however, the fog cleared away and they found themselves on the eastern side of Waygats Strait, sailing about half a league from shore on a wide, calm sea fifty fathoms in depth. Jan wrote that it looked like the Spanish sea in color and general atmosphere. The water was so clear along the coast that they could perceive the crabs at the bottom at a depth of eight fathoms. He at once christened it the New North Sea, and reported without hesitation that it undoubtedly led to China and Japan, the countries of the Far East which were nearby. Everyone was jubilant, and Jan himself was in seventh heaven, as the two small cannon on each ship were fired, the prince's flag hoisted, and the trumpet sounded in a triumphant salute. They were sure that they had reached their goal.

However, they now began to feel that winter was approaching, because for the first time since they had passed the North Cape in June, it was dark enough at night to see the stars, although the moon was not yet visible. They knew winter would come rapidly, so it was necessary to make haste. Nervously they began to survey the Siberian shore, to locate and sound harbors and havens for the next voyage.

The New North Sea, into which they had sailed with such high hopes, now proved to be full of floating ice, with some bergs so large and deep that they were grounded on the bottom. They reassured themselves with the theory that this ice had been discharged into the New North Sea from the great Ob River, which they felt sure lay just ahead, as described long ago by the earliest Flemish explorers in those regions, Oliver Brunel and Isaac Massa. Everywhere they saw great herds of seals and groups of walruses sunning themselves on the ice, and multitudes of sea fowl that nested on the isles along the shore. The two little Dutch ships had penetrated into a world which they believed had hitherto been unknown to Western Europe. They did not know that the English had been there half a century earlier.

August was slipping away, and they knew from their White Sea experience that they should get back and round the North Cape into the Atlantic in September if they did not wish to be caught in the dread Arctic winter. It was at this time that they came to an island about a league long, lying half a league offshore. It had much green growth, lakelets of fresh water, good anchorages and a safe, land-locked harbor. They also saw evidences of animal life, and of course the birds were everywhere. They disembarked and found many rock-crystals, which were used for optical and other industrial purposes and also had value in the jeweler's trade of that time. The island looked so promising that they named it Staten Island in honor of their parliament, the States General.

They still continued to sail eastward through the floating ice, keeping a sharp look-out for signs of human habitation on the shores and for the sails of *lodkas* at sea, but they met nobody. "We hoped with God's help to find a wide and open sea through which would be an unhindered free passage to China," wrote Jan. From August 8, 1594 on, he wrote at length all the reassuring arguments he could think of to convince himself that the wide, open route to China lay just ahead. All aboard were keyed up to a high pitch of expectation, and when they found what they took to be a navigational marker in the form of a stone cairn on an islet their hopes rose even higher, in spite of the icebergs and floes in their path. Jan asserted that this ice had been discharged into the New North Sea from the inlets and streams of the mainland, and repeated that the Tartars were accustomed to make the passage to the Orient even during the winter.

On August 9, 1594, he wrote apprehensively that the Arctic winter would set in on September 20th (by the calendar of that time), when the sun would pass to the south side of the equinoctial line. On that same August day, the New North Sea once more became clear of ice, and the two ships pressed forth boldly, sailing both day and night. Jan ended his long and rather vacillating entry for that day with an apostrophe to the Almighty in an exalted vein, saying that after so many centuries during which the Northeast Passage had been shrouded in mystery, at last benign Providence had vouchsafed to reveal it, and before the little squadron returned to their homeland it might be granted to them, by divine Grace, to discover the secret route to China.

At Last, the Ob River?

ON THE NEXT DAY, Wednesday, August 10, 1594, he made another detailed entry which reflected his feelings of excited anticipation. He recounted that they sailed steadily eastward along the coast with a good wind, encountering no ice and making good soundings as they went. They encountered the mouth of a river at about thirty-eight degrees east of Waygats Strait, to which Jan now referred as the Straat Nassau; this they unhesitatingly identified as the beginning of the delta of the Ob. Jan expressed disappointment that no *lodkas* were within sight, as they had been in the other navigable estuaries they had seen. Since they had no charts, but only the written reports of Isaac Massa and Oliver Brunel to guide them, the pilots did not realize that what they took to be the beginning of the great River Ob was only the mouth of the little Kara, which marked the boundary between Russia and Siberia. As far as is known, this error was not made clear until the map of Isaac Massa was published in Holland in 1612, although at that very time the Muscovy Company in London had secret maps of the area, drawn by their own early explorers, of which the Dutch were ignorant. All that Jan had to go by, however, were the confused chronicles of Dutch voyagers, without any definite bearings, sketches or instructions. In a burst of wishful thinking, he confidently asserted that the northernmost point of Asia, the Cape of Tabin, undoubtedly lay eastward, just across the delta on the east bank of the River Ob. Once they had rounded this Cape, the Strait of Anian would be discovered not far beyond. They sailed steadily all that night and the next day along a flat green coast, with good soundings and little ice, while on shore they observed deer, birds, and once a group of three men. Jan continued to be meticulous in his descriptions, overconfident in his expectations. Ahead of them the coast extended in a northeasterly direction, and they were by now sure that they had discovered the route to China.

Prows Pointed Homeward

H o w e v e r, the wind veered to northeast, which prevented any further progress. It was late in the season, the skippers and supercargos looked grave, and a decision had to be made: in view of the headwind, they would turn around and set their course for the Netherlands. On August 11, 1594, Jan recorded this conclusion. It must have been with mingled feelings that he ended the entry with fervent thanks to the Almighty for granting them success in their quest, and worded his prayer for a safe homeward journey.

From August 1, 1594, when the New North Sea was suddenly discovered, until August 11th, when it was decided to discontinue explorations and to sail home, Jan Huyghen van Linschoten seemed to be in the grip of a positive, unquestioning conviction that they had reached their goal, that they were at last sailing in the great warm sea which led on to China. In his euphoria he had no hesitation in setting down the "facts" which he considered to be irrefutable.

He knew his record would be read critically as a public document. Therefore, he must have been careful in what he said; his self-deception was sincere. Moreover, the official journal of the voyage must have been read and approved by the fleet commander, and must have expressed the views of the officers and crew. It was not, of course, the first time that wishes had been mistaken for horses—and since they were so far from home, who could dispute their account?

The Westward Voyage

W i t h the apogee of his enthusiasm now past, as they turned westward Jan continued to record his careful observations, under the heading "to the west of the River Ob." He calculated their latitude as 71 degrees, and noted that at night they saw the moon and some stars for the first time since they had passed the Lofoten Islands, off the Atlantic Coast of Norway on their eastward course. Clearly, it was high time they were leaving the Arctic.

On the misty, rainy Sunday afternoon of August 14, 1594, sailing against a northwesterly wind, they sighted Waygats Island, and soon they were picking up the landmarks which they themselves had set there as navigational guides. Because of their previous careful sounding and coasting, they were able to sail forward in the perilous Strait in spite of heavy weather and fog. However, the going was so difficult that, though they had been carrying little sail, they finally anchored under the lee of the Island of Idols and let the storm blow itself out. On August 15th they emerged from the Strait, little realizing how lucky they were to have got past that bottleneck before it should become choked with ice.

A Nearly Disastrous Reunion

J A N continued conscientiously to record every detail of the homeward voyage, charting the same course they had covered in their other direction. The voyage was proceeding uneventfully when suddenly one morning two sails were sighted on the horizon. Everyone took the two vessels to be *lodkas*, but as they neared Jan saw that they carried topsails. To everyone's delight, they were seen to be the two Amsterdam ships commanded by Willem Barentsz. The two little squadrons sailed eagerly toward each other like two parties of children dashing together heedlessly. Suddenly they came to their senses, but they remembered that they were in uncharted seas too late, for they were surrounded by shoals with dangerous reefs. It was only with the greatest difficulty that they managed to extricate themselves from their peril, and to find safe waters in which to celebrate their reunion. When at last they found themselves together in clear, deep water, they discharged their cannon amidst cheers from all hands and many shouted greetings from ship to ship. Barentsz came aboard the *Swan* for a happy reunion, and for the first time they learned of the fortunes of their brethren.

Barentsz's Report

I N C O N T R A S T to the good reports of Superintendent Nay's squadron, the Amsterdammers had only defeat and frustration to recount. Barentsz informed them that, after picking up the coast of Nova Zembla at 73 degrees, 25 minutes north latitude on July 4th, he had made progress along the coast until July 13th; but then he was blocked by great ice fields and was driven backwards. The two ships struggled on, and by July 31st they had reached an archipelago which he called the Islands of Orange, about 80 degrees north latitude, at the extreme northern tip of Nova Zembla,

THE CATASTROPHIC TEMPEST *in the Azores, which devastated Spanish shipping, as described by Linschoten. The violently tossed ship in the background and the terror of the people on shore are vividly rendered.*

Quem capiant cœlum lymphęque salubria tellus.
Quęque novo semper gramine parturit.
Quę facile admittat gremio et producat alendo
Quod peregre intulerit provida cura solo:
Fanum Helenę capiat teneatq; nisi arctius ingens.
Orbe procul nostro clauderet oceanus.
Hoogerb.

Insula D.Helena
ubertate et aqu
inhabitata ; hic
tium, sita in al

Het Eylant van Sa
lucht. vruchtbaerheyt
onbewoont . een goede
leggende op die h

A. não Sᵃ Maria
Souta Capitayna

CHART OF ST. HELENA ISLAND, *one of several which Linschoten drew to illustrate the* Itinerario. *A competent cartographer,*

he made many maps and charts. Note the entire fleet of *naos* in the foreground, and the people and animals roaming the hills ashore.

SHIP ROUNDING THE CAPE. *A Portuguese nao of the Carreira da India is shown fighting for survival against one of the overwhelming black tempests off the Cape of Good Hope.*

ERNARDUS PALUDANUS, osmopolite, the scholarly Town Doctor of Enkhuizen, collaborated with Linschoten in writing nd publishing his books of ravel. He had a museum containg tens of thousands of curios nd specimens from all over the vorld.

ETRUS PLANCIUS, Protestant minister and famous as a cargrapher and geographer, was an nstigator of early Dutch voyages o the Orient and a rival of Linchoten in attempting to reach hina through the Arctic Northst Passage.

LINSCHOTEN'S SHIP CAUGHT IN THE ARC-
TIC ICE. *It was only by good luck that the ship escaped
being frozen solid or ground to pieces between ice floes.*

THE PINNACES *of Linschoten's fleet were the scouts
and pathfinders for the larger vessels.*

MEN KILLED BY POLAR BEAR. *Busy search-ing for crystals, two men with hammers and chisels were set upon by a bear, which killed them both.*

BARENTSZ RELICS *discovered in a ruined hut in Nova Zembla late in the last century; abandoned there in 1597, they are now in the Rijksmuseum, Amsterdam.*

THE DROMMEDARIS TOWER at *Enkhuizen*. *The squatly formidable brick stronghold was constructed by Emperor Charles V to
protect the harbor of Enkhuizen, which was the strategic key to the
control of the Zuider Zee. It was a familiar landmark and a proud
monument for all the citizens of the town, including Jan van Linschoten.*

at the margin of the Kara, or Tartarian, Sea. To the north lay only an unbroken barrier of solid ice which it would have been impossible to attack. Clearly, if a warm polar sea lay beyond, it was not accessible by this route. The theory of Petrus Plancius, if not disproved, certainly could not at this point be demonstrated to be correct.

The exhausted crew, after having carried on a very gallant struggle, now gave up the fight. Barentsz, while not admitting defeat, conceded there had been a setback, and on August 1st he pointed the prow for home. Yet even though he had been turned back, he had made an impressive effort, and any modern navigator familiar with the handling of small sailing craft will credit his crew with an almost superhuman performance. Without charts or any records of previous voyages, faced with unfamiliar variations in the performance of his compass, and with no means of arriving at longitudinal measurements, they had battled with sail and oar against great seas, strong coastal currents, unpredictable squalls, gales and freakish fogs, in waters full of dangerous, floating icebergs and floes and punctuated with many reefs and islets.

Barentsz's log showed that in twenty-five days his hundred-ton ship, the *Messenger,* and its little fishing-smack consort had been forced to "put about" eighty-one times during a voyage of about 1700 miles. The bearings and distances which he recorded in his journal have now been separately checked over the same courses with modern instruments by both Russian and British navigators, and his calculations have been found to be almost precisely correct; this is striking proof of the competence of that extraordinary seaman.

The dejected Amsterdammers then sailed cautiously back down the west coast of Nova Zembla to try to meet the returning *Swan* and *Mercurius.* Barentsz's orders had been to rejoin the Zeelanders if he were blocked on his northern thrust, and he loyally proceeded to do so, sailing to meet them instead of lying in wait at the rendezvous they had agreed upon for September. This gallant sailor generously joined in celebrating the great achievement of his more fortunate colleagues, and from then on he co-operated heartily in exploring and charting the still partly unfamiliar waters between Waygats and the White Sea.

A Dutch Victory

ON SEPTEMBER 12, 1594, near to home, at the Dogger Bank, they were electrified to learn from a passing herring buss the news of the great victory that Prince Maurice had won over the Spaniards at Groningen. The next day their squadron passed through the herring fleet, which was convoyed (in case of English attack) by two Dutch warships, and they broke out all the flags and pennants which they carried—especially the proud standard of the House of Orange.

Home Once More

ON SEPTEMBER 14TH, their Superintendent, Cornelis Corneliszoon Nay, on the *Swan*, signalled farewell to his consorts and took a course southeast by south to his home port in Zeeland, while the *Mercurius* and the two Amsterdammers steered on a more easterly path toward Texel.

On September 16th, they sailed with a spring tide into the Helder. They were home again, after a voyage of three months and ten days—a mere summer cruise compared to the immense voyages of the *Carreira da India*. Jan closed his official report with his expression of thanksgiving for such a speedy and fortunate voyage "to the Lord God to whom alone is the Honor, Power and Glory from now unto eternity, Amen."

A Signal Honor

JAN SUBMITTED his written report of the voyage to the States General, and soon thereafter he received an invitation which was the greatest of honors: His Excellency, the Stadtholder, Prince Maurice of Orange-Nassau, and the Raadpensionaris, Johan van Oldenbarnevelt, wished to hear his report at first hand, and to discuss it with him.

The feelings of the young explorer from Enkhuizen, who had, during the thirty-two years of his life, progressed from the humble status of an innkeeper's son to become a member of the ruling oligarchy of his town (via points in the fabled East and in the rugged Arctic), can hardly be compassed in a simple statement, although he himself wrote of the interview later in a matter-of-fact way. The command to an audience with the nation's rulers must have filled him with delight and jubilation, and he must have felt rewarded and appreciated at last for all his careful work, intensive effort, and great hardships, as he journeyed down to The Hague for his interview.

In his personal colloquy with his liege lord and the Grand Pensionary, Jan must have acquitted himself brilliantly. He was in the full flush of enthusiasm after the success of the first Arctic voyage in finding, as he supposed, the long-sought Northeast Passage, and he was possessed of boundless confidence in the undertaking. Without doubt he was able to impart some of this conviction to his noble interlocutors.

To the North

Jan's Appointment for the Second Voyage

THE STATES GENERAL soon decided to equip a substantial second expedition to complete the attempt to reach China via the Northeast Passage. In the atmosphere of great optimism that surrounded the project, the two heads of the Dutch State personally nominated as *Opper Commis*, or chief supercargo, none other than Jan Huyghen van Linschoten. In many respects this position was that of actual command of the fleet, for while the admiral, vice-admiral and captains were responsible for navigation and discipline, the word of the *Opper Commis*, who represented the dominant mercantile element, was ordinarily final. In addition to being responsible for the trade and finance of the fleet, Jan would also be the diplomatic representative of the United Provinces. His rank and authority were further enhanced by his being again designated to write the official report of the undertaking for the States General.

The appointment of the thirty-two year old Enkhuizer to this position of command aroused the jealousy of the contentious Reverend Petrus Plancius of Amsterdam, who had until then enjoyed the position of supreme arbiter in matters of cartography and navigation. He was furious, and all the more so since he had derided the feasibility of the eastward Waygats route to China and had been the chief promoter of the direct northerly route across the Pole, to the west of Nova Zembla. Although his theory had suffered a defeat, Petrus Plancius could not now bring himself to stand aside, but importantly busied himself by assuming the role of chief adviser to the expedition, supplying much information regarding the coasts of Tartary, Cathay and China, which he had gathered for the most part from classical sources and which was, needless to say, of very questionable value.

Plancius had been so dogmatic in his earlier geographical assertions that he took Jan's success and Barentsz's failure as a personal affront, and in his usual overbearing style questioned the veracity of Jan's report of the first voyage. Therefore, in the opening paragraphs of his report of the second voyage, Jan frankly referred to the animadversions of the *Predikant* and, in a dignified comment, asked his readers to weigh his account for themselves.

Jan's Marriage

DURING this winter of heady success, when he and everyone else in the Netherlands believed that the first expedition to the north had discovered the Northeast Passage to the Indies, Jan was happy as he had never been before. To crown the respect which was generally felt for him, he had been received in private audience by both the Stadtholder and the chief executive; and three months before he was to sail on the second expedition, he was married to Reinu, the daughter of his friend and protector, Meinert Semeyns. As we have previously observed, this marriage set malicious tongues wagging when, within five months of the ceremony, a little daughter was born—but in the absence of any details all speculations have to end there. Jan and Reinu were prominent citizens and no doubt easily lived down any gossip. They were to spend the rest of Jan's life together and to retain their positions of dignity and respect in their town.

Plans for the Expedition

THE STATES GENERAL decided to fit out a well-equipped fleet of seven ships to sail to China through the Straat Nassau, as Waygats Strait was now grandly called. Two vessels would be from Zeeland, two from Enkhuizen, one from Rotterdam, and two from Amsterdam; since the Amsterdammers had favored the northerly route which had been found impracticable, they now would have to follow the lead of the Zeelanders, as Jan did not fail to remark. The only concession granted to the Plancius theory of open water around the Pole was that, once Cape Tabin had been rounded, two fast despatch boats were to carry the news home and to take their course north of Nova Zembla.

The superintendent, or admiral, would once again be Cornelis Corneliszoon Nay, who had commanded the fleet which made the successful voyage in 1594; the vice-admiral would be Brandt Tetgales, of Enkhuizen, who had been skipper of the *Mercurius* on the first trip. François de la Dalle was to be the assistant supercargo, and Splindler or Spindler, the Slav, would again be the chief interpreter. The entire undertaking, although under the auspices of the States General, was obviously dominated by Balthasar de Moucheron. The personnel included most of those who had made the previous voyage. Amsterdam would be represented by Barentsz, Jakob van Heemskerk, and Jan Corneliszoon Rijp, all of them able mariners, but unfortunately aligned with the Reverend Petrus Plancius and his geographical theories.

Although the Stadtholder signed the commissions, the States General lent its authority, and the individual States furnished the ships, armament, food and crews, the trading cargoes and working capital were all donated by various companies of merchant adventurers who supported the enterprise in the expectation of future profits. These commercial bodies all had their own representatives aboard. For example, Jan Huyghen van Linschoten, Heemskerk and Rijp were the agents of the Associated Merchants of Holland and West Friesland. This complicated organization of control was typically Dutch, and resulted in the same division into cliques and factions which was characteristic of the national economy. Thus Jan, as the commercial representative of West Friesland, was in the same group with the Amsterdammers, because West Friesland was a part of the Province of Holland. Yet his own sympathies, as well as the interests of the Enkhuizen merchants, tended toward the Zeelanders, who were the rivals of the Hollanders. At the same time, in his official capacity as *Opper Commis* he represented the Seven United Provinces.

Written instructions from the States General to the *Opper Commis*, or chief supercargo of the voyage, and to François de la Dalle as his deputy, were formally drawn up under five headings. They particularly emphasized the need for the establishment of good diplomatic relations with the authorities of the oriental lands the expedition would reach, and enjoined upon their representatives the duty of scrupulously correct treatment and the utmost consideration toward oriental powers in matters concerned with trade. The supercargos were instructed to try to establish sound, permanent trading contacts, to learn what exports from the Netherlands would be salable in China and what Chinese products could be imported into the Netherlands, and to investigate and to report upon their prices. They were charged with the duty to observe and report upon the customs, manners and religious practices of the natives. They also were to make note of all harbors and anchorages and to record prevailing or seasonal winds, tides and currents.

Any navigators and merchant adventurers with experience in the Arctic realized that expeditions there were possible only in the late spring and summer months. A long voyage was necessary to reach the Straat Nassau, which was now realistically considered as the starting point for the crucial push to the New North Sea, past the delta of the River Ob, and around the Cape of Tabin to the Straat Anian. Therefore it was imperative to sail from Texel not later than the first of May. It would, in fact, be wiser to get to Kilduyn Island by that date, and to lie there at anchor in the hope of an early thaw, so that no time would be lost in case of favorable weather conditions. None of the responsible heads of the expedition denied the logic of this reasoning.

Delays and Handicaps

HOWEVER, the Dutch had an incurable habit of setting up committees to handle simple administrative details, and an incorrigible urge to negotiate and compromise between wrangling provincial and municipal factions. Their arguments lasted almost up to the final moment, on July 2, 1595, when the conglomerate fleet finally sailed fromTexel. Only about sixty days were left of the summer, in which to sail from the Netherlands all the way through the Kara Sea, before the perilous winter season set in. No saboteur plotting to wreck the voyage could have contrived matters more adroitly for his purpose. It would have been better to have done as the Portuguese used to do in such a situation—admit that the fleet had "missed its voyage" and wait until the following year.

While one delay after another held up the sailing of the squadron and vital time was fast ebbing away, the zealous young *Opper Commis* must have been in torture. Later, in writing his report to the States General, he could not refrain from mournfully hinting that the undertaking was half doomed before it had even sailed.

It was unfortunate for the project that the plan of developing the Northeast Passage had assumed such a promising aspect after the voyage of the previous year that it was taken up at the highest level and became a national affair. No longer could wise Balthasar de Moucheron, strong financier though he was, dominate its execution. The plan gave promise of power and profit to the whole United Provinces, and hence became a universal bone of contention. His Excellency, Prince Maurice of Orange-Nassau, and Johan van Oldenbarnevelt, the Grand Pensionary, were fencing for control of it. The Amsterdammers who had originally derided the idea had succeeded in forcing their way into the undertaking.

The new nation was at the moment in a precarious economic situation. Its carrying trade in the Baltic and the Gulf of Finland was protected, but its extensive and profitable freight traffic and commerce with the Spanish peninsula, and with the Atlantic Islands, West Africa and Brazil under Portuguese charter, although still surviving, had been crippled by Philip II. The nation's economy was now largely kept going by the fruits of its piracies and, strangely enough, by its profits from the sale of food and war supplies to its enemies, the Spanish army in Flanders and the Spanish fleet in Spain.

The great adventure undertaken by the Amsterdammers, largely initiated by Petrus Plancius, of sending a fleet under Cornelis de Houtman around the Cape of Good Hope to Java, as counselled by Jan Huyghen van Linschoten, had not yet borne fruit. The squadron had now been gone for two years, and the only news of it had been in the form of disquieting reports from Lisbon. Everyone thought that the undertaking had failed (as indeed, it nearly had).

With De Houtman's voyage almost given up as a failure, their only hope of reaping the immense profits of Oriental trade seemed to lie in the possibility of developing the Northeast Passage. This had suddenly become of paramount interest to the rulers of the United Provinces, who were faced by the necessity of solving their economic dilemma somehow. At the same time, in the large cities of Amsterdam and Rotterdam, the merchant adventurers feared that they might become subordinated to their trade rivals in Zeeland and West Friesland, and therefore they joined the enterprise as lustily as, upon other occasions, they had swarmed, cutlass in teeth, over the bulwarks of rich galleons in the Narrow Seas.

The Belgian Traders

ONE OF the queerest facts about this grim internal struggle was that it was not, in fact, between Dutchmen. At that time, the few important Dutch merchants had little knowledge of any foreign trade except for their experience as freighters in the North Atlantic under charter. They had traded on their own largely in Scandinavian produce, herring, and salt. Now, the Amsterdammers who were so vigorously fighting the Zeelanders were not Dutchmen, but Belgian refugees from the occupied provinces of the South Netherlands like Petrus Plancius, Willem Usselincx, and Isaac Le Maire, who had chosen Amsterdam for their headquarters not because they were Calvinist or Lutheran zealots (except perhaps for Petrus Plancius), but because war conditions had made Antwerp and Flanders no longer tenable as a base for their foreign trade. And their rivals in Zeeland were also Belgian refugees.

Johan van Oldenbarnevelt, the Grand Pensionary, himself a Dutchman, supported the Belgian traders of Amsterdam against their Belgian rivals in Zeeland, who were under the protection of Stadtholder Count Maurice of Orange-Nassau. The only born Dutchmen engaged in the complicated economic struggle were the West Frieslanders of the towns of Enkhuizen and Hoorn, who were trade competitors of Amsterdam and dedicated supporters of the Stadtholder.

The plan for the northeast expedition had been initiated by the dynamic Balthasar de Moucheron, and he had given primacy in it to his adopted state of Zeeland, using Enkhuizen as a secondary support against the aggressive and overbearing Amsterdammers. Yet, paradoxically, when it came to outfitting the second expedition after the apparent triumph of the first, De Moucheron had met with reluctance and resistance in the government of his own province of Zeeland, which had grudgingly given him only the inferior, 175-ton *Griffoen* and an 80-ton flyboat. At the same time, Amsterdam supplied Barentsz and Heemskerk with three ships, including the new, 200-ton *Winthondt* (or, in English, *Greyhound*).

The skippers, pilots and supercargos of the fleet were the same able individuals who had made the first voyage the year before, brilliantly executing two separate dashes, one to the north and the other to the east.

A Bad Start

AT LAST, the fleet sailed, and it seemed as if the angry gods showed ill will from the very start. As soon as they reached the Atlantic Ocean, the wind set in an unfavorable quarter and remained there, so that they had to tack almost all the long distance to the North Cape. Some of the ships were neither fast nor weatherwise, and sailed poorly into the wind. Especially was this true of the *Griffoen*, which had been furnished by the State of Zeeland. Unfortunately, this awkward and sluggish vessel was the flagship of the fleet, and had aboard it not only Admiral Cornelis Corneliszoon Nay, but the second supercargo, François de la Dalle, who was their expert in Russian affairs, and Christoffe Splindler, the chief Russian interpreter.

The two Zeeland ships had been extensively reconditioned for their hazardous voyage, and neither ship had been in good condition, to judge from the extent of the repairs that had to be undertaken. François de la Dalle himself complained that the two ships supplied by Zeeland were very inferior. Both vessels had an outer wooden sheath, or skin, built over the original hull, and the space between the two was filled with a composition of sulphur and *harpuis*, a mixture of pitch-tar and rosin. It is amazing to note that the clumsy *Griffoen* was also the carrier of the merchandise belonging to Balthasar de Moucheron, the originator and guiding spirit of the whole enterprise. That the ship was such a poor one was due to the pettifogging of the short-sighted Zeeland politicians, who were influenced by De Moucheron's jealous trade rivals in his own town of Veere and in neighboring Middelburg to attempt to hamper his competition.

Jan made his conscientious daily entries in the log regularly, from the day they sailed out from Texel, perhaps quieting his doubts in the performance of this responsible task. He recorded the courses steered, the direction of the winds, the general state of the weather, and the canvas carried. Whenever an observation by instrument was carried out, he entered it as "guessing" in his account. Jan was aboard the Enkhuizen ship *Hoop* (or *Hope*, in English), where his cabin was set up in much the same manner as it had been on the first northern expedition, with his desk on gimbals and his chair firmly lashed to the floor, and a swinging oil lamp to provide some illumination.

To the North

Northward Progress

I T W A S N O T until July 23rd that there was a landfall, and on that day Jan sighted the Lofoten Islands, off the Norwegian coast, already covered with snow. On the next day the mariners sighted their first sail, which proved to be the Enkhuizen ship of Roelof Janszoon, bound from the White Sea to Amsterdam. The *Griffoen* hailed it and sailed close, carefully aiming and attempting to throw to them a precious packet of letters to be taken back to the Netherlands. However, because of the heavy seas, the cast missed its mark, and the bundle fell into the ocean. The two ships then had to part and continue on their separate courses, to the great disappointment of the men of the *Griffoen*, who had hoped to send back word to their wives and families. They continued their slow progress northward, tacking again and again, and on one day even having to retrace their course and sail southward with shortened sail in a heavy storm. On July 29th they sailed close to a dead whale, covered with ravening sea fowl, and on the 30th they were surrounded by a school of frolicking whales. On August 2nd, a whole month out from Texel, they passed snow-covered Tromsö Island, and hence knew themselves to be about forty leagues west of the North Cape, the promontory on an island off the north coast of Norway that was a well-known landmark to all navigators in the arctic seas.

On the next day, still sailing northeastward in a heavy rainstorm about two leagues off Tromsö Island at about 69 degrees north latitude, the *Griffoen* suddenly crashed upon a hidden, uncharted reef. There was consternation aboard the ship, but it stood fast. Fortunately a heavy, false oak prow had been built as an icebreaker in front of the ship's bow, and had been extended down into what was called a loose keel, a strong extra planking which sheltered the real keel. Had it not been for that, the hull would have been shattered, but instead only the protective timbers were damaged. Luckily there was no sea running at that time. There was very little wind, but soon it shifted to a moderate gale from the northeast. By backing the sails, the ship was manipulated so as to slide off the reef; once free, the carpenters reported no water in the hold, to the very great relief of all aboard.

Then they sighted two yachts southward bound and sailing very close to the shore, but Admiral Nay did not risk approaching them; he concluded from the way they hugged the coast that they were Norwegian or Danish craft, familiar with their perilous course, and probably merely carrying stockfish from the White Sea to the Danish-controlled port of Bergen, in Norway.

A Close Escape

ON THE NEXT DAY, August 6th, the fleet was suddenly struck by a heavy storm from the southeast, with immense waves and a thick fog. Before the visibility was lost, the admiral signalled a northwest course to port. The *Griffoen* was following this course with little sail set when suddenly, in the mist and only a few hundred yards away, there appeared on the port side, speeding along on its starboard tack, the big Amsterdammer, the *Winthondt*, whose skipper was Willem Barentsz. A collision seemed inevitable, but Skipper Nay luffed with the *Griffoen*, hoping to fall astern of the *Winthondt* and let it cross his bow. By this maneuver they avoided a head-on crash, but the *Griffoen* now bumped heavily side-on against the other Enkhuizen ship, the *Hoop*, which was sailing in a parallel course. The *Griffoen*'s *zwaard* was swept away, and the mizzen mast went by the board, carrying with it into the sea the ship's galley and the skipper's cabin. Almost identical damage was suffered by the side-swiped *Hoop*, on which Jan was serving.

It seemed a miracle that no damage was done to the hull of either ship, and this escape was perhaps due to their heavy double sheathing. If a ship had been sunk in that boiling sea and cold, sweeping gale, no one could have survived. Jan grimly remarked that this was the second time the Amsterdammers had failed to heed orders. (By the time Jan's journal was published, in 1601, Skipper Willem Barentsz had met a hero's death in the Arctic, and it would hardly have seemed proper to refer to the well-known fact that, although he was a superbly skillful handler of a sailing ship, he was nevertheless so daring as to be judged reckless. It was because of this reputation that, on the next Amsterdam expedition to the North, sent out in 1596, Barentsz was appointed Head Pilot instead of Skipper, since the insurance carriers and the merchant adventurers whose trading cargoes were on board were fearful of the risks he would take with a ship.)

Jan gave thanks to Providence for their miraculous escape, and remarked philosophically that as soon as there was a calm a new mizzen could be stepped and new deck-houses constructed. In that time of wooden ships, the versatile ship's carpenters were frequently called upon to perform emergency repairs at sea which would today challenge the skill of a master shipwright. Because of this, relatively high rank and pay were given to a ship's carpenter, who was, for example, many grades superior to a surgeon —if and when a surgeon was aboard, which was seldom.

To the North

Beyond the North Cape

ON AUGUST 7TH, having now been five weeks en route, and having at last passed beyond the North Cape, the squadron of seven ships was overhauled by the Enkhuizen ship of Jacob Jochemszoon which had sailed from Texel just two weeks after them. He was carrying freight for the White Sea, and then would take a cargo of Muscovy products directly to Venice, picking up a cargo there for Enkhuizen. This was a fairly typical voyage for a Dutch merchant ship at the time, if it was fast, had a strong complement, and carried at least eighteen heavy cannon to permit it to qualify as a *straatvaarder*, that is, a ship that could penetrate the Strait of Gibraltar and run the gauntlet of Moorish galleys in the Mediterranean.

As Skipper Jochemszoon expected to be back in Enkhuizen by October, Jan and François de la Dalle gave him packets of letters and reports to deliver for the fleet. These were, in fact, delivered on October 16, 1595, while the *Hoop*, the first ship to return, did not reach Texel until October 26th, ten days later.

On August 9th they were overhauled by an Amsterdam ship bound for the White Sea under Skipper T. G. Varcken, who had left Texel at the same time as they had, and whom they had last seen off the Lofoten Islands struggling, like themselves, against the unfavorable weather. On the same day they saw a Norse or Danish ship sailing before the wind from the White Sea, bound for Bergen, and then later another on the same course, but flying the English flag and also no doubt homeward bound.

It was disconcerting to Jan, who knew how far ahead their own goal lay, to see these various merchant ships already sailing home, their Arctic business done for the year, while the Netherlands squadron had not even begun its mission. They now were sailing day and night, trying to make up time, with all sail spread and with generally good winds. The waters were uncharted except for the maps Jan had drawn in the previous year, but because of the constant daylight they were able to press on for twenty-four hours a day, keeping lookouts at the mastheads and sounding constantly. However, on August 17th they encountered a great, jumbled, high ice field which stretched to the north as far as they could see, lying athwart their course, but with open lanes of water reaching eastward. They took the sun with their instruments, and guessed their position to be about 70½ degrees north latitude; they thought they were about twelve leagues from Nova Zembla. All day long they coasted the ice field, for about twenty-five leagues. Everyone was dispirited and discouraged, for the endless floe seemed as substantial as land. They feared that this showed they would not be able to complete their voyage; and they also feared that they would find a similar obstacle in the New North Sea. Apparently it did not occur to them that the ice would block the Straat Nassau, and that they might never even have a chance to reach the New North Sea.

On the next day, August 18th, they decided to try to crash a path through the ice, since the floe seemed thinner and softer. They had a favorable wind and were able to break through, so they made some progress. Jan and the others began to pick up courage, although the signs were far from encouraging. Jan noted that in these same waters the year before they had seen no ice; but the past winter had been extraordinarily severe, which probably explained the present appearance of floes. He recognized the shorelines of the islands of Mauritius and Orange, both named in honor of Count Maurice; then they picked up the land of New Walcheren and calculated hopefully that they were perhaps about nineteen leagues to the north of the Straat Nassau.

The Ice-Bound Strait

SEVEN WEEKS after weighing anchor at Texel, on Saturday, August 19, 1595, the flotilla at last reached the strait. Only a scant fortnight of possible weather remained, during which they had to sail hundreds of miles through the New North Sea, past Cape Tabin to the Strait of Anian, or else face the rigors of nine winter months of darkness in the bleak Arctic.

To Jan's despair, the mouth of Nassau Strait was so piled up with huge blocks of ice that it was impossible to tell where the shores left off and the channel began. No strait seemed to be there. Perplexed and frustrated, the nine ships huddled together before the mountain of ice, and then Admiral Nay ordered them to seek shelter behind a cape on the Island of Idols, where there was clear water and a good anchorage free from the current. As they lay there during the night in deep dejection, unable to sleep, a strong east wind sprang up and began to drive more of the floating ice from the New North Sea into the strait with resounding crashes. The wind and the icebergs pushed the ice that had blocked the strait out into the open water. At dawn, the officers saw that the fleet was being hemmed in and trapped, and that it would soon be crushed against the shore. Anchors were hastily lifted and sails set to the strong wind; fortunately, by taking quick action they managed to sail back into relatively open water. Icebergs and smaller blocks of ice were tossing and plunging in the stormy sea, colliding with thunderous impact. A more frightening and sinister experience could not have been imagined, especially in contrast to the rosy dreams of success which the leaders of the expedition had been entertaining.

To the North

Coasting Along Waygats Island

THAT MORNING, against a cold north wind with snow and hail, they coasted north along Waygats Island, which Jan had christened Enkhuizen Island, casting the lead and always on the alert for reefs. After a long time thus spent, they were delighted to see a *lodka* lying at anchor in a little bay, and they made for it at once. However, at this moment the Admiral had the bad judgment to discharge a cannon to call the ships' council to come aboard the *Griffoen* for a conference; this frightened the Russian crew, and they rushed aboard the *lodka* and hastily sailed away. Jan then took a boat's party ashore to see if they could find any natives, but they discovered only fishing nets and some leather sacks made of walrus hide which were full of evil smelling but valuable train oil, made from boiled-down walrus fat. Many objects which had been dropped in a hurry also lay about. A native sled loaded with pelts was on the shore, but there were no reindeer in sight. The landing party refrained from taking any of the abandoned gear, and left behind some bread and cheese as a peace offering.

The skippers, pilots and supercargos gathered aboard the flagship to discuss the situation. They decided to send a longboat into the Straat Nassau to see if there was any channel along either shore. Jan offered to lead an armed exploring party across the interior of Waygats Island to the northern shore, opposite Nova Zembla, in order to see if there were any huts, settlements or camps to be found anywhere. He also wanted to explore the northern coast to learn what the ice conditions were in the very wide upper strait which was known as Straat Kara; in the previous year this had been found to be much less navigable than the Straat Nassau, and consequently few soundings or explorations had been made. However, under the unexpected and disheartening new conditions in which they found themselves, Jan hoped that an open passage might be found there.

Exploring the Island

THUS, early on Monday, August 21, 1595, Jan and his exploring party of fifty well-armed men set out against a cold north wind with snow and hail. Although they crossed the island in several directions, they saw no habitations nor any sign of a permanent station. They did, however, come upon a camp near the shore, with many recent footprints of men, women and children all around, as well as sleds, hides, pelts, and even arrows and tools which evidently had been dropped hastily as the people fled. Jan took care not to disturb any of their arrangements nor to appropriate any belongings, and again left bread, cheese, some knives and other trifles as further evidences of good will.

At the northern coast of Waygats Island, on the shore of Kara Strait, they were disappointed to see no open water at all, but only great, tumbled ice floes that stretched away as far as they could see. At several places along the beaches they saw the fresh carcasses of dead walruses which had obviously been killed by hunters and from which the tusks, hides and some bones had been stripped; Jan knew that the men who had made the kill must intend to boil down the carcasses for oil. Moreover, this would have to be done promptly, for otherwise the bears and foxes would have a feast, and there would be nothing left to process into train oil. Therefore Jan deduced that the walrus-hunting parties must be hiding somewhere in the vicinity. At a number of points along the shore there were stone caches holding leather bags of train oil, well covered by piles of rocks. However, since the bears had a keen sense of smell, were possessed of enormous strength, and had a certain mischievous, destructive ingenuity, these cairns could afford only temporary protection for the oil-bags while the band of armed hunters was near. It was evident that at some time during the summer the Russian traders would come in *lodkas* to barter for these accumulations of oil.

As Jan had learned on his previous voyage, the *lodkas* would carry the skins of oil to the White Sea markets, where they would be auctioned off to English and Dutch merchants, as the oil was in strong demand by the manufacturers of soap in northern Europe. The ivory of the walrus tusks was mostly sold in the Russian market, where it was highly prized. There was little European demand for walrus hides, as they did not tan well, but the Samoyeds valued them highly, cutting them into strips and using them for many purposes.

In the camps which Jan now inspected there were bundles of various pelts, including wolf, fox, sable, seal, and some bearskins which must have been trapped on Nova Zembla or the mainland and held for the arrival of the trading *lodkas*. Some of these furs were of superior quality and would bring good prices in European markets. This was, of course, of interest to François de la Dalle and to the other De Moucheron veterans, who had been accustomed to trading no farther east than the White Sea ports and at the markets in Wardhuis and Kilduyn, where they bought train oil and pelts from the *lodkas*. Now they saw at first hand how the hunters operated who supplied the *lodkas* with their so-called Muscovy products. Whether it would pay the Dutch to procure these products at the source would be a moot question. It was only recently that the Grand Duke in Moscow had taken any interest in subjugating the migrant and barbarous Lapps, Finns and Samoyeds who subsisted so precariously along the outer fringes of his realm. He had already contested the claims of sovereignty of the Danes over trading and fishing in the area, and it probably would be more politic under present conditions for the Dutch to continue to buy in the White Sea, under license from the court at Moscow, rather than to try to compete with the Russians in the polar seas. However, if the plan of seizing and fortifying Waygats Island came into effect, then an entirely new economic and political pattern would develop which would have to be dealt with in due time.

The Blocked Strait

BUT JAN HAD a more pressing problem before him than the petty economy of the Muscovy trade. He was fully aware that he was largely responsible for the safety of seven ships, with many thousands of silver pieces of eight and much costly merchandise aboard, and crowded with merchants, artisans and soldiers. The fleet was at a dangerous anchorage on a rocky lee shore, exposed to fierce Arctic gales and in danger of being crushed by enormous masses of floating ice. Some way must be found quickly to get through the Straat Nassau and into the safety of the supposedly warm and ice-free New North Sea that lay so few miles to the east.

Finding the passage blocked at the strait had dealt an even more crushing blow to Jan than to his colleagues, because he had been completely confident, after his experience of the year before, that the passage would be unhindered. Besides, he was more enthusiastic and more deeply committed to achieving the Northeast Passage to India than any of the others. He was much more altruistic and imaginative than most of his colleagues, and also, in a way, more naive. He and the courageous, reckless Barentsz stood out in contrast to the selfish, unenterprising mediocrities who were their mates, except perhaps for François de la Dalle, who was also a man of superior character and comported himself well in the crisis.

The assurances of the friendly *lodka* captains on the previous voyage had been a factor in Jan's feeling of certainty, and now he was extremely anxious to interrogate some of the natives through François de la Dalle to learn how to thread a passage through the ice. Another desperate question was just how much more navigating time was left before they would risk being firmly locked into the ice—if, indeed, they had not already exceeded that time limit.

It seemed to Jan that his world and all his expectations were in danger of collapse, and he was at his wit's end to know what to do next. In his fervent prayers that a way might be opened for them we have no way of knowing whether he addressed himself to the Catholic saints as mediators in his private devotions, as had been his custom of old, or to the new

Calvinist God to whom in his official report he so often made petitions
and gave thanks. Though his prayers were not answered, later he was to
feel grateful and relieved that the wisdom of Divine Providence had kept
the expedition from getting far into the Kara Sea, where they would
probably have perished, meeting the same fate that befell the first English
polar explorer, the bold Sir Hugh Willoughby, who froze to death with
all his crew when his ship was caught in the Arctic ice.

It is true that a year later Barentsz and Heemskerk with eighteen men
incredibly managed to survive through a polar winter by dint of superb
fortitude and wise leadership, as also did some whalers at Spitsbergen
under somewhat comparable conditions. However, in the situation in
which the fleet of Cornelis Corneliszoon Nay found itself, it is hardly
likely that any could have escaped death on the icy shores of Waygats
Island. As set forth in his report of September 15, 1595, Jan finally humbly
admitted that it was not God's will that the fleet should pass beyond the
Straat Nassau on this voyage.

A Russian Shumen

HOWEVER, for the present Jan was still frantically seeking a way forward. When the longboat had come back with a discouraging report of
its attempt to skirt the shore of Waygats Island, he sent it out again to try
to get through the Strait, but the ice so closed in on the boat that the
crew had to leave it on shore and come back to the ship by land. The next
day another longboat, sent to retrieve the one that had been abandoned,
returned to report that a Russian *shumen*—evidently a corrupted word
meaning a craft somewhat smaller than a *lodka*—lay offshore at the mouth
of the Strait, and its crew were cooking a meal on the beach.

Jan hurried there with François de la Dalle and found some of the crew
skinning a walrus, while others were boiling porridge in an iron pot over
a driftwood fire. When De la Dalle addressed them in Russian, they responded in a friendly fashion; they said they were from the White Sea,
and had spent the summer on Nova Zembla fishing and walrus hunting.
In exchange for some good Dutch bread and cheese, the Russians offered
Jan's party a delicacy of frozen marrow of reindeer bones which the
explorers found delicious. Some of the men wore ornaments that looked
as if carved from walrus ivory, but they explained to De la Dalle that it
was in reality mammoth ivory, which the natives recovered from the
carcasses of prehistoric mastodons buried for many centuries in the frozen
swamps; this was a commodity in which the natives traded in considerable
volume.

The Russians told Jan's party that they had had a very unsatisfactory year because an unusually long and severe winter had frozen up the area until late in the spring. This information was of great interest to Jan, especially when he learned that in contrast the previous winter had been unusually mild. This explained the navigability of the Straat Nassau in 1594 and its ice-locked condition in 1595. The Russians said that the winters were extremely variable; and, although it was only after mild winters that the Strait was ice-free, it generally was passable in summer. They also said that the northern strait (Kara Strait) almost always remained frozen even throughout the summer. Jan asked how much more time they would have before the hard winter set in, and the answer was ten weeks. However, there must have been a misunderstanding in the translation, for the Dutch knew that the sun would pass below the equatorial line at the equinox in September, and the Arctic winter would then set in.

The Russians said that the Samoyeds on Waygats Island only hunted and fished there in the summer and then went south to pass the winter in the pine forests where fuel was plentiful. Jan asked them to assure the Samoyeds of Dutch friendliness. Although the head man with whom they talked was himself a Russian colonist from the White Sea, he was able to tell De la Dalle much of interest regarding the Samoyeds, who differed greatly from the pastoral Lapps or Finns, whose mode of life Jan had observed at Kilduyn Island. Jan learned that they would not dare be anywhere near Waygats Island or the Straat Nassau after September or before May. He informed Jan that in November and December the sun disappeared entirely, and the dim twilight, called daylight, lasted only two or three hours. Not only was the cold utterly unbearable then, but the constant blizzards could stifle a man, throw him off his feet, and make it impossible to see further than five steps ahead. He said that if hunters were caught by an early winter, they would not dare to go even ten feet from a hut without holding onto a rope.

This was, of course, of great interest to Jan and De la Dalle in view of the plan to set up a barracks and a fort at Waygats Island. Another piece of military information was that the back country where the Samoyeds spent the winters was passable only when frozen over, when the natives travelled in reindeer-drawn sleds and the Russian officials, when they visited the area, used dogs to pull their sleds. In the summer, the whole area was a vast swamp over which they could not pass. He also said that there was no timber or forest growth except far in the interior, because the land was perpetually frozen two feet below the surface. This information not only made it apparent that it would be impossible to fortify the Straat Nassau, but also gave a grim warning to the Dutch as to the peril the fleet would be in if they tarried much longer in those waters.

The Russians in the *shumen* had a quantity of walrus tusks and furs, but they declined to sell them, saying that they were in a group with three other *lodkas* for which they were then waiting, and they could not dispose of their catch without the consent of their partners. They made one statement to which Jan gave great significance. They declared that each year several *lodkas* set out from Colmogro Island, where their own home was. They sailed through the Straat Nassau across the Kara Sea to the mouth of the vastly wide and long River Ob, up which they sailed to a river called the Gilissy (Yenissay), where they traded ivory, pelts and train oil for linen and other commodities. They spent the winter there, returning to Colmogro (Kholmogóry, now Archangelsk) only the following summer. The people in that far country were, they said, Christians like themselves and of the Greek persuasion. This account made a great impression upon Jan, as also did the statement that the Kara Sea never froze, and that the ice in it was discharged from the various large rivers that emptied into it. Jan was much heartened by this information.

Through the Strait

ON RETURNING to the fleet, Jan learned that another longboat had just come back with the news that the Straat Nassau now appeared to be open, and it was decided to try to sail through to the Kara Sea. On the next day, August 25, 1595, there was a strong west wind blowing directly into the Strait, and at noon the entire fleet boldly sailed into the passage. Although there were some floating ice floes, and some ice piled up along the shores, the squadron steered its way through and entered the open Kara Sea. They had not progressed far, however, when, to their consternation, they saw ahead of them, in the shape of a half-moon, a vast wall of piled-up ice reaching from the shore, stretching across their path and enclosing them. The entire Kara Sea seemed choked with ice. Much alarmed, they turned about and, working against wind and tide, managed to get back into the Straat Nassau; they anchored for the night close to the shore, between the two capes which Jan in the previous year had named Twist Hoek and Cruys Hoek, where they found some shelter from the west wind. Feeling trapped, they passed an apprehensive night praying for divine aid to enable them to escape from their predicament.

On the next morning, August 26, 1595, the strong west wind began driving ice into the Strait, and before long a high wall was piled up at the eastern end of the Straat Nassau where it debouches into the New North Sea. This wall extended from the Cape of Twist Hoek across to Maelson's Island and closed the exit as effectively as a stopper in a bottle. By the Grace of God, as Jan described it, the fleet was lying to the west of Twist Hoek. The current for some reason began to flow very strongly westward through the Strait in opposition to the wind, so that along the north shore of the Strait there was a strong westward push that kept the eastward, wind-driven ice away from the shore. Steering cautiously, the seven ships floated down this ice-free channel, carrying against the strong head wind only a rag of sail sufficient to maintain enough headway to respond to the rudder.

And Back

I T W A S with heartfelt thanks to Providence that Jan saw the last of the drifting string of vessels hug the shore past De Moucheron's Hoek and then hoist sail to get back to the fairly safe anchorage they had so confidently left on the previous day. When the *Hoop* had swung out of the Straat Nassau and hoisted sail, Jan looked back in the vessel's wake and perceived that there were two strong currents flowing through the Strait, one hurtling eastward and the other westward, struggling against each other "just as they do in the Strait of Magellan," as he remarked in his journal.

The next day, August 27, 1595, Jan saw that the west wind had finally driven so much ice into the Straat Nassau that it was completely filled up from shore to shore, and he realized then how narrow had been their escape. Then the gale suddenly shifted to the south and began to drive the ice across the bight in which the fleet was anchored; the ships had to weigh anchor and creep close to the shore, where they were huddled together in only three fathoms of water, so that, Jan said, they were only by God's Grace kept from striking bottom. They realized it was only by Divine Mercy that they were being preserved. Jan noted that, although it was a clear, sunshiny day, somehow the sun's rays seemed to have no warmth. During the night it was so cold that new ice formed to the thickness of a finger over the old ice, and not only was the rigging ice-covered, but the water vat on the *Hoop* froze. Jan noted that no one got much sleep that night, since all were so worried by the way the ice was relentlessly being blown farther and farther into the bight in which they were now trapped.

Trapped in Ice

T H E N E X T D A Y , August 28, 1595, was one of torture for all, because the ice now had been driven about the ships and encircled them like a belt. It was so firm that Jan wrote he could have walked from the *Hoop* to shore without getting his feet wet. The ships all were frozen in, but not yet to the point of being crushed by pressure, and everyone realized that they were dependent upon God's mercy and if they could only hold their position until the wind changed they might still hope to escape destruc-

tion. Again it was a bitterly cold, sleepless night, but since it now began
to rain heavily, Jan nursed the hope that the wind would change.

On August 29th, the rain ceased and a heavy fog set in, but the gale
continued to blow from the south, veering to southwest. Jan noted that
all they could do was to pray to God for mercy and hope that the pressure
on the hulls would not increase. On the morning of August 30th, the wind
changed to northerly and caused the ice to drift westerly, seawards; in a
short time the fleet again was in open water, and before long there was a
wide ice-free area between the anchorage and the receding ice.

Open Water Again

THE RELIEF of the crew was very great, for all realized how close to
overwhelming disaster they had been, and that it was only Divine Providence that had spared the fleet. At noon the wind shifted strongly to east,
and before long the sea around them was completely void of ice. Now that
the fearful crisis had passed, the reaction of all the crews was that this
could only be a temporary respite. They should not tempt providence by
continuing to run such risks, but should take advantage of their present
liberation from the ice to sail homeward.

A Group of Samoyeds

ON THAT AFTERNOON, a scouting longboat returned with a report
of having seen from a distance a group of natives encamped on the mainland south of the Straat Nassau. The next morning, Jan sent two boats to
make contact with the Samoyeds and to establish friendly relations. He
sent along Michiel, the Slav interpreter from Amsterdam, and gave him a
list of items about which to question the natives; particularly he was to
ask when the great winter gales would come, and when navigation would
become impossible in the ice-bound seas. He was especially to find out all
possible details regarding the New North Sea. The emissaries succeeded in
getting on friendly terms with the natives, after some tense moments of
distrust had been overcome, but the interpreter, who was not very intelligent, had difficulty in clearly understanding and translating some of
the answers to his queries, and the information he brought back was confused and contradictory.

In order to try to clear up these questions, on the next morning, Sep-
tember 1st, Jan and François de la Dalle were rowed to the camp of the
Samoyeds bearing gifts of knives, bread, cheese and brandy. François de la
Dalle asked in Russian to meet the headman, who proved to be cordial and

informative. From him they learned that winter would begin within three weeks, and at the latest four, and that total darkness would prevail not long after. He also confirmed that in the winter the straits and inlets would be frozen solid, so that hunters could travel safely across the ice from the mainland to the islands; in some years the water remained frozen throughout the summer, so that then the west to east passage by ship was impossible. He declared that there was a warm sea to the east of Nova Zembla which bordered on the land of the Tartars through which the River Ob flowed, and that they, like the Samoyeds, paid tribute to the Grand Duke of Moscow.

What particularly interested Jan and François de la Dalle was his statement that, after a five-day journey by water to the east through the warm Kara Sea (the New North Sea), an immense open sea would be reached. They understood him thus to describe the North Pacific Ocean near China, and accordingly they were much heartened. Once more they had elicited from the confused natives, who were anxious to please, the answers which they unconsciously inspired and which they wanted to hear. This was the third time that Jan and his colleagues had, in their intensity, deluded themselves when thus questioning the Samoyeds or the Russians. As the old proverb says, "What men hope, men gladly believe."

Again Through the Strait

STIMULATED by this encouraging information, Jan learned with elation on rejoining the fleet that a longboat which had been sent in the morning to scout the situation in the Straat Nassau had brought back news that a south wind had that day cleared the Strait of ice. The admiral had decided that if it were still clear in the morning, they would try once more to sail through to the New North Sea and thence eastward to Cape Tabin.

The next morning, September 2nd, was clear, with a good south wind, and the fleet immediately weighed anchor and sailed through open water to the mouth of the Straat Nassau. Finding the passage clear, they sailed past Maelson's Cape, well into the Strait, but when about half way through they had to cast anchor behind Cross Cape because the south wind was blowing so strongly that they were afraid of being driven ashore.

The New North Sea

ON THE NEXT MORNING, September 3rd, they entered the New North Sea, which they found ice-free, warmer, and of a deep blue color;

when they sounded, they could find no ground even at 110 fathoms. As far as the horizon, the sea stretched out shining and clear, so with high hopes they set their course northeasterly and bowled along with a spanking southwest breeze. Jan buoyantly told the others that it reminded him of the similar situation on the voyage of the previous year, when they had been able to sail at will through the same area. Everyone was in high spirits, the fleet sailed merrily along with a fair wind and all sails spread, and the land of Cathay seemed to be just over the rim of the sea.

The Ice Barrier

BUT SHORTLY AFTER NOON they suffered a great shock, for ahead of them, stretching from north to south, completely blocking their path, lay another immense field of ice, with a high wall of jumbled, mountainous blocks in its seaward side. Jan said in his report that none of them had ever before seen such a formidable barrier piled up of mammoth, menacing masses of jagged ice. He and his shipmates were plunged into despair, for they had all been convinced that the Kara Sea was clear except for the floating ice discharged into it from the great rivers. They now realized that the immense spread of ice that lay before them was the frozen surface of the New North Sea itself.

Lost in the Fog

SINCE the gale was driving them steadily toward the wall of ice, the admiral signalled the fleet to come about and sail into the wind. It was now obvious that their only course was to sail back again to the Straat Nassau. They had hardly established their new direction when the other ships of the squadron were blotted out from Jan's gaze by a sudden heavy fog that blanketed the sea, and no ship could see any of its mates. Immediately they sounded their trumpets and discharged muskets, and by continuing to do so they managed to keep apart and yet together. Despite the fog, the southwest wind blew strongly, and the ships dared not furl their canvas because of the icy lee shore which lay so near.

But as the day wore on and they continued their steady southwesterly course, they realized that they must be driving toward the Siberian coast and began to listen anxiously for the sound of breakers along that rocky shore, with its outcroppings of reefs and shallows. The fog thickened, the wind which had tossed up a heavy sea became a shrieking gale, and as the ships tore along the skippers gradually took in their canvas, thankful at least that the sea about them was clear of ice.

The admiral had never established any set of sound signals by which to issue orders to the fleet in a fog, either by trumpet call or shots, to establish a change of course, uniform setting of sails, or anchoring. Therefore all the seven ships could only plunge along blindly in the same formation they had been following prior to losing sight of one another. Each ship continued its endeavor to keep with the others by alternate signalling and listening, and each one constantly sounded the lead and kept one lookout far forward and another at the masthead. It was not possible accurately to locate the source or direction of the signals between ships, but when the pounding and crashing of ice-laden surf upon a rocky shore became audible, each skipper knew that danger lay straight ahead, and each hurriedly took in all sail and began to drift. The lead showed that the depth of the sea was shoaling rapidly; shouts were exchanged from ship to ship, and soon the order was passed from one to another to drop anchor. Now at least they knew they had succeeded in keeping together, though their danger was still extreme. They had no idea where they were, and everyone felt a sense of fright, dejection and helplessness in the fog.

Saved by a Miracle

W H A T was their astonishment, then, when the fog lifted in the late afternoon, to find that they had blindly cast anchor in the familiar haven of Staten Island, the safest anchorage on the whole coast. Jan said with conviction that a real miracle had been vouchsafed them; the Lord had answered their prayers by taking them by the hand and leading them to this safe harbor. Miracle or not, the fleet had no more than adjusted its anchorage in the haven after the fog had lifted than a wild storm burst from the northwest, setting up a heavy sea and driving a great mass of ice through the Straat Nassau into the New North Sea. The giant currents which raced just beyond their snug harbor would have crushed the entire flotilla against the Siberian coast had they not somehow come in the blind fog to the one safe anchorage available.

Staten Island lay just beyond the eastern mouth of Straat Nassau, and Jan peered toward the Strait as he crouched in the crow's nest at the masthead of the *Hoop*. The driving hail almost blinded him, but by protecting his eyes he could see, in momentary lulls in the storm, that the storm-lashed, ice-laden current debouching easterly from the Straat was met by the powerful tide from the New North Sea pouring irresistibly westward, and a great maelstrom was created. Icebergs and myriads of frozen blocks swirled madly in it, and all seven vessels would have been sucked down and battered to bits had they been caught up by the storm while entering the Strait. Jan was filled with mixed horror and thankfulness as he saw what might have been their fate.

To the North

On September 4, 1595, because the storm had forced ice into their harbor, they shifted the position of the ships to a narrow, reef-filled channel between Staten Island and the mainland; for greater safety, the vessels were moored side by side and lashed together by ropes.

Disagreement about Next Move

THE ADMIRAL then called a meeting of the officers and supercargos to settle upon a code of auditory signals to use in the future, in case of fog or snow or darkness. At the same time, he asked for frank discussion as to whether, now that they were east of the Straat Nassau, they should try once more to sail eastward across the New North Sea in an attempt to reach their goal. The general opinion was that, in consideration of the lateness of the season and particularly because of the extraordinarily heavy amount of ice in that year, they would be butting their heads against a wall, as Jan put it. He also piously said, in his official report, that it obviously was not the Divine Will for them to try to carry on the voyage farther at this time, and it would be tempting Providence to try to do so. The Amsterdammers, led by bold Willem Barentsz, dissented from this opinion. They demanded that they should now sail north, along the eastern coast of Nova Zembla to its northern tip, and then sail northeast, as had been advocated by Petrus Plancius and tried by Barentsz in the previous year. Barentsz clashed openly with the admiral about this, accused him of timidity, and threatened to leave the fleet with the Amsterdam contingent of three ships and go it alone. Some of the other skippers intervened and tried to make peace, but Barentsz was belligerent, remained defiant in his attitude to the admiral, and would not be pacified. Consequently the meeting broke up in disagreement without having arrived at a decision.

Hunting Parties Ashore

ON SEPTEMBER 5, 1595, the storm continued. When word of the discussion in council leaked out to the crews, much dissatisfaction was expressed at the idea of persisting further in the voyage. A number of rabbits and other game had been observed on land, and in order to divert the men the admiral gave permission for hunting parties to go ashore. A few of the returning hunters brought back some "mountain crystals" which they found imbedded in rocks along the coast, and an order was immediately issued granting leave to any groups who wished to prospect further for these symmetrically formed pieces of clear, transparent quartz which were akin to the "iceland spar" and "greenland spar" then in commercial demand for optical and decorative purposes.

On September 6, 1595, several parties went ashore to try to collect crystals and dispersed in little groups along the seaside. A pair of sailors who were kneeling intently chiselling out a crystal were suddenly set upon and killed by a bear which had padded up to them unnoticed. Both men had been well liked, and the effect of this accident upon the crews was demoralizing.

The seamen were bored and frustrated, many of them were suffering from scurvy, and all of them had been frightened by the recent close escape of the fleet. Now they became unruly and almost mutinous as they foresaw what privations and dangers would lie ahead if the officers hesitated any longer to sail homeward. Soon it would be too late, if indeed it was not already so. The ice had begun to pile up all about Staten Island, the Straat Nassau was choked with it, and many felt that they already had delayed too long and now were trapped.

Escape Through the Strait

ON SEPTEMBER 8TH, the admiral called another meeting of the Council and an angry debate ensued in which the Amsterdammers still stood out for wintering in the Arctic. Barentsz had a heated exchange with the admiral, although he was reminded that, under their orders, he was to obey Nay's command. However, on September 9, 1595, when the state of the ice seemed promising for an escape, the fleet lifted anchors and sailed for the Strait. Skirting the shore to avoid the ice, the *Griffoen*, the admiral's ship, and the Rotterdam yacht both ran aground on hidden reefs. All the boats of the fleet were recruited to try to tow them; both vessels jettisoned ballast, water, beer barrels and other heavy cargo, and set out anchors by which they finally warped themselves free. Jan recorded that this, too, had a disturbing effect upon the seamen. It was only with the greatest difficulty that they now made their way along the coast for the short distance to the Strait, moving into every opening in the ice, availing themselves of every favoring current or breeze, placing kedge anchors on the floes all along, and using long oars or sweeps to maneuver the ships.

On September 11, 1595, they worked their way into the Strait. Here, stranded on the shore, they found a dead whale, and Jan gathered and brought aboard the *Hoop*, as curiosities, its immensely long lower jawbones. (He later was to present one of these to the Town of Enkhuizen, where it was suspended in the Municipal Building, and the other he was to give to his birthplace, Haarlem, where it was mounted on the inner wall of the City Hall.)

Once more the flotilla took anchorage in a protected inlet. They had barely done so when a great storm arose from the west, and the Strait became a raceway, with very high waters which spread far out beyond the shore. The vessels put out all their anchors and doubled the cables, and for two days the skippers hardly dared hope to hold from hour to hour. Fortunately the bottom was good ground and the anchors held, but they passed two days of great anxiety, praying constantly for safety as the jagged masses of ice hurtled past, each one easily capable of cutting their straining cables or tearing a fatal gap in their hulls.

However, on September 14th, the western wind which had swept the ice at breakneck speed through the Strait veered to easterly, and the skippers seized what was probably the last opportunity to escape. They at once lifted anchors, spread sails, and sped hurriedly through the Strait. It was foggy, there was snow and hail in the air, and the shores on both sides were buried in snow. It was the middle of September, and they knew well that they should already be out of the Polar Seas. They had already overstayed their time.

The admiral and most of the captains obviously had no hope left of achieving the northeast passage; they considered it worse than a risk to try any longer. Willem Barentsz, who was pilot major of the fleet and also in command of the *Winthondt*, had tried to arouse a spirit of adventure in the other captains. However, in this case the daring man of genius was frustrated and harshly repressed by the cautious mediocrity, Admiral Nay, who, as it happened, was right.

Barentsz's Attempts to Continue

ON THE NEXT MORNING before sunrise, Barentsz began independently to warp his vessel out through the ice and shamed the others into following. With great risk and toil, they made progress in the channel between the island and mainland, but soon another council was called. The discouraged commanders were terrified by the lateness of the season and the frightful winter which would soon set in. All they wanted was an excuse to abandon the adventure. They voted to make one more try, but the next day, another council was called. The daring Barentsz was now frantic, and urged that they swing around and try to get through to the New North Sea by following the northern route, along the west coast of Nova Zembla which he had attempted to take the previous year. Despite his fervor, the council voted that it was too late; moreover, the admiral stated that Barentsz's plan was not in accordance with their explicit orders from the States General.

This was a convenient excuse, and it met with the support of the others.

Barentsz then begged the admiral to be allowed to call for volunteers from the fleet to stay with only two ships to try to get ahead and to prepare to remain all winter if necessary. However, the others would not agree, as they feared to seem, by contrast, lacking in enterprise and hardihood. The next day, the tireless Barentsz went ashore alone and walked all over Enkhuizen Island, studying the channel and testing the tides and currents, but he had scarcely returned before the admiral's ship weighed anchor and led the fleet in retreat. They all anchored off shore during the night. However, the next morning Barentsz set his topsail and weighed anchor, steering back for the Straat Nassau hoping to stimulate some of the others to follow. The admiral naturally did not permit this.

Jan's Statement

TO PROTECT their reputations and to excuse themselves with the States General, the council asked Jan, as the official chronicler and chief instigator of the voyage, to draw up a statement justifying their withdrawal. This he adroitly did. He entitled the document "Protest," and put as good a face as possible upon the failure. Although presumably addressed to the Stadtholder and States General, it really was directed to Almighty Providence, to which Jan assigned all responsibility. "Inasmuch as it has pleased the Lord God not to permit the present voyage," he wrote, "they find themselves compelled because of the time that has elapsed to discontinue the navigation at this time." Barentsz and the second Amsterdam captain, Janszoon, at first declined to sign this document, but finally yielded and did so.

The implication was that in the ensuing spring the fleet would again set forth on its search for the route to China. Jan's great opportunity had been lost, and the adventure entered upon with so much confidence was a failure. This was inevitable, for in their ignorance they had undertaken the impossible. In making the attempt, Jan and his associates had neglected in no respect to try to carry out their orders. Great courage, superb seamanship, and untiring devotion to duty, all had been expended. But neither they nor any other of their contemporaries could conquer the invincible, icy Arctic. They had done their best.

Homeward Bound

ONCE CLEAR AGAIN of the Straat Nassau, the defeated Argonauts set their course for home on September 16, 1595. Jan continued meticulously to enter in his journal the details of the wind, the weather and sea, the course, the islands they passed, the sails they saw, the storms that assailed them, and the dangers they detected and avoided.

At dawn on October 8, 1595, the flotilla was at about 73 degrees north latitude, had cleared North Cape, and was sailing due west into what is now called the Norwegian Sea. The wind was northeast, and was aiding the fleet to fight the warm North Atlantic Drift, which here had a strong easterly flow. The two yachts which had been in their company were now nowhere to be seen, and the admiral signalled to them to shorten sail in the expectation that the yachts would overhaul them. However, although it was clear weather the two small boats were not sighted all day.

The Hoop *Ahead*

AT DUSK a snow storm struck the fleet, and the wind veered to north. As soon as it became dark, the *Hoop* changed its course, put on full sail, and, despite the gale, drove southwesterly through the night. The ship was now in the Atlantic Ocean, and there were no navigational dangers.

On the next morning there was no visibility because of the snowfall, and when the storm cleared up at noon the fleet was not in sight. Instead of waiting for the others, Jan kept to his homeward course with all sail set in a good northerly gale. The *Hoop* was a newly built ship and much faster than the *Griffoen*, the flagship, to whose pace the fleet had been restricted. By pushing along alone, Jan arrived at Texel in seventeen days, on October 26, 1595, while the *Griffoen* did not reach its harbor in Veere until November 20, 1595, having taken twenty-three days more than the *Hoop*. Barentsz and the three Amsterdam ships kept company with the fleet, and hence they also were three weeks behind Jan in reaching Texel.

Jan the Spokesman

IT APPEARS quite improbable, considering Jan's character and his close relationship with the admiral and François de la Dalle, that he would have left the fleet without their agreement. Now that the project had proved a failure, and because the details of its execution had met with vehement objections from Barentsz, it was essential for the directors of the expedition to get in the first word with the governmental authorities, who would be shocked by the failure. They probably were by now expecting the arrival of one of the Rotterdam yachts, which had been assigned to bring back the good tidings that Cape Tabin had been reached as planned.

The unexpected return of the whole fleet which had sailed away with such fanfare would disappoint and probably enrage the speculators who had put their capital in it, and they would lend willing ears to Barentsz's complaints. Their unsuccessful return, after such great promises, would deal a heavy blow to the prestige and influence of Balthasar de Moucheron. Also, since a large amount in government funds had been expended unprofitably in the venture, the Stadtholder and the Grand Pensionary, both politically sensitive to criticism, would be driven to make a scapegoat of De Moucheron.

Therefore it was essential to get word of their turning back to Balthasar de Moucheron before it was made public. It was customary, as we have seen, that a ship which had been sent out under the auspices of the States General was held incommunicado in the harbor upon its return until its officers had submitted their logs and journals to representatives of the sponsoring body and until the complement and cargo had been inspected by them. Only after official approval were the men paid and allowed ashore, and in cases such as this, in which national interests were involved, the crew were first required to take an oath of secrecy concerning the events of the voyage. However, since the *Hoop* was an Enkhuizen ship, and since most of the cost of the voyage had been contributed in that city, we may be certain that Jan found a way to get in touch with Balthasar de Moucheron and his Enkhuizen friends the moment his ship anchored at Texel.

Jan was, for every reason, the best qualified officer to speak for his fellows and to present the facts in a favorable light. However, as was to be expected, when the storm of public criticism broke he was publicly accused of coloring his report in favor of C. C. Nay, François de la Dalle and himself.

It took great courage for Jan to step into the breach. The year before, with his natural candor and naïveté, he had been jubilant in christening islands, capes and other geographical features of the area with the names of his sponsors and friends, in the conviction that his expedition had achieved for the Netherlands in the Arctic what Columbus, da Gama and Magellan had done elsewhere. His assurance had been so infectious that the great leaders of his country had accepted his assumption at face value, perhaps because the eager simplicity of his character, together with his personal modesty, rendered all the more convincing his claims on behalf of the Arctic project. Even at the height of his prestige, he had countered the arrogant insistence of Petrus Plancius with restrained assurance. Now, although the second expedition had failed to reach its goal, his confidence in the project's ultimate feasibility gave him the fortitude necessary to withstand the flood of vituperation and derision which was poured upon him by a nation which always was quick to trample upon a fallen hero.

As soon as the *Hoop* had come to anchor at Texel, it was the unpalatable task of Jan to report at once, personally, to Count Maurice and to the

Grand Pensionary. He was still completely confident of the soundness of the plan to reach China by the Northeast Passage, and urged the authorities to send out the fleet again in the spring of 1596. He emphasized that the Russians were accustomed to making the passage through Waygats Strait (the Straat Nassau) annually, and he suggested that two scouting yachts should be sent forward ahead of time to observe the routes taken by the Russian *lodkas.*

Jan a Father

UPON HIS RETURN Jan had a private preoccupation which must have distracted him from his official worries, for when he had sailed from Texel, on July 2, 1595, his bride of three months was expecting a child in August. Jan learned upon his arrival at Texel that he was the father of a daughter, Marietje, named after his own mother, and baptized on August 24, 1595.

Duties as Chief Supercargo

IT WAS SOME MONTHS, however, before he could be released from his official duties as chief supercargo for the fleet of seven richly laden vessels. In that capacity he had legal and fiscal responsibilities, along with his colleague François de la Dalle, not only to the States General but also to the States of Zeeland and Holland and to the municipal admiralties of Middelburg, Rotterdam, Amsterdam and Enkhuizen. This congeries of national, provincial and city legislative bodies, all somewhat overlapping, and each jealous of the other, is an example of the incredibly complicated way in which all government business was carried on in the United Provinces. Energetic and courageous as were the talented Dutch people, their achievements were limited by their clumsy and inefficient form of administrative organization, which has been aptly described as "organized disorder."

Moreover, Jan and De la Dalle also had accepted the responsibility of acting as legal representatives on the cruise for the various private associations of merchant adventurers who held joint ownerships in the trade cargoes carried by the fleet. All parties, both official and private, were dissatisfied with the results of the undertaking, and the two supercargos were targets of much grumbling and many complaints. This made their task far from pleasant, and at times Jan was under great strain. However, his experience as supercargo in the previous year's voyage, although it had been a much smaller squadron, his two years as representative of the German firm of Welser in the complicated salvage operation in the Azores, and his long service as accountant for the Archbishop in Goa, all now stood him in good stead.

CHAPTER IX

Burgher and Savant

The Scapegoat

THE AUTUMN OF 1595 was not a happy one for Jan in Enkhuizen, although he must have gotten some surcease from his public harassments by the new comfort of having his own home with a wife and little daughter. His position as the discredited chief commissioner of the returned fleet was anything but pleasant, but even less comfortable was the situation in which he found himself as the fiscal agent or factor in the expedition for the several syndicates made up of groups of private merchants. Naturally, there had been some damage to the trading merchandise for which Jan had been responsible, and the assessing of averages and the adjustment of liquidations was not always amicable. Tedious and complex though it was to redistribute the disembarked goods to their owners upon payment by them of assessed charges, there were few persons better qualified than Jan to handle this delicate transaction, because of his experience in apportioning the losses and making the adjustments upon the merchandise salvaged from the wrecked "Ship of Malacca" in the Azores.

Many of his friends and connections had invested in the fleet, and although they really were fortunate to be assessed only for expenses and receive most of their capital back, nevertheless they had originally cherished such high hopes of making handsome profits (based largely on Jan's sanguine forecasts) that the fiasco stung them to an unjust sense of outrage. They could hardly have been criticized for complaining, however, since even the Heads of State had endorsed the speculation, having themselves been carried away by Jan's optimism. But the politicians adroitly stepped aside and let Jan be the scapegoat for all. There has been speculation as to whether the ancient nursery rhyme "Jan Huyghen," today still recited in a laughing chorus by dancing children, was composed by detractors of Linschoten in derision at his Humpty Dumpty–like fall from high position with the collapse of the second polar expedition. The persistence of such children's rhymes through the centuries has been demonstrated in many cases. In it, the ridiculed Jan Huyghen is mockingly depicted as a cask which has swelled beyond normal dimensions, has burst its hoops, and thus has collapsed into a jumble of loose staves. The historical origin of the satirical refrain cannot be traced, but it may well date from 1595, when the vindictive subscribers to the syndicates made Linschoten the butt of scathing criticism for the failure of the venture.

However, when the Amsterdammers, inspired by the indomitable and frustrated Barentsz, joined in the chorus and blamed the Enkhuizen admiral and the Zeeland skippers for pusillanimity in not having pushed eastward through the ice, then the old feud broke out between Amsterdam and Zeeland. Soon Jan had his partisan defenders at home. He and De la Dalle had never lost their conviction that somewhere not far behind the frozen zone there sparkled a calm, blue, iceless sea on which they could safely sail to Cathay, and even their detractor Petrus Plancius himself held strongly to this belief.

Frustration

DESPITE the complaints of the disgruntled shippers whose speculation had turned sour, and disregarding the many jeers and taunts which Jan had to face, there still were many people who shared his belief that once through the Waygats Strait one could sail unimpeded over the Kara Sea (Jan's New North Sea) to the Strait of Anian and on to Cathay.

But Balthasar de Moucheron, the father of the plan, now had lost faith in it and refused to invest any further capital in the venture. His defection had the effect of deterring any further investment by Zeeland or Enkhuizen maritime entrepreneurs. In vain Jan pointed out how the Portuguese pioneers in the fifteenth century had also met with initial disappointments in their attempts to reach the Orient by sea, and how by persistence they had eventually succeeded and had reaped an enormous reward. His argument was that the Russian luggers knew a route through Waygats Strait and made annual voyages through the ice via the Kara Sea to the mouth of the Ob River.

He and a group of associates lobbied and pleaded with the States General to provide them with two small, light-draft pinnaces to permit them to make a scouting voyage to learn this Russian route, which then could be followed by an appropriate expedition. They managed to get a bill introduced to this effect, but it was buried in committee. The States General did, however, pass a substitute bill promising to pay the sum of 25,000 florins to any explorer who might at his own expense find the Northeast Passage to China. However, Jan could not persuade any leader to try to raise funds to fit out such a squadron in the hope of winning the award.

Amsterdam's Tenacity

ALTHOUGH the Zeelanders and West Frieslanders had lost heart, the tenacious Amsterdammers, under the urging of the Reverend Petrus Plancius, sent out a third expedition. On May 10, 1596, two little ships set out for the Arctic Circle from Amsterdam with China as their objective. They carried with them costly fabrics and other choice European merchandise to meet the high standards of Chinese importers, as well as impressive presents for the officials in the ports they hoped to reach. One flyboat was under the command of Jan Corneliszoon Rijp, who was skipper and factor for the goods that a syndicate of merchants had laden in it. The skipper of the other ship was Jacob Heemskerk Henderickszoon, who likewise was supercargo. He had sailed with Linschoten's unsuccessful voyage of 1595.

It is surprising that Willem Barentsz had only the position of chief pilot of this latest polar expedition, but it is understandable that the prudent Amsterdam merchants, having in mind only the profit from the adventure, did not dare entrust their investment to the hands of this dynamic zealot, in whose lexicon there was no such word as "fail." Nevertheless, Barentsz was the activating force of the expedition. Cautious Captain Rijp always disagreed with him and insisted on sailing on a safe course, which eventually netted him nothing but saved him hardship and risk, although he did discover Spitsbergen and Bear Island along with Barentsz. Heemskerk, on the other hand, encouraged the aspiring Barentsz and was sympathetic to his daring. Rijp lost the confidence of Plancius after his failure and no longer was favored by him.

The Saga of Barentsz

JAN AND DE LA DALLE were excited and dejected when their rivals Barentsz and Heemskerk sailed for the third time to try to seize the prize from them, and they were sure that the Amsterdammers would succeed. However, the polar expedition of 1596 was caught in the ice in northeastern Nova Zembla. After wintering there Barentsz managed spectacularly to guide the survivors, including Heemskerk, back to Kilduyn with the merchandise in two small, patched-up boats; however, he lost his own life due to exhaustion. The epic of all three of Barentsz's heroic polar expeditions was published in 1598 in Amsterdam by a survivor, Gerrit de Veer, who incidentally voiced the Plancius faction's viewpoint. De Veer attacked Linschoten's account of his two expeditions, but he was forced by the Dutch authorities to retract. De Veer's book was widely translated in European languages because it depicted the victorious struggle of Barentsz and Heemskerk for survival in the Arctic winter. In 1871 a Norwegian whaler discovered the ruins of the hut where Barentsz and Heemskerk had spent ten agonizing months of Arctic winter with sixteen men. The contents of the hut were, after almost three centuries, in a good state of preservation, and now are on exhibition at the Rijksmuseum in Amsterdam. They include a letter, signed by all the crew and addressed to whom it might concern, giving the details of their adventure. There also were books, manuscripts, arms, tools, utensils, a clock, navigating instruments, and many articles of clothing. This constituted a treasure trove for historians because it answered many questions regarding sixteenth century maritime usages.

The failure of the expedition of Heemskerk and Barentsz was not such a blow to public feeling as the previous Arctic fiascos had been, for in the meantime Cornelis de Houtman's expedition to Java, although severely battered, had managed to reach home again. The Dutch now felt that the treasures of the Orient were within their grasp along the Cape route, and consequently, instead of grumbling over past failures, they once more took heart. It was to be the beginning of their Golden Age.

The Dutch Renaissance

IN THAT SAME YEAR OF 1596 when Barentsz made his last attempt to reach the Orient by way of the Northeast Passage, a joint Anglo-Dutch expedition sacked Cadiz, the citadel of Spain's commercial empire, and among the aggressors were many Enkhuizers. It was in that year that King Philip II of haughty Spain entered a plea of bankruptcy and repudiated his debts with a whining, face-saving declaration, thereby ruining all the merchants who had trusted him. But Enkhuizen flourished more than ever, and a bad debt there was a rare occurrence.

As early as 1592 the windmill had been used to furnish the power to saw logs, and in 1596 a much improved planing mill was invented and set in motion near the Zaan River, which still remains a district of milling and lumbering; it was at that time a busy shipbuilding center. In 1597,

Burgher and Savant

Stadtholder Maurice drove the Spanish forces southward, Spanish control of Rhine navigation was broken, and the rich German river traffic was now free to flow into the Netherlands again. Wood was once again rafted down the great river from the Black Forest, and huge trees from Germany and Scandinavia were planed into ship timbers. Rope mills, tar sheds, sail yards, net factories, carpenter shops, smithies, all worked overtime turning out the small, efficient Enkhuizer yachts, flyboats and herring busses, which required much smaller crews than the freighters of competing nations, had a shallower draft, and were so sturdily constructed that they outlasted the craft of other maritime peoples. The freighting trade of Enkhuizen expanded accordingly—as did trading activities all over the United Provinces.

An Antwerp refugee merchant had once said, with some justice, "Until we came to Amsterdam, the Hollanders were barely able to pay for the maintenance of their dykes." Now, however, although the southern refugees still inspired and guided them, the Dutch themselves were on the move; this was true in the West Friesland ports and in the rising metropolis of Amsterdam. The activities of Dutchmen were widespread, and among Dutchmen Jan van Linschoten, now an influential citizen of Enkhuizen, held a position of authority, being a man who had traveled far and apparently knew the whole world.

Dutch cargo ships continued to carry timber from the Baltic, iron from Sweden, grain from Danzig and Riga, stockfish from Norway and Iceland, wine, olive oil and marble from Italy, figs, dates and valuable carpets from the Levant, dried currants from Greece, in a never-ending pageant of merchantmen that proudly flew the Dutch colors in every part of the world. Now, however, instead of merely freighting merchandise for the accounts of other countries, Dutch carriers took a hand in the transactions; from being simply ship-owners they became merchants and bankers. No longer was the Groot Visscherij (the "great fishery" of the herring trade) the sole support of Enkhuizen, for now the whole wide world was open to the enterprising mariners from the Zuider Zee.

From Enkhuizen, from Amsterdam, and from some other Dutch ports, expeditions put to sea to try their luck in the Spanish Indies—the Caribbean Ocean, including the Spanish Main and Mexico. They usually carried flour, wine, oil, clothing, tools, arms, and other indispensable supplies to the lonely Spanish overseas colonists, and bartered these commodities for gold dust, sugar, tobacco and cotton—that is, so long as they were admitted as peaceful traders. However, if difficulties were made, their cannon came into play. Since they were commissioned by the Stadtholder as privateers, they were at liberty to seize any enemy craft that crossed their path. If they failed to "catch a fish," as capturing a Spanish prize was called, they could always take on a profitable load of salt at a West Indian island or from "the Caraques," by which the coast of Venezuela was meant.

In some cases they met disaster, as when the colonial authorities invited the crew to bring their merchandise ashore in a peaceful fashion and then fell upon them and seized both goods and men. Outrages of this sort naturally entailed retaliation on the part of the Dutch, who would soon send a squadron of warships to demand satisfaction. The Dutchmen even became so bold as to attack the Spanish foe in his greatest strongholds, as happened in 1607 when Heemskerk, of Arctic fame, was killed while attacking and destroying the Spanish fleet at Gibraltar. The epitaph upon his tomb in Amsterdam says (translated into English):

> Heemskerk, with ice and iron alike at strife,
> Left here his limbs, his flag, his fame—
> and at Gibraltar his life.

To the Indies

IN 1597, when the heroic but unsuccessful Polar expedition of Barentsz and Heemskerk returned home, the people of Amsterdam were in no hurry to continue the Northeast adventure, though both Plancius and Heemskerk still believed in the Arctic route to China, and Jan, as we know, was heart and soul in favor of it. In the summer of 1597, however, when the De Houtman expedition returned from the first Dutch voyage to the East Indies, all public interest in any other route than the Cape died a quick death.

The triumphant homecoming from Java had another side, for only eighty-nine men came back out of the original crew of 284; the round trip had lasted two years and four months, and the commercial results of the expedition were meager. However, the trip had been made, and it was confidently expected that future expeditions would do better. This was certainly Balthasar de Moucheron's idea, for he hired the De Houtman brothers away from Amsterdam and hurriedly sent them off again to the East Indies for his own account in an attempt to reap the fruits of their pioneer voyage. It is not known whether Linschoten was involved in this venture. Let us hope that he was not, for like Antonio in The Merchant of Venice and also like King Philip of Spain, De Moucheron was to suffer from a series of misfortunes; this expedition had one maritime disaster after another and eventually failed expensively. Yet the second fleet that Amsterdam sent our shortly after De Moucheron's squadron had sailed had dazzling success. Half the fleet of eight ships was back in Amsterdam within fifteen months with an enormously profitable cargo, to be followed soon by the rear guard with an equally rich consignment. General exultation prevailed, and in the Amsterdam wharf district two thoroughfares were named Bantam Street and Pepper Street.

The Treasurer of Enkhuizen

BY THE YEAR 1597, only two years after his crestfallen return from the Arctic, Jan had regained status and had been appointed Treasurer of the City of Enkhuizen. This post was by no means a sinecure, but was an important and lucrative position of influence and responsibility. The city had valuable endowments and perquisites which had originally been granted by the Emperor Charles V, including remunerative taxes upon all shipping in the Zuider Zee; in addition, it was engaged in various current enterprises. Consequently Jan was in a position to profit by the immediate boom that developed in the East Indian spice trade. He was now a member of the ruling oligarchy of the town whose members at once became an active factor in the oriental market. Because of the nationwide interest in the Indies, Jan's prestige was once more great, for he, more than any other man in the United Provinces, possessed full knowledge and sound data concerning the Far East. His informative publications about the Portuguese and Spanish overseas empires in both hemispheres were the sole reliable printed sources of guidance for the northern maritime countries which now were actively challenging the Hispanic monopolies. Also, when in 1598 Lucas Waghenaer published in Enkhuizen his *Enkhuizer Zeekaertboek*, which was a popular edition of his famous *Mariner's Mirror*, he duly acknowledged his indebtedness to his friend Jan Huyghen van Linschoten for assistance in preparing the part devoted to the navigation of the Arctic Seas.

The Overseas Adventurers

AS SOON as it became evident that the combined naval forces of Portugal and Spain were unable to prevent outsiders from using the Cape route to the East Indies, a general outburst of activity swept the young Republic. Consequently in 1598—the same year in which King Philip II, now almost a forgotten man in Holland, was buried in the now famous crypt at the Escorial—several expeditions were sent out to various destinations, all of them intent upon gaining profit in the tropics where hitherto Portugal and Spain had enjoyed a complete monopoly. Some went to try their luck in the East Indies, while others ventured along the African shores or across the Atlantic to the Caribbean or to Brazil and the River Plate. Each expedition was determined to do business if possible peacefully, but if necessary by force. Even the salt trade, which used to ply to Setúbal, had to go much farther afield now, since Setúbal had been forbidden to the Dutch by royal decree. Now well-armed flyboats from Enkhuizen sought the salt beds at the Portuguese Cape Verdes or in the West Indies for salt for the packing sheds of the Herring City.

In that same year two squadrons independently tried their luck at negotiating the terrible Strait of Magellan in an attempt to reach the Spice Islands along the western course. The first one, with Dirk Gerritszoon "China" along as an expert on that country, was scattered all over the Pacific; one of its ships reached Japan, thus preparing the way for Dutch penetration into that remote and secluded empire. The other, efficiently led by Olivier van Noort, succeeded in circumnavigating the globe, the first time this feat had been accomplished by the Dutch.

It was also in the dynamic year of 1598 that a Greenland Company was chartered by the States General for the purpose of whaling, and there was other activity of this kind proposed or under way. Linschoten's advice was probably sought in this connection, in view of his experience in both southern and northern waters. However, such enterprises were kept completely secret, since every trading company was afraid of its competitors.

The expeditions to West Africa were so numerous that the States General, which in the beginning had encouraged them, not only decided to withhold support but actually to discourage them, since they wished to avoid excessive competition which might spoil both the buying and selling markets. This excessive competition was precisely what ruined business for the all too numerous East India companies, some of which had made a fair start; the bottom was knocked out of the spice business when the companies bid up prices to acquire spices and then had to sell their wares in a glutted buyer's market at home for less than they had paid for them. In a few years as many as twenty-one Dutch fleets, totaling sixty-one ships, competed to buy spices in the Indies upon the seller's terms. A financial panic ensued, there were bankruptcies on all sides, and a dangerous depression set in. All trade was practically suspended for fear of further financial disaster.

The United East India Company

IN THIS dangerous and lamentable state of affairs, the States General, under Oldenbarnevelt's leadership, decreed a temporary embargo on all navigation to the Indies. This measure was followed, in 1602, by the creation of a licensed stock company under an exclusive charter. Existing companies were allowed to join it with their share prorated according to the value of their invested capital. Separate divisions of this national corporation, called chambers, were established in the respective provinces, each one being represented proportionately on the main board of directors under government supervision. Control in the board lay in the hands of the Amsterdam Chamber, which held 3,700,000 shares of stock. Zeeland came second with 1,300,000. The other two Chambers were divided between Hoorn with 550,000 and Enkhuizen with 250,000 shares, and Delft with 450,000 and Rotterdam with 175,000 shares.

This strong, monopolistic organization came to be known as the United Chartered East India Company, in Dutch abbreviation the "V.O.C." It was given semi-sovereign powers, including its own military and naval forces as well as the power to conclude treaties with native states and rulers within the company's grant of territory, which was to extend from the Cape of Good Hope in an eastward sweep to the Strait of Magellan, both passages being reserved for the V.O.C. to the exclusion of all others.

Among some of the prominent shareholders were Petrus Plancius and Isaac le Maire; the Semeyns family were also shareholders, probably acting on the advice of Jan van Linschoten, who was now recognized in all the Netherlands as the leading authority on matters pertaining to trade with the East. Balthasar de Moucheron, whose importance had dwindled as a result of his chain of misfortunes, was not listed among the shareholders.

Of the V.O.C. buildings in Enkhuizen, some are still extant and are among the landmarks of the old city.

The board of over forty directors was too unwieldy for efficiency, and therefore an executive committee of seventeen actually administered the company's affairs. They were popularly called the "Heeren XVII," or Seventeen Lords. Eight of them were from Amsterdam and nine from all the other chambers, which made the preponderance of Amsterdam almost unassailable. No stockholders' meetings were held and no reports were sent out; the meetings of the committee of seventeen were secret. Shareholders, however, had little to complain about, since in the fifth year of its existence the V.O.C. paid a 75 percent dividend.

Orders to the Governor General in the Indies were "to exclude all other European traders . . . by such means as may be necessary." These instructions were carried out to the letter and beyond by the early governors, who succeeded in securing for the company an extremely strong position in both the military and the commercial sense. In order to create scarcity after the devastating effects of the boom and slump in the market that had preceded the organization of the V.O.C., the governors had whole spice islands burned out and in other areas had all the trees chopped down in order to maintain the price of nutmeg or mace at the level deemed proper by the committee of seventeen.

The company's governors participated in local administration only by directing and controlling the native rulers. They were not interested in converting the natives to Christianity, since commercial profits were their sole objective. Therefore Japan preferred them to the Portuguese, whose proselytizing efforts they resented. In other Eastern countries the Dutch at first ingratiated themselves by supporting the local Buddhist and Moslem clergy against the Portuguese missionaries, and they also encouraged the local monarchs to seize Portuguese trading stations and merchant ships. However, after a few years, when the Dutch had gained sufficient control both of the exports and of the intra-India trade, the native rulers discovered with dismay that they had been backing the wrong horse, and were now and henceforth firmly in the grasp of the powerful "Koempeni."

The English, too, were at first welcomed by the V.O.C. as allies in overcoming the Portuguese, but before long they found themselves regarded as interlopers. The aim of the chartered monopoly was to eliminate all competition, so, as soon as possible, allies were eliminated as well as enemies; both got in the way of the policy to "buy cheap and sell dear." At the same time, the V.O.C. saw that production was reduced to the scarcity level in order to maintain high prices. These high-handed methods, of course, could not fail to arouse opposition, but as long as substantial dividends kept on rolling into the Netherlands the company could afford to ignore any protests.

Holland to the Fore

AT THIS POINT the Netherlands no longer was an oppressed and long-suffering country; now the tables were turned, and Dutch aggression threatened to tear the Spanish and Portuguese empires to pieces. A tremendous amount of privateering developed in all waters and on every coast where the two Hispanic empires once waxed rich. In the field of piracy too, unrestrained competition was felt as a drawback, and consequently the idea of a monopoly on privateering was put forward.

At the instigation of Willem Usselincx, one of the southern refugee businessmen, the formation of a Dutch West India Company was now being considered, with the double aim of attacking the enemy and of building up a Dutch colonial empire in the Americas. In 1606, Linschoten was appointed to a distinguished committee to study this possibility, using the East India Company as a model. However, negotiations with Spain for peace or at least a truce of some duration were impending—the truce was put into force in 1609 for twelve years—and all aggressive activities had to be suspended in view of this situation; hostilities were not renewed until 1621. A West India Company was then actually founded, but Jan was no longer there to take part in it.

A Citizen of Consequence

ALTHOUGH Jan did not live to see all this growth come to its greatest flowering in Holland's Golden Century, he at least witnessed how the Republic was growing strong, wealthy and independent of outside assistance, and his home city of Enkhuizen was attaining great prosperity. As for his own position, he must have counted among the best people in town as a citizen of property and weight, in addition to being a man of considerable learning and vast experience. Because of this, he was named as a trustee of the Enkhuizen Hospital in 1606, and in the following year his wife, Reinu, became "House Mother" of the city alms house. Such posts of control in public charities were customarily filled by persons of wealth and position, being considered as a mark of distinction. The boards were self-perpetuating, and it was impossible to become a member unless one was socially acceptable and politically compatible with the regents. Since they were well aware of their importance, these dignitaries enjoyed having their portraits painted in a group; such paintings, especially those by Frans Hals and Rembrandt, are very well known. Unfortunately, no such group portrait survives in which either Jan or Reinu is depicted. Jan's only portrait is the engraving which was used as the frontispiece of his *Itinerario* and is also found in that position in the present work.

In 1610 Jan applied to the States General for the renewal of his copyright, or exclusive license, to publish his *Itinerario;* he also petitioned for an annuity, in recognition of his services to the nation in supplying to the early expeditions to the East Indies the sailing directions and commercial information which had been so important in their success. The States General granted the renewal of copyright, which cost them nothing, but denied the petition for a pension, saying that the applicant had already been well compensated by the royalties on the sale of his books! There may have been political reasons for this refusal; but it should also be remarked that generosity has never been a special characteristic of the Dutch.

Jan's wanderlust no longer moved him to join the adventurers who left Enkhuizen and other Dutch ports to seek their fortunes or to see the world. Now a burgher of consequence, he could enjoy the comforts of his placid homeland without worry—good wine, beer, and tobacco with long clay pipes at every hearthside, and on the well-laden tables butter, cheese, eggs, meat and fish in profusion. Whenever the need arose to travel within the boundaries of the Republic, he did not have to depend on a leaky, fetid nao or a rolling, plunging flyboat or yacht, but could embark upon a snug, spacious, horse-drawn canal boat from which, pipe in hand, he could view the luminous green pastures and prosperous farmsteads at a placid rate, taking, for example, something like ten unhurried and comfortable hours to get from the Bank at Amsterdam to the States General at The Hague. While he stayed peacefully at home his encyclopedic knowledge of products, routes, markets and currencies must have been of unique value to the Enkhuizen chamber of the V.O.C. His wide knowledge of the outside world also must have given him an important place among the intelligentsia of Enkhuizen, as was shown by the warm and friendly odes dedicated to him in his published works. And we may safely assume that at least a part of the Latin correspondence of the learned Dr. Paludanus with savants in all the cultural centers of Western Europe must have been directed to his co-author, Jan Huyghen van Linschoten. Jan's list of foreign correspondents was undoubtedly not limited to scholars in the Protestant countries of the north, for the astute Cornelis Claeszoon, his publisher, had had the *Itinerario* translated into Latin by a Catholic scholar who had smoothed over certain controversial passages and omitted others, so that the book was rendered acceptable and was read by the Catholic world.

When viewed in the light of his time and his surroundings, Jan must appear as a steady man and husband, without major vices. However, the virtuous scorn which he expressed in the *Itinerario* of the sensuality and voluptuousness of Portuguese Eurasian society in Goa, while ringing true, may have been demanded by his publisher as an additional spicy feature of the book for which Claeszoon himself could decline all responsibility, knowing it could not fail to stimulate public attention in a way only comparable to certain passages in the Old Testament.

There is no trace of Jan's little daughter, Marietje Jansdochter van Linschoten, beyond the entry of her baptism. Her name was not mentioned in her mother's will, which was drawn up in 1613, in which the only beneficiaries were her three children by her first husband. Infant mortality was very high in those days, and it is obvious that little Marietje did not survive childhood. Jan Huyghen van Linschoten thus left no descendants.

The Publications

THE OFFICIAL LICENSE granting the author full copyright was dated 1594. In the course of the next two years his first and best group of manuscripts were published together in one volume, but in all probability the parts were also for sale separately. Priority had to be given to the *Reysgeschrift*, which was prepared with the utmost speed in order to accompany Cornelis de Houtman on his first voyage to the Indies in 1595, and consequently that extremely useful compendium of practical sailing directions bears the same date. Next came the *Itinerario* proper, followed by the chapters on Spain and Portugal, and finally the *Beschryving*, all of these being dated 1596. It may be safely assumed that both author and publisher agreed upon this reversed order of publication because of the pressing need for the *Reysgeschrift*.

A great number of Dutch reprints followed this first edition, in 1604, 1614, 1623 and 1644. There was a complete English translation in 1598, as well as English and German versions of the *Itinerario* in the same year. Two Latin editions were published in 1599; French translations appeared in 1610 and 1619. These numerous editions show that Linschoten must have stirred the minds and imaginations of scholars and ordinary readers in many countries.

In the meantime, being deeply impressed with Padre José de Acosta's book, *Historia natural y moral de las Indias*, Jan decided to have his own works more or less supplemented by a Dutch version of it; he called his translation *Historie Naturael ende Morael van de Westersche Indien* (Moral and Natural History of the West Indies). In this connection it should be observed that, up to about 1800, "Las Indias" was generally used in Spanish when "America" was meant, because of Columbus's error in thinking he had reached the Indies when he came to the Antilles; hence the Caribbean world is still called "The West Indies" and the first natives of the Americas "Indians." Jan's translation of Acosta's book was meant only for Holland, since the work was available in practically all countries in various languages; his translation has never been reprinted.

Jan's belated publication on the polar expeditions of 1594 and 1595 also had but little success. As we know, it had been part of his assignment to report to the Stadtholder and to the States General, and upon his return he prepared a manuscript to be published in a more attractive way than any official account. Maps and engravings, the latter by the brothers Joannes and Baptista à Doetechum, were to illustrate the book in the same charming way as the *Itinerario*, this time embellished with the coats of arms of Enkhuizen and the various other cities and provinces that had participated in the venture. Not forgotten were the remarkable Arctic fauna, nor the Samoyed and Lapp villages as portrayed in Jan's sketchbook.

However, when Jan came to look for a publisher he found the tide had turned. The public was full of enthusiasm regarding the successful trade with the Indies and was still avidly devouring his descriptions of those wonderlands, but was totally uninterested in his defensive account of his Arctic adversities. Besides, such northern exploits had already been related in an engaging way by a member of the Barentsz expedition that had spent the winter in Nova Zembla, and now this entertaining narrative, by one Gerrit de Veer, was put out by Jan's own former publisher, Cornelis Claeszoon, who was a close associate of the Reverend Petrus Plancius and saw no utility in editing the arguments of one of the learned man's fiercest opponents, as Jan now was.

It was only after the East India fever had somewhat subsided that Jan succeeded in finding a publisher willing to risk bringing out his manuscript. This was Gerard Ketel, of Franeker, Friesland, who brought out *Naar het Noorden* (To the North) on January 1, 1601. The book was dedicated to Prince Maurice, the Stadtholder, and to the Mighty Lords the States General of the United Provinces of the Netherlands. Despite its undoubted merit, which is recognized by modern historians, this disquisition upon what was then considered the past history of a failure did not gain the favor of the public, and today very few copies of the original edition are in existence.

Jan's last publication was a translation of a communication which was directed in 1609 by the King of Spain to the Duke of Lerma concerning the banishment of the Moriscos, or Christianized Moors, who constituted a very important industrial element in the Spanish economy. This brief social study, published by Jacob Lenaertsz Meyn, of Enkhuizen, in 1609, was read with great attention at that period. However, it has added little to Jan's fame, which was chiefly based on his *Itinerario*, and its accompanying works.

Certain students of Shakespeare have interpreted some lines in *Twelfth Night* which make reference to a world map as having been inspired by the English edition of the *Itinerario*, which was, as we have seen, published in London in 1598. If this interpretation is correct, it illustrates the degree of popularity which Linschoten's book must have enjoyed throughout the civilized world of his day.

What is believed to be his signature has been found written on the cover of a copy of Ramusio's *Navigazioni*. That, together, with his portrait at the age of thirty-two, is about all he has left us of a personal nature. Only a few legal records of transactions to which he was a party other than in his capacity as Town Treasurer exist to help give an idea of the day to day events of his life.

The Olive Branch

GRATIFYING TRIBUTE to his standing and nation-wide prestige was paid him in 1611, the year of his death, by his hitherto implacable adversary, the Reverend Petrus Plancius. This learned gentleman was preparing a last effort to reach China via the North Pole (on the basis of theories now considered futile, if not grotesque), and he invited Jan Huyghen van Linschoten to appear before the States General as a witness in favor of that scheme. When his messenger arrived in Enkhuizen, Jan was confined to his bed in what was to be his last illness. It is to be hoped, however, that the olive branch from his former opponent arrived in time to let the dying man savor of this, his last wordly triumph.

Apart from the date of his death in February, 1611, no details of Jan's last illness are known, and there is no indication of how long he had been sick. According to modern standards of longevity, his death was a premature one, but in seventeenth-century Europe, with its unceasing epidemics and plagues, with the lack of domestic sanitation and the backward medical practices of the day, his life-span was probably not below average. For example, although Dr. Paludanus himself lived to the advanced age of eighty-three, he buried four wives and most of his children.

No doubt Jan was zealously attended in his illness by his friend the Town Doctor, and one can learn from his professional practices, as set forth by himself in the *Itinerario*, how little beneficial effect his ministrations and nostrums probably had in preventing the demise of his colleague. Yet at that time Paludanus was already sixty-one years old, and he was to survive his younger co-author by over a score of active years.

Jan's will is still extant and shows that he left a substantial fortune to his widow, Reinu, who was also wealthy in her own right.

For a historian who visits modern Enkhuizen, much remains of Jan's historic period, but apart from the simple marble plaque of commemoration marking his burial place in the Wester Kerk, there is no memorial erected by his fellow citizens to the gifted geographer and cosmographer to whom all Holland owed so much.

Even though modern Enkhuizen prides itself upon being the birthplace of Paul Potter, the painter, the town reserves its highest honors for the memory of Linschoten's friend and associate, Bernardus Paludanus. In the Church of Saint Pancras (or Zuider Kerk), there is an elaborate memorial erected to Paludanus by his heirs. Upon it is carved so lengthy an epitaph that it almost amounts to a biography. A stone to his memory is also inserted in the wall of the old Weigh House, now a museum, in which there is a seventeenth-century chamber of the local surgeons' guild, although this organization apparently was founded some years after the death of Paludanus in 1633. Also, a copy in oil of the original portrait of Paludanus, which is in the Frans Hals Museum in Haarlem, hangs in an honored place in the Town Hall.

Although it is difficult for the modern reader to feel any regard for the intelligence of Paludanus after reading his turgid, pedantic prose and hilariously absurd theories of medicine—hilarious even though it represented the orthodox professional thinking of his time—nevertheless he must have been a person of character and understanding to whom respect should be shown.

His quick recognition of the talents of Linschoten, with whom he so generously co-operated and whom he so loyally supported in his days of adversity, show him to have been a man of perspicacity and integrity. His steadfast refusal of a professorial chair at the University of Leyden at a higher stipend and with great dignity shows that he was a man of unique independence of mind.

Within recent years, his *Album Amicorum,* or autograph book, has been discovered, containing the signatures and apothegms of many of the contemporary celebrities of Europe whose fame has endured.

Moreover, the catalog of his famous museum has been unearthed and has been given professional admiration in informed centers for its orderly biological, botanical and zoological classifications by the great pioneer in the natural sciences, who lived long before the days of Linnaeus and Buffon.

The honors paid Paludanus by his fellow townsmen redound also to the credit of Jan Huyghen van Linschoten, to whom the learned doctor accorded such friendly respect.

The old metropolis, now reduced in population to a quarter of its former size and completely bereft of importance, has nourished a warm appreciation of its golden past and has preserved not only its archives and relics, but also many of its picturesque towers, ramparts and other ancient structures.

The massive old warehouse, or *Peperhuis,* of the East India Company has been renovated and converted into a vast provincial Zuider Zee Museum, in which are displayed the vestiges of the ancient sea-farm communities of former times, most of which now stand far from water amidst the farmlands where once the Zuider Zee sparkled or raged.

Public-spirited and proud of its history as ancient Enkhuizen is, nevertheless the memory of Jan Huyghen van Linschoten has been allowed to die out, and his name is not even mentioned to the thousands of tourists who annually visit the delightful old seaport which three centuries ago hailed him with pride.

It is gratifying, however, that through the scholarly care of the Linschoten Society the record of his great achievements has been restored and his memory rescued from oblivion. For the erudite series of historical works published by the Linschoten Society not only is read by patriotic Dutch students in that exceptionally literate country, but the chronicles are also enjoyed in every foreign country where scholars are at work. The fascinating historical series may be found in the more important public libraries of the United States, as well as in the collections of universities and colleges.

Bibliography

THE BOOKS AND ARTICLES consulted by the author have now been transferred from the McKew Parr Library at Chester, Connecticut, to form part of the McKew Parr Collection known as "Magellan and the Age of Discovery" in the library of Brandeis University, at Waltham, Massachusetts, where they are available for research. The bibliography has been arranged in subject-matter divisions according to the chapters of the book, and is headed by a list of the basic editions of Jan Huyghen van Linschoten's own works.

Abbreviations used for the periodicals cited are: MM, *The Mariner's Mirror*; HT, *History Today*; Am. Hist. Rev., *American Historical Review*; Nat'l Geog. Mag., *National Geographic Magazine*; and Geog. Rev., *Geographical Review*.

The Works of Jan Huyghen van Linschoten

THE FOLLOWING authoritative modern editions of Linschoten's works were published by the Linschoten-Vereeniging of The Hague, Netherlands (*see* Preface):

Van Linschoten, Jan Huyghen (H. Kern, Ed.). *Itinerario: Voyage ofte schipvaert van Jan Huyghen van Linschoten naar Oost ofte Portugaels Indien, 1579–1592*, eerste en tweede deel. The Hague, 1910.

Bibliography

Ibid. (S. P. L'Honore Naber, Ed.). *Reizen van Jan Huyghen van Linschoten naar het Noorden, 1594–1595.* The Hague, 1914.

Ibid. (C. P. Burger, Jr., and F. W. T. Hunger, Eds.). *Itinerario: Voyage ofte schipvaert van Jan Huyghen van Linschoten naar Oost ofte Portugaels Indien, 1579–1592,* derde deel: *Beschrijvinghe van de gantsche custe van Guinea, Manicongo, etc.* The Hague, 1934.

Ibid. (J. C. M. Warnsinck, Ed.). *Itinerario: Voyage ofte schipvaert van Jan Huyghen van Linschoten naar Oost ofte Portugaels Indien, 1579–1592,* vierde en vijfde deel: *Reysgheschrift van de navigatien der Portugaloysers.* The Hague, 1939.

Ibid. (H. Terpstra, Ed.). *Itinerario: Voyage ofte schipvaert van Jan Huyghen van Linschoten naar Oost ofte Portugaels Indien, 1579–1592.* 3 vols. The Hague, 1955, 1956, 1957. (A modern re-editing of the complete Itinerario.)

Early Editions

Van Linschoten, Jan Huyghen. *[Itinerario] His Difcours of Voyages into ye Easte & West Indies, deuided into foure Bookes.* John Wolfe, London, 1598. (This first English edition is not in the Parr Collection.)

Van Linschoten, Jan Huyghen. *[Itinerario] Navigatio ac Itinerarivm Iohannis Hvgonis Linscotani in Orientalem sive Lvsitanorum Indiam Descriptiones etc.* The Hague, 1599.

Van Linschoten, Jan Huyghen. (T. De Bry, Ed.) *[Itinerario] Americae Pars Quarta.* Frankfurt, 1599.

Van Linschoten, Jan Huyghen (T. and I. De Bry, Eds.) *[Itinerario] Indiae Orientalis.* Frankfurt, 1601.

Van Linschoten, Jan Huyghen. *[Itinerario] Histoire de la Navigation de Jean Hvgves de Linfchot Hollandois aux Indes Orientales, avec annotations de B. Paludanus, Docteur en Médecine etc.* Deuxiefme édition augmentée. Amsterdam, 1619.

Ibid. Troisième édition augmentée. Amsterdam, 1638.

Modern English Edition

Van Linschoten, Jan Huyghen. (Dr. Arthur Coke Burnell, Ed. Vol. I, Dr. Pieter Anton Tiele, Ed. Vol. II.) *[Itinerario] The Voyage of John Huyghen van Linschoten to the East Indies.* 2 vols. The original Phillips translation. Hakluyt Society, London, 1885.

Introduction

Anson, G. *Voyage Round the World.* London, 1840.

Bamford, P. W. *The Procurement of Oarsmen for French Galleys (1660–1748).* Am. Hist. Rev., Washington, 1959.

Bibliography

Beaglehole, F. C. *Journals of Captain James Cook on his Voyages of Discovery* London, 1955.

Boxer, C. R. *The Manila Galleon 1565–1815*. HT, London, 1958.

Esparteiro, A. M. *A Higiene nas Náus de Viagem em Meados de Seculo XVIII.* Lisbon, 1958.

Lynam, E. *Richard Hakluyt and his Successors*. London, 1946.

Masefield, J. *Sea Life in Nelson's Time*. New York, 1937.

Mason, F. van W. *Manila Galleon*. New York, 1962.

Pigafetta, A. *Magellan's Voyage Around the World* (Robertson edition). Cleveland, 1906.

Powell, I. G. *Early Ship Surgeons*. MM, London, 1923.

Powell, I. G. *The Early Naval Lieutenant (1580)*. MM, London, 1923.

Purchas, S. *Hakluytus Posthumus* or *Purchas his Pilgrimes*. London, 1905–07.

Roddis, L. H. *James Lind, Founder of Nautical Medicine*. London, 1951.

Schurz, W. L. *The Manila Galleon*. New York, 1939.

Taylor, E. G. R. *The Original Writings and Correspondence of the Two Richard Hakluyts*. 2 vols. London, 1935.

Waters, D. W. *Limes, Lemons and Scurvy in Elizabethan Times*. MM, London, 1955.

Walter, R. *Anson's Voyage Round the World*. London, 1928.

CHAPTER I

Background and Boyhood

Boonenburg, K. *De Zuiderzee*. Amsterdam, 1956.

Boonenburg, K. *Houten Schepen*. Enkhuizen, 1957.

Bowen, M. *Holland*. New York, 1929.

Fransen, Dr. J. *Schoon Enkhuizen*. Amsterdam, 1946.

Heide, G. D. van der. *Zuyder Zee Archaeology*. The Hague, 1961.

Kerkmeijer, J. C. *De Historische Schoonheid van Hoorn*. Amsterdam, 1946.

Norel, K. *De Haringstad*. Enkhuizen, 1946.

Prime, K. F. *Geschiedenis van Antwerpen*. 25 vols. Antwerp, 1927.

Rogers, J. K. T. *Holland*, London, 1889.

Stirling, Maxwell W. *Don Juan of Austria, 1547–1578*. 2 vols. London, 1883.

van Loon, H. W. *Golden Book of the Dutch Navigators*. New York, 1938.

Wedgwood, C. V. *Guillermo el Taciturno, Principe de Orange, 1533–1584*. Mexico, 1947.

Wegg, Jervis. *Decline of Antwerp under Philip II of Spain*. London, 1924.

Zuiderzeemuseum de Enkhuizen. *Glorie van Hindeloopen*. Enkhuizen, 1958.

Bibliography

CHAPTER II

Apprenticeship in Spain and Portugal

Spain

Altamira, R. *History of Spain*. New York, 1949.

Altamira y Crevea, R. *Historia de España*. 5 vols., Barcelona, 1913.

Altamira y Crevea, R. *Historia de la Civilización Española*. 4 vols. Madrid, 1935.

Chauno, H. & P. *Seville et l'Atlantique (1504-1650)*. 4 vols. Paris, 1955-1956.

Diaz y Perez, N. *Monumentos e Historia de Badajoz y Caceres*. Barcelona, 1887.

Doussinague, J. M. *La Politica Exterior de España Siglo XVI*. Madrid, 1949.

Duchesne, R. P. *Compendie de la Historia de España*. Madrid, 1764.

Ehrenberg, R. *Capital and Finance in the Age of the Renaissance*. London, 1928.

Fisher, Godfrey. *The Brotherhood of St. George at San Lucar de Barrameda*. London, 1953.

Gebhardt, D. V. *Historia General de España y de sus Indias*. 7 vols. Habana, 1864.

Gwynne, P. *The Guadalquivir, Its Personality, People and Associations*. London, 1912.

Madariaga, S. de. *Spain*. London, 1930.

Mariana, J. de. *Historia General de España*. Madrid, 1678.

Mariéjol, Jean H. *Philip II, First Modern King*. London, 1933.

Meyerstein, E. H. W. *Troubles of Devonshire Mariners in Spanish Ports, 1550*. MM, London, 1949.

Pike, R. *Seville in the XVI Century*. Am. Hist. Rev., Washington, 1961.

Prescott, Wm. H. *The Reign of Philip II, King of Spain*. 3 vols. Philadelphia, 1875.

Smith, R. S. *The Spanish Guild Merchant, 1250-1700*. Durham, 1940.

Valladares, D. A. *Vida Interior del Rey D. Felipe II*. Madrid, 1788.

Watson, R. *Reign of Philip II, King of Spain*. London, 1794.

Wroth, L. C. *An Elizabethan Merchant*. San Marino (Calif.), 1954.

Portugal

Azevedo, J. L. de. *Epocas de Portugal Economico*. Lisbon, 1947.

Birago, Gio. Bat. *Historia della Difunione del Regno di Portogallo della Corona di Caftiglia*. Amsterdam, 1647.

Boxer, C. R. *Some Early Portuguese Bills of Lading*. MM, London, 1939.

Blount, Edward. *History of the Uniting of the Kingdom of Portugal to the Crown of Castile*. London, 1600.

Brochado, Costa. *D. Sebastião o Desejado*. Lisbon, 1941.

Bibliography

Cortesão, A. & Mota, A. T. *Tabularum Geographicarum Lusitanorum*. Lisbon, 1960.

Esaguy, J. de. *O Minuto Vitorioso de Alcacer Quibir 1578*. Lisbon, 1944.

Faria, Vicomte de. D. *Antonio Prieur de Crato, XVIII Roi de Portugal*. Lausanne, 1917.

Faria y Sousa, M. de. *The History of Portugal to 1698* (Tr. by Capt. J. Stevens). London, 1698.

Gois, D. *Lisboa de Quinhentos*. Lisbon, 1937.

Livermore, H. V. *A History of Portugal*. Cambridge, 1947.

Livermore, H. V. *Privileges of an Englishman in the Kingdom and Dominions of Portugal*. London, 1954.

Lodge, R. *The English Factory at Lisbon*. HT, London, 1932.

Machada, J. F. *Historia de Portugal*. Lisbon, 1951.

Matos, L. de. *Les Portugais en France au XVIe Siècle*. Coimbra, 1952.

Monino, A. R. *Viaje a España del Rey Don Sebastian de Portugal*. Valencia, 1956.

Nowell, Chas. E. *A History of Portugal*. New York, 1952.

Neufville, L. de la. *Histoire Générale de Portugal*. 2 vols. Paris, 1700.

Penrose, B. *Travel and Discovery in the Renaissance (1420–1620)*. Cambridge (Mass.), 1952.

Prestage, Edgar. *Portugal a Pioneer of Christianity*. Watford, 1933.

Prestage, Edgar. *The Portuguese Pioneers*. London, 1936.

Queiros Veloso, J. M. de. *A Perda da Independencia*. Lisbon, 1940.

Queiros Veloso, J. M. de. *O Interregno e o Breve Reinado de D. Antonio*. Lisbon, 1953.

Rau, Virginia. *Subsidios para o Estudo das Feiras Medievais Portuguesas*. Lisbon, 1943.

Renouard, Y. *O Grande Comercio do Vinho da Idade Media*. Revista de Historia, São Paulo, 1953.

Rogers, F. M. *The Obedience of a King of Portugal*. Minneapolis, 1958.

Rogers, F. M. *The Travels of the Infante Dom Pedro of Portugal*. Cambridge (Mass.), 1961.

Rogers, F. M. *Victory at Azemmour*. Lisbon, 1960.

Rubio, J. O. *Felipe II y Portugal*. Madrid, 1927.

Serrão, J. W. *Portuguesas no Estudo de Toulouse*. Coimbra, 1954.

Severin de Faria, M. *Noticias de Portugal Offerecidas a Dom João IV*. Lisbon, 1655.

Seyner, Fr. A. *Historia del Levantamiento de Portugal*. Zaragossa, 1644.

Silva, J. G. de. *Stratégie des Affaires à Lisbonne entre 1595 et 1607*. Paris, 1956.

CHAPTER III

The Outward Voyage

Balen, W. J. van. *Hendrik de Zeevaarder*. Amsterdam, 1962.

Boxer, C. R. *Portuguese Roteiros (1500–1700)*. MM, London, 1934.

Bibliography

Boxer, C. R. *Um Roteirista Desconhecido do Seculo XVII, Dom Antonio de Ataide*. Lisbon, 1934.

Broek, J. C. *Letter from Olivier van Noort, Ist Dutch Circumnavigator, 1598–1601*. Minneapolis, 1957.

Brown, L. A. *The Story of Maps*. Boston, 1949.

Castro, J. C. de. *Roteiro do Atlantico Norte*. Lisbon, 1957.

Christy, M. *The Voyages of Captain Luke Foxe, of Hull, and Captain Thomas James of Bristol*. London, 1893.

Coolhaas, W. Ph. *Pieter Van den Broecke in Azie*. The Hague, 1962.

Corney, B. *The Voyage of Sir Henry Middleton to Bantam and the Moluco Islands*. London, 1856.

Cortesão, A. *Ciencia Nautica e o Renascimento*. Lisbon, 1949.

Daniel, G. *As Rotas Maritimas do Atlantico*. Boletin da Sociedade de Geografia de Lisboa, Lisbon, 1961.

Farina, F. *Historia de la Navegación*. Madrid, 1950.

Findlay, A. C. *Sailing Directory for the Ethiopic or South Atlantic Ocean*. London, 1875.

Figueroa, R. P. de. *Las Cosas que los Pilotos Ha de Saber para Bien Nauegar* Cadiz, 1867.

Fonseca, Q. de. *Diarios da Navegacão da Carreira da India*. Lisbon, 1938.

Foster, W. *John Jourdain's Journal of a Voyage to the East Indies, 1606–1617*. London, 1905.

Foster, W. *The Voyage of Nicholas Downton to the East Indies, 1614–15*. London, 1938.

Foster, W. *The Voyage of Sir Henry Middleton to the Moluccas, 1604–1606*. London, 1943.

Foster, W. *The Voyages of Sir James Lancaster to Brazil and the East Indies, 1591–1603*. London, 1940.

Foster, W. *The Voyage of Thomas Best to the East Indies*. London, 1934.

Franco, S. C. *Historia del Arte y Ciencia de Navegar*. 2 vols. Madrid, 1947.

Fryke, Christopher and Schweitser, C. *Voyages to the East Indies*. London, 1929.

Gillis, J. M. *U.S. Naval Astronomical Expedition to the Southern Hemisphere*. Washington, 1855.

Gray, A. *The Voyage of François Pyrard of Laval*. London, 1889.

Hewson, Comdr. J. B., R.N.R. *History of the Practice of Navigation*. Glasgow, 1951.

IJzerman, J. W. *Journael van de Reis naar Zuid Amerika door Hendrik Ottsen, 1598–1601*. The Hague, 1918.

Keuning, J. *De Tweede Schipvaart der Nederlanders naar Oost-Indie*. 6 vols. The Hague, 1938, 1940, 1942, 1944, 1947.

Landstrom, Bjorn. *The Ship*. New York, 1961.

Lavarende, J. de. *Romantische Scheepvart*. Amsterdam, 1960.

Lello e Irmão. *Caravelas, Naus e Galés de Portugal*. Porto, 1950.

Leybourn, W. *Introduction to Astronomy and Geography*. London, 1675

Lloyd, C. *Ships and Seamen*. Greenwich (England), 1961.

Luard, C. E. *Travels of Sebastien Manrique, 1629–1643*. London, 1926

Bibliography

Markham, C. R. *The Voyages of Sir James Lancaster, Knt., to the East Indies* London, 1877.

Moreland, W. H. *Peter Floris, His Voyage to the East Indies.* London, 1934.

Nance, R. M. *Sailing Ship Models.* MM, London, 1924.

Oliveira e Sousa, J. de S. *Regimento que se Deu a João de Saldanha 1585.* Porto, 1944.

Oliver, S. F. *The Voyage of François Leguat of Bresse, 1690–98.* London, 1890.

Pereyra, C. *La Conquista de las Rutas Oceanicas.* Madrid, 1929.

Prottengeier, A. E. *From Lisbon to Calicut.* Minneapolis, 1956.

Quintella, I. de C. *Annaes da Marinha Portugueza.* 2 vols. Lisbon, 1839.

Raper, H. *Practice of Navigation and Nautical Astronomy.* London, 1842.

Rego, A. de S. *Viagems Portuguesas a' India.* Lisbon, 1954.

Rodrigues, Visconde de. *Roteiro da Navegação e Carreira da India.* Lisbon, 1940.

Rouffer, G. P. & IJzerman, J. W. *De Eerste Schipvaart der Nederlanders naar Oost-Indie, 1595–97–98.* 3 vols. The Hague, 1915, 1925, 1929.

Sanceau, Elaine. *Caminho da India.* Porto, 1948.

Santa Eulalia, J. de. *Viagem do Marquez de Tavora.* Lisbon, 1751.

Santa Maria, G. di. *Prima Speditione all' Indie Orientali.* Rome, 1666.

Satow, E. M. *The Voyage of Captain John Saris to Japan in 1613.* London, 1900.

Silveira, L. *Itinerario de Sebastião Manrique.* 2 vols. Lisbon, 1946.

Sinclair, W. F. *The Journey of Pedro Teixeira.* London, 1901.

Skelton, R. A. *Explorers' Maps.* New York, 1958.

Taylor, A. H. *Carrack into Galleon.* MM, London, 1920.

Taylor, E. G. R. *The Troublesome Voyage of Captain Edward Fenton, 1582–83.* London, 1959.

Temple, R. C. *The Travels of Peter Mundy.* 4 vols. London, 1905, 1914, 1919, 1936.

Unger, W. S. *De Oudste Reizen van de Zeeuwen naar Oost-Indie, 1598–1604.* The Hague, 1948.

Vascóncelos, F. de. *Armadas de Carreira da India (1560–1590).* Lisbon, 1938.

Vascóncelos, F. de. *Doze Episodios da Historia da Marinha Portuguesa.* Lisbon, 1953.

Vascóncelos, F. de. *Navios dos Descobrimentos e Navegações dos Portugueses, XVI e XVII Seculos.* Lisbon, 1957.

Vascóncelos, F. de. *Pilotos das Navegações Portuguesas XVI–XVII.* Lisbon, 1942.

Villiers, A. *By Way of Cape Horn.* London, 1930.

Villiers, A. *The Way of a Ship.* London, 1954.

Weider, F. C. *De Reis van Mahuen de Cordes door de Straat van Magalhaes naar Zuid-Amerika en Japan, 1598–1600.* 2 vols. The Hague, 1923–24.

Wroth, L. C. *Way of a Ship.* Portland, 1937.

Bibliography

CHAPTER IV

Goa

Africa and Brazil

Balen, W. J. van. *Hollandsche Kapers.* Leiden, 1942.

Balen, W. J. van. *Nederlands Voorhoede.* Amsterdam, 1946.

Blake, J. W. *Europeans in West Africa (1450–1560).* London, 1941–42.

Boxer, C. R. *The Dutch in Brazil (1624–1654).* Oxford, 1957.

Boxer, C. R. *Salvador de Sa.* London, 1952.

Brett, J. A. *The Levant Company's Factory in Aleppo.* HT, London, 1962.

Brown, R. *The History and Description of Africa.* London, 1895.

Colby, R. *Madagascar, the Great Island,* HT, London, 1962.

Embid, F. P. *Los Descubrimientos en el Atlantico y la Rivalidad Castellano-Portuguesa.* Seville, 1948.

Dias, G. S. *Os Portuguesas em Angola.* Lisbon, 1959.

Foster, W. *The Red Sea and Adjacent Countries in the XVII Century.* London, 1949.

Hanke, L. *The Portuguese in Spanish America.* New York, 1962.

Luiz, D. F. de S. *Os Portuguezes em Africa, Asia, America e Oceania.* 3 vols. Lisbon, 1848.

Naber, S. P. L. *Beschryvinghe ende Historische van het Gout Koninckrijck van Gunea.* The Hague, 1912.

Ratelband, K. *De Westafrikaanse Reis van Piet Heyn (1624–1625).* The Hague, 1959.

Ratelband, K. *Reizen naar West-Afrika van Pieter van den Broecke (1605–1614).* The Hague, 1950.

Saunders, J. J. *The Caliph Omar: Arab Imperialist.* London, 1961.

Slessarev, V. *Prester John, the Letter and the Legend.* Minneapolis, 1959.

Stanley, H. *A Description of the Coast of East Africa and Malabar.* London, 1865.

Welch, S. R. *Africa do Sul sob Dom Manuel.* Laurenço Marques, 1950.

Welch, S. R. *Europe's Discovery of South Africa.* Cape Town, 1935.

Welch, S. R. *Portuguese and Dutch in South Africa (1641–1806).* Cape Town, 1951.

Welch, S. R. *Portuguese Rule and Spanish Crown in South Africa.* Cape Town, 1950.

Welch, S. R. *South Africa under King Manuel (1495–1521).* Cape Town, 1946.

Welch, S. R. *South Africa under John III (1521–1557).* Cape Town, 1948.

Welch, S. R. *South Africa under King Sebastian and the Cardinal (1557–1580).* Cape Town, 1949.

Bibliography

Goa: The China Sea

Almeida, A. C. de. *Cousas da India e do Japão*. Coimbra, 1957.

Boxer, C. R. *A derrota dos Hollandeses em Macau, 1622*. Lisbon, 1928.

Boxer, C. R. *As Viagems de Japão e seus Capitaes-Mores 1550–1640*. Macao, 1941.

Boxer, C. R. *Capitais Gerais e Governadores de Macau 1557–1770*. Macao, 1944.

Boxer, C. R. *Cornelis Speelman and Growth of Dutch Power in Indonesia 1666–1684*. HT, London, 1958.

Boxer, C. R. *Fidalgos in the Far East*. The Hague, 1948.

Boxer, C. R. *Jan Compagnie in Japan 1600–1817*. The Hague, 1936.

Boxer, C. R. *Jesuits at the Court of Peking*. HT, London, 1957.

Boxer, C. R. *Portuguese Commercial Voyages to Japan 1630–1639*. London, 1934.

Boxer, C. R. *South China in the Sixteenth Century*. MM, London, 1953.

Boxer, C. R. *The Affair of the Madre de Deus*. MM, London, 1929.

Boxer, C. R. *The Christian Century in Japan*. Berkeley, 1951.

Boxer, C. R. *The Great Ship from Amacon*. Lisbon, 1959.

Brazão, E. *Relações Diplomaticas de Portugal e China*. Lisbon, 1949.

Chandhuri, K. M. *The East India Company and its Shipping, Early XVII Century*. Cambridge, 1963.

Collis, M. *The Land of the Great Image*. London, 1943.

Cortesão, A. *The Suma Oriental of Tomé Pires, The Book of Francisco Rodrigues*. London, 1944.

Dartford, G. P. *Malacca: Emporium of the Eastern Trade*. London, 1960.

Foster, W. *The Embassy of Sir Thomas Roe to the Court of the Great Mogul, 1616–1619*. London, 1899.

Foster, W. *The John Company*. London, 1926.

Guerriero, J. T. de V. *Jornada de A. Coelho de Mação a Goa*. Lisbon, 1732.

Hall, D. G. E. *A History of South-East Asia*. London, 1955.

IJzerman, J. W. *Dirck Gerritsz Pomp (1544–1604)*. The Hague, 1915.

Meilink-Roelofsz, M. A. P. *Asian Trade and European Influence in the Indonesian Archipelago between 1500–1630*. The Hague, 1962.

Milo, T. H. *Portuguese Trade and Shipping with the Netherlands after the Discoveries*. Lisbon, 1961.

Morse, H. B. *East India Company Trading to China*. 4 vols. Cambridge, 1926.

Sloos, D. A. *De Nederlanders in de Phillippijnsche Wateren*. Amsterdam, 1898.

Staunton, G. T. *The History of the Great and Mighty Kingdom of China*. London, 1854.

Tavernier, J. B. *Six Voyages en Turquie, en Perse et aux Indes*. 3 vols. Paris, 1679.

Torchiana, H. A. van. *Tropical Holland*. Chicago, 1921.

Vidart, L. *Descubrimiento de Oceania por los Portuguesas*. Madrid, 1896.

Winstedt, R. O. *History of Malaya*. Singapore, 1935.

Worcester, G. R. G. *The Chinese War Junk*. MM, London, 1948.

Wroth, L. C. *Early Cartography of the Pacific*. Providence, 1944.

Bibliography

Goa: The Colony

Agencia do Ultramar. *Fundação do Estrado da India em 1505.* Lisbon, 1955.

Andrada, J. F. de. *Dom João de Castro.* Paris, 1759.

Andrade, A. A. de. *Traditional Anti-Racialism of Portugal's Civilizing Methods.* Lisbon, 1954.

Archer, M. *India and Archaeology.* HT, London, 1962.

Bacon, L. *The Lusiads.* New York, 1950.

Badger, G. P. *The Travels of Ludovico di Varthema.* London, 1863.

Baião, A. *Itinerariãos da India a Portugal por Terra.* Coimbra, 1932.

Balen, W. J. van. *Naar de Indische Wonderwereld.* Amsterdam, 1942.

Ballard, G. A. *The Downfall of Portugal in the East.* MM, London, 1926.

Barros, J. de. *Da Asia de João de Barros e de Diogo de Couto.* 24 vols. Lisbon, 1777–88.

Bernardino, F. G. *Itinerario da India por Terra Ate' a Ilha de Chipre.* Lisbon, 1953.

Botelho, S. *O Tombo do Estado da India.* Lisbon, 1868.

Boxer, C. R. *Antonio Telles em Goa.* Lisbon, 1938.

Boxer, C. R. *Novas da India Oriental Portuguesas e Hollandeses.* Lisbon, 1928.

Boxer, C. R. *The Portuguese in the East.* (Chapter in *Portugal and Brazil.*) Oxford, 1953.

Boxer, C. R. *The Surprisal of Goa's Bar.* London, 1930.

Burton, R. F. *The Lusiads.* 2 vols. London, 1880.

Camoëns, L. de. *The Lusiads.* New York, 1950.

Carruthers, D. *The Desert Route to India.* London, 1928.

Correa, G. *Lendas da India.* 8 vols. Lisbon, 1858.

Correira, G. da S. *Historia da Colonisação Portuguesa no India.* Lisbon, 1948.

Couto, D. do. *D. Paulo de Lima Pereira.* Lisbon, 1765.

Couto, D. do. *Decada Quarta da Asia.* Lisbon, 1602.

Couto, D. do. *Soldado Pratico.* Lisbon, 1790.

Cura, J. R. *Los Establecimientos Europeos en las Indias Orientales.* Paris, 1825.

Dames, M. L. *The Book of Duarte Barbosa.* 2 vols. London, 1918–1921.

Davies, D. W. *Dutch Seventeenth Century Overseas Trade.* The Hague, 1961.

Faria y Sousa, M. de. *Portuguese Asia.* 3 vols. London, 1695.

Faria y Sousa, M. de. *Asia Portuguesa.* 6 vols. Porto, 1945.

Felner, R. J. *Subsidios para a Historia da India Portugueza.* Lisbon, 1868.

Ficalho, Conde de. *Garcia de Orta e o seu Tempo.* Lisbon, 1886.

Fonseca, J. N. da. *Historical and Archaeological Sketch of the City of Goa.* Bombay, 1878.

Ford, J. D. M. *Letters of John III (1521–1557).* Cambridge (Mass.), 1931.

Ford, J. D. M. *Letters of Court of John III.* Cambridge (Mass.), 1933.

Freitas, F. S. de. *Do Justo Imperio Asiatico dos Portugueses.* Lisbon, 1960.

Garcia, J. I. de A. *Archivo de Relação de Goa Seculos XVII, XVIII, XIX.* Nova Goa, 1872.

Gokhale, B. G. *Indians and the British.* HT, London, 1963.

Bibliography

Gonçalves, J. J. *Os Portugueses no Sião*. Lisbon, 1957.

Grey, E. *The Travels of Pietro della Valle in India*. London, 1891.

Kimble, G. H. T. *Esmeraldo de Situ Orbis*. London, 1936.

Lagoa, Visconde de. *Glossario de Antiqua Portuguesa Ultramarina*. 4 vols. Lisbon, 1953.

Lagoa, Visconde de. *Grandes e Humildes na Epopeia Portuguesa do Oriente*. Lisbon, 1942.

Lagoa, Visconde de. *Grandes Viagems Portuguesas*. Lisbon, 1951.

Lagoa, Visconde de. *Peregrinação de Fernão Mendes Pinto*. Lisbon, 1947.

Lobato, A. *Fundamentos da Presença de Portugal na India*. Lisbon, 1954.

Lopes de Castenheda, F. *Historia do Descobrimento & Conquista da India*. 4 vols. Coimbra, 1924, 1928, 1929, 1933.

Luz, F. M. da. *Las Cidades e Fortalezas nas Partes da India*. Coimbra, 1952.

Luz, F. P. M. da. *Conselho da India*. Lisbon, 1952.

Major, R. H. *India in the Fifteenth Century*. London, 1858.

Markham, C. R. *The Life and Acts of Don Alonzo Enriquez de Guzman*. London, 1862.

Martinho, J. A. *Os Portuguesas no Oriente*. Lisbon, 1938.

Martins, J. F. F. *Crónica dos Vice-Reis e Governadores da India*. Nova Goa, 1919.

Martins, R. *Historia das Colonias Portuguesas*. Lisbon, 1933.

Pannikar, K. M. *Asia and the Western Dominance*. London, 1953.

Pannikar, K. M. *Malabar and the Dutch*. Bombay, 1931.

Pannikar, K. M. *Malabar and the Portuguese*. Bombay, 1929.

Parr, C. M. *So Noble a Captain*. New York, 1953.

Penrose, B. *Goa—Ranha do Oriente*. Lisbon, 1960.

Pissurlencar, P. *Portugueses e Maratas*. Nova Goa, 1926.

Pissurlencar, P. S. S. *Rigimentos des Fortalezas da India*. Goa, 1951.

Pissurlencar, P. *Tentativo do Portugueses para a Occupação do Conção*. Lisbon, 1955.

Reynal, Abbe. *Settlement and Trade of the Europeans in the East and West Indies*. 8 vols. London, 1783.

Ribeiro, L. *Registo da Casa da India*. 2 vols. Lisbon, 1954–55.

Ribeiro, S. *Conquista do Reyno de Pegu pelos Portuguezes*. Lisbon, 1762.

Robertson, W. *The Knowledge Which the Ancients Had of India*. London, 1802.

Robusto, R. W. *Goa, Terra Indo-Portuguesa*. Porto, 1953.

Rodrigues, C. M. M. S. *Portuguese Overseas Provinces*. Lisbon, 1954.

Ryley, J. H. *Ralph Fitch: England's Pioneer to India and Burma*. London, 1899.

Salazar, O. *Goa and the Indian Union*. Lisbon, 1954.

Saldanha, M. J. G. de. *Historia de Goa*. 2 vols. Nova Goa, 1925–26.

San Roman, Fray A. *Historia General de la Yndia Oriental*. Valladolid, 1603.

Sarmento, S. C. M. M. *Portugal in India*. Lisbon, 1953.

Silva, J. D. *Efemerides do Imperio Colonial Portugues*. 2 vols. Lisbon, 1940.

Soares, J. P. C. *Bosquejo das Possessoes Portuguesas no Oriente*. Lisbon, 1851.

Tenreiro, A. *Itinerario*. Lisbon, 1762.

Bibliography

Trigueiros, L. F. *O Homen Portugues na Cultura dos Descobrimentos*. Porto, 1960.

Vascóncellos, F. de and Boxer, C. R. *Andre Furtado de Mendonca*. Lisbon, 1955.

Viterbo, S. *Viagems da India a Portugal por Terra*. Coimbra, 1898.

Goa: Ecclesiastical

Badger, G. P. *History of the Imams and Seyyids of 'Oman*. London, 1870.

Baiáo, A. *A Inquisição de Goa*. 2 vols. Lisbon, 1949.

Boxer, C. R. *Christians and Spices—Portuguese Missionaries 1518-1658*, HT, London, 1958.

D'Orsey, Rev A. J. D. *Portuguese Discoveries, Dependencies and Missions in Asia and Africa*. London, 1893.

Horthemels, D. *History of the Inquisition at Goa*. London, 1688.

Jesuitas. *Jesuitas*. Rome, 1961.

MacLagan, Sir E. *Os Jesuitas e o Grão Mogul*. Porto, 1946.

Martins, J. F. F. *O Misticisimo Religioso ao Serviço da Expansão e do Dominio Portuguese no Oriente*. Lisboa, 1938.

Martins, Rocha. *O Apostolo das Indias S. Francisco Xavier*. Lisbon, 1942.

Rego, A. da S. *Historia das Missões do Padroado Portugués do Oriente*. 11 vols. Lisbon, 1947-55.

Rogers, F. M. *Geo-Theo-Politics in the Age of Discovery*. Cambridge (Mass.), 1960.

Rogers, F. M. *O Sonho de Unidade entre Christãos Ocidentais no Seculo XV*. Bahia, 1960.

Rogers, F. M. *The Quest for Eastern Christians*. Minneapolis, 1962.

Rogers, F. M. *The Western Dream of Christian Indies*. Cambridge (Mass.), 1960.

Santos, L. dos. *Projecção Cultural do Christianismo na India Portuguesa*. Lisbon, 1961.

Goa: Nautical

Ballard, G. A. *Early European Rivalry in the Indian Ocean*. MM, London, 1928.

Ballard, G. A. *Rulers of the Indian Ocean*. MM, London, 1927.

Ballard, G. A. *The Arrival of the Dutch and British in the Indian Ocean*. MM, London, 1926.

Ballard, G. A. *The Century of Portuguese Supremacy in the Indian Ocean*. MM, London, 1925.

Ballard, G. A. *The First Plan of European Dominion in the Indian Ocean*. MM, London, 1924.

Ballard, G. A. *The Navigators of the Indian Ocean Prior to the European Domination*. MM, London, 1924.

Ballard, G. A. *The War of the Arabian Sea*. MM, London, 1925.

Bibliography

Botelho de Sousa, A. *A Historia das Guerras no Mar e no Além Mar.* 2 vols. Lisbon, 1940.

Botelho de Sousa, A. *Historia Militar Maritima da India 1589–1669.* 2 vols. Lisbon, 1930–1948.

Botelho de Sousa, A. *Subsidios para a Historia Militar Maritima da India.* 4 vols. Lisbon, 1930–1956.

Boxer, C. R. *European Rivalry in the Indian Seas, XVI–XVII Centuries.* MM, London, 1928.

Boxer, C. R. *Naval Actions between the Portuguese and Dutch in India, 1654.* MM, London, 1928.

Boxer, C. R. *Nuño Alvares Botelho e sua Armada.* Porto, 1928.

Boxer, C. R. *Una Desconhecida Victoria Naval Portuguéz no Seculo XVII.* Lisbon, 1929.

Castro, D. J. de. *Primeiro Roteiro da Costa da India.* Porto, 1843.

Castro e Almeida, E. de. *Archivo de Marina e Ultramar.* Coimbra, 1908.

Ferrand, G. *Instructions Nautiques et Routiers Arabes des XV et XVI Siècles.* Paris, 1921–23.

Gonçalves, Julio. *Os Portuguesas e o Mar das Indias.* Boletim da Sociedade de Geografia de Lisboa, Lisbon, 1947.

Hornell, James. *A Tentative Classification of Arab Sea-Craft.* MM, London, 1942.

Hornell, James. *The Sailing Craft of Western India.* MM, London, 1946.

Hornell, James. *The Tongue and Groove Seam in Gujarate Boats.* MM, London, 1930.

Moore, Alan. *Craft of the Red Sea and Gulf of Aden.* MM, London, 1920.

Pannikar, K. M. *India and the Indian Ocean.* London, 1945.

Villiers, A. *Passage in a Red Sea Dhow.* MM, London, 1954.

CHAPTER V

The Homeward Voyage

Albion, R. G. *The Timber Problem of the Royal Navy.* London, 1952.

Anderson, R. C. *Comparative Naval Architecture (1670–1720).* MM, London, 1921.

Anderson, R. C. *Dutch Three Deckers, 1682.* MM, London, 1929.

Anderson, R. C. *Early Books on Shipbuilding and Rigging (1536–1720).* MM, London, 1924.

Artinano, G. *Arquitectura Naval Española.* Madrid, 1920.

Barbosa, A. *Historia da Ciencia Nautica Portuguesa.* Porto, 1948.

Boxer, C. R. *Portuguese East Indiamen in the Early XVII Century.* MM, London, 1940.

Boxer, C. R. *The Tragic History of the Sea, 1589–1622.* London, 1959.

Cervin, R. de G. B. *Galleons and "Q" Ships in Spanish Conspiracy against Venice, 1618.* MM, London, 1934.

Bibliography

Cooper, Ernest R. *The Davis Back-Staff or English Quadrant.* MM, London, 1944.

Gould, R. T. *John Harrison and his Timekeepers.* MM, London, 1935.

Harries, H. *Nautical Time.* MM, London, 1928.

Lane, F. C. *Economic Meaning of the Invention of the Compass.* Am. Hist. Rev., Washington, 1963.

Lane, F. C. *Venetian Naval Architecture, 1550.* MM, London, 1934.

Lane, F. C. *Venetian Ships and Shipbuilders of the Renaissance.* Baltimore, 1934.

Lopes de Mendonca, H. *Navios Portuguesas nos Seculos XV e XVI.* Lisbon, 1898.

Lopes de Mendonca, H. *P. F. Oliveira e a sua Livro da Fábrica das Náos.* Lisbon, 1898.

May, W. E. *The History of the Magnetic Compass.* MM, London, 1952.

Moll, F. *The History of Wood Preserving in Shipbuilding.* MM, London, 1926.

Nance, R. M. *The Venetian 16th Century Merchant Ship.* MM, London, 1914.

Palacio, D. G. de. *Instrucción Náutica Para Navegar.* Madrid, 1944.

Pires, D. *Viagems et Naufragios Célebres.* 4 vols. Porto, 1937.

Riesenberg, Felix. *Under Sail.* New York, 1937.

Roiz, P. *Libro de Reloges Solares.* Valencia, 1575.

Smith, F. G. W. & Sisson, R. F. *Shipworms, Saboteurs of the Sea.* Washington, 1956.

Sottas, D. J. *Messageries Maritimes de Venise aux XIV et XV Siècles.* Paris, 1938.

Sousa, V. *Trabalhos Náuticos dos Portuguezes, XVI–XVII Seculos: Marinharia e Constructores Navaes.* Lisbon, 1898–1900.

Syria, P. de. *Arte de la Verdadera Navegación.* Valencia, 1602.

Vascóncelos, F. de. *A Cruz de Ordem de Cristo na Marinha Portuguesa.* Lisbon, 1951.

Vascóncelos, F. de. *Armadas da Carreira da India de 1560 a 1590.* Lisbon, 1938.

Vascóncelos, F. de. *Pilotos dos Navegações Portuguesas dos Seculos XVI e XVII.* Lisbon, 1942.

Villiers, A. *Monsoon Seas.* New York, 1952.

Welch, J. J. *Textbook of Naval Architecture.* London, 1893.

Wiel, A. *The Navy of Venice.* London, 1910.

Wroth, L. C. *The Way of a Ship.* Portland (Me), 1937.

CHAPTER VI

The Atlantic Islands

Bell, D. *Elizabethan Seamen.* Philadelphia, N.D.

Boehrer, G. C. *Franciscans and Portuguese Colonization in Africa and the Atlantic Islands.* The Americas, Washington, 1955.

Bibliography

Brown, A. S. *Madeira, Canary Islands and Azores.* London, 1913.

Chapman, A. B. W. *The Commercial Relations of England and Portugal (1487–1807).* London, 1907.

D'Almeida, G. *Ilha de S. Miguel, Descobrimento et Diversas Noticias.* Ponta Delgada, 1885.

Dyer, F. E. *The Elizabethan Sailorman.* MM, London, 1924.

Grey, C. *The Merchant Venturers of London, Far Eastern Trade and Piracy, XVII Century.* London, 1932.

Hahn, Emily. *The Azores.* The New Yorker Magazine, New York, 1959.

Laughton, J. K. *State Papers Relating to the Defeat of the Spanish Armada, 1588.* London, 1894.

Laughton, L. G. C. *English and Spanish Tonnage in 1588.* MM, London, 1958.

Laughton, L. G. C. *Gunnery, Frigates and the Line of Battle 1620.* MM, London, 1928.

Lewis, M. *Armada Guns: A Comparative Study of English and Spanish Armaments.* MM, London, 1942.

Mattingly, Garrett. *The Armada.* Boston, 1959.

McGrath, P. *Merchant Shipping in the XVII Century.* MM, London, 1954.

Mees, J. *Histoire de la Découverte des Iles Açores.* Gand, 1901.

Naval Project. *Galeones y Flotas del Peru y Nueva España.* Madrid, 1720.

Navarrete, D. M. F. *Disertación sobre la Historia de la Náutica.* Madrid, 1846.

Oliveira, F. *Arte de Guerra do Mar.* Lisbon, 1937.

Ommanney, F. D. *El Océano.* Mexico, 1953.

Raleigh, W. *The Principal Navigations, Voyages, Traffiques, and Discoveries of the English Nation.* London, 1903–5.

Rawlinson, H. G. *The Flanders Galleys between Venice and England.* MM, London, 1926.

Ribeiro, O. *A Ilha de Fogo.* Lisbon, 1954.

Roux, A. *Ships and Shipping.* Salem, 1928.

Taylor, E. G. R. *A Regiment for the Sea.* MM, London, 1963.

Twiss, Sir T. *Black Book of the Admiralty.* 5 vols. London, 1876.

van Loon, H. W. *Ships and How They Sailed the Seven Seas.* New York, 1935.

Waters, D. W. *Art of Navigation in Elizabethan England.* New Haven, 1958.

CHAPTER VII

Home Is the Sailor

Aubery, L. *L'Histoire de Hollande et des Autres Provinces-Unies.* Paris, 1697.

Beekman. *Geschiedkundige Atlas van Nederland.* (16 portfolios of maps, 37 vols. of text.) The Hague, 1942.

Blok, P. J. *History of the People of the Netherlands.* 5 vols. New York, 1898.

Bosman, W. *Coast of Guinea.* London, 1705.

Carus-Wilson, E. M. *The Merchant Adventurers of Bristol.* London, 1928.

Bibliography

Duikes, G. *The Golden Age of Amsterdam*. HT, London, 1957.

Gernez, D. *Lucas Janszoon Wagenaer 1584*. MM, London, 1937.

Geyl, P. *Netherlands in the XVII Century*. London, 1961.

Geyl, P. *The Revolt of the Netherlands 1555–1609*. New York, 1958.

IJzerman, J. W. *Dirck Gerritsz Pomp 1544–1604*. The Hague, 1915.

Markham, C. R. *The Natural and Moral History of the Indies*. London, 1879.

Mollema, J. C. *Geschiedenis van Nederland*. 4 vols. Amsterdam, 1939.

Motley, J. L. *History of the United Netherlands*. 4 vols. London, 1860.

Motley, J. L. *Rise of the Dutch Republic*. 2 vols. London, 1856.

Parker, J. *The Merchant Explorer*. Minneapolis, 1961, 1962, 1963.

Philips, J. D. *Gezigten van Steden, Kerken Gebouwen in de Vereen Netherlanden*. Amsterdam, 1703–1756.

Rowen, H. H. *The Ambassador Prepares for War 1669–1671*. The Hague, 1957.

Willan, T. S. *The Russia Company 1553–1603*. Manchester, 1956.

Willan, T. S. *The Muscovy Merchants of 1555*. Manchester, 1953.

CHAPTER VIII

To the North

Anderson, Comdr. W. R. *The Arctic as a Sea Route of the Future*. Nat'l Geog. Mag., Washington, 1959.

Backer, J. *Seal Hunting off Jan Mayen*. Nat'l Geog. Mag., Washington, 1948.

Bartlett, R. A. *Servicing Arctic Airbases*. Nat'l Geog. Mag., Washington, 1946.

Bond, E. A. *Russia at the Close of the XV Century*. St. Petersburg, 1875.

Calvert, Comdr. J. F. *Up Through the Ice of the North Pole*. Nat'l Geog. Mag., Washington, 1959.

Christy, M. *Captain William Hawkeridge in Search of a North-West Passage in 1625*. MM, London, 1927.

Conway, W. M. *Early Dutch and English Voyages to Spitzbergen in the Seventeenth Century*. London, 1902.

Costa, Rev. B. F. de. *Sailing Directions of Henry Hudson*. Albany, 1869.

Crouse, N. M. *In Quest of the Western Ocean*. New York, 1928.

Ellis, Henry. *Voyage de la Baye de Hudson Fait en 1746–47*. 2 vols. Paris, 1749.

Frank, R. Jr. *Flashing Harpoons*. New York, 1958.

Frank, R., Jr. *Frozen Frontier*. New York, 1961.

Frank, R., Jr. *Ice Island*. New York, 1951.

Gilson, M. P. *A Woman's Winter on Spitsbergen*. Nat'l Geog. Mag., Washington, 1928.

Gosch, C. C. A. *Danish Arctic Expeditions, 1605 to 1620*. London, 1896.

Gould, L. M. *The Polar Regions in their Relation to Human Affairs*. Geog. Rev., New York, 1958.

Grey, I. *Ivan the Terrible and Elizabeth of England*. HT, London, 1962.

Bibliography

Keuning, J. *Petrus Plancius* (*1552–1622*). Amsterdam, 1946.

Knutsen, W. *Milestone in my Arctic Journeys*. Nat'l Geog. Mag., Washington, 1949.

Lalor, Lt. W. G. *Submarine through the North Pole*. Nat'l Geog. Mag., Washington, 1959.

Mackenzie, A. *Voyage to the Pacific Ocean in 1793*. Chicago, 1931.

Markham, A. H. *The Voyages and Works of John Davis, Navigator*. London, 1878.

Markham, C. R. *Life of John Davis, the Navigator 1550–1605*. London, 1889.

Markham, C. R. *The Voyages of William Baffin*. London, 1880.

McFee, W. *Sir Martin Frobisher*. London, 1928.

Mirsky, J. *Elisha Kent Kane and the Seafaring Frontier*. Boston, 1954.

Mirsky, J. *To the Arctic, the Story of Northern Exploration*. London, 1949.

Mowat, Farley. *Ordeal by Ice*. Boston, 1960.

Murphy, H. C. *Henry Hudson in Holland*. The Hague, 1909.

Naber, S. P. L. *Beschryvinghe van der Samoyeden Landt en Spitsberghe by Hessel Gerritsz*. The Hague, 1924.

Naber, S. P. L. *Henry Hudson's Reize*. The Hague, 1921.

Naber, S. P. L. *Reizen van Wm. Barents, Jacob van Heemskerck, Jan C. Rijp*. 2 vols. The Hague, 1917.

Neatby, L. H. *In Quest of the Northwest Passage*. New York, 1958.

Nicholson, N. L. *Resources of the Arctic*. Geog. Rev., New York, 1952.

Nunn, G. E. *Origin of the Strait of Anian Concept*. Philadelphia, 1929.

Parker, John. *The Strait of Anian*. Minneapolis, 1956.

Parry, W. E. *A Voyage for the Discovery of a North-West Passage—1819–1820*. London, 1899.

Parry, W. E. *Journals of the 1st, 2nd & 3rd Voyages for the Discovery of a North-West Passage—1819–1825*. 5 vols. London, 1828.

Platt, R. *A Visit to the Living Ice Age*. Nat'l Geog. Mag., Washington, 1957.

Rolt-Wheeler, F. *Quest of the Western World*. New York, 1921.

Rundall, T. *Narratives of Voyages towards the North-West*. London, 1849.

Sheppard, T. *The Old Dutch Whalers*. MM, London, 1939.

Stefansson, V. *The Three Voyages of Martin Frobisher in Search of a Passage to Cathay and India by the North-West, 1576–8*. London, 1938.

Stirling, M. W. *Nomads of the Far North*. Nat'l Geog. Mag., Washington, 1949.

van Loon, H. W. *Golden Book of the Dutch Navigators*. New York, 1938.

Veer, Gerrit de. *The Three Voyages of William Barents to the Arctic Regions, in 1594, 1595 and 1596*. London, 1876.

Veer, Gerrit de. *A True Description of Three Voyages by the North-East*. London, 1853.

Wagner, H. R. *Spanish Voyages to the Northwest Coast of America in the Sixteenth Century*. San Francisco, 1929.

White, A. *A Collection of Documents on Spitsbergen and Greenland*. London, 1856.

Winsor, J. *Narrative and Critical History of America*. 8 vols. Cambridge (Mass.), 1889.

Zenzinov, V. M. *With an Exile in Arctic Siberia*. Nat'l Geog. Mag., Washington, 1924.

CHAPTER IX

Burgher and Savant

Akveld, L. M. *Jornal van de Reis van Piet Heyn naar Brazille en West Afrika 1624–25*. Groningen, 1962.
Balen, W. J. van. *De Ontdekking van de Wereld*. 2 vols. Amsterdam, 1932.
Barker, J. E. *The Rise and Decline of the Netherlands*. London, 1906.
Davies, D. W. *A Primer of Dutch Seventeenth Century Overseas Trade*. The Hague, 1961.
Ligtenberg, C. *Willem Usselincx*. Utrecht, 1914.
Motley, J. L. *Life and Death of John of Barneveld*. 2 vols. London, 1874.
Reus, G. C. K. de. *Administrativen van Niederlandsch-Ostindischen*. The Hague, 1894.
Rowse, A. L. *Sir Nicholas Throckmorton (1560)*. HT, London, 1962.
Tawney, R. H. *Business and Politics under James I*. HT, London, 1958.
Temple, R. C. *Papers of Thomas Bowrey, 1669–1713*. London, 1925.
van Loon, H. W. *Fall of the Dutch Republic*. New York, 1924.
Vere, F. *Salt in Their Blood—The Famous Dutch Admirals*. London, 1955.
Wilson, C. *Profit and Power*. London, 1957.

Index

Index

Index

Index

Index

Index

Index

Index

Index

Index

Index

Index

About the Author

Charles McKew Parr brings to the writing of history and biography an unusual background, for he has been a successful businessman and politician as well as a student and scholar.

He was born in Baltimore in 1884 of a family that settled in Maryland in Lord Baltimore's day. He attended Boys' Latin School and then went to West Point. But deafness disqualified him for military life, and he entered upon a business career which has taken him all over the world. Eventually he became chairman of the board of the Parr Electric Company and the Parr Marine and Export Company, and a governor of the National Association of Electrical Distributors.

During World War I he was a Trade Adviser with the War Trade Board, a Special Assistant to the Secretary of State, and a foreign agent in Spain. During World War II Mr. Parr served as a dollar-a-year man with two Washington agencies.

Because he believed strongly that businessmen should participate in government instead of criticizing it, he entered local politics and served as a Representative and as a Senator in the Connecticut State Legislature. His chief interest during these years has been the improvement of libraries. He is a member of the Governor's Commission on Libraries for the State of Connecticut. He has been active in the Connecticut Library Association and has served as a trustee of his local library. The children's room in the Chester Public Library has been named for him.

Many volumes from his own extensive library have been given to various universities. The books are in many languages, of which Mr. Parr reads at least seven (he learned Dutch at the age of seventy to make proper use of the archives in Holland when he was doing his research for Linschoten).

In 1962 Chester celebrated McKew Parr Day and the whole town paid him honor. In that same year he was made a Doctor of Laws by the University of Bridgeport. He is also a Commander in the Knights of Christ, the oldest military order in the world. This order was conferred on him by the Portuguese government for the scholarship that went into the writing of Mr. Parr's previous book, a biography of Ferdinand Magellan.

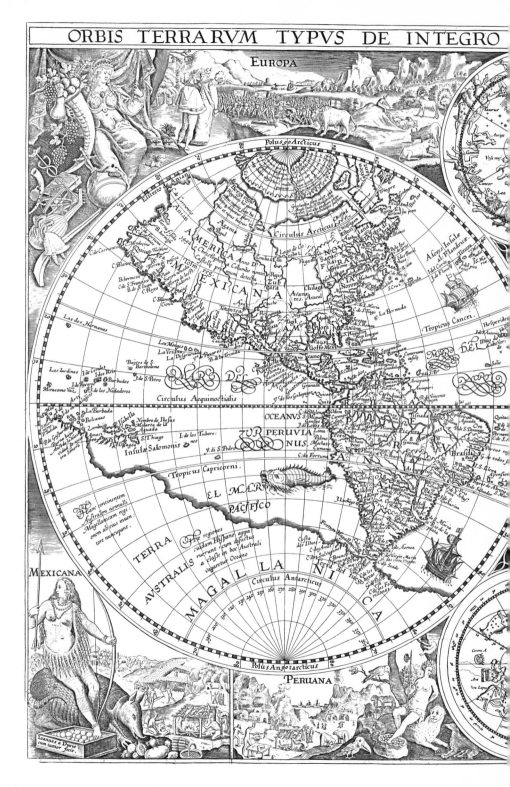

ORBIS TERRARVM TYPVS DE INTEGRO

THIS MAP *is the famed Orbis Terrarum of Petrus Plancius*